# NEW NATIONAL AND POST-COLONIAL LITERATURES

**Also by Bruce King**

*Derek Walcott and West Indian Drama/'Not Only a Playwright But a Company'/The Trinidad Theatre Workshop 1959–1993*
*V. S. Naipaul*
*\*Three Indian Poets: Ezekiel, Ramanujan and Moraes*
*Coriolanus*
*\*Modern Indian Poetry in English*
*The New English Literatures: Cultural Nationalism in a Changing World*
*History of Seventeenth-Century English Literature*
*Marvell's Allegorical Poetry*
*Dryden's Major Plays*

**Books edited by Bruce King**

*West Indian Literature*
*The Later Fiction of Nadine Gordimer*
*Post-colonial English Drama: Commonwealth Drama since 1960*
*The Commonwealth Novel since 1960*
*Contemporary American Theatre*
*\*A Celebration of Black and African Writing*
*Literatures of the World in English*
*Introduction to Nigerian Literature*
*Dryden's Mind and Art*
*Twentieth Century Interpretations of 'All for Love'*

**Series edited by Bruce King**

*Modern Dramatists*
*English Dramatists*
*\*Published by Oxford University Press*

# NEW NATIONAL AND POST-COLONIAL LITERATURES

## An Introduction

EDITED BY
BRUCE KING

CLARENDON PRESS · OXFORD

Oxford University Press, Great Clarendon Street, Oxford OX2 6DP

Oxford New York
Athens Auckland Bangkok Bogota Bombay
Buenos Aires Calcutta Cape Town Dar es Salaam
Delhi Florence Hong Kong Istanbul Karachi
Kuala Lumpur Madras Madrid Melbourne
Mexico City Nairobi Paris Singapore
Taipei Tokyo Toronto Warsaw
and associated companies in
Berlin Ibadan

Oxford is a registered trade mark of Oxford University Press

Published in the United States
by Oxford University Press Inc., New York

The several contributors 1996
Introduction and editorial matter © Bruce King 1996

First published 1996

First published as a Clarendon paperback 1998

British Library Cataloguing in Publication Data
Data available

Library of Congress Cataloging in Publication Data
New national and post-colonial literatures: an introduction / edited
by Bruce King.
Includes bibliographical references (p.  ).
1. Commonwealth literature (English)—History and criticism.
2. English literature—20th century—History and criticism.
3. Commonwealth countries—In literature.   4. Developing countries—
In literature.   5. Indigenous peoples in literature.
6. Decolonization in literature.   7. Nationalism in literature.
I. King, Bruce Alvin.
PR9080.N49   1996
820.9'9171241—dc20   96–31090
ISBN 0–19–871040–2
ISBN 0–19–818484–0 (Pbk)

3 5 7 9 10 8 6 4 2

Printed in Great Britain
on acid-free paper by
Bookcraft Ltd,
Midsomer Norton, Somerset

PR
9080
·N49
1998

*In memory of Ken Saro-Wiwa (1941–1995)
and to Rhonda Cobham Sander, David
Dabydeen, and Derry Jeffares for their
friendship, ideas, and help at various times*

# Preface

THIS book is an introduction to the new national literatures in English and such branches and offshoots as writing by exiles, Third World feminists, and post-colonial theorists. This is not, however, a survey of the history, major works, and major writers of each of the national literatures and their overseas branches. There are now too many significant texts, writers, nations, and critical theories for such a survey; another kind of map is necessary. Instead the focus is on such topics as the relationship between literature and language, creolity, colonialism, nationalism, cultural pluralism, and 'marginalized' groups within a nation. The approach is comparative. Contributors have been asked to write essays that are useful to the beginner as well as the specialist, and they have been asked to examine the main concerns, opinions, and theories that have shaped discussion. While not avoiding generalizations, most essays are also grounded in the works, ideas, and contexts of the creative writers who made or are making the new literatures. Some contributors use an impersonal academic tone, others appear more committed, but each is personally involved in the new literatures and the problems of post-colonialism.

The book will introduce the reader to most of what is said and felt to be of significance. It will, for example, explain the lineage of national to Commonwealth to post-colonial literary criticism. Besides familiarizing readers with significant writers, concerns, and contexts, the contributors often question received opinion. The essays at times disagree with each other, and my Introduction often takes a different perspective from the contributors, but given the range of opinions and positions in the noisy world of literary criticism this is a more unified collection of essays than might be expected. The contributors share similar concerns and respect each other although holding different views and specializing in different areas. Many of the essays have been influenced by discussions among the contributors or with the editor. Both the beginner and specialist should find much to think about.

B. K.

# Contents

*List of Contributors*                                            xi

### PART I. INTRODUCTION

1. New Centres of Consciousness: New, Post-colonial, and
   International English Literature                                3
   *Bruce King*

### PART II. ENTANGLED ROOTS

2. Language, Orality, and Literature                             29
   *Chantal Zabus*

3. Psychology, Creolization, and Hybridization                  45
   *J. Michael Dash*

4. The Internationalization of Literatures                      59
   *Vinay Dharwadker*

### PART III. SETTLERS, COLONIALS, AND NATIONALISTS

5. Pioneers and Settlers                                        81
   *Aritha van Herk*

6. Colonial Literatures                                         102
   *W. H. New*

7. 'Forging the Conscience of Their Race': Nationalist Writers  120
   *C. L. Innes*

### PART IV. POST-COLONIALISM AND ITS DISCONTENTS

8. Plato's Cave: Educational and Critical Practices             143
   *Helen Tiffin*

9.  The Post-colonial Project: Critical Approaches and Problems   164
    *Gareth Griffiths*

10. Post-colonial Critical Theories   178
    *Stephen Slemon*

    PART V. BRANCHES, SITUATIONS, AND DIFFERENCES

11. Exiles and Expatriates   201
    *Chelva Kanaganayakam*

12. Diasporas and Multiculturalism   214
    *Victor J. Ramraj*

13. Post-colonial Women Writers and Feminisms   230
    *Ketu H. Katrak*

14. Paper Tracks: Indigenous Literatures in Canada, Australia, and New Zealand   245
    *Adam Shoemaker*

*Bibliography*   263

*Index*   303

# List of Contributors

J. MICHAEL Dash (University of the West Indies) has published *Literature and Ideology in Haiti* (1975), *Jacques Stephen Alexis* (1982), *Haiti and the United States* (1988), *Édouard Glissant* (1995), and translations of francophonic Caribbean literature.

VINAY DHARWADKER (University of Oklahoma) has co-edited, with A. K. Ramanujan, the *Oxford Anthology of Modern Indian Poetry* (1994) and edited Ramanujan's *Collected Poems* (1995). *Sunday at the Lodi Gardens* (1994) is his first volume of poetry.

GARETH GRIFFITHS (University of Western Australia) is author of *A Double Exile: African and West Indian Writing between Two Cultures* (1978), co-author of *The Empire Writes Back* (1989), and co-editor of *The Post-colonial Studies Reader* (1995).

C. L. INNES (The University, Canterbury) is author of *The Devil's Own Mirror: The Irishman and the African in Modern Literature* (1990), *Chinua Achebe* (1990), *Woman and Nation in Irish Literature and Society* (1993), and co-editor of *The Heinemann Book of Contemporary African Short Stories* (1992).

CHELVA KANAGANAYAKAM (Trinity College, University of Toronto) is author of *Structures of Negation: The Writings of Zulfikar Ghose* (1993).

KETU H. KATRAK (University of California—Irvine) is the author of *Wole Soyinka and Modern Tragedy* (1986).

BRUCE KING is author of *Derek Walcott and West Indian Drama* (1995), *V. S. Naipaul* (1993), *Three Indian Poets* (1991), *Modern Indian Poetry in English* (1987), *The New English Literatures* (1980), and other books.

WILLIAM NEW (University of British Columbia) is author of *Articulating West: Essays on Purpose and Form in Modern Canadian Literature* (1972), *Among Worlds: An Introduction to Modern Commonwealth and South African Fiction* (1975), *Dreams of Speech and Violence: The Art of the Short Story in Canada and New Zealand* (1987), *A History of Canadian Literature* (1989), and editor of *Four Hemispheres: An Anthology of English Short Stories from around the World* (1971), *Canadian Writers before 1890* (1990), and many other publications including *Critical Writings on Commonwealth Literature: A Selective Bibliography to 1970* (1975).

VICTOR J. RAMRAJ (University of Calgary) is author of *Mordecai Richler* (1983) and editor of *Concert of Voices: An Anthology of World Writing in English* (1995) and the journal *Ariel: A Review of International Literature*.

ADAM SHOEMAKER (Queensland University of Technology) is author of *Black Words, White Page: Aboriginal Literature 1929–1988* (1989), *Mudrooroo: A Critical Study* (1993), and co-editor of *Paperbark* (1990).

STEPHEN SLEMON (University of Alberta) is co-editor of *After Europe: Critical Theory and Post-colonial Writing* (1989).

HELEN TIFFIN (University of Queensland) is co-author of *The Empire Writes Back* (1989) and co-editor of *After Europe* (1989), *Past the Last Post: Theorizing Post-colonialism and Post-modernism* (1991), and *The Post-colonial Studies Reader* (1994).

ARITHA VAN HERK (University of Calgary) is author of a book of essays, *A Frozen Tongue* (1992). Her often prize-winning novels include *Judith* (1978), *The Tent Peg* (1981), *No Fixed Address* (1986), *Places Far from Ellesmere* (1990), and *In Visible Ink* (1991). She edited *Alberta Rebound: Thirty More Stories by Alberta Writers* (1990) and co-edited *West of Fiction* (1983).

CHANTAL ZABUS (Université Catholique de Louvain) is author of *The African Palimpsest: Indigenisation of Language in the West African Europhone Novel* (1990).

PART I

# INTRODUCTION

CHAPTER ONE

# New Centres of Consciousness: New, Post-colonial, and International English Literature

BRUCE KING

The Age of Postcolonialism was brought about by the new political and economic importance of former colonies after the Second World War and the rapid spread of communications and international business during the last third of the twentieth century. Local cultures in the process of modernization and undergoing the crisis of identity that accompanies hasty transformation were increasingly, if uneasily, in direct contact with an expanding Western culture and economy themselves undergoing mercuric changes including their relationships to former colonies and their own crisis of identity. The results were liberating, energizing, at times contradictory, as traditions crumbled and were constructed.

During the first phase national political and cultural liberation was the goal. In the second phase cultural and economic liberation became the ideal for groups and movements within and across national boundaries, including black nationalism, feminism, and recent immigrants, each of which claimed its own literature. Although a similar process could be seen in the cultures of other former imperial languages, it was in English-speaking nations that this development most rapidly and visibly took place. 'English literature' now meant such writers as Wole Soyinka, Chinua Achebe, Nadine Gordimer, J. M. Coetzee, Derek Walcott, V. S. Naipaul, Margaret Atwood, Michael Ondaatje, Les Murray, Salman Rushdie, Vikram Seth, Anita Desai and Janet Frame, none of whom was British, American, or even Irish. As English was the main international language of business, science, politics, travel, education and social change, even nations that were not former English colonies produced English-language writers. The new national literatures, national multicultural literatures and International English literature were parts of a developing urban global culture, produced by international politics, communications and a world-wide economy, which included a heightened awareness of difference partly to assert identity. (Nostradamus' lost prophecy *Theorizing a Global Culture*)

That English literature has changed radically since about 1960 is obvious; less clear is the nature of this new literature especially as the various descriptive terms have their own historical and political contexts. Many nationalists, Americans and cultural radicals regard

'Commonwealth' as a passing phase of British neo-colonialism. Others regard Post-colonial as an American and New Left ignorance of national differences that also disregards the continuing links between many English-speaking nations. International, Global, or World English homogenizes and suppresses differences. New Literatures indicates that post-colonialism is a further development of the decolonization and the changed cultural perspective that followed the Second World War; 'New' reminds us that the literatures of the former colonies are still not known or much studied abroad, in contrast to 'post-colonial' or 'global' which assume that familiarity with a few texts allows generalizations and the right to theorize. An objection is that New Literatures continues the drawing of national cultural boundaries during a time of the lowering of barriers and the criticism of nationalism. A further objection to the term New Literatures is that they have long histories, although their prominence on the world's cultural map is recent.

They did not seem old or neo-colonialist to many writers of the 1950s who struggled to create an authentic modern national literature in former English colonies where there were few readers, teachers, publishers, or critics interested in local writing. Nissim Ezekiel's poem 'Enterprise' might be read as an allegory about the small band who consciously set out to create a modern Indian poetry in English: 'It started as a pilgrimage | The sun beat down to match our rage. | . . . We lost a friend whose stylish prose | Was quite the best of all our batch. | . . . Some were broken, some merely bent. | . . . Home is where we have to earn our grace.'[1] Derek Walcott, who sees the Caribbean poet's task as Adamic in giving a new world names and identity, associates the excitement of his generation with Wordsworth's at the French Revolution: 'There is a force of exultation, a celebration of luck, when a writer finds himself a witness to the early morning of a culture that is defining itself, branch by branch, leaf by leaf, in that self-defining dawn.'[2]

## HISTORY

The new national literatures began with the first European explorations overseas; language, culture, literature, and education developed along with trade, domination, administration, and settlement. Explorers, traders, conquerors, travellers, and pioneers were some of the early European writers. There was a parallel literature written by non-

[1] Nissim Ezekiel, Collected Poems 1952–1988 (Bombay: Oxford University Press, 1989), 118.
[2] Derek Walcott, The Antilles: Fragments of Epic Memory (New York: Farrar, Straus, & Giroux, 1993) ('The Nobel Lecture', unpaginated).

Europeans who came into contact with European expansionism. Of interest as examples of how cultures view each other, the literature of cultural contact[3] remained the subtext of other themes as settlement and colonization began to produce writing specifically by and about the colonized, administrators, and settlers. The intricacies of such early pioneer and settler writing are discussed in the following pages by van Herk and many of the issues remain current. The English diarist or letter writer attempting to make sense of life in the colonies had to describe what had not been described before, and had to do so with the vocabulary and assumptions of Europe; often the only likely readership was European. Yet the act of filling a page, of describing a space, of populating it with local characters and manners, was the start of a new national literature.

Artists in such societies often felt they were stranded in distant provinces of the Empire far from the sources of light, culture, and patronage; creative writers debated the contrasting virtues of a new world versus the old. Much of the literature of the colonial period was about problems of settlement, and the societies they produced. The literature of the early settlers and colonials which was formerly thought of as a history of recording local fauna and flora, or as adapting alien manners and art-forms to new environments, has more recently attracted attention for its social and political implications, as can be seen in New's essay. South Africa is an example of how settlement was often built on continuing injustice and conflicting claims. Eventually elsewhere the distinctions between colonized and settlers became less sharp as new local societies and nations began to emerge with their own élites, classes, regions, immigrants, minorities, and other characteristics.

Colonial literature often treats of manners, morals, politics, religion, and most other interests of European literature, except that such concerns are explored within the possibilities, contrasts, and cultural hierarchies of local societies and their relationships to Europe. Most colonial and early independence fiction is written within the conventions of realism and social comedy.

Colonial government also created the outlines of a future modern state. Nationalist cultural assertion, discussed by Innes, political independence, and various post-colonial challenges to the new nation-states followed. The West Indies, where few of the original natives survived, exemplifies the creation of a new Creole society from a diversity of cultures and peoples, a topic central to Dash's essay and perhaps the central and most debated theme of this volume, as the relationship between abstract ideas and social realities is bound to be awkward and filled with tensions.

---

[3] See Mary Louise Pratt, *Imperial Eyes: Travel Writing and Transculturation* (London: Routledge, 1992).

While conditions and production varied at different places and times, the new literature was mostly ignored, or thought to be without interest, except by a few local intellectuals, and there was seldom a market or welcoming context for it. To be a serious writer with opportunities for publication and recognition meant leaving the colonies, which were felt to be provincial and unsupportive of local arts. Claude McKay, Jean Rhys, C. L. R. James, Samuel Selvon, George Lamming, and V. S. Naipaul are among the West Indian writers who became expatriates. Many Canadian, New Zealand, and Australian writers, such as Katherine Mansfield or Christina Stead, became expatriates and were regarded as part of the international modernist movement although they retained a sense of personal national identity. Some writers, such as the Australians Henry Handel Richardson and Martin Boyd, never really settled and their lives were characterized by continual movement between home and abroad.

Those who pull up their roots tend to become exiles, nostalgic for a now idealized culture of their origins, or cosmopolitans, like Christina Stead. Many well-known late colonial and Commonwealth writers were conflicted by or tried to blend their internationalism and longings for home. Too often, when, as in the case of Patrick White, they returned home, they were regarded by nationalists as alien élitists unconcerned with the problems of local society. Yet it was often the returning exiles, such as A. D. Hope in Australia and Nissim Ezekiel in India, who led the new literatures towards international standards and modern intellectual concerns. Even today many of the better Australian authors, such as Thomas Keneally and Frank Moorhouse, are criticized by those who insist on local subject matter.

The Second World War was followed by the collapse of the European empires, the granting of independence to and the conscious cultural decolonization of former colonies. This movement included such British Dominions as Canada and Australia, which were already independent but where British culture was regarded as superior and people still thought, and were taught, of England as 'home', their land of origin. Many artists and intellectuals returned home from abroad to become leaders in the creation of a new national culture.

The model, however, became India, Africa, and the West Indies, where there was a political struggle for self-rule and independence. Major writers of this period, including Achebe, Soyinka, and Walcott, tend to be concerned with problems of bi-culturalism, the relationship of nationalist cultural assertion to universalism, as well as critically examining what their newly independent nations were doing with their freedom. How could one reconcile cosmopolitan awareness, standards of judgement, and scepticism with the need to see the world through local, rather than alien, eyes? How could local folk culture be integrated with modern art? Such conflicts were never resolved and give the new literatures their strength. Younger writers, educated after national independence, feel such problems less pressingly and treat local society as a given, a reality with a diverse life of its own. The conflict between modernization and asserting a separate usable past, however, remains central to most national literatures and the various post-colonial movements that followed. It could be argued that the international literature of post-colonialism, in all languages, is based on the conflict between what is perceived as the traditional culture of the past and incorporation into a global modern culture.

While the large body of writing that appeared at the time of decolonization resulted as much from increased educational, social, and economic opportunities as from political concerns, the critical reception was usually informed by the politics of nationalism. Discussions of the new literatures are still shaped by themes of the long period of cultural assertion and opposition that was part of the context of political independence. And many of the themes—the need for a national language, history, and culture—have been continued by such movements as feminism, ethnic separatism, and gay rights, which might be thought of as micro- or pan-nationalisms that have a similar dynamism and logical structure to nationalism and use similar means to create a unified political movement.

Looked at historically the nationalist period has been followed by post-colonialism, a time when the unity of the state is being challenged by other kinds of identification, as discussed in essays by Ramraj, Katrak, and Shoemaker. Nationalism assumed that the people were one and shared similar interests, but this was mostly a way of uniting diversity. In practice many groups were ignored, had other interests, or continued to be repressed. In some parts of the world independence led to far greater repression. The logic and language of liberation and decolonization were therefore continued by the new regionalists, minorities, and other excluded groups.

The comparative history of the new literatures remains a future task. So far there has only been one tentative sketch.[4] While there are now histories of the English-language literatures of many countries including Australia, Canada, New Zealand, India, Ghana, and even such smaller states as Zimbabwe, much needs to be done. Nigeria, the most productive and significant black African nation, lacks a literary history, and at

---

[4] Bruce King, *New English Literatures: Cultural Nationalism in a Changing World* (London: Macmillan, 1980).

present the only West Indian literary history available consists of the essays in my *West Indian Literature*.[5]

Literary histories reflect three phases of post-colonial culture. Earlier histories, including K. R. Srinivasa Iyengar's *Indian Writing in English* (1962) and H. M. Green's *A History of Australian Literature* (1961), tend to be inclusive, uncritical, and favourably biased towards realism and nationalist politics. M. K. Naik's *A History of Indian Writing in English* (1982) and Leonie Kramer's *The Oxford History of Australian Literature* (1981) belong to the second period which takes a more selective, critical position, often influenced by modernist standards, the New Critics, and F. R. Leavis. Histories of the first period usefully discuss minor and non-'creative' authors and are chronological and aware of cultural context, while later histories usually consist of analytical essays on significant authors. During the third phase, histories—such as Terry Sturm's *The Oxford History of New Zealand Literature in English* (1991)—are influenced by such concerns as Critical Theory, multiculturalism, feminism, and native peoples. The important writers of the second period are likely to be treated during the third period as white male European-oriented élitists. A nationalist stick is used to beat the 'internationalist' poetics of the modernist canon, while a Third Worldist, sometimes Marxist, version of post-colonialism is used to deconstruct the 'nationalist' canon. The often expanded and revised *Literary History of Canada* offers many archaeological levels of cultural assumptions. Anthologies of the new national literatures follow a similar pattern with earlier ones using specific cultural references as a basis for inclusion, later anthologies tending towards a local modernist canon, and more recent volumes promoting writing by women, immigrants, and native peoples, often in their own languages or varieties of English.

Although the literatures have long histories, their 'take off'—the time when they first gained attention because of their vitality, originality, quality, and quantity—occurred during the mid-twentieth century when modernism blended with nationalist concerns in the writings of such writers as Patrick White, George Lamming, Walcott, and Soyinka. A similar development occurred slightly earlier in French with L. S. Senghor and Aimé Césaire. The next phase, post-colonialism, coincided with post-modernism as can be seen in Rushdie's *Midnight's Children* and Naipaul's *In a Free State*. The obvious parallel is the Latin American magical realists.

Is this the age of post-modernist post-colonialism? Literary critics have generally rejected the linkage of post-modern eclecticism, with its European notions of exhaustion and the end of history, to the vitality and

---

[5] Bruce King (ed.), *West Indian Literature* (Basingstoke: Macmillan, 1979; 2nd edn. 1995).

challenges of the post-colonial. European post-modernism is seen as the result of post-imperial cultural relativism, non-European post-modernism is thought to be the result of bringing many local traditional cultures together in a modern state and global economy. A better argument is that periodizations are abstractions that ignore or conflate too much. From a stylistic perspective the problem is not so simple. Vikram Seth's *A Suitable Boy* is a self-consciously traditional novel written against the kind of fabulation practised by Rushdie, but Seth's deliberate use of older literary manners and form itself might be regarded as characteristically post-modern. Or it could be seen as doing what artists have always done in finding models in the art of the past. In Gordimer's recent books, Walcott's *Omeros* (1990), and Naipaul's *The Enigma of Arrival* (1987) and *A Way in the World* (1994), the mixing of genres, the blend of fiction and autobiography, the self-reflexivity, and the re-examination of their earlier work and its influences might be regarded as a significant post-colonial variant of post-modern tendencies. The twilight of the Empire and its literary traditions are being revisioned through re-examined memories and the construction of new mythologies.

The similar histories of the new literatures and commentary about them suggest that they share in the continuous international circulation of ideas and intellectual fashions. Writing in dialect, in some form of social realism, in modernist and post-modernist styles appeared in most colonies or new nations shortly after becoming fashionable in Europe and the United States, as did literary criticism justifying the style as authentically, even uniquely, nationalist or post-colonial. This suggests that the new literatures are still related to a shared, now globalized, European and American culture. Hélé Béji's *Désenchantement national: Essai sur la décolonisation* (1982) although about Tunisia expresses post-nationalist concerns familiar to many English-language intellectuals. Given the increasing rapidity and ease of international communications how could it be otherwise?

Does this mean that the new literatures are overseas branches of good old Brit Lit Ltd.? No, because the local literatures have themselves become self-generating, taken on new themes, and by now have their own traditions, models, characteristics, history, and affiliations as well as being grounded in national or regional life. Rather than looking over one's shoulder at the great tradition of English literature, a young West Indian writer is more likely to suffer anxieties of influence from Walcott, V. S. Naipaul, Wilson Harris, Kamau Brathwaite or Earl Lovelace. Lawrence Scott's *Witchbroom* (1992) even includes acknowledgements to its many Caribbean literary influences. Ben Okri's models range from the previous generation of African writers through the classics of nineteenth-century European fiction and current Latin American magic realists. Rather than dialectics of home and abroad, native and alien, it is more accurate, if more difficult, to think of the new literatures as participating in a continually changing movement of artistic, cultural, and political influences which produce new states of consciousness at different times and places. While sharing in some West Indianness each West Indian writer will be different as a result of his or her unique experience. The difficulty is finding the right balance between discussion of such specificity, national tendencies, and the international developments that are part of post-colonialism and globalization.

The problem, however, was always there. At what point did pioneer writers in Australia or Canada become Australian or Canadian? Why are West Indian or Indian authors long settled in England not considered British writers? What does one do about the current jet-setters that regularly divide their time between several countries? Some think of themselves as national authors, others as international or 'world' writers.

### NATIONALISM AND INTERNATIONALISM

Imperial powers import and are changed by the cultures they colonize; the international cultural market has let the Barbarians into the former imperial centres. The boomerang offers an analogy to describe how an imperial culture is taken abroad, adapted, and then returns to influence future generations. England and the United States are experiencing their own internal decolonizations and their writers are at present influenced by the new literatures and cultures. Everyone wants to be a cultural métis or post-colonial. The debate about multiculturalism has its parallels in renewed Welsh and Scottish nationalism and in an interesting, if complicated, discussion about Anglocentricity and provincialism in literary studies.[6]

The new English literature, however, is not just the Empire writing back; its authors include Eastern Europeans and Asians, whose origins are outside the English-speaking world. As English has become an international language, literatures in English are being written by Russians, Thais, and Japanese. Current discussions of post-colonialism and multiculturalism seldom face this, although the issue has been raised by Joseph Brodsky and must occur to anyone considering such a writer as Nuruddin Farah for whom English is also a foreign language. The internationalization of English literature overlaps with, and perhaps should be seen as encompassing, Commonwealth, Post-colonial, and multicultural literature.

[6] Robert Crawford, *Devolving English Literature* (Oxford: Clarendon Press, 1992).

For many writers, however, questions about nationalism, race, even colour, are not of prime importance as the arts have their own languages, their own cultures, and are international. Walcott is West Indian, Seamus Heaney is Irish, both are highly 'national' writers concerned about their own language and culture; both also believe that poets share a metalanguage of poetry which is used to name, define, and celebrate the world. Many artists claim that emotions or artistic conventions are universal as they are based on common human characteristics such as the heartbeat, breathing, or feelings of loss. Writers also often make a distinction between form, which they see as universal, and subject, which they regard as local and particular. Most modern theorists reject such simple, rule-of-thumb distinctions, but criticism has been unable to balance universalism and creative concerns with the national and political contexts of the new literatures. Discussion of the national literatures and internationalism somehow goes astray. The terms of the discourse are not right to handle the ways in which ideas and influences circulate while societies and individuals remain distinct. Curiously we have far less trouble discussing such entangled developments in music, painting, or genetics.

Although nationalists see decolonization as resulting from local actions, the struggle against imperialism was and is international, an alliance between nationalism and the Left. That such movements succeed, and that we have a resulting literature, is usually the consequence of international politics, economics, marketing, and opinion. Yet each national literature is different and its branches are different from each other. Ezekiel writing from cosmopolitan Bombay will see a different India from Jayanta Mahapatra in provincial Orissa. David Dabydeen is a British West Indian writer; Austin Clarke is a Canadian West Indian writer; Earl Lovelace is a Trinidadian West Indian writer. The realities they know and experience are different. But they all share in and make use of a larger culture of English and European literature. Attempts to diagram the complexities of such cross-pollenizations are doomed to failure if only because the historical circumstances keep changing as has the paradoxical nature of colonialism and post-colonialism.

One agent of change is the United States, the new liberator, the new imperialist. The role of the United States during and after the Second World War meant that liberal free-trade capitalism would replace imperial preferences, and colonies would become independent nations often dependent on American aid, trade, and cultural influences. Thus began a period of rapid Americanization, including American literary models, that at first seemed liberating and modernizing but soon was felt to be neo-colonialist. Much of what is thought of as post-colonial has some connection to American influences on education, art, opportunities, and social attitudes.

The United States has long offered alternatives to British political, cultural, and literary models for writers and intellectuals in what are now the new nations. An example of the way the United States opened new directions was the influence of American underground publications on the group associated with *Tish* in Vancouver. The San Francisco poets introduced a generation of young Canadians—Frank Davey, Fred Wah, George Bowering—to 'Open Field' poetics. If at first this meant imitation of the American tradition of Ezra Pound, W. C. Williams, Charles Olson, and Robert Creeley, it also showed writers how to use their own voices, local materials, and contemporary popular culture. Instead of the traditions of the past and a high culture associated with Europe, a literature based on local realities was possible, yet it was also a literature connected with what was happening on the contemporary literary scene. Soon their poetry became Canadianized in subject matter as they learned to use their own lives and interests. Their Open Field poetics became post-modern open, sometimes playful, forms, and took on other influences, especially deconstructionist theory. In Robert Kroetsch's *Seed Catalogue* (1986) we can see how such multiple influences resulted in a new avant-garde regionalism. Davey, Kroetsch, and other *Open Letters* contributors have led the discussion of what might be thought of post-nationalist Canadian literature.[7]

The new national literatures did not just come from finding some usable past in native traditions or the 'little culture' of the folk; the catalyst was as much the assimilation of the latest contemporary styles in contrast to what was felt to be an outdated British colonial tradition. Often the styles were from the American and French avant-garde. Kirkby's *The American Model* includes excellent essays by Australian poets about ways American poetry has influenced them, why, and in what ways Australian poetry remains distinctive.[8]

Modern nationalism itself is a product of Romanticism with its idea of the nation as the folk having their own state, culture, language, even religion. There is a tendency by critics and some writers to see the new literatures in terms of a simple opposition between, on the one side, the language and culture of the colonizer, and on the other resistance by some native language and culture. Even the most supple discussions too often resort to ahistorical assumptions of native versus the imported. Detailed knowledge of literary and cultural history provides a corrective. There has long been a circulation of influences of a much more complex kind than the simple polarities of present theories; influences and models do not move in one direction. African independence movements in-

---

[7] See Frank Davey, *Post-national Arguments* (Toronto: University of Toronto Press, 1993).
[8] Joan Kirkby (ed.), *The American Model* (Sydney: Hale & Iremonger, 1982).

fluenced American and Canadian minorities and women during the 1960s, then Americans influenced the Commonwealth with 'minority' liberation movements. The process can be seen in Margaret Atwood's writings at the time of *Surfacing* (1972) and *Survival* (1972), the latter being the critical theory behind the former. African liberation movements and Frantz Fanon's psychological theories about the need for violence as part of liberation are clearly as much influences as were attempts to define Canada's distinctness from such then current ideas of the New World American Adam. Atwood's African models seem in turn to be part of the late 1960s counter-culture in the United States, a set of attitudes which *Surfacing* both assumes and criticizes, but in which it shares. *Surfacing* and *Survival* articulated a sense of how Canadians, because of their history, environment, and social choices, felt unlike their neighbours to the south. Atwood's books soon became a model for other Commonwealth writers, especially in the 'white' Commonwealth. The influence of Africa on American and European music, and the way a partly Africanized Western music has influenced modern African music, shows how the arts circulate, crossing and recrossing boundaries, to create new, unique forms of culture.

There is also an increasing circulation of influences between the new national literatures, especially within the Commonwealth. The short stories of Frank Sargeson, a New Zealander, showed Australian poets ways of reproducing common lower- and middle-class speech. Rushdie's *Midnight's Children* showed Australian, Indian, and African novelists how post-modernist fabulation and self-reflexivity could be given national political dimensions and used allegorically. The line of transmission was from Günter Grass and Gabriel García Márquez through Rushdie to such Commonwealth novelists as Syl Cheney-Coker, Alex Miller, and Amitav Ghosh. The continual movement of writers within the Commonwealth means that ideas, models, and literary techniques rapidly become transnational and transcultural. African authors teaching in the Pacific islands influence Pacific island writing. While such influences are usually between writers in the same language, they have at times crossed languages, as with the influence of Aimé Césaire on E. Kamau Brathwaite within the Caribbean.

Although this collection of essays is concerned with writing in English, there is often a parallel colonial, national, or post-colonial literature in non-European languages which has its own complex relationship to the literatures of the past. In India or Africa colonization led to modern European-influenced literatures in local languages before there was an interesting modern literature in English. Many of these modern literatures became very good, and their writers discovered Verlaine, Valéry, surrealism, and T. S. Eliot before local English-language writers did. Such

Indian English poets as Dilip Chitre and Arun Kolatkar are also major writers in Marathi. Mazisi Kunene belongs to a modern tradition of Zulu poets; his translations of his poems into English are often magnificent poetry. There is a still unrecognized circulation of influences between modern local-language literatures and European-language literatures. Cross-cultural literary influences can be seen in the poetry of A. K. Ramanujan and Mahapatra and in the plays of Soyinka. Cross-pollenization takes place in various ways. After Kofi Awoonor began to write poetry based on translations from Ghanaian oral verse, Kofi Anyidoho, who although younger was brought up in a family where Ewe traditions remain alive, found ways to use a traditional world-view along with oral forms and expressions in his English-language poetry.

Just as there is no clear dividing line between the new national literatures in English and their overseas branches in the United States or England, so there is no clear division between the new national literatures in English and in local languages. Some authors write in more than one language and others are at home in several languages, but because of education or personal circumstances write only in one. Kamala Das writes poetry in English and prose in both English and Malayalam, a southern Indian language; when she began writing poetry there were no modern Malayalam poets and her English-language education in northern India left her unable to handle the complex forms of traditional Malayalam verse. Mehrotra says that for the Indian English-language poet no one language is foundational with the others being superstructural; many cultural languages coexist and continually change roles in the writer's creative imagination. A source of strength in the new literatures is the ways in which linguistic, artistic, moral, and mental structures are present in various combinations, fusions, conflicts, and contradictions. Such terms as resistance, multiculturalism, creolity, and modernization isolate and fetishize some characteristics of the new literatures at the expense of others. The comments of writers about their own work and society are useful correctives. A diversity of views about African literature and culture can be found in essays by Soyinka, Achebe, Njabulo Ndebele and interviews by Duerden and Pieterse and Wilkinson.[9]

MARKETS

The rapid development of the new literatures can be explained in terms of the economics and sociology of publishing. The creation of new

---

[9] Wole Soyinka, *Myth, Literature and the African World* (Cambridge: Cambridge University Press, 1972); id., *Art, Dialogue and Outrage,* ed. Biodun Jeyifo (Ibadan: New Horn Press, 1988); Chinua Achebe, *Morning Yet on Creation Day* (London: Heinemann, 1975); id., *Hopes*

nations brought about a demand for school and university syllabuses with local content thus creating a market. Nationalist critics at first reluctantly and then energetically saw the value of a comparative approach and of international associations to promote the new literatures. Many of the standard earlier works of literary criticism reflect this period of discovering commonalities, and much worthwhile criticism is still produced by journals of Commonwealth literature and as a result of conferences of the various branches of the Association of Commonwealth Literature and Language Studies. The Commonwealth critics' network—to which some contributors to this book belong—remains important in exchanging news about up-and-coming writers, in sharing ideas, and in resisting the takeover of the new literatures by American and Americanized intellectuals whose vision is limited to their own 'post-colonial' cultural wars. Good interpretative criticism, and creative writing, can be found in such journals as *Wasafiri* and *Ariel*, or is published by Dangaroo Press, Bayreuth African Studies, and the University of Queensland Press. The many special issues of *Kunapipi* (also published as Dangaroo Press books) are themselves part of the history of this field. Too often post-colonial theorists and those readers just discovering the new literatures are unfamiliar with the long continuing discussion and criticism by both creative writers and scholars that has characterized Commonwealth literary studies.

National independence and decolonization also brought about independent local publishing houses. Instead of Oxford University Press or Penguin being directed from England there were now locally owned companies with their own policies. As the local companies needed to sell their books abroad and the British companies linked up with the local companies, the result was an international, global flow of publications. The economics of publishing (like the economics of the automobile industry) made a global market necessary. As local economies grow so do the publishing markets. India is the third largest English-language market in the world. Some literary firms have told me that over half of their sales are to the Commonwealth. As local publication becomes easier and overseas success more likely, there are more writers. The days are over when many Australians or West Indians had privately to publish and sell their own works. Once a Rushdie or Vikram Seth has a success, publishers look for the next big success.

As English has become an international language, there is also an international market beyond the former British colonies. Because of the

*and Impediments* (London: Heinemann, 1988); Njabulo S. Ndebele, *South African Literature and Culture* (Manchester: Manchester University Press, 1994); Cosmo Pieterse and Dennis Duerden (eds.), *African Writers Talking* (London: Heinemann, 1972); Jane Wilkinson, *Talking with African Writers* (London: James Currey, 1992).

international readership the best-known works of the new literatures are likely to be novels that have as their subject matter the grand themes of decolonization, racial and cultural conflict, or disillusionment with independence. Plays, poetry, and fiction that require familiarity with a national culture, history, or society are less likely to travel well. (There are also fewer introductions to such genres; one of the few is my *Post-colonial English Drama* (1992).) Vikram Seth's *A Suitable Boy* (1993) was a breakthrough in being an international success while consciously avoiding the translation of Indian words and concepts into English. While British and American English are still the international norms, increasingly readers of Rushdie, Walcott, Soyinka, Saro-Wiwa, and other writers are faced by unfamiliar words, idioms, dialects, and languages.

## THE POST-COLONIAL, OTHERS, AND DIFFERENCE

The increasing internationalization of the literary market, discussed here by Dharwadker, has parallels in the development of rapid communications, ease of transportation, massive immigration, and lowering of national boundaries to foreign workers. Not only do ideas and tastes move around the world rapidly, but so do people. Not long ago Ezekiel, Dom Moraes, Adil Jussawalla, or R. Parthasarathy felt they had to choose between exile or living in India. A trip to England was expensive. Now students and writers fly back and forth. Vikram Seth is an example of the new internationalism or globalization. Whereas earlier diasporas felt uprooted there are now diasporas that are really rooted both here and there (unlike the immigrant's nostalgia for home in the past). Even expatriates have a different perspective from the international expatriate of the past. Younger Indian writers, such as Agha Shahid Ali, Meena Alexander, Amitav Ghosh, and Sujata Bhatt, live or have lived in many countries. There are now diaspora literatures of those who are acculturated but not fully assimilated in foreign lands and these are difficult to place in national literary traditions.

Within such diasporas, discussed by Ramraj, there are distinctions between the internationalized cultural élite, immigrants who feel exiled, and those raised abroad who have retained or developed a renewed sense of ethnicity. As Kanaganayakam's essay shows there are distinctions between kinds of exiles. Practical politics may require rainbow coalitions, but within England there is a clear distinction between writers who consider themselves Africans, British West Indians, Black Britons, or Indians. The common characteristic is a multiple consciousness, a feeling of participating in several cultural groups or traditions without being fully at home.

Paradoxically the development of new national economies linked to the international market and communications contributed to the rise of a new regionalism and pan-nationalist minority movements. The formerly sad, impoverished, isolated colonies of the Empire now have thriving regional communities capable of supporting local literary journals and publishers that are very much in contact with the rest of the world and plugged directly into an international distribution network through television, Internet, and jet aeroplanes. One result is a new cultural regionalism with its own versions of the avant-garde. Sections of the global network allow the writer from Manitoba or Alberta who is ignored in New York to be read and discussed in Australia, Sri Lanka, or Germany. Feminist, gay, and 'diaspora' literatures might be regarded as pan-movements which gain part of their strength from the access to readers, publicity, and critics across national boundaries made possible by the new global market.

Until about 1980 criticism of the new literatures was largely impressionistic and historical, concerned with such problems as the relationships between the literatures and European literature, and influenced by the politics of national or racial cultural assertion. Such criticism had a close relationship to the creative literature and reflected the concerns found in previous generations of writers. The earlier literature of nationalistic cultural assertion had by the generation of Achebe, Soyinka, and Naipaul become complicated as writers began to ask: what exactly is this new nation, what is its relationship to its various social groups, and why has it already become so disillusioning? The grand period of decolonization and cultural assertion was already a time of renewed alienation and questioning; critics were often divided between wanting to join the celebration of independence and celebrating those who were sceptically examining the results. Unfortunately this close relationship between criticism and literature was bypassed as the theorization of literature and culture began to dominate the teaching of the humanities. Paradoxically, the nature and history of the new literatures was challenged by post-colonial studies, which view most high cultural forms as politically implicated and likely to be complicit with imperialism or social injustice. The essays by Tiffin and Griffiths discuss some of the resulting problems.

Post-colonial should mean the period beginning with national independence in contrast to the colonial, but in recent theory the new nations are regarded sceptically as neo-colonialist. One of the ironies of recent literary history is how the new national literatures had barely begun to find a place on the cultural map before they were shoved aside, or said to be oppressive and dominant, by the post-colonial deconstruction of national culture. In the process the study of post-colonial theory replaced the study of post-colonial literature.

Such theory has more often been concerned with the West's view of the Other, or how European views have influenced Third World writers, than with actual writing from the new nations. Said's *Orientalism* (1978) is the model for critics intent on showing that even benign, well-intended, progressive Europeans writing about non-Western culture share the guilt of imperialism since, the argument goes, their involvement, their very glance, must be shaped by prejudices and stereotypes and any contribution made to knowledge will be complicit in cultural imperialism; even sympathetic research into the culture of the Others contributes to Western cultural and political imperialism by mapping the territory for invasion of and colonizing the Other's assumptions about himself.[10] Only theorists are apparently immune from Western Panendemic Cultural Imperialism. Is not their view of the West their own Other?

Such theory assumes that all writing, whether an administrative document or a novel, is an ideological construction, a devious means of either conscious political persuasion or the symbolization of unconscious prejudices and desires, from which it is necessary to tease out the hidden politics.[11] Those who believe that all of life is political will regard works of art primarily as political texts. There has been surprisingly little examination of the assumptions, of what is inscribed in the methodology, but analysis has been damaging. Lowe has an especially delicious chapter on the absurdities of what she terms 'The Desires of Postcolonial Orientalism: Chinese Utopias of Kristeva, Barthes, and *Tel quel*'.[12] This influential group of French progressive intellectuals started with the notion that 'the Chinese language' and therefore culture was feminine and from that bit of silliness built a theory of China as a woman's paradise. Jeff Lewis shows how attempts to de-Orientalize Australian culture impose still another Western Orientalism on the East.[13]

Maughan-Brown's discussion of Kenyan literature is perhaps the most successful application of a political-discourse approach because his study is firmly grounded in historical details and empirical sociological analysis.[14] As there has been little detailed research into the actual social contexts, cultural networking, and literary careers of writers and influential movements beyond the studies by Wren, Walmsley, and King, discussion of the new literatures tends to be historically uninformed.[15] Theories

---

[10]   Gauri Viswanathan, *Masks of Conquest* (New York: Columbia University Press, 1989).

[11]   Fredric Jameson, *The Political Unconscious* (Ithaca, NY: Cornell University Press, 1981).

[12]   Lisa Lowe, *Critical Terrains* (Ithaca, NY: Cornell University Press, 1991).

[13]   Jeff Lewis, 'Putu Goes to Paris: Global Communication and Australian Imaginings of the East', *Kunapipi*, 14/3 (1994), 54–75.

[14]   David Maughan-Brown, *Land, Freedom and Fiction* (London: Zed, 1985).

[15]   Robert M. Wren, *Those Magical Years* (Washington: Three Continents Press, 1991); Anne Walmsley, *The Caribbean Artists Movement 1966–72* (London: New Beacon Books, 1992); Bruce King, *Modern Indian Poetry in English* (New Delhi: Oxford University Press, 1987); id., *Derek Walcott and West Indian Drama* (Oxford: Clarendon, 1995).

have been created from the top down; literary criticism with a precise awareness of social differentiation would be an ideal worth pursuing. Local literary and intellectual journals offer a corrective to simplified generalizations. A subscription to the excellent *Southern African Review of Books* is perhaps the best introduction to the complexities of South African literature and cultural politics.

Ahmad offers a useful perspective on current slipshod eclectic theorizing of the post-colonial.[16] Ahmad situates the current anti-'orientalism' as itself an 'orientalism' produced by the Western counter-culture and New Left of the 1960s and 1970s which romanticized the Third World while ignoring the actual social, economic, and political realities of the former colonies. The homogenization of the Third World into an idealized movement of resistance to imperialism is another example of the West ignoring the specificity of alien societies and cultural products while, by 'othering' the Third World, also ignoring what is common to humanity. To claim, for example, that a Hindu or Muslim does not have similar desires for personal liberty or economic advancement to someone in the West contributes to the perpetuation of feudalism, tyranny, and neo-colonialism. Just as non-Western cultures are highly differentiated, socially and economically complex, so their internal liberation and potential liberation from alien economic power often requires assimilation of Western technology and thought. For Ahmad, imperialism brought the benefits of modernization along with new injustices.

In *The Mimic Men, The Overcrowded Barracoon, Among Believers*, and other works, Naipaul looks sceptically at various nationalist movements, finding them without sufficient economic basis for actual national liberation, deluded by a rhetoric of revolution while lacking the material means of social change, or simply a guise for continuing aspects of feudalism and local oppression. Naipaul's writing, with its concern for utility, consciousness of the material basis of society and culture, and identification with India and the Indian diaspora, offers a thorough, if at times too pessimistic, examination of the problems of late colonialism, nationalism, and the post-colonial. In *A House for Mr Biswas* (1961) Biswas at first cannot escape from the grinding poverty and oppressive society of rural farming, needs to acquire the means of survival in the modern world, eventually masters a trade, and by acquiring possessions and a career is enabled partly to fulfil his ambitions of 'paddling' his own canoe. Biswas's problems could be seen as analogous to colonial societies as they strive for independence and self-development. There is the need for the economic basis for such independence and for attitudes that go with it. Naipaul's remarks about cultural nationalism are at times

---

[16] Aijaz Ahmad, *In Theory* (London: Verso, 1992).

confusing as they have different contexts and his own thought has changed, but the basic assumption is that without the economic means, mastery of skills, awareness of market, rationality, and an acceptance of what is required in the modern world, talk of liberation remains talk obscuring continuing dependency. This also means that much of the world will remain dependencies of stronger political and economic powers. Walcott, however, warns against confusing economic with cultural dependency; art gives permanence and status to otherwise unrecognized, unshaped and changing cultures.

Too often theoretical studies are concerned with the supposed political evils or hidden imperialism of Shakespeare, Kipling, and Jane Austen. Soyinka, Walcott, or Gordimer seldom figure in such studies, or if they do are implied to be neo-colonial élitists. Achebe, Ngugi wa Thiong'o, or Brathwaite might be cited, but only in their more nationalist cultural assertions or as part of an attack on the portrayal of the non-European world by such writers as Joseph Conrad, Joyce Cary, or Graham Greene. Theory itself colonizes literature; like other exploitative aliens it needs to be resisted while learning from it. Ashcroft, Griffiths, and Tiffin in *The Empire Writes Back* (1989) show how theory is applicable to the new literatures, but they too construct a demonized European tradition against which the empire is rebelling.

Post-colonial cultural studies often are concerned with pan- or micro-nationalisms such as gender or black studies. While using discourse analysis such -isms depend on many of the characteristics of nationalism. Like nationalism such -isms are modernizing movements which attempt to create unity through the construction of a usable past (including a history of victimization, heroes, and enemy Others), a national language, and the assertion of a cultural uniqueness which has been suppressed. Just as nationalist movements are led by groups which claim to represent the people but are themselves élites in the process of formation that are soon challenged by those who feel left out from the resulting political gains, so the new -isms have fragmented with, for example, black and Third World feminists arguing that they are not represented by white middle-class feminists. In the process post-colonial has shifted its meaning from the study of new national literatures to a deconstruction of the nation in which various social groups within—whether new or older—nations are said to be distinctive cultures, usually oppressed by dominant groups.

If the concept of national literatures ignores diversity of cultures and identities within a state's boundaries, post-colonialism often homogenizes the non-Western into a Third World Other or becomes a metaphor for any cultural study of any subject in any language. See Kam Tam reviewing *Past the Last Post: Theorizing Post-colonialism and Post-*

*modernism* objects, 'by privileging post-colonial writing as dominant post-colonial cultural text, the book is basically revealed as élitist. . . . Where are the pulp fictions? Where are the films? The television?'[17] A review in the *Times Literary Supplement* shows how the concept post-colonial has become unanchored from its original historical and political situation and is seen as analogous to any form of resistance to supposed straight white male national norms: 'Hallam's reassessment of Sodom from the committed point of view of the Sodomite reads like the post-co-lonial reappropriation of a once-subject people. Focussed and purpose-ful, his account of oppression is, *ipso facto*, a record of resistance.'[18] The reviewer here makes explicit what is often assumed in much post-colonial criticism, where certain groups considered formerly oppressed or mar-ginalized are engaged in resistance. Linda Hutcheon's 'Introduction' (1995) to an issue of *PMLA* concerned with 'Colonialism and the Postcolonial Condition' brilliantly summarizes recent directions in post-colonial theory, but ignores creative literature and the views of creative writers. Only one of the seven essays in the issue is a reading of an English-language post-colonial text; the rest are concerned with theory, literature in other languages, and the 'homoerotics' of Orientalism. Many readers might feel that the new English literatures were better served when they were marginal to the academic profession and before criticism was assumed to have a political purpose.

Class and sexuality are part of the sociology and psychology of the arts, but are seldom treated by literary critics with the care or precise do-cumentation that is needed to 'place' a person or text in context. Instead of detailed research to understand the role of social differences in culture, vague notions of group or class are used to deny the authenticity of an author or literary work, assert their complicity in some injustice, or praise some writers as authentic marginal voices. Attempts to qualify the study of the post-colonial through 'positionality'—analysis of Ethnicity, Class, Gender, and Sexual Preference—often begin with conclusions inscribed in their assumptions and methodology. Once you set out to find injustice or anything else in literature you will find it. At its best the study of 'positionality' recognizes that literature is filled with what older critics termed ambiguities and ambivalences having conflicting moral, cultural, social, and psychological origins. Whereas examination of positionality has often made colonial literature appear more interesting, it has too often been applied reductively, or to make simplistic assertions about value, to more recent texts.

---

[17] See Kam Tam, *Span* 33 (May 1992), 152–4. (Review of Ian Adam and Helen Tiffin (eds.), *Past the Last Post: Theorizing Post-colonialism and Post-modernism* (New York: Harvester Wheatsheaf, 1991).)

[18] Gregory Woods, 'Aimless Snippets', *Times Literary Supplement* 5 Feb. 1994, p. 10.

Reductionism is inherent to critical approaches that use the arts for other purposes; the actualities of lives, personalities, texts, and complex situations are ignored in favour of group labels. Even such terms as diversity and difference ignore uniqueness and particularity; theorists who treat the individual as a creation of language and society are bound to be distrustful and unsympathetic towards that which cannot be easily classified. A problem with such formulae, beyond the importation of new prejudices in place of the old, is that subsequent critics must devote energy discussing and qualifying them, as I have here, and the study of literature becomes the study of theory or a quarrel about social justice.

The basic problem with nationalism, post-colonialism, and other conceptual terms is that attempts to define difference usually result in an essentialism, a stereotype, or an idealization. The authors of *Éloge de la créolité* distinguish between exteriority (nativist, racist, indigenist, polarized, imitative, or oppositional) and an interiority that results from full acceptance of the Creole as 'the *interactional or transactional aggregate* of Caribbean, European, African, Asian and Levantine cultural elements, united on the same soil by the yolk of history'. After defining diversity as a 'relative cohabitation' between populations they rapidly move down the road of abstractions towards ethnic separatism, micro-nationalism, generalized Others, a sentimental primitivism, and abandonment of the forms of Western democracy for some idealized authentic politics. Creoleness expresses itself through language, especially orality and folk literature and is 'buried in our collective unconscious'; without learning the cultural traditions of the past 'it is difficult for collective identity to take shape'. 'Our writing must unreservedly accept our popular beliefs, our magico-religious practices, our magic realism,' 'For us there are no *formal freedoms*.' While the authors want to share in the world's modern culture they have provided a recipe for a cultural nationalist reactionary dictatorship. Perhaps the nature of language, with its binary structures, makes it impossible to explain the complexities of culture?[19]

### CHANGE

Cultures change, have always changed and have been influenced by other cultures. Unchanging cultures ossify and become sterile. In *Things Fall Apart* Achebe carefully makes the reader aware that the traditional Igbo culture which Okonkwo claims to represent varied from clan to clan and

---

[19] Jean Bernabé, Patrick Chamoiseau, and Raphaël Confiant, *Éloge de la créolité/In Praise of Creoleness*, bilingual edition, trans. M. B. Taleb-Khyar (Paris: Éditions Gallimard, 1993), 87, 95, 97, 101, 117.

was always changing. Achebe is against the notion of African culture as stasis. Okonkwo's flaw is his rigidity, his failure to adapt. Where preservation of the clan or group is the first priority, obsession with cultural traditions can be dangerous. Kwame Appiah shows how the diversity of African cultures has been obscured by a Pan-Africanism which in itself has been influenced by radical ideologies, while Africa's long, deep relationship to the intellectual life of the United States and Europe has been hidden by nationalist and Pan-African constructions of an African tradition. Gilroy finds the roots of much 'black' ideology in Hegelian philosophy; he claims that modernity results in a black Atlantic culture that transcends ethnicity and causes a double consciousness. Olive Senior's impressive *Arrival of the Snake-Woman and Other Stories* (1989) moves between finding a usable past in traditional rural Jamaican communal mores and a powerful feminist argument about individual independence in the modern world.

Culture is influenced by technology. Arshia Sattar says that television (especially since satellite transmissions) is more a global influence than international business or any political imperialism. If you turn off the sound you can see that Indian singers, dancers, actors, and other entertainers share a similar body language based on MTV. Regardless of what language is being spoken or sung, communication is through a common visual language derived from America. Western media also shape the kind of message; if you can watch CNN's on the spot coverage, you are unlikely to keep tuned to a government broadcast of carefully censored news designed to shape public opinion.[20] Such cultural changes help to explain the attractions of nativism, ethnicity, nationalism, and other forms of separatism. As nations and groups are brought closer together with shared desires, tastes, and ideas, the more likely they are to be conscious of and assert differences. The attraction of an increasing universal consumerist liberal culture intensifies the stresses of social change, while the pains and disappointments of acculturation and assimilation challenge self-identity and produce re-ethnification.

It is possible that we best can learn about literary and cultural traditions and influences by considering the history of popular music or jazz. Most traditional arts were themselves in the past the products of a creative use of alien influences. Both music and art history show how ideas, techniques, styles, and movements are taken from one place to another, change in their new environment, and find patronage and a role in local societies while continuing to remain in touch with newer outside influences. Traditions are yesterday's changes; the cultural is always intercultural. The intercultural should be seen from the inside, as part of

[20] Arshia Sattar, 'Does Television Exist If You Don't Watch It?', *Literary Criterion* [Bangalore], 28/4 (1993), 62–71.

a society's creative adaptation and synthesis, rather than an alien imposition. Artists, whether professional Yoruba drummers or Western-trained composers, always creatively respond to their environment in producing new forms suitable for their time. The city is where various groups and cultures come together to produce something new.

It is said that post-colonial theory is the product of an expatriate élite addressing a Euro-American academy predisposed towards post-structuralist analysis and seeing the world in terms of progressive and reactionary movements. Replies to post-colonial theories within the Commonwealth and Third World are usually themselves attempts to claim a bit of the action—to create a space, say, for the white Commonwealth, or for local nationalists and Marxists—while resisting what is thought of as another form of cultural imperialism. When claims of being a victim are a means of political and cultural power it is to be expected that everyone should want to be a victim, but the real interest in the new literatures is their world-wide success rather than a continuing colonial heritage of failure. Often modern national cultures have developed more successfully than the local economies and politics, although some nations, such as Canada, Australia, and India, have also become economic giants. Many of those advocating de-Orientalization and post-colonialism might be thought rather among the favoured than the victims.

It is time to reconsider some current notions of resistance. Many writers, including Wole Soyinka, and Jack Mapanje, have been imprisoned or forced into exile as a result of actual political struggle against the tyrannies of their governments; others, notably Salman Rushdie, have lived in fear of their lives because of their writings. Ken Saro-Wiwa was often imprisoned for his criticism of corruption and tyranny in Nigeria; due to his leadership in defending the Ogoni people he was killed by the government. They are the brave, the rebels, the resisters. Too often others, especially literary critics, have assumed the honours of the struggle against colonialism and post-colonial tyrannies.

While much theory appears antagonistic towards the complexities and achievements of the better writers, post-coloniality recognizes that nations are mental, social, and political constructions that change according to circumstances. In a time of massive immigration, rapid international communication, and the increased demands by minorities, national cultural boundaries are less stable than in the past and notions of national identity are changing. Some writers, such as Bharati Mukherjee in the United States and Neil Bissoondath in Canada, argue for assimilation; Claire Harris and Marlene Nourbese Philip insist on their black and female group identity in Canada; others, especially those raised in England such as David Dabydeen, Fred D'Aguiar, and Caryl Phillips, claim a bi-national, black, or British West Indian identity. The history of the Jews, or of the Irish abroad, might explain such ambivalence; even when there is assimilation without the obvious distinctiveness of skin colour, groups formerly regarded as inferior are likely to experience continuing prejudices that result in a sense of difference.

It is probable that the age of post-colonialism is already over; post-colonialism is said to mask continuing colonialism, a way to appropriate Others for Western culture, a stage towards global analysis. A major interdisciplinary symposium on international post-colonialism was as much concerned with a critique of the idea of the post-colonial as with its theory.[21] The clever are abandoning the ship, for globalization theory, transculturalization, positionality, and detailed social history. There will, however, always be a conflict between traditionalists wanting to construct an ideal past and modernizers embracing change; usually this takes the shape of nationalist (or regionalist) versus internationalist or cosmopolitan. Change, however, has been taking place since the beginning of time and all cultures are mixtures of other cultures. The essays by Zabus and Dash indicate some of the ways this takes place. There has always been trade, travel, communication, imitation, influences, and cross-pollenization; Amitav Ghosh's *In an Antique Land* (1992) shows the extensive international trade and cross-cultural influences that existed for centuries between Asia and Africa before the time of European imperialism. The traditionalist is usually also a modernizer, but one who seeks to construct a usable cultural past while desiring modern politics and technology. Nostalgia for a supposed past is especially appealing during times of rapid change, but most societies keep their difference as they modernize.

The new literatures are products of change, often have change as a subject, and each literature has writers who are traditionalists and those who are modernizers. Simplistic polar opposites such as traditionalists and modernizers are, however, misleading about writers or writing. Achebe is nostalgic for a past when clan society was supposedly complete in itself, but he does not believe in the efficacy of the rituals of the past. Soyinka, the modernizer and cosmopolitan, believes that Yoruba ritual works, that Yoruba myths apply to modern life. As Maja-Pearce has argued, Achebe's world is secular, rationalist; Soyinka's is sacred, still influenced by the gods.[22]

Discussion of the new literatures, and their offshoots, tends towards two basic positions: the political prejudges language, influences, and even choice of artistic forms; while for those more concerned with artistic

---

[21] Francis Barker *et al.* (eds.), *Colonial Discourse/Postcolonial Theory* (Manchester: Manchester University Press, 1994).

[22] Adewale Maja-Pearce, *A Mask Dancing: Nigerian Novelists of the Eighties* (London: Hans Zell, 1992).

competence, ideological issues are a distraction and often wrong. Theories totalize, create orthodoxies, and attract those who want political power. Aesthetic, formalist, and functionalist approaches often ignore the indirect social and political contexts of the arts. For many people recognized culture and cultural forms express social identity, hierarchies, community, and even political legitimization; thus there are always fights over canons, taste, styles, and levels of culture. In new nations and among some minorities where institutional bonds and power are weak the argument is strongest concerning the symbols and history of cultural authenticity. Such quarrels may or may not be meaningful to most creative artists who, using many different forms, symbols, and histories, are too sophisticated to be neatly categorized throughout their development. There is by now a long history of politicized commentary on the new literatures in which minor authors are praised for their folksiness, orality, depiction of the poor, use of traditional forms, or being the voices of the people. The best writers have seen instead that they needed to learn the forms and styles of European and world literature as ways to begin and develop.

The dialogue, however, is important as mastery of international standards must be accompanied by the creation of a personal voice and other resources only available through consciousness of local society and culture. Many artists creatively use the tension between both positions. For Walcott all art and life begins in imitation; all culture starts in mimicry. The artist has a double consciousness; in watching himself imitate he initiates a new vision. Because of its many influences and the character of local life there is a distinctive Caribbean culture; the artist's job is to give it form and make people aware of it.[23] Ned Thomas gets at the heart of the matter:

The colonial or provincial neurosis is always to look for approval to some distant centre, and even the protest against this dependent condition is still controlled by that which it reacts against: no reagent is a free agent. But whatever creates a new centre of consciousness is truly liberating, and this is what love does: it endears places to us, surrounds them with an air of glory, creates a centre from which we can look outwards, in Donne's phrase 'makes one little roome, an everywhere'.[24]

[23] Derek Walcott, 'The Caribbean: Culture or Mimicry?', *Journal of Interamerican Studies and World Affairs*, 16/1 (Feb. 1974), 3–13. Republished in Robert D. Hamner (ed.), *Critical Perspectives on Derek Walcott* (Washington: Three Continents Press, 1993), 51–7.

[24] Ned Thomas, *Derek Walcott: Poet of the Islands* (Cardiff: Welsh Arts Council, 1980), 21.

# PART II

# ENTANGLED ROOTS

CHAPTER TWO

# Language, Orality, and Literature

CHANTAL ZABUS

When the British settled or colonized various parts of this planet, they did not know that their tongue was going to be (metaphorically) twisted, bloated, shrunk, pulled out, severed, mangled, hacked. If they had known, they might have thought twice about the future use of this fleshy muscular organ and the language it carried—English.

If English did at all change in the process of colonization, it did not move overnight from good to bad to worse or from the elegiac innocence of the homy English cottage to the hyper-communicative experience of the 'global village'. Most of its contemporary plasticity as an international lingua franca was already inscribed in its own hybrid beginnings. Whether by the original owners of the language or by its post-colonial co-owners, English has always been put to various uses.

When the Irish writer James Joyce argued that his last work, *Finnegans Wake* (1939), was 'traduced into jinglish language', he was attempting to deconstruct the language of colonial England, which had subordinated Eire to its control for some 700 years. The Anglo-Irish struggle, however, belies easy comparison to the colonization of Africa which, unlike the colonization of the European peoples, is compounded by race and slavery. In the case of the settlement of the Caribbean islands or of Canada, imperialism is further complicated by the partial or complete retrenchment of the native inhabitants.

English has either ousted the indigenous languages altogether, as it had done with Celtic in the fifth and sixth centuries, or it has inexorably transformed them, along with the social arenas where they were in use. Post-colonial societies inevitably bear the stamp of such transformations. Although it is often argued that such societies moved 'from tribe to nation' or from an 'oral' to a 'written' culture, it also makes sense to view them as hosting multiple worlds and syncretic phenomena existing side by side: the old and the new; the industrialized cities and the traditional rural areas; the oral and the written; the mother tongue and the 'stepmother tongue'; along a continuum, as it were.

## THE EAR IS SHAPED LIKE A QUESTION MARK: THE ISSUE OF ORALITY

It is indeed difficult to dismantle paradigms that are traditionally paired off, however antithetically, such as East vs. West; oral art vs. the novel; the communal spirit vs. individualism. However, the tendency is now towards disaggregating origins and the oral, or what I would venture to call the past-oral, as so-called oral societies are always associated with a bucolic, nostalgic era. Some argue that to be authentically African, for instance, African novels in English have to be leavened with the appropriate yeast of orality; others will argue that English is instrumental in prolonging the life of ancestral genres like the epic, the initiation story, and the fable through modern art-forms such as the novel. One can indeed see the oral tales of allegedly 'tribal' societies and the adventure stories in Euro-American popular or mass culture as the 'syllables and broken fragments of some single immense story' which is told again and again, variously, human interpretation being what makes it look different.[1] Despite such arguments in praise of continuity, questions of orality inevitably pop up when discussing post-colonial societies.

### THE CLASH OF TWO TITANS: SPEECH AND WRITING

Ironically, it was when the newly independent societies had snatched English away from its ancestral home and were shedding the relics of the past-oral that Western theoreticians pointed to the evils of print culture and the neo-orality of this *fin de siècle* and end of millennium. The extremely acoustic technology of electronics could indeed be said to provide non-linear and possibly richer forms of communication, thereby reviving older oral forms. In their move from orality to neo-orality, however, some societies short-circuited the middle stage of the written word so that, from this quasi-Darwinist perspective, writing is seen as some sort of missing link.

Without prior consensus, Lévi-Strauss's *La Pensée sauvage* (1962), Goody and Watt's extended article on 'The Consequences of Literacy' (1962), and McLuhan's *The Gutenberg Galaxy* (1963) were all published at approximately the same time, thereby providing a convenient watershed date for the demotion of print culture in the West. Havelock surmised that the deadening hand of print was held responsible for

---

[1] Fredric Jameson, *The Political Unconscious* (Ithaca, NY: Cornell University Press, 1981), 105.

splitting the history of human culture between pre-Gutenberg script and post-Gutenberg text. Such over-valorization of speech over writing has since been endorsed by Zumthor or challenged by the deconstructionist Jacques Derrida, who argues that Western culture is nostalgically yearning for a certain kind of 'authentic' speech and has imposed idealizations derived from standardized writing back onto speech.

The theoretical cleavage between speech and writing was crystallized by Ferdinand de Saussure, who, in his *Course in General Linguistics* (1916), divided language into *langue*, the idealized grammatical form, recently rebaptized as 'the code', and *parole*, i.e. what goes on in real language interactions or 'the message'. Post-colonial linguists have argued that Saussurian linguistics has marginalized the social by bracketing the 'message' in order to concentrate on the 'code'. Ashcroft, for instance, proposes to redress this imbalance by focusing on the message and reinstating the *parole*. He goes so far as to construe the history of European literary theory as an arena where the participants are locked in a 'gladiatorial contest over the ownership of meaning'.[2] As the contest is between margins or periphery and the centre, between language variants and a standard code, the post-colonial discourse in English has been labelled a 'counter-discourse'.

However radical Ashcroft's position may be, the post-colonial linguistic programme is certainly more humane than MIT linguist Noam Chomsky's act of universalization in his *Aspects of the Theory of Syntax* (1965), where he posits an ideal speaker-listener, in a completely homogeneous speech community. Post-colonial theory thus views language as a human behaviour and the 'ethnography of speaking' as a new area of critical inquiry.

RETRIEVING THE ORAL IN LITERATURE

Attitudes towards orality diverge. At one end of the spectrum, oral texts continue to be seen as the unlettered country cousins of literature. At the other end, orality is the nurturing support of print. For instance, the African oral poem or 'song' is considered as the best basis of modern printed African poetry in English or in translation (Okot p'Bitek, Mazisi Kunene, Gabriel Okara, and Kofi Awoonor) as opposed to the more print-based poetry of Soyinka and Okigbo. The Ghanaian poet Kofi Awoonor's 'Dirge' is a 'copy' miming the song genre. According to

[2] Bill Ashcroft, 'Constitutive Graphonomy: Post-colonial Theory of Literary Writing', in Stephen Slemon and Helen Tiffin (eds.), *After Europe: Critical Theory and Post-colonial Writing* (Sydney: Dangaroo, 1989), 59.

Haynes, it could pass as a printed translation into English from Ewe, Awoonor's native tongue, except that there is no Ewe original. Awoonor's instruction that the dirge 'be Sung to slow drumbeats of ten-second intervals' hints at the idea of the poem as oral performance and, more largely, at the origins of literature out of oral verbalization.

The simultaneous retrieval and embedding of oral material in literature reflects a certain ideological positioning, as such a retrieval had conventionally been carried out by non-native scholars. In the case of Africa, the traditional oral material had been recorded in the first half of the nineteenth century by mostly Protestant missionaries, colonial governors, travellers, soldiers, and well-meaning field researchers possessed of an innate or acquired capacity for scientific observation. R. S. Rattray's collection *The Ashanti Proverbs* (1916), gingerly subtitled *The Primitive Ethics of a Savage People* (!), is a case in point. So, to record oral material such as proverbs in a novel is to take proverbs away from the folklorist, weird-object approach to African ethnology.

Chinua Achebe's recording of some 27 and 129 *ílú* or Igbo proverbs in *Things Fall Apart* (1958) and in *Arrow of God* (1964), respectively, was motivated by the need to preserve the residual 'glory of Igbo oratory'. In his introduction to the revised edition of *Arrow of God* (1974), he 'hopes that African writers will make use of them [proverbs] in dialogue, for which they were originally intended'.[3] One such proverb is used early in *Things Fall Apart*: 'Our elders say that the sun will shine on those who stand before it shines on those who kneel under them', which is directly traceable to an original Igbo *ílú*.[4]

Taking their cue from Achebe, the Nigerian troika of Afrocentric critics—Chinweizu, Jemie, and Madubike—was later to identify the essential basis of inspiration, form, and decisive behaviour of African literature as *oratoria* as opposed to *literatura*, as if these were the star-crossed lovers of two rival families. That they may be siblings in an incestuous relationship is more like it, as illustrated by Wole Soyinka's *The Forest of a Thousand Daemons* (1968), which is an adaptation of Yoruba writer D. O. Fagunwa's *Ògbójú Ode Nínú Igbó Irúnmalè* (1938). The 'oral' quality of the written text is such that the readership is also an audience, a kind of co-author or what Zumthor has called a listener-author ('auditeur-auteur'). This text has been argued (e.g. by Wilkinson) to be self-referential, as it reflects on the possible extinction of the oral tradition and the urgency of reducing it to writing. The main protagonist Akara-Ogun tells the author in a metafictional comment not to 'delay it till another day lest the benefit of

---

[3] Chinua Achebe, *Arrow of God* (1964; rev edn. London: Heinemann, 1974), pp. vii–viii.
[4] Chinua Achebe, *Things Fall Apart* (London: Heinemann, 1958), 5.

it pass you over . . . . there is this fear that I may die unexpectedly and my story die with me. But if I pass it on to you now and you take it all down diligently, even when the day comes that I must meet my maker, the world will not forget me.'[5] The theatrical version of the text by Wale Ogunyemi in *Langbodo* (1977) is an attempt to restitute the Yoruba text or 'copy' to the realm of orality or what is called 'secondary orality', that is, theatre.

Interestingly, eating and telling, whether proverbs or stories, are intimately connected: 'When I [Akara-Ogun] have done with eating, I will lay my tongue to the tale of my second journey, and that story is even more delectable than the one that has gone before.'[6] Proverbs, Achebe tells us in *Things Fall Apart*, 'are the palm-oil with which words are eaten'—(in Igbo) 'Ilú ká n'èjí èrí úkà.'[7] Like a cola-nut, the word is chewed, manducated before it is passed on by word of mouth onto the page. If the mouth is the voicing organ of orality, the ear is the privileged receptacle of oral culture.

DIONYSIUS' EAR

The labyrinthine construction of the ear may be an index to the possible distortion of the received message so that orality may be a reactionary obstacle to progress. Although the Somali novelist Nuruddin Farah was educated to respect the works of the great Somali poets of the Ogaden and has made ample use of oral texts as in *Close Sesame* (1983), he is fully aware of the negative role orality can play in a dictatorship. In *Sardines* (1982), a Somali poet notes that the organ of oral culture—the ear—is shaped like a question mark. The ear is here the debased organ of the barely literate General's police system. The General's 'ear-service' is so tyrannical that there exist no written reports and a phone call suffices to issue an arrest warrant. As literacy is a threat to the oralized power-system, all of Farah's rebels are what Derek Wright called 'revolutionaries of the written word'. As rebels against despotism, they risk, as in *Sweet and Sour Milk* (1979), being confined to the General's 'Dionysius' Ear', after the ear-shaped cave where Dionysius the Elder, who in the fourth century BC controlled Syracuse, held as prisoners those who resisted him. Farah thus sees writing as a means to end dictatorship. Writing is here associated with permanence but also, to some extent, with land-surveying and map-making, as the pen charts out new shores of relative certainty and the watery rumours of hearsay ebb away, at least for a while.

[5] Wole Soyinka, *The Forest of a Thousand Daemons* (1968; Edinburgh: Nelson, 1982), 8.
[6] Ibid. 34.    [7] Achebe, *Things*, 4.

## WRITING WITH AN ACCENT

When 'the Empire writes back to the centre', it does so not so much with a vengeance as 'with an accent', by using a language that topples discourse conventions of the so-called 'centre' and inscribing post-colonial language variants from the 'margin' or 'the periphery' in the text. Such variants result from the transformation of language through local use, itself the result of social change. Yet the inscription of variants within a text often goes beyond the mere recording of such a transformation. The writer then no longer imitates what is happening as a result of social change but uses language variance as an alibi to convey ideological variance.

The methods used to 'write with an accent' and to convey ideological variance cover a whole panoply of devices, generally designated as 'indigenization' or 'nativization', which are themselves part of larger, conscious strategies of decolonization or what the authors of *The Empire Writes Back* called abrogation and appropriation. The Indian writer Mulk Raj Anand has used Indian locutions that are rendered directly into English and his way of writing has been described in terms of a fast, galloping 'tempo', which Raja Rao in his preface to *Kanthapura* (1938) defined as 'the tempo of Indian life', which 'must be infused into one English expression . . . we, in India, think quickly, we talk quickly, and when we move we move quickly; there must be something in the sun of India that makes us rush and tumble and run on.' Upon closer scrutiny, it turns out that Anand's 'Indian English' is made of transliterations or calques from Urdu and Punjabi. Raja Rao in *The Serpent and the Rope* (1960) has, for his part, attempted to employ Sanskrit rhythms in English but his experiment has been deemed a failure, possibly because it is an overly conscious, nationalistic nativization of English that finds no tangible echo in the linguistic arena.

### TWO WAYS OF SHADOWING: CUSHIONING AND CONTEXTUALIZATION

Concretely, one may wonder what constitutes an Indian tempo or an African rhythm. Cushioning (after the common device used by translators to 'cushion' e.g. Middle French medical terms with their Latin equivalents) consists in tagging an English calque onto the indigenous word as in the oft-cited pair '*obi* or hut' from *Things Fall Apart*. Here the English translation 'shadows', i.e. provides a fainter representation or adumbration of, the Igbo word *obi* or homestead. Although such a method, if carried to extremes, can syncopate the meaning of a text, it is effective in preventing the use of culturally misleading expressions (e.g. 'reception hall' or 'sitting room') and in avoiding the glossary or footnote. *Things Fall Apart* amply testifies to this method: 'the elders or *ndichie*'; '*eze-agadi-nwayi*, or the teeth of an old woman'; '*jigida*, or waist beads.'[8] The explanatory item can stretch its shadow over a whole phrase, as in the Indian writer R. K. Narayan's *The Vendor of Sweets* (1967): 'a *kapalam*, a vending bowl made of a bleached human skull.'[9]

Generally, cushioning fills the (cultural, linguistic) gap between the word and its referent, between *obi* and hut, and, paradigmatically, between two worlds that were forcefully brought into contact. One can indeed see in the proximity of these inter-referential signs a step towards a reciprocal creolization, as a way of being 'at once a native and alien', after Bharati Mukherjee's phrase. This method's general premiss is that English can be if not the direct conveyor of African or Indian culture, at least the pointer that explains African or Indian culture and metonymically signals cultural difference.

Contextualization is another method of shadowing. It consists in surrounding the indigenous word with a halo, an area of immediate context that involves the reader in some sort of guessing game. For instance, R. K. Nayaran in *The Man-Eater of Malgudi* (1962) introduces the Indian word *rakshasa* in italics without further explanation. Speculation as to what it means runs high until it is defined much later as 'a demoniac creature who possessed enormous strength, strange powers, and genius, but recognized no sort of restraints of man or God. . . . "Every *rakshasa* gets swollen with his ego." '[10] Contextualization, like cushioning, is a way of grappling with the untranslatable.

The demands on the reader of post-colonial literatures are quite heavy. It is probably because Achebe sensed that such a reader would be 'no longer at ease' that he deleted one sentence in Igbo from *Arrow of God*. In a name-calling match, a girl is answered by her brother: ' "it kills little girls," said Nwafo. "I did not ask you, ant-hill nose." "You will soon cry, *Usa bulu Okpili*." '[11] We may suppose that Achebe deemed the latter Igbo phrase ('the moon kills little boys') too burdensome and, in the revised 1974 edition, he sacrificed the Igbo retort to ensure clarity for the non-Igbo reader.

RELEXIFICATION

This is a more radical method of inscribing language and ideological variance in a text in that it forces English to carry the weight of the

---

[8] Achebe, 9, 25, 49.
[9] R. K. Narayan, *The Vendor of Sweets* (Harmondsworth: Penguin, 1967), 125.
[10] R. K. Narayan, *The Man-Eater of Malgudi* (Harmondsworth: Penguin, 1962), 95–6.
[11] Achebe, *Arrow of God* (1964 edn.), 3.

colonized culture and attempts to convey indigenous concepts, thought-patterns, structures, and rhythms, and even linguistic features of the mother tongue. The most daring experiments in relexification have taken place on African soil and its most controversial practitioner is one of Africa's and Nigeria's gentlest poets, Gabriel Okara, in his one and only novel *The Voice* (1964).

Okara has thus relexified the English 'he is timid' into 'he has no chest' or 'he has no shadow', its equivalent in Ijọ, Okara's native tongue. 'Inside', one of his most innovative concepts in *The Voice*, harks back to the Ijọ *biri*, meaning the inner hall of one's integrity and connoting 'soul' or 'spirit'. When such innovations affecting the lexis and the meaning of the language are extended to the syntax, the result may be both stilted and alluring as in 'Who are you people be?'. In 'To every person's said thing listen not', the postponement of the negative can be traced to Ijọ sentence-construction: 'kími gbá yémọ̀ sè pòù kúmọ́' (literally: Man-say-things-all-listen not). The many double- and triple-barrelled coinages such as 'surface-water-things' can be traced to Ijọ: 'ọ̀gọ̀nọ̀ béní yèámọ̀' (literally, up-water-things); 'Coming-in people' from: 'súọ́ bómíní kimiamọ' (come-in-people).[12] Needless to say, Okara does not render language change in Nigeria, as, for instance, Ken Saro-Wiwa or Buchi Emecheta do, but bends the English language and uses its pliability to assert Ijọ culture.

Inherent to Ijọ (and most sub-Saharan African languages) is the process of reification, that is, the fact of converting a person or an abstract concept into a 'thing'. Hence Okolo's confusion of mind ('Okolo' means 'the voice' in Ijọ) is given the quality of thingness and is likened to 'a room with chairs, cushions, papers scattered all over the floor by thieves'. Word-repetition in 'Izongo laughed a laugh', 'the black black night', or 'the cold cold floor' all go back to most West African languages as well as to pidgins and creoles but also to the reiterative technique used in the Bible, in the black spoken church sermon, and in jazz improvisation.[13] But when Okara writes about the 'frustrated eyes, ground-looking eyes, harlots' eyes, nothing-looking eyes, hot eyes, cold eyes',[14] he is doing more than just using the inner resources of Ijọ; he is resorting to the formulaic (to help recall) and the flowing *copia* characteristic of traditional oral narrative that is always accompanied by the story-teller's voice modulations, tonal punnings, facial contortions, and flamboyant gestures.

Relexification alone cannot fully explain what is meant by 'tempo' or 'rhythm' but it largely contributes to the author's 'accented' enunciation in the text, which is here the site of ideological variance.

---

[12]  Gabriel Okara, *The Voice* (London: Heinemann, 1964), 26, 7, 34, 27.
[13]  Ibid. 76, 35, 76, 77.      [14] Ibid. 80.

AUTO-TRANSLATION

Relexification is also used when writers translate themselves. The Kenyan Ngugi wa Thiong'o is the first African writer to dramatize auto- (or self-) translation as a stage beyond writing in European languages and as a conceptual step towards African-language writing. He indeed translated his Gĩkũyũ novel *Caitaani-Mũtharaba-inĩ* into *Devil on the Cross* (1982) and the play *Ngaahika Ndeenda* (written with Ngugi wa Mirii) into *I will Marry when I Want* (1982). The auto-translator ceases to be an eternal guest in his own work, and feels 'at home' in the mother tongue. He also encourages his people's participation in an indigenous-language literature and sets the stage for the simultaneous development of African writers and their proper audience.

'Writing with an accent' is actually how the Iranian-born writer Taghi Modarressi, who now lives in the United States, described his translation into English of his own Persian novels such as *The Pilgrim's Rules of Etiquette* (1989). Modarressi's literal translations of Persian idiomatic expressions leave a tangible trace of the foreign in the English text. Phrases like 'nobody chopped any chives for him'; 'dust be on their heads'; 'trying to be the bean in every soup'; or 'he didn't possess any more than a sigh' clearly suggest another language than English.[15] This is characteristic of works by Eastern exiled writers, whether in English like Salman Rushdie's *Shame* (1983) or in translation (i.e. from the Arabic) like Tayeb Salih's *Season of Migration to the North* (1976). It applies, to some extent, to all those writers 'exiled in English', after Nasrin Rahimieh's phrase, but also to what is still called 'Black British writing', a controversial category which lumps together writers living in Britain like Linton Kwesi Johnson (Jamaica), David Dabydeen (Guyana), Timothy Mo (China), Kazuo Ishiguro (Japan), and Ben Okri (Nigeria). This 'new internationalist' writing is on the rise and is vibrating with new accents and rhythms.

POLYRHYTHMS

Whether on African soil or the Indian subcontinent, English is seen as a pale, livid corpse or zombie brought back to life through infusion (Rao), emulsion (Achebe), blood transfusion (John Pepper Clark, who is Ijọ) and even surgical transplantation (Okara). Ngugi may then have a point when taking Achebe, Okara, and the more eccentric Tutuola to task for injecting 'black blood' into the foreign language's 'rusty joints'.[16]

---

[15] Taghi Modarressi, *The Pilgrim's Rules of Etiquette* (New York: Doubleday, 1989), 19, 20, 24, 31.
[16] Ngugi wa Thiong'o, *Decolonizing the Mind* (London: James Currey, 1986), 7.

Concomitant with these reviving techniques there is a robust language solidly anchored in the sun-drenched African or Indian soil like Yoruba or Hindi to give it life anew. One may then wonder how English fares in the Caribbean, where no native language survived after the almost complete annihilation of the Amerindians, i.e. the Taino, Siboney, Carib and Arawak peoples. English is the site of criss-crossings between Spanish, French, Asian languages, and others like Ashanti, Kikongo, and Yoruba, which were imported through the slave trade.

THE ISLE IS FULL OF NOISES . . .

In *The Four Banks of the River of Space* (1990), the doyen of Guyanese letters, Wilson Harris, begs us to 'listen to the voice of the flute. It sings and it tells in the English language; yet solid (however whispering) music gives the Word that echoes in one's frame, as one kneels, uncanny twists, uncanny spirals, that relate ancestral tongues, Macusi, Carib, Arawak, Wapishana pre-Columbian tongues that have been eclipsed.'[17] Although Harris's language is said to secrete within it the tongues of ancient peoples, such ancestral languages are not linguistically embedded in the deep structure of the English narrative. The return to such sources can therefore only be mythical.

The Barbadian George Lamming in *The Pleasures of Exile* (1960) has used the vast metaphor provided by Shakespeare's *The Tempest* to theorize Caliban's curse into the need to 'Christen Language afresh'[18] and thereby explode Prospero's old myth—what Wilson Harris called in 'Explorations' 'the homogeneous imperative'. Caliban's dream-statement that 'the isle is full of noises' translates into the Creole polyrhythms that in turn reflect in the very texture of the texts the multiple instabilities of the Caribbean.

The erection of a spoken vernacular as a national language with its canon of written literature has always been a goal of liberation movements. It is therefore not surprising that the Jamaican historian and poet Edward Kamau Brathwaite should mention Dante Alighieri's *De vulgari eloquentia* (1304) in his *History of the Voice* (1984). Indeed, Dante's Defence in Latin for the recognition of his own Tuscan vernacular is not dissimilar to Ngugi's statement, *Decolonizing the Mind* (1986), in which he bids farewell to English and embraces Gikũyũ and KiSwahili as the medium for his creative writing. Caribbean writers like Brathwaite and John Hearne have endeavoured to rehabilitate the 'bare foot' language or Patwah of Jamaica and erect it as a 'nation language'.

[17]    Wilson Harris, *The Four Banks of the River of Space* (London: Faber & Faber, 1990), 44.
[18]    George Lamming, *The Pleasures of Exile* (1960; London: Allison & Busby, 1984), 118.

This community-born 'nation language' is informed by the language of slaves, indentured labourers, and servants brought in by the *conquistadores* and now thrives alongside English, Hindi, varieties of Chinese, and residual African languages. Brathwaite sees this creolized medium as the 'submerged area of that dialect which is more closely allied to the African aspect of experience in the Caribbean'.[19] Caribbean texts are therefore peppered with etymons and roots from 'owa rial Afrikan langgwij' (from the Cassidy and Lepage spelling system but, strangely enough, it could as well come from *Finnegans Wake*). For instance, the African substratum of Creole may be seen in *myal*, as in Erna Brodber's novel of the same name (1988), from the Hausa *maye*, meaning 'sorcerer, wizard' but also 'intoxication' and 'return'.

In Brathwaite's *The Visibility Trigger* from *X/Self* (1987), a poem like 'Poor Cyaaan Tek No Moore' duly features lines from an Akan dirge— 'dam, damirifa due'. But he also uses Rasta phrases, the most common being 'iani' or 'i-and-i' to refer to I, my, we, and us, as in 'Poem for Walter Rodney'—'those night beast a babylon who heiss us on sus | but that worst it is the blink | in iani own eye.'

David Dabydeen's poems in *Slave Song* (1984) are meant, he says, 'to be spoken aloud, not read silently . . . [for] gestures naturally and spontaneously accompany oral delivery'.[20] In 'Song of the Creole Gang Women', he attempts to bring out the brokenness and brutal physicality which he sees inherent in Creole, 'like the rawness of a wound': 'Wuk | nuttin bu wuk | Maan noon an night nuttin bu wuk | Booker own me patacake | Booker [the same as in Booker Prize] own me pickni. | Pain, nuttin bu pain | waan million tous'ne acre cane. | O since me baan—juk! juk! juk! juk! juk!'[21] Creole is here on a par with performance, whose kinetic dimension is often entrapped in the fixity of the printed text, much to Dabydeen's regret.

The task of Caribbean writers, whether living in the Caribbean or in exile or alternating between England and home like Caryl Phillips, is to find a voice of their own from the tangled ethnic strands mingled contrapuntally, as in Caribbean music. The many migrant registers come as fractured as the land masses that make up the islands: Trinidadian nation-forms like *grand charge*, picong, robber talk; kaiso (or calypso), 'dread talk'; what Brathwaite has termed the dislocations of Bird, Dizzy, and Klook; the rootsical vibes of Bob Marley, the sound-structure of Rastafarian drums in Jamaican reggae; and Don Drummond's trombone which can be heard in Derek Walcott's 'Blues'. They all contribute to

---

[19] Edward Kamau Brathwaite, *History of the Voice: The Development of Nation Language in Anglophone Caribbean Poetry* (London: New Beacon Books, 1984), 13.
[20] David Dabydeen, *Slave Song* (Mundelstrup: Dangaroo Press, 1984), 13.
[21] Ibid. 14, 16.

shape the *riddim* of Caribbean nation language and to explode Babylo-
nian English ('Babylon' is synonymous with capitalism, the police, 'the
system') which continues to castigate the Rastafari language of resistance
and subversion and through it, the mystical wisdom of Jah. However, the
universalizing thrust of the 'nation language' ideology seems to ignore the
fact that the various patois of the islands are often mutually unintelligible.

Such explosions and 'throwing of words' also translate into the politics
of 'noise' as in Vic Reid's 'noise in the blood' in *Nanny Town* or, as
Carolyn Cooper has pointed out, in the megawattage noise evoked by
Bob Marley in 'Bad Card' from his *Uprising* album (1980): 'I want to
turn up my disco I Blow them to full watts tonight I In a rub-a-dub style.'
'Noise', conventionally deemed unpleasant, loud, and unwanted, has
been aptly described by Brathwaite as a decorative energy, a 'congrega-
tional kinesis', ranging from use of scrapes and shak-shak to the long roll
of the drum. Obviously, 'noise' is meant to be heard and enhances the
histrionics of performance.

'Dub' (from 'to double') or 'performance-poetry' originated in Jamaica
and emerged out of reggae culture. Many dub poets are professed
Rastafarians. Yet, the term 'dub poetry' was coined by the least affiliated
with Rastafari and the most distrustful of the 'Haile Selassie thing',
Linton Kwesi Johnson a.k.a. LKJ, to describe the musical talkover of the
reggae DJs or 'toasters' or MCs of the 1970s, which led to North
American rap. Although its core practitioners are Jamaicans (Louise
Bennett a.k.a. Miss Lou, Mutabaruka, Oku Onuora, Mikey Smith, and
Jean Binta Breeze), dub has a Trinidadian sister in Brother Resistance's
'rapso' and it is now an international movement based mainly in Kingston, London (e.g. Benjamin Zephaniah), and Toronto (e.g. Lillian
Allen), not to mention Native Canadians.[22] The dub poets see themselves
as the modern urbanized successors of the African griot voicing a sound-
poetry that transfers the story-telling event from its ancestral African
form to a modern structure of electronic communication (musically,
from the bass drum to the bass guitar or the synthesizer bass) and uses
the African-derived 'call-and-response' pattern ('jamma songs'). As
sound-poetry, it can only be apprehended with the help of audio-visual
technology ('teknalagy'), for the printed word, considered as deprived of
sound and therefore dead, fails to render the 'voiceprint' of performance.
It also raises scriptural problems about how to signal Creole and ideological problems about the status of the language of performance which,
like the popular culture it carries, gets 'no respect' from intellectuals who
are 'high' not with *kaya* or *ganja*, the 'holy herb', but with Gutenberg-
obsessed theory.

[22] Christian Habekost, *Verbal Riddim: The Politics and Aesthetics of African-Caribbean
Dub Poetry* (Amsterdam: Rodopi, 1993), 15–89.

Such problems also befall EnPi (NP or Nigerian Pidgin), which is now the mother tongue of several million Nigerian locutors. Outside of the use of Pidgin in poetry, the Ogoni writer Ken Saro-Wiwa has experimented *in vitro* with an amalgamation of Kana (his native tongue), Pidgin, Standard Nigerian English, and broken English. The result of such alchemy is, by Saro-Wiwa's own admission, 'rotten English'. Sozaboy (soldier-boy) expresses himself in this discordant post-Civil War idiom in *Sozaboy* (1985): 'I was thinking to myself how I am lucky to be with Bullet in the same company. Because to talk true, I like am plenty. Na very fine man. And e' sabi almost everything. And e' no dey make *gra-gra*. All him things na *je-je*. And if you no know sometin and you aks am he will take time to explain to you.'[23] This may serve as a basis for stylistic innovation in the same way that Vic Reid in *New Day* (1949) and Sam Selvon in *The Lonely Londoners* (1956) laid the foundations for the use of Creole in Caribbean third-person narrative, at a time when Creole was still associated with degeneracy, linguistic self-hatred, and intellectual backwardness.

FOURTH WORLD VOICES

The absence of a true creolizing process in the 'Fourth World' has produced another variety of writing in English. Such literatures have been marked by what the Aboriginal writer Colin Johnson has called 'cultural and genocidal imperialism'. Significantly, in 1988 Johnson discarded, as an anti-bicentennial gesture, his Anglo-Celtic 'whitefella name' to rebaptize himself Mudrooroo Narogin, after his birthplace in Western Australia.

Facing the impossibility of retrieving a language which is now extinct, Mudrooroo decided to supplement Australian History with the Aboriginal story in his novel *Doctor Wooreddy's Prescription for Enduring the End of the World* (1983), which deals with the last Tasmanian Aboriginals. The book attempts to reconstruct apocryphal characters like Wooreddy and chronicle the first contacts between the European prisoners and the Bruny Island Aboriginals, the way Canadian George Bowering reconstructed the Indians' responses to George Vancouver's Pacific expedition in *Burning Water* (1983). Also, in the context of the New Zealand Land Wars, the Maori novelist Witi Ihimaera has reconstructed in *The Matriarch* (1986) the Maori leader Te Kooti's campaign against European settlement, while giving the floor over to a Maori woman, traditionally not permitted to engage in debating skills in male-dominated gatherings or *hui*.

[23] Ken Saro-Wiwa, *Sozaboy: A Novel in Rotten English* (Port Harcourt: Saros International, 1985), 87.

In 'White forms', Mudrooroo has argued that 'as a literature of the Fourth World . . . it must and does deal with the problems inherent in this position and it must be compared to similar literatures, for example the American Indian [ironically also called First People] . . . not . . . to the majority literature'. As such, his own *Master of the Ghost Dreaming* (1991), which plays the 'Cockney-accented Aboriginal English' of Fada and his efforts 'to find and keep his aitches'[24] against his rival Jangamattuk's Yoruba-and-Pidgin-informed 'english', withstands the comparison with, for instance, the Native Canadian writer Ruby Slipperjack's *Honour the Sun* (1987), in which he positions a young girl, Owl, at a cultural and linguistic crossroads: her native (Cree) culture, a nineteenth-century Christian culture, and a twentieth-century modern literacy. Both novels, in their own way, point to the future minorization of Standard English in the formation of many indigenous 'Englishes' within an increasingly polyrhythmic space.

### THE PEN AND BEYOND: ORALITY AND GENDER

Whereas Western gynocriticism heralds the pen(is) as responsible for the fathering of texts and the female ink/milk as a possible lubricant for the blank page, the search for a post-colonial, female language beyond the ears, mouth, and other organs of patriarchy remains problematic. Significantly, the first part of Erna Brodber's novel *Jane and Louisa Will Soon Come Home* (1980) is called 'Voices' to refer to the heterophony of disembodied voices on the Jamaican scene. Most of the novel is in 'nation language' as opposed to the Standard Jamaican English of the upwardly mobile khakhis or light-skinned Jamaicans. As the middle-class woman narrator Nellie moves out of the *kumbla* (i.e. the cocoon of the worm but also the disguise that fools the enemy), she also moves deftly towards what Wilentz has called 'a more holistic language . . . at once Caribcentric and feminist'. As Nellie returns from abroad, she sees people 'waiting, Perhaps for language'.[25]

The Maori writer Patricia Grace foregrounds 'a way of talking', which gives the title to one of her short stories, by representing colloquial talk, not as a deviation from the standard norm but as a network of solidarities; a web of sorority. Keri Hulme, who describes herself as a 'mongrel' with a *taha Pakeha*, i.e. a side that is European, and grew up speaking corrupt Maori, writes what she calls 'bicultural poetry'. Her

---

[24] Mudrooroo Narogin, *Master of the Ghost Dreaming* (Sydney: Angus & Robertson, 1991), 8.
[25] Erna Brodber, *Jane and Louisa Will Soon Come Home* (London: New Beacon Books, 1980), 41.

original ancestral language Ngai Tahu is practically extinct today but her English is nevertheless sprinkled with Maori words and she makes use of old forms such as the *waiata roha* (love song) or the *oriori* (lullaby) as in her poem. 'Nightsong for Te Pipiwharauroa', which also incorporates a *whakatauki* or proverb. Her fellow-poet Henare Dewes, of Ngati Porou and pakeha ancestry, uses Maori words (mostly food items) in her poem 'Whakarongo' (or 'Listen') that are left untranslated: 'Who will gaff the tuna stream | and tickle nga tarante | and collect the kina | kantai and pipi | pick the puha and bittercress | set the hinaki | make the bread to buy the kai | for te Huatahi | eh! . . . who!'

In her novel *the bone people* (1983) Keri Hulme has her heroine Kerewin use an unusual blend of Elizabethan archaisms and contemporary vernacular interspersed with Maori proverbs and dialogues: ' "E korero Maori ana koe?" "He iti iti noa iho taku mohio," she answers blandly.'[26] The glossary at the end of the book provides the translation: 'Do you speak Maori?'—'I understand a bit.' By foregrounding the concept of *aroha*, i.e. love, care, compassion, and support, she runs counter to the *mana* or the prestigious power of the great, championed by Ihimaera. The search for land, the much disputed object of the Land Wars, is here a quest for a room of one's own against the breast of *Papatuanuku* or earth mother. Yet, here as in other post-colonial women's novels, the language of post-patriarchy is not linguistically tangible as yet.

The feminization of language, if any, seems to go hand in glove with its dehierarchization through the representation of colloquial talk and what Cooper has called the 'vulgar' body of popular culture whose language, like that of woman and performance, has been inferiorized. *Lionheart Gal* (1986), as it documents in Creole/English the ideological development of the (Jamaican) Sistren Theatre Collective, stands 'between' fiction and research data, illustration and testimony, text and story. Carolyn Cooper's own piece of criticism on *Lionheart Gal*, partly in English, partly in Creole, testifies to the possible, alternative future for the language of criticism but also to an in-between feminine positioning, a meandering refusal of closure. It remains, however, an experiment. If academic English is bound to change at all, it is likely to get increasingly Americanized, as is British English whose local varieties, which Henry Higgins in G. B. Shaw's *Pygmalion* could effortlessly recognize, are being supplanted by urban variants of the North American dialect.

Women have also tried to reconnect with the 'mother tongue', i.e. the tongue of the 'mother-culture', and develop some sort of female 'voiceprint' within a system that denied their sisters access to functional

---

[26] Keri Hulme, *the bone people* (Wellington: Spiral, 1983), 57.

literacy. Two Hausa/Fulani women poets, Hauwa Gwaram and Hajiya 'Yarshehu from northern Nigeria, have published *Alkalani A Hannun Mata* (*A Pen in the Hands of Women*) (1983), a collection of Hausa verse or *wakoki* that are broadcast on local radio stations in an attempt to reach secluded Muslim women without requiring them to leave their homes. Such works are likely to have an impact that novels like Zaynab Alkali's *The Stillborn* (1984), studded as it is with Hausa words and precious cultural references, cannot hope to have.

In post-colonial societies, radio and television are indeed busy taking orality out of the past or rather tap(p)ing orality out of the past and broadcasting it into the future. The immediate future is inevitably one of hybridity and errancy, as the babble of many tongues and various Englishes has its first go on the waves, well over the seas and beyond our Gutenberg galaxy. Yet, if an 'after Babel' were to be conceived, beyond this neo-oral end of millennium, the 'Newspeak' is likely to be an 'international English' that may cease to vie for the absolute ownership of meaning.

# CHAPTER THREE

# Psychology, Creolization, and Hybridization

## J. MICHAEL DASH

> Melange, hotchpotch, a bit of this and a bit of that is how newness
> enters the world. It is the great possibility that mass migration gives
> the world, and I have tried to embrace it.
>
> (Salman Rushdie)

It is nothing new to say that Salman Rushdie's novel *The Satanic Verses*
is a transgressive work. This is precisely how it was seen in 1989 by
Islamic fundamentalists who deemed its contents heretical. Yet for the
novelist the transgressive nature of his work did not lie in its irreverent
attitude to Koranic orthodoxy. It lay elsewhere. It is the novel's 'embrace'
of 'newness' that Rushdie saw as the true daring of that literary text. *The
Satanic Verses* may well be notorious because it is one of the growing
number of contemporary works that marks a departure from the romance of the traditional in order to celebrate 'hybridity, impurity, intermingling, the transformation that comes of new and unexpected
combinations of human beings, cultures, ideas, politics, movies, songs'.[1]
In describing his secular, cosmopolitan novel as 'a love-song to our
mongrel selves', Rushdie is acknowledging the force that the ideas of
creolization and hybridity have acquired at the end of the twentieth
century.

The idea of society as an integrated culture, organically whole, insu-
lated by language and tradition from the relentless advance of modernity
and its supposedly alienating values, has now become unpersuasive.
Instead, the notion of timeless tradition has given way to a view of all
societies as caught up in a process of contact, change, and transformation. This realization has had a devastating effect on many of our
received ideas. The reassuring dichotomies of 'primitive' as opposed to
'modern', of 'periphery' as opposed to 'centre', have yielded a pervasive sense of the cross-cultural that has increasingly undermined the concepts of cultural difference or otherness. In a world gone inexorably

---

[1] Salman Rushdie, *Imaginary Homelands* (Harmondsworth: Penguin, 1992), 394.

cosmopolitan, the ideal of Creole identities is seen as transcending earlier myths of race and nation. As Ashcroft, Griffiths, and Tiffin declare in *The Empire Writes Back*, 'cross-culturality [is] the potential termination point of an apparently endless human history of conquest and annihilation justified by the myth of group "purity" '.[2]

Even if the process of creolization is now seen as a global phenomenon, the term does have a special meaning for the Americas in general and the Caribbean in particular. Recognition of the especially intense nature of cultural and racial hybridization in the Caribbean as a prelude to the universalization of heterogeneous societies is explicit in James Clifford's remarkable critique of traditional anthropological practice, *The Predicament of Culture*. In his brief but insightful readings of Caribbean writers, he declares that the Caribbean has become the paradigm for modern, syncretic cultures everywhere which have been turned into urban archipelagos. 'We are all Caribbeans now in our urban archipelagos.'[3] In making this assertion, Clifford is alluding to the destructive yet unpredictably creative nature of the colonial enterprise in the Caribbean.

Plantation slavery and later schemes of indentureship left in their wake diverse groups of people cut off from their communities of origin. Because of the extermination of the native peoples in the Caribbean, the archipelago became a *tabula rasa* which underwent total repopulation for the purposes of working the plantations. Manned by wholly introduced populations, the Caribbean was unlike both the settler colonies of Canada and Australia and the imperial possession that was India. Nor was it like the colonies of Africa where tribal units were subjected to the colonizer's sense of a civilizing mission. Caribbean plantations were the prototypes of modern industrial plants in which European capitalism produced totally unintended cultural entities out of the need to exploit cheap labour.

The use of the term Creole from the outset points to the unpredictable nature of this particular system of economic exploitation. Creole has traditionally been used to distinguish that which is created in the colonies which is neither native nor derives directly from the culture of origin. It is used to describe both someone born in the colonies and some new cultural or linguistic forms created from the juxtaposition of diverse populations. The term already suggests the later hypothesis of creolization that the oppressed and the exploited were not merely the passive victims of an oppressive system but rather, through a pattern of apparent consent, opposition, and overt resistance, managed to create unpre-

---

[2] Bill Ashcroft, Gareth Griffiths, and Helen Tiffin, *The Empire Writes Back* (London: Routledge, 1989), 36.

[3] James Clifford, *The Predicament of Culture* (Cambridge, Mass.: Harvard University Press, 1988), 173.

cedented cultural transformations from a series of dialectical relations that united oppressor and oppressed.

One of the sociological commonplaces used to describe the Caribbean is that of a multiracial Creole community or an ethno-cultural melting pot. While there is a great truth in these clichés regarding post-plantation Caribbean society, they suggest a serene cultural wholeness which conceals the truth about turbulent societies formed from the colonial process. Indeed, there is a sense in which the notion of a Creole society is used in a populist way by governments in order to minimize class and ethnic complexities in various countries. It is no coincidence that the idea of a Creole identity has gained importance whenever there has been a surge of nationalist idealism in the Caribbean. The Creole model suggests a homogenizing process that, in the official view, creates a unified nation from the past of plantation slavery. Because of this ideological appropriation of the term, the notion of creolization still remains ill-defined and fraught with ambiguities. Some of the best writing and theorizing about creolization has insisted on the dynamic and unpredictable nature of the process. As Nigel Bolland argues, 'Creolisation then, is not a homogenizing process, but rather a process of *contention* between people who are members of social formation and carriers of cultures, a process in which their own ethnicity is continually re-examined and redefined in terms of the relevant oppositions between different social formations at various historical moments.'[4]

The strength of the Creole hypothesis, however, has always been its emphasis on the creative potential of plantation society. In this regard it has always been a more attractive and promising model than other theories of post-plantation societies that concentrated on their negative and uncreative aspects. Two models of Caribbean society that have been opposed to the Creole concept are the plantation model and plural society model. In the case of the former the plantation persists as an exploitative and destructive entity that prevents the emergence of new social and cultural forms. Such a model puts great emphasis on the morbid relations between the dominant authoritarian system and the passive subordination of the majority. The notion of pluralism is an equally pessimistic one as it focuses on racial difference and social confrontation rather than on contact and interdependence. Because they deny the dynamic nature of post-plantation society as well as the inventiveness of the diverse ethnic groups, both models are simplifying and reductionist. They condemn Caribbean societies to being mere adjuncts to imperialist metropoles.

[4] Nigel Bolland, 'Creolisation and Creole Societies', in A. Hennessey, *Intellectuals in the Twentieth-Century Caribbean I* (Basingstoke: Macmillan Caribbean, 1992), 72.

Both these views of post-colonial societies as hopelessly dependent and incapable of transcending their brutal beginnings leave out of account the question of culture and the role it plays in a community's collective psychological survival. It is, therefore, no coincidence that the most articulate and passionate proponents of the ideas of creolization have been writers. The theorizing of a Creole model by the Barbadian poet and historian Edward Kamau Brathwaite is very important to the development of the idea of creolization. Brathwaite's work is marked by a critique of dependency theory and a celebration of resistance in Caribbean folk culture. In his theories of Creole society he argues for process and transformation over structures and stasis. Despite the fact that his emphasis is invariably on the transformation of African retentions in Caribbean folk culture, his general perspective usefully points to the creative exploration of society and culture outside of simplifying notions of power and dependency. As he persuasively argues in his essay 'Caribbean Man in Time and Space', 'The plantation . . . does not contain all that is planted. Therefore it is essential that our concepts and models, when made and applied, should be applied not only to the outer field of reality, but to our inscapes equally.'[5]

Even as Brathwaite was attempting to develop his model of Creole society in response to theories that were inadequate to account for changes in post-plantation society, Guyanese novelist and theoretician Wilson Harris had already begun to explore the 'inscapes' of Caribbean societies in order to demonstrate the psychological strategies that had been devised for coping with the assaults of what Brathwaite calls 'the outer plantation'. In a lecture delivered in February 1970 in Guyana entitled 'History, Fable and Myth in the Caribbean and the Guianas', Harris outlined his critique of traditional historical approaches to developing societies and developed his notion of the internal corrective responses that allowed the dominated to survive beyond their victimization. Harris chose as his model for the process of psychic reordering the most disadvantaged ethnic group in the Americas, the aboriginal peoples. For Harris, the process of creolization seems to begin with the group's imaginative efforts to circumvent historical tragedy.

There are two vital aspects to Harris's formulation of the idea of cultural metamorphosis. First, he directs attention away from the individual as the basic unit of society. Secondly, he is more interested in exploring the inner dimension of the group's opposition to the dominant culture than in direct explicit challenges to the system. It is not the stubborn defiance of the maroon that attracts Harris's attention. Rather, it is the dialectical relationship between victor and victim, exploiter and

<hr>

[5] E. K. Brathwaite, 'Caribbean Man in Time and Space', in *Carifesta Forum* (Kingston: Institute of Jamaica, 1976), 202.

exploited, that provokes his imaginative exploration. Invariably, Harris in his theoretical model uses terms like 'gateway consciousness' or 'threshold consciousness' to signify a complex process of accommodation and transformation between oppressor and oppressed that forms the essential dynamic of an emergent Creole culture. As Harris himself put it: 'the imagination of the folk involved a crucial inner re-creative response to the violations of slavery and indenture and conquest.'[6] Literature, then, functions as a form of critical thought for Harris, allowing for the exploration of areas of human experience that are unavailable to the historian or anthropologist.

The other major writer to explore this aesthetic of renascence and metamorphosis is the poet Derek Walcott. Walcott's work abounds with images of the painful yet glorious emergence of space, character, and consciousness from the mean, petty, and circumscribed. The persona of the 'shabine' as racially indeterminate, the ambiguous yet all-encompassing legacy of the sea, the ideal of fortunate travelling, and the conception of the Caribbean as a New World Mediterranean all point to Walcott's desire to transcend the fragmented to celebrate the process of a Creole wholeness. Without a real penchant for theorizing, Walcott seems to project his critical thought through his poetry. His one important essay that tackles the issue of creolization is 'The Muse of History'.

This 1974 essay is as much an indictment of literature as political propaganda and the view of history on which it is based as it is a celebration of what Harris had earlier called a spirit of 'renascence' in the Americas. Like Harris, Walcott is exploring in this polemical work the aesthetic possibility of transcending a conception of history that imprisons those who adopt it as well as those who reject it. In his critique of 'the prophets of bitterness' and their jaundiced view of the past, Walcott suggests that there is a spirit of inventiveness and renewal in the New World that makes history irrelevant. As he boldly declares, 'amnesia is the true history of the New World'.[7] To illustrate this aesthetic of renewal, Walcott cites the examples of a number of poets from the Americas: Whitman, Césaire, Neruda, and Perse. They all are praised because of the spirit of elation or exuberance in their work.

This essay strongly argues that the Caribbean in particular and the Americas as a whole provide an especially challenging and liberating context for the creative artist. It is a context which, despite its brutal beginnings, permits the artist to rethink old hierarchies, to experience an openness to influences from everywhere, and to explore the emergence of

[6] Wilson Harris, *History, Fable and Myth in the Caribbean and Guianas* (Georgetown: Ministry of Information and Culture, 1970), 12.

[7] Derek Walcott, 'The Muse of History', in *Carifesta Forum* (Kingston: Institute of Jamaica, 1976), 114.

new forms of hybridity. As is the case with Wilson Harris, Walcott is impatient with the reductionist views of political ideologies. The ideal of the 'unencumbered' poet 'carrying entire cultures in his head' is characteristic, for Walcott, of all forms of linguistic and cultural activity in the New World. For instance, the process of linguistic creolization, of the free and spontaneous intermingling of words and ideas, is seen as exemplary of the Creole sensibility which radically rethinks notions of originality, genealogy, and mimicry. If linguistic creolization in the Americas is indicative of an irrepressible spirit of renewal, the same is true of religion. In 'The Muse of History' he examines the adoption of Christianity by African Americans not in terms of a form of abject submission but rather as an example of 'cunning assimilation'. In hymns, spirituals, and the blues Walcott sees the practice of repetition, allusion, and improvisation as the slave imaginatively 'wresting God from his captor'. This process, concludes Walcott, represents the true beginning of imaginative literature.

There are two crucial aspects of Walcott's reflections in this essay that are central to his view of creolization. These are the collective nature of the response to imaginative challenges and the sense of incompleteness of the creative act. In two of his most successful later dramatic poems, Walcott extends these ideas. The main joke of the poem 'The Spoiler's Return', which satirizes the materialism and corruption of oil-rich Trinidad, is that the dead calypsonian who returns is a decomposing composer ('I decompose, but I composing still').[8] Not only is the individual authorial voice undermined in this way but the poet/calypsonian must survive by feeding off others like the bedbug of one of his best-known calypsos. The image of poet as parasite not only wittily illustrates a kind of acute self-awareness, it hints strongly at the kind of intertextuality and interrelating that Walcott sees as the defining mode of the Creole sensibility. The same ideas are again apparent in the more explicit meditation on poetic creativity 'The Schooner Flight'. Repeatedly in this poem Walcott refers to the inextricable bond between individual and communal—'I loved you alone and I loved the whole world'; 'I have no nation now but the imagination'; 'either I'm nobody or I'm a nation.' The 'nobody – nation' tension in the poem is a simple formulation that lies at the heart of the process of creolization. The poem ends with an extended image of unpredictable, multiple branching that extends throughout the world. There is no 'one island' but 'so many islands | As many islands as the stars at night | on that branched tree'.[9]

[8] Derek Walcott, 'The Spoiler's Return', in The Fortunate Traveller (London, Faber & Faber, 1982), 53.
[9] Derek Walcott, 'The Schooner Flight', in The Star-Apple Kingdom (New York: Farrar, Straus, Giroux, 1979), 19.

The extent to which what is seen as intense and all-encompassing in the Caribbean has become a global phenomenon is suggested by Walcott when Shabine declares, 'this earth is one I island in archipelagoes of stars'. In so doing, Walcott checks the tendency to create a Creole essentialism which would turn the Caribbean into a centre of exemplary creolity. The ultimate aim of Walcott's imaginative enterprise is the dissolution of categories like centre and periphery, classic and modern, sameness and otherness. In this regard, much of what is imaginatively suggested in Walcott's creative work is given fuller critical elaboration in the critical writing of the Martiniquan novelist and critic Édouard Glissant.

The relationship between these two writers is a long-standing one. Walcott used Glissant for his epigraph to *Another Life* and Glissant is fond of citing Walcott's 'Sea in History' to evoke the complex relationships between past and present in the region. Both writers also acknowledge St John Perse as a major precursor. Glissant is the only Caribbean writer to have given sustained theoretical attention to the idea of creolization. In his *Caribbean Discourse* he describes creolization as a concept that does not glorify 'the composite nature of a people' since 'no people has been spared the cross-cultural process'.[10] He sees the need to deconstruct the category 'creolized' as constituting a half-way point between pure extremes. His dissatisfaction with the term 'Creole' is evident in his recent work where 'relation' is used. The influence of Glissant's ideas on the 'Créolité' movement in Martinique is undeniable and reveals the importance of the ideal of creolization for societies like Martinique that are small, dependent, urban, yet resist being swept unprotestingly into assimilation within a metropole. The recent use of Chaos Theory by the Cuban novelist Antonio Benitez-Rojo in his *The Repeating Island* is yet another indication of the need to theorize creolization in terms of concepts that would loosely be categorized as post-modern.[11]

A treatment of Walcott's ideas and their relation to the post-modern is beyond the scope of this essay. Nevertheless, there is an important overlap between the post-modern and creolization. Linda Hutcheon points to the crucial relationship between post-colonial writing and post-modernity in *A Poetics of Postmodernism*, when she notes that excentric discourses like post-colonialism have had an 'important impact on the post-modern'.[12] There is nothing overtly post-modern in Walcott's use of language or poetic structure. However, as Rei Terada persuasively argues in *Derek Walcott's Poetry: American Mimicry*, Walcott's poetry

[10] Édouard Glissant, *Caribbean Discourse* (Charlottesville: University of Virginia, 1989), 138.
[11] Antonio Benitez-Rojo, *The Repeating Island* (Durham, NC: Duke University Press, 1992).
[12] Linda Hutcheon, *A Poetics of Postmodernism* (London: Routledge, 1988), 71.

'dramatizes' the post-modern without 'enacting' it.[13] His obsession with displacement, wandering, and incompleteness constitutes a vital link with post-modern poetics. Recently, Walcott has come perilously close to acknowledging a link with the post-modern when, in 'Caligula's Horse', he questions authorial intention and describes poetic language as a form of textual wandering which puts meaning constantly at the mercy of detour, accident, and error. 'That is one part of the poetic process, accident as illumination, error as truth, typographical mistakes as revelation.'[14]

With the poetry of Walcott, the idea of creolization enters a particularly complex theoretical phase. No longer can one rely on the old platitudes of cultural fusion and melting pot. The Creole model that is emerging lies, as Wilson Harris once presciently observed, in 'the arts of the imagination'. It is based on a vision of dynamic, indeterminate, and unstable cultural and linguistic interplay. Increasingly, the word 'translational' is being used to describe the creolizing aesthetic. For instance, in praising the poetry of Césaire and Perse, Walcott remarks on the 'appearance of translation from an older epic' that gives a special force to these Caribbean poets. Already, Walcott may have been announcing his own major poetic effort at giving the 'appearance of translation'[15] in his epic work *Omeros*. In making this observation, Walcott attacks both the notion of the original as transcendental point of reference and imitation as debased version of the foundational text. The poet then is neither a spokesman for the original nor does he master the precursor's text but enters into a translational relationship with a chain of resonances released within a literary tradition. This view of a translational practice which might be either intralingual or interlingual depends on a process of linguistic restatement, mutation, and adaption that has clear socio-cultural implications. This calling into question of the diachronic or historical linearity and privileging of synchronic interplay reveals the important overlap that exists between creolization and post-modern theorizing.

Post-modernism offers a general theoretical context that allows creolization and hybridity to evolve with a reinforced philosophical grounding. In particular, translational theories share with a Creole poetics the rethinking of traditional hierarchies and the assumption of binarist thought. In the same way that the process of creolization favours reversals, contradictions, and recombinations, and calls into question the idea of sacred origins and pure beginnings, so post-modern thought challen-

---

[13] Rei Terada, *Derek Walcott's Poetry: American Mimicry* (Boston: Northeastern University Press, 1992), 214.
[14] Derek Walcott, 'Caligula's Horse', in Stephen Slemon and Helen Tiffin (eds.), *After Europe* (Sydney: Dangaroo Press, 1989), 138.
[15] Walcott, 'The Muse of History', 120.

their destination is an occasion for great joy. Susanna Moodie's description of arriving in Canada is euphoric, almost transcendent. 'As the clouds rolled away from their grey, bald brows, and cast into denser shadow the vast forest belt that girdled them round, they loomed out like mighty giants—Titans of the earth, in all their rugged and awful beauty—a thrill of wonder and delight pervaded my mind. The spectacle floated only dimly on my sight—my eyes were blinded with tears—blinded by the excess of beauty.'[15] Moodie's attributions of sublimity to the Canadian landscape can be read in the context of her arrival after a long and uncomfortable journey; they are in ironic contrast to her later descriptions of the 'iron winter' of 1833 when she reports that 'the rigour of the climate subdued my proud, independent English spirit, and I actually shamed my womanhood and cried with the cold'.[16] The experiences that settlers endure are often in such direct contrast to the initial moment of sighting, described in such painterly transcendence.

Similar joy is reflected in the arrival of settlers to Australia, who project onto the landscape a combination of relief (that the journey is over) and aesthetic beauty. Sarah Midgley and Richard Skilbeck, for instance, both extol the romance and beauty of the country that they can see from the deck of the ship. A great number of 'sighting' descriptions are available for Australian settlers, thanks to Charlwood's collection *The Long Farewell: Settlers under Sail* (1981), but not all approach their destinations with the same picturesque eulogy. Worried about the penetrability of a landscape that they must soon enter and, in their own sensibility, subdue, the 'new-found' land does not always seem so hospitable to those settlers still spectators from the deck of a ship. Indeed, it can appear to be barren and rocky, a forbidding rather than inviting aspect. Hassam breaks these descriptions down to a sequence of features directed by the congruency of voyage and arrival to its effects.[17] The reliance on narrative as one way of trying to inscribe order through the cultural assumptions implicitly carried by the settlers is even more evident. Searching for evidence of 'civilization', the arriving passengers signal their own quotidian assumptions. If there are houses and fields, the projected settlement looks to be promising, for the inscription of 'civilization' is already evident.

All of these descriptions are inflected by the subject positions of the writers of these diaries and journals. Not only the material position of the impending settlers impinges on their narrative, as Hassam points out,[18] but their education and occupation, the 'cultural relativity of the

[15] Moodie, *Roughing it*, 22.

[16] Susanna Moodie, *Life in the Clearings versus the Bush* (New York: Dewitt & Darenport, 1853), 106.

[17] Hassam, 'Writing the Coastline', 202–3.

[18] Ibid. 204.

discourses available to them',[19] including, of course, their class, gender, and their occupational trajectory. Emigrants who packed and carried the cultural weight of Victorian England to a new settlement emblematized the contradictory nature of settlement itself. They sought an idealized 'new world', but were encumbered with the baggage of their past. Afflicted by what McCormick effectively describes as 'the Victorian vice of cant',[20] the educated or cultured settler could not easily shake the imposition of imperial condescension; early verse and narrative reeks of that mothball association. Thus, settler and pioneer writing is, by virtue of its occupation of displacements, by virtue of its contradictory desires, more heavily inflected by space and time than any other post-colonial writing.

But what were the components necessary to the production of settler writing? Was it so condensed as to be complete in what McCormick suggests are 'some of the necessary conditions for the writer—an interested audience, a sense of direction, and, in a new country and a new people, an inexhaustible theme'?[21] The necessary conditions of any literary production go beyond the writer, to projected audience, printer, text, and actual reader. Writing, publishing, and the reception of that writing are influenced and inflected by 'geographical, economic, political, and cultural features peculiar to . . . time and society'.[22] What the settlers brought with them bespoke influence much more than what they observed around them. What they wrote was pre-inscribed by a trajectory that moved from official description to interpretative literary construction. And it is essential to remember that early writing was directed backwards, to a European audience; it was not a matter of settlers writing for settlers themselves.

To begin with, there were official narratives, fulfilling the function of the report or dispatch, and pretending to a governmental distance. Early Australian narratives focus on describing life in Botany Bay, as with Watkin Tench's *A Narrative of the Expedition to Botony Bay* (1789) and Phillip's *The Voyage of Governor Phillip to Botany Bay; with an Account of the Establishment of the Colonies of Port Jackson and Norfolk Island* (1789). While Phillip enacts an 'officially acceptable interpretation of the settlement',[23] other such accounts can be read as either official or quasi-official to the extent that they are considered accurate repres-

---

[19] Hassam, ' "As I Write" ', 46.

[20] E. H. McCormick, *New Zealand Literature: A Survey* (London: Oxford University Press, 1959), 19.

[21] Ibid. 22.

[22] Elizabeth Webby, 'Writers, Printers, Readers', in *The Penguin New Literary History of Australia* (Ringwood: Penguin Books, 1988), 113.

[23] Robert Dixon, 'Public and Private Voices', in *The Penguin New Literary History of Australia*, 126.

entations, and most are coloured by pre-constructed eighteenth-century European ideas about how both the natural and cultural world should be ordered. Questions of representation become heavily torqued by the cultural and political relativity of the discourses available to these diarists. For Edward Jerningham Wakefield, who set down his experiences, with considerable enthusiasm, in *Adventure in New Zealand* (1845), the greatest appellation was to be 'a gentleman in every sense of the word',[24] and he applies that approbation to Maori, whaler, and missionary alike, if he feels that they merit such praise. He also provides his readers, from the point of view of a commercialist, with a detailed rendering of the quarrels between the government and the New Zealand Company, a friction frequently repeated by various companies and governing bodies throughout the outposts of the Commonwealth. Ernest Dieffenback's *Travels in New Zealand* (1843) is less impressionistic, leaning toward a scientific mode of description and interpretation. As befitted one who was a naturalist and surgeon, his concretized descriptions are lengthy and explicit. But the contrasting history of these early authors is telling: Dieffenback, the scientist, returned to Europe; Wakefield, the commercialist, stayed in New Zealand. That division between science and mercantilism might be said to play out the perpetual struggle of the settler colony and her writings.

The accounts of explorers and adventurers fall between official reports and adventure tales. They were not so much a part of the settler impetus as they were prefigurations of that experience; at the same time, such journals and accounts influenced subsequent texts, particularly those memoirs that were barely concealed travel writing. Travel, adventure, and settlement were inextricably connected, and any attempt to separate their texted apprehensions into genres is fraught with the tangled and transgressive nature of writing in a seemingly uninscribed context. Certainly, the explorers' journals 'catered to the growing interest in narratives of frontier adventure' in Canada, Australia, and New Zealand.[25] Such published accounts played into and encouraged a newly awakening interest if not pride in the grandeur and difficulty of the landscape—whether reflected in Canadian Alexander Henry's *Travels and Adventures in Canada and the Indian Territories between the Years 1760 and 1776* (1809); or Thomas Mitchell's *Three Expeditions into the Interior of Eastern Australia* (1838); or George Forster's description of New Zealand in his *Voyage round the World* (1777). These 'expedition' reports deploy a combination of landscape description with hardship lament, coded within a romantic heroic quest motif for a particular physical grail, a grail composed of the landscape itself, but constructed

[24] Edward J. Wakefield, *Adventure in New Zealand* (London, 1845), 23.
[25] Dixon, 'Public and Private Voices', 132.

to act as metaphor for something greater: 'civilization and settlement' as ultimate goals. These journals were frequently over-inscribed to appeal to a European audience's social expectations of wilderness and its concomitant desolation; the writer or recorder's words were edited to enhance their acceptability to a readership that was interested in distanced description rather than the intense discomfort of personal experience, and almost contemporaneous with the explorer's accounts were missionary or church journals, which sought to convert at the same time as they described.

Whatever expectations helped to produce the official or the religious record, the close congruency between settler writing and travel writing reflects the extent to which the settler becomes so by virtue of his or her travelling. Travel writing was particularly appetizing to the European audience, which craved varieties of adventure, and much early writing was willing to appease that hunger. Anna Bronwell Jameson recorded her adventures in *Winter Studies and Summer Rambles in Canada* (1838), a beautifully subversive work comprised of a journal written to an absent friend, which captures the physical distinctiveness of the Canadian landscape. Various of these traveller-writers were of and from Europe and they returned to Europe, but their travel records succeeded in reaching past a mere collation of experience. George Heriot published *Travels through the Canadas* (1807); Paul Kane, more famous as an artist than a writer, published his Canadian *Wanderings of an Artist* (1859), which offers vivid visual and textual descriptions. The experience of North American travel was bolstered by travellers' accounts of northern North America by Charles Dickens, Anthony Trollope, Rudyard Kipling, and Samuel Butler. While many in the world wanted to travel, it seemed the whole world wanted to read travellers' tales, wanted to be able to participate without leaving the comfort of the strictured Victorian armchair.

As might be expected, then, early literary production in the colonies was inevitably not books so much as letters, sketches, occasional verse, stories, and reviews in newspapers and other local instruments. The earliest records, letters, were the main means of communicating with family and community left behind in Europe. That letters were copious and lengthy, full of information and description, speaks to their potential for publication; and epistolary hands expected an audience beyond their immediate recipient. Australian convict Thomas Watling (*Letters from an Exile at Botany-Bay, to his Aunt in Dumfries*, 1794) advises his aunt to publish his letters if doing so will be in her interest; the most energetic yet sensitive of epistolary descriptions of settler Australia is available in *The Letters of Rachel Henning* (1969) and in the letters of Eliza Brown, who 'reinstated a Victorian ideal of domesticity in the new land, according to a contemporary cult of femininity which allocated the "cultiva-tion" of a domestic space as women's work. The definitions and pro-scriptions for achieving that space and constituting oneself a lady within it were stretched and made very flexible by their new environment.'[26] Much of the interesting memoir material available is written by women, who seemed aware of their role as recorders of experience, particularly personal experience, but who had no pretensions to being published writers. Such texts by women have been discounted and marginalized in 'high art' canon formation, and many have only recently been redis-covered.

Their prose documents enhance the interesting question of the delinea-tions of gender, genre, and writing. In particular, the descriptive nar-rative that called itself the 'sketch' highlighted 'the difficulty of making rigid distinctions between fiction and non-fiction'.[27] This cross-genre inscription selected and magnified a particular scene or incident, often combining diary notations with a botanical, natural, and adventurist slant, which enabled intimacy as well as vivid documentary detail. As Gerson and Mezei have shown, the sketch was an adaptive form, particu-larly for women's practical and imaginative occupation of a new country.[28] From 1791 to 1796, Elizabeth Posthuma Simcoe, wife of the first Lieutenant Governor of Upper Canada, kept a diary that combined sketches, notes, and narrative, all sharply discriminatory according to the English norm she was accustomed to. Elizabeth Simcoe enjoyed a priv-ileged position; class and education shaped the response of many diarists to the settlements they observed, but seemed to live above rather than within.

More satisfying are those memoir/notes from women settlers who did remain, making a home in the colony: Australian Louisa Anne Mere-dith's *Notes and Sketches of New South Wales* (1844) and *My Home in Tasmania* (1852) are mirrored by Canadian Catharine Parr Traill's *The Backwoods of Canada: Being Letters from the Wife of an Immigrant Officer; Illustrative of the Domestic Economy of British North America* (1836). Her *Female Emigrant's Guide* (1854) is a survival manual, combining recipes for soap and tea with practical advice. Traill's *Cana-dian Wild Flowers* (1868), an illustrated botanical guide, matches Meredith's *Tasmanian Friends and Foes: Feathered, Furred, and Finned: A Family Chronicle of Country Life* (1880), which includes coloured plates of Meredith's own drawings. In their inception and execution,

[26] Delys Bird, 'Women in the Wilderness: Gender, Landscape and Eliza Brown's Letters and Journal', *Westerly*, 36/4 (Dec. 1991), 37.
[27] E. Webby (ed.), *Colonial Voices: Letters, Diaries, Journalism and Other Accounts of Nineteenth-Century Australia* (Brisbane: University of Queensland Press, 1989), p. xvi.
[28] Carole Gerson and Kathy Mezei (eds.), *The Prose of Life* (Toronto: ECW Press, 1981).

these works argue for that most salubrious of settler writing's accomplishments—to describe the previously unencountered, with as much detail as the hungering mind can figure.

While all of these writers employed current literary conventions to describe their experiences, there is an individual edge to each one's approach, giving rise to comparisons such as those which address the differences between Catharine Parr Traill and her sister Susanna Moodie. Traill's writing is considered 'plainer, more seemingly objective, more idiomatic, more adept at recording dialect, hence more acceptable to twentieth century taste', while Susanna Moodie, through her concern with literary form and structure (*Roughing it in the Bush* and *Life in the Clearings versus the Bush*), appears to be 'more estranged by language from the place she made her home. It is for this predicament that she became a paradigm of the Canadian frontier mentality.'[29] The confusion of these literary personae with their writing is common in critical evaluations of settler texts. What we can assert is that these 'notes and sketches' were pragmatic portraits of the environment that these women had to adjust to and bespeak both their extraordinary flexibility and their sharp observation, whatever their position, of their social and physical surroundings.

That mixture of naturalistic detail with social and political observation, both record and invention, underscores the impossibility of labelling these works in terms of strict autobiography, travel narrative, or fiction. Mary Hannay Foott's *Sketches of Life in the Bush, or Ten Years in the Interior* (1872) employs the memoir frame to contain bush tales—often romantic or moralistic—of love or bravery. Australian Emma Macpherson argues that a 'lady's point of view' is better able to give a sense of daily life in the colonies than that of male authors, who focus on providing great tracts of information. Certainly, New Zealand's first 'lady novelist', Isabella Aylmer, in her *Distant Homes; or The Graham Family in New Zealand* (1862), treads carefully on domestic sentiment as well as detail, and 'provided the model for the pioneer-emigrant novels which ran from the setting out in England to the final stages of settling in "Maoriland" '.[30] Louisa Anne Meredith's *Notes and Sketches of New South Wales* and *My Home in Tasmania* deliberately engage with the minutiae of what she calls 'the simple realities around us'. Meredith's 'veranda diorama' establishes what Dixon so accurately describes as 'the female subject at the physical centre of the domestic environment, which becomes a point of reference from which to judge the public world'.[31]

---

[29] W. H. New, *A History of Canadian Literature* (London: Macmillan, 1989), 55, 56.
[30] J. C. Reid and G. A. Wilkes, *Australia and New Zealand* (University Park: Pennsylvania State University Press, 1970), 186.
[31] Dixon, 'Public and Private Voices', 135.

This veranda position continues to be a literal trope in Australian writing; Fiona Giles's collection of short stories by nineteenth-century Australian women, called *From the Veranda*, addresses that notion: 'The verandah extends the domestic into social life; it is marginal to both, but through the fiction becomes central, mediating between private and public worlds, and breaking down the division between them.' So that while the domestic has made women's stories seem insubstantial, women wrote and published short stories (often as sketches) in great numbers in the nineteenth century. They were, argues Giles, predictable for their moral intention, but remarkable for their 'detailed account of Australian conditions and . . . practical difficulties'.[32] And these early writings laid the groundwork for the excellent work of Barbara Baynton and Katharine Susannah Prichard, who wrote, without romanticizing, about women's experience in the bush; their very presence gestures toward the linguistic signification of women within Australian discourse.[33] It is also important to note that out of the early settler writings of women came an apprehension that marriage and freedom were not necessarily compatible. For example, Catherine Helen Spence's *Handfasted*, which suggested alternatives to the institution of marriage, was completed in 1879, but never published until 1984. Perhaps in that spatial silencing resides the real voice of settler writing by women.

Nineteenth-century Canadian women worked from within the domestic sphere as well; those who ventured outside that sphere 'were mostly impelled to do so in the name of good works', and they entered the literary arena with diffidence. Yet, along with their hard labour as immigrants, they did charity work and contributed to education; their stories 'bear witness to the rapidly transforming historical, social, and publishing conditions of Canada'.[34] Certainly, women's writing of this period offers historical documentation along with explicit response to a frequently daunting environment, overall emphasizing the importance of family and community as well as issues, such as suffrage and temperance, germane to women. Both Dixon and Webby point out that this material underscores the practicality and energy of writing women, who had to satisfy both the physical demands of pioneering and their own determination to record their experiences. Even when sentiment overwhelmed good sense, as with the later novels of Canadian suffragist Nellie McClung (*Clearing in the West* (1936) and *The Stream Runs Fast* (1945)), the energy of pioneer women and the

---

[32] Fiona Giles (ed.), *From the Veranda: Stories of Love and Landscape by Nineteenth Century Australian Women* (Victoria: McPhee Gribble Publishers, 1987), 1, 2.

[33] Schaffer, *Women and the Bush*, 23.

[34] Lorraine McMullen and Sandra Campbell (eds.), *Pioneering Women: Short Stories by Canadian Women* (Ottawa: University of Ottawa Press, 1993), 3, 6.

extent to which they enabled the agricultural settlement of the colonies are integral.

Most early literary writings wrote back to the Empire in both imaginary and actual ways; these works, highly coloured renderings of romantic imposition, were frequently printed in England. Thomas Wells's *Michael Howe, the Last and the Worst of the Bushrangers of Van Diemen's Land* (1818) was the first Australian literary work to be printed, at its author's expense: the romance of the bushranger aroused considerable local interest. The first volume of poetry, Barron Field's *First Fruits of Australian Poetry*, appeared in 1819 and, whatever its colonial pretensions, did make an effort to describe the Australian landscape. The earliest novel, by Anna Maria Murray, *The Guardian: A Tale, by an Australian* (1838), declared itself as being written by an Australian, both literally and pseudonymously, as well as melodramatically. The earliest Canadian novel (although Canada as a political entity did not yet exist), Francis Brooke's epistolary *The History of Emily Montague* (1769), has been described as a typical arcadian version of garrison life by a woman who spent five years with her husband, chaplain to the British garrison, at Quebec City. The first New Zealand novel, Major H. B. Stoney's *Taranaki: A Tale of the War* (1861), was a ponderous and romanticized version of the Maori wars. Ellen Clacy's *A Lady's Visit to the Gold Diggings of Australia* (1853) promised that combination of gentility and new experience perfectly suited to a European audience's curiosity; her *Lights and Shadows of Australian Life* (1854) dealt with the romantic subjects of bushrangers, station, convicts, and, not least, emigration.

Thus, the colonies became a setting, a literary site, in itself an important declaration. Although privately printed volumes were notoriously vanity in their production and pretension, these works argued for the glimmerings of settler literature, that it was possible and perhaps necessary to write in a newly settled country.

That declaration was a step forward, despite the imposition and propagation of mannered literary conventions. As W. H. New argues, 'the stories in all the separate colonies were affected by similar aesthetic fashions: the romance of history, the morality of poverty and other problems, the role of Providence as the author of the future, the effect of sublimity [as experienced in Nature] on the soul'.[35] Examples of this aesthetic abound. The first English-language novel by a writer born in Canada was the work of a woman, Julia Catherine Hart's *St. Ursula's Convent; or The Nun of Canada* (1824); typically, it is a sentimental and rather contrived account of seigneurial life in Quebec. Frontier and historical romance was popular, and the success of writers like James

---

[35] New, *Canadian Literature*, 74.

Fenimore Cooper and Sir Walter Scott encouraged employment of the form. In Canada, Major John Richardson was the primary romance writer of his time; his lengthy and intricate novel *Wacousta; or The Prophecy: A Tale of the Canadas* (1832) combines verifiable history with elements of the revenge tragedy and Gothic romance. The novel reverses inscribed expections of civilization and wilderness; Wacousta is a white man who has assumed the identity of an Indian and his attack on civilization is motivated by dark revenge. Even post-settler texts resort to the costume Gothic. So the fashion for sentimental romances of money, morality, and marriage, although not directly connected to the settler experience, served as urban reflections of the pressure of developing social aspirations. Rosanna Leprohon's *Antoinette de Mirecourt; or Secret Marrying and Secret Sorrowing* (1864) is about a young Canadienne who flouts social mores and marries against her parents' wishes; her subsequent unhappiness teaches her a great lesson. May Agnes Fleming's romantic tales about poor women who marry prosperous men were extensively serialized in Canada and the United States. While not settler writing as such, these novels reveal the extent to which imperial sensibilities governed the fiction that was popular during and after the settler wave.

The division between those stories that nodded to prevailing tastes by concerning themselves with 'courtship and society, love and money, class and honour', and those that dealt with the male attributes of bravery and honour, appeared to be in the gender that the writer dared to occupy.[36] Australian women writers of meta-domestic fictions often employed a male pseudonym, such as, for example, Edith Lyttelton, who used the pseudonym of G. B. Lancaster. Despite the hold of English culture over most of these writers, reflected in their tendency to elevate the European over the indigenous, their settler experience is inescapable and persists in edging out from under the camouflage of romance, as with, for example, Rosa Praed's *An Australian Heroine* (1880) and *The Romance of a Station* (1889), both based on her experience of living on a station in Queensland. The assiduous depictions of these women's writing are essential to contemporary readers' apprehension of settler life.

There was critical complaint that early settler writing was merely travel writing in disguise. Frederick Sinnett's 1856 essay 'The Fiction Fields of Australia' suggests the agricultural motif, concerned with matters of growth and settlement, as a more fruitful reading of settler experience than the peripatetic trope of travel. It was true that narratives which pretended to be fiction combined autobiography with descriptions of

[36] Elizabeth Webby and Lydia Wevers (eds.), *Happy Endings: Stories by Australian and New Zealand Women, 1850s–1930s* (Port Nicholson: Allen & Unwin, 1987), p. viii.

flora, fauna, and climate, mating personal experience and observation with fiction. These texts often included a strange assortment of narrative utensils: yarns, anecdotes, games, natural characteristics, and even instructions for identifying various plants and animals. Alexander Bathgate's *Waitaruna* (1881) and Dugald Ferguson's *Bush Life in Australia and New Zealand* (1893) and *Mates* (1911) explore the New Zealand pioneer hero as a man of industry and determination, carefully resistant to the baser temptations of colonial life. George Chamier's *Philosopher Dick* (1891) is a sprawling and elaborate narrative which veers between cheap philosophizing and satire, and which combines diaries and letters with the story of an English migrant who feels, melodramatically, that he has abandoned civilization in coming to New Zealand. Such a mix of tone and structure is typical of the pioneer novel, which critics claim had as its objective the need to make coherent an incoherent trajectory of experience.

And so these texts are difficult to delineate in terms of either their genre or their motivation. Australian Charles Cozens's *Adventures of a Guardsman* (1848) is considered an autobiography of a gentleman convict, but its embellishments push it into the realm of fiction. Alexander Harris's *Settlers and Convicts; or Recollections of Sixteen Years Labour in the Australian Backwoods* (1847) features the staple fictional characters of convicts, bushrangers, and squatters, but its description of the physical landscape, along with its advice and suggestions for potential immigrants, gives it the trajectory of a guidebook. Catherine Helen Spence's *Clara Morison: A Tale of South Australia during the Gold Fever* (1854) goes beyond the travel or guidebook trope by focusing on the inner conflicts of her characters; for all that it is a domestic novel, it seeks to provide a 'faithful transcript of life in the Colony', particularly during the gold fever. And arguments over whether Tucker's *Ralph Rashleigh* (published in 1952, but set in the 1820s and written, apparently, in the 1840s) is fiction, non-fiction, or a convict memoir continue; both cautionary tale and guidebook advice are presented, combined with elements of picaresque experience easily relatable to convicts and bushrangers.

If the natural world serves as a stock character in pioneer narrative, there are also human figures which recur in Australian, Canadian, and New Zealand literature. The bushranger and the squatter both epitomize one who has stepped past social constraints. Loosely tied to them is the character, both positive and negative, of the remittance man, sent to the colonies either to improve himself or to be conveniently erased from a respectable family. Of the settler figure there are two: the newly arrived emigrant, hapless in his ignorance and idealism, contrasted to the seasoned and hard-working settler who envisions a bright future for his children if not himself. And not least, there is the mysterious untamed hero, who somehow succeeds in uniting the fierce determination of a fighter and adventurer with the finer sensibilities of an artist.

If these characters were oddly sorted, their employment underscored many of the clichés held by Europeans about colonial types. At the same time, writers succeeded in imparting a good deal of genuinely new (previously unencountered) and, to a European audience, interesting information. For Sinnett to complain that antipodean—and by extension all colonial—novels were merely 'books of travel in disguise' was to reflect a cross-genre fact that actually made these texts both unusual and successful. These settler writers mixed their own experience with natural and social observations, combined descriptions of travel and settlement with fictional motivation, so that the texts they produced may not have been 'high art' but were valuable social and cultural documents that succeeded in gesturing toward, if not interrogating, the unusual aspects of the new colonies.

Versification, with all its attendant topicality, worked from both sentiment and officially sanctioned social occasions: anniversaries and funerals, ceremonial solemnities. The peculiar institution of the 'poet's corner' in periodicals stood side by side with the tradition of political satire, which was immediately relevant to these inhabitants of a frictioned political moment. Written for and from the moment, rough verse or song reflected the interests of the community audience, particularly epitomized by Banjo Paterson (*Old Bush Songs* (1905)), who, according to Cliff Hanna,[37] serves as the bridge between the bush song and the literary ballad, with its more direct reference to Europe as cultural authority. The famous 1890s feud between Banjo Paterson and Henry Lawson arose, at bottom, from this cultural schism: Lawson's resistance to authority is rooted in an emotional and idealized support for the underdog while Paterson swung toward a heroic and well-mounted national figure. Although the argument is that both eulogize the bush worker, that pioneer of the environment, it is more accurate that both rely on a romanticization of the 'bush' itself to portray their pioneer position. Without that beautifully inscribable landscape, its combined seductiveness and potential for both malleability and violation, as Annette Kolodny would argue, the ballad fell back on the weary figure of the lone bushman, and its text becomes a victim of the legend that it intends to enhance. Most important of literary poets was Charles Harpur, native-born Australian of convict parents, who 'deliberately attempted to write epics and tragedies using Australian material'.[38] His determination to be

---

[37] Cliff Hanna, 'The Ballads', in *The Penguin New Literary History of Australia*.
[38] Webby, 'Writers, Printers, Readers', 118.

an authentic poetic voice for Australia was undercut by his reliance on traditional verse forms and techniques; still, he was one of the first to utilize the Australian landscape.

In New Zealand, the conception of the poetic sensibility was in direct opposition to the pragmatic industriousness of settler life; that poetry should concern itself with abstract rather than concrete details of physical life was over and over again exemplified by poets seeking to imitate their colonial forebears. C. C. Bowen's *Poems* (1861), Frederick Napier Broome's *Poems from New Zealand* (1868), Alfred Domett's *Ranolf and Amohia* (1872), and Thomas Bracken's *Musings in Maoriland* (1890) were all versifications that resisted the very energy of the place out of which they arose. Poetry was expected to be refined and rhetorically high flown, representing a separation of art and experience. Sadly, these colonial couplets did not capture the energy and eloquence of prose diaries and letters.

In Canada, versification addressed both occasional and political moments. The dual cultural settlement of French and English gave rise to expression of those conflicting impulses; at the same time as verses were penned praising the beauty and wealth of the country, scathing satires spoke to the colony's political tensions. Much political friction afflicted the northern North American settlement: the English expulsion of the Acadians in 1755, the English defeat of the French in the 1759 Battle of the Plains of Abraham, the war of 1812, when the United States invaded Canada, the failed rebellions of 1837, and, not least, the Riel rebellion of 1885. As W. H. New notes, 'after the Rebellions of 1837, literary commentary takes primarily journalistic and lyric forms; political analysis appears in essays, political experience in song'.[39] Even Susanna Moodie wrote lyrics designed to inspire loyalty during the 1837 rebellion. Initially, of course, sentimentalism ruled, but it moved toward a new Romanticism, which nevertheless imitated the conventions of the European poem, employing the landscape as metaphor, but within a stilted formal convention that negates the very energy and wilfulness of the world that the settlers knew.

Australia's settler writing is deeply inflected by the convict experience. The tension between forced settlement (or exile) and settlement by choice is clearly present in early writing, and sometimes the differentiation between those who chose to go to Australia and those who were sent is textually permeable. Early settler texts from Australia reflect a determined unruliness, one which seeks to combine the images of Australia as a depraved and disorderly felons' colony and as a trim and flourishing garden. Convicts portrayed themselves as exiles; they were portrayed by

[39] New, *Canadian Literature*, 37.

others from a rhetorical position determined to expose convict recalcitrance as a reinforcement of the disciplinary mode. Thus, Richard Johnson's *An Address to the Inhabitants of the Colonies, Established in New South Wales* (1794) is a combination of official hectoring and moral bludgeoning. The constructed and constrained rhetoric surrounding the convicts was indirectly supported by even the letters and memoirs of gentlewomen (wives of churchmen, officials, and military officers), whose pastoral and domestic ideology was deeply scored by the disciplinary aspects of Australian settlement.[40] Marcus Clarke's famous if melodramatic *His Natural Life* (1874) is the ultimate novel delineating convict experience; it convincingly evokes the terrible suffering of penal servitude.

No writing could escape its delineated social and political sphere; connected to that framing is the extent to which settler displacement gave permission for transgression and transformation of one's subject position. As Susanna Moodie notes:

the sight of the Canadian shores had changed them [her fellow passengers] into persons of great consequence. The poorest and the worst-dressed, the least-deserving and the most repulsive in mind and morals exhibited most disgusting traits of self-importance . . . They talked loudly of rank and wealth of their connexions at home, and lamented the great sacrifices they had made.[41]

Just so does Thomas Watling in his *Letters from an Exile at Botany-Bay, to his Aunt in Dumfries* portray himself as an artist whose sensibilities are offended by penal servitude. Thus, settlers too could seek to transform themselves with rhetoric, if not behaviour, as if emigration offered an opportunity for rebirth.

The pastoral expansion of the 1820s and 1830s was very much encouraged and abetted by various writers seeking to 'sell' Australia to free immigrants, and their narratives are a combination of accounts and descriptions determined to make Australia an attractive destination for settlers. William Charles Wentworth's *Statistical, Historical, and Political Description of the Colony of New South Wales* (1819) sought to make available pertinent enthusiastic facts; Joseph Lycett's art in *Views in Australia* (1824) presented the Australian landscape in a manner recognizable to Europeans; James Atkinson's *An Account of the State of Agriculture and Grazing in New South Wales* (1826) acted as a record of what it was like to farm in New South Wales. Extolling sport and adventure, along with the pastoral frontier (with Australian details of animals and plants), these texts sought to exploit the craving for and the popular interest in a frontier mythology that encouraged so many settlers to emigrate.

[40] Dixon, 'Public and Private Voices', 131.
[41] Moodie, *Roughing it*, 31.

Various settlers record their meeting with and apprehension of the peoples who inhabited the lands that the settlers were appropriating, although there is a marked resistance to any recognition that the original inhabitants were being dispossessed by the settler colonies. In New Zealand, George French Angas conducted an anthropologically inspired journey in search of 'memorials of the skill and ingenuity of a race of savages', resulting in *Savage Life and Scenes*.[42] Edward Shortland's *Traditions and Superstitions of the New Zealanders* (1854) continued the momentum that sought to analyse, record, and describe Maori life. Richard Taylor occupies a firmly disapproving missionary position in his *Te Ika a Maui* (1855), and Sir George Grey's *Mythology and Traditions of the New Zealanders* (1854) takes on the avuncular and paternalistic tone of one who has gathered this material merely because it could be useful to those who needed to have official dealings with the Maoris. And Arthur S. Thompson's ambitious *The Story of New Zealand: Past and Present—Savage and Civilized* (1859) sought to provide a comprehensive record of the colony and its original inhabitants. The Maori wars of the 1860s coincided with the spread of settlement in New Zealand; while much writing of that period was polemical and periodic, a few accounts tried to convey the complex and bitter struggle. J. E. Gorst's *The Maori King* (1864) is a diverse and observant account of events and their initiating policies; T. W. Gudgeon's *Reminiscences of the War in New Zealand* (1879) traces, very directly, the campaigns themselves. Fiction, on the other hand, resorted to the conventions of the historical romance as a thin cover for a racist polemic, as with, for example, Major B. Stoney's *Taranaki: A Tale of the War*. John Logan Campbell follows the path of pioneer narrative toward a sympathetic if condescending portrayal of the Maori in *Poenamo* (1881); F. E. Maning, in his memoirs, *History of the War in the North* (1863) and *Old New Zealand* (1863), encapsulates the misconceptions that Europeans had of the Maori people.

Most early depictions, including Thomas Mitchell's *Three Expeditions* (1838), treat the Australian Aboriginal people as 'troublesome' and attribute hostility and defiance to them. The settler assumption that natives must be 'civilized' underwrites their distempered approach to the original inhabitants; it was only through such attributions of otherness that they could justify a superior impetus. This unreflexive and racist arrogance, cloaked in colonial sincerity, is from a contemporary point of view both despicable and laughable, but inasmuch as these early texts, with their combination of personal observation, history, anthropology, and social inflection, sought to articulate the 'new' colonies, they repres-

---

[42]   George French Angas, *Savage Life and Scenes* (London: Smith, Elder, 1847), 26.

ent both a subject position and the particular perspective of the settler world. In Canada, the many aboriginal peoples and languages made a comprehensive investigation or recording of stories and customs diffi-cult, but the work of American ethnologist and anthropologist Franz Boas initiated studies later continued by Edward Sapir. The publication of Indian and Inuit myths in English was problematic; the extent to which they were simplified and reduced had much to do with notions of propriety. Missionaries tended to slant retellings of Indian tales toward the cautionary; literary, religious, and children's narratives tended to censor native earthiness. Again, the narrative position of the inscriber inflected the resultant texts. Captivity journals could be considered even more suspect, for they exaggerated the heroism and fortitude of the captives at the expense of their aboriginal captors.

In Australia, Aboriginal cultures were textually represented as either objects of anthropological studies, or in myth and folk-tales primarily intended for children.[43] This implied infantilization appears to be a feature of settler attitudes toward the indigenous peoples they are intent on displacing, whether in New Zealand, Canada, or Australia; the gap between early settlers and their apprehension of aboriginal peoples is emphasized by the European separation of word and body, a separation which, as Stephen Muecke explains so beautifully,[44] does not enable the inscriber to understand the country within which both word and body exist. Thus, settler accounts of indigenous peoples, their religion, and mythology are deeply suspect, at the same time that they reveal a distinct proclivity to collapse the original inhabitants of the land with the land and its resistance to settlement.

The essential question for settler writing remained that bugbear of 'suitable material'. Do indigenous geography and landscape, native ani-mals and original inhabitants, not to mention the particular demands of trying to construct a material future within a difficult-to-imagine-and-even-apprehend frontier make suitable material for a written text? This eternal question probably plagued the colonial writer, who had more opportunity for self-reflexivity, rather than the settler or pioneer writer with less leisure to contemplate the rigours of his or her meta-intellectual life, but it was nevertheless the Rubicon between texted and untexted experience. As Webby argues, 'the belief that new countries lacked the depth of culture and length of history required for the higher literary genres would seem to explain why most of those attempting poetry and tragedy set their works outside Australia',[45] while diarists and travel

---

[43] See Susan Sheridan, 'Women Writers', in *The Penguin New Literary History of Australia*.

[44] Stephen Muecke, 'Aboriginal Literature: Oral', in *The Penguin New Literary History of Australia*, 32.

[45] Webby, 'Writers, Printers, Readers', 119.

writers were happy to inscribe the country they found themselves trying to see. This general insistence on setting as cultural anointment is an odd conflation, but one that is again and again evident in early settler writing. Often enough character and conflict, even the very cadence of lines of poetry, come out of the writer's immediate environment—Canada, Australia, or New Zealand—but they have been transplanted onto and into another location. The end result is that settler writing frequently suffers from the powerful discomfort of displacement, the writer's inscribement undercut by the constraints of expectation. Thus, early texts that encapsulate the development of nascent colonies generally bespeak themselves as purveyors of the adventure and hardship variety, with events and characters depicted in black and white strokes more than subtle shades of grey. And certainly, they were directed back 'home', to a European audience, with its particular expectations and presuppositions.

The national declension of such writings—is it Canadian if the writer does not remain in Canada?; is it Australian if the text is written by a British adventurer?—must be more permeable than has been generally determined. As Elizabeth Webby argues, since it was often necessary for such works to be published and particularly read in England, the whole enterprise of literary production and reception is made more complex than the geographical place out of which such work arises. And that complexity argues for a settler writing that occupies the uneasy cusp of between and becoming.

The goal of these books as warnings and sales pitches for would-be emigrants, combined with their authors' individual positions as settlers or returned settlers, commercial entrepreneurs or government officials, sets up this writing as problematic for both its impetus and its execution. While it refuses to adhere to notions of literature as generically classifiable, it nevertheless invites speculation as to the energy and potency of writing in a new settlement, writing that by virtue of its unusual environment, could not adhere strictly to the established literary rules that would second each text to a definition. The composition of settler writing argues that the moment that can be identified as an awakening of indigenous literature is somewhere on the continuum between the settler's text and the national text, a national text happy to employ a particular vernacular, the moment when the speech of a country is given a space in which to hear itself.

The composition of any settler narrative, then, is inflected by both the journey and its self-conscious process, the arrival and its concomitant disappointments or euphorias, and the subsequent act of 'settling' which is coloured by the trajectory of those previous experiences. Hassam asserts that 'what the diarist . . . finds is that the narrator is, like the spatial occasion, purely specular, purely graphological. The narrator exists as an outcome of narration.' This astute observation has a direct bearing on all further occasions of narration which seek to relate the settler or pioneer experience. If 'the destination evoked at the end of the travelling is testament . . . to [a] desire for self-presence',[46] pioneer or settler writing can be seen to assert a particular facet of this subject position. The question is, though, can the text actually accomplish this self-presence, or is it merely another aspect of the journey's process, another strategy to subjugate experience to a more manageable form? Settler writing is, then, very much a product of the process of displacement that the migrant imposes on him- or herself, desired and desirable displacement perhaps, but nevertheless a displacement that can be accounted for (and made more amenable) with the tentative order of narrative and verse. Hassam's analogy between a geographical journey and a spiritual journey, with the destination as a place of reconciliation[47] for travel literature, gestures toward the same desire for reconciliation in pioneer and settler writing, a writing incorporating and enjoying displacement, inevitably serving as a vehicle by which the act of 'settlement' appears to enable, if never accomplish, some kind of closure or unity.

[46] Hassam, ' "As I Write" ', 40, 45.
[47] Ibid. 41.

CHAPTER SIX

# Colonial Literatures

## W. H. NEW

### COLONIAL, COLONIST, COLONIZER, COLONIZED

The term 'colonial' applies most readily to a political condition of
dependency, whether passively accepted or actively enforced. It also
alludes to the conditions of literary and material production in dependent societies and to the sets of attitudes that reconfirm these conditions:
attitudes and preconceptions about value, authority, and social priority
that in practice reflect the norms of the controlling culture. From this
general condition has arisen the metaphoric use of the terms 'colonial'
and 'colonialism'—whereby the language of political empires is applied
to real or perceived power relations (and power discrepancies) between
the sexes, among races and classes, and between centres of political and
economic influence and their 'marginalized' peripheries. While the
rhetoric of European imperial expansion often constructed the colonies
as the vigorous future—the leading edge of discovery, the site of untouched nobility and unlimited opportunity—the economic and political
realities of Empire nevertheless left control in European hands. Because
access to power constitutes a principal criterion that distinguishes the
'colonial' and the 'colonized' from any alternative condition (e.g. 'self-
determination'), the term 'colonial' is now generally associated with
derivativeness, imitativeness, and ineffectuality.

'Colonial literatures' reflected this ambiguity. While they repeatedly
showed signs of resistance to the status quo, they tended also to accept
the conventional rhetoric of future greatness—thus reiterating in aesthetic practice the political dilemma of dependency. The colonial mind at
once regarded the norms of Empire as an unacceptable imposition ('low-
est and last, with his areas vast, | And horizon so servile and tame, | Sits
the poor beggar Colonial | Who feeds on the crumbs of her [i.e. the
Empire's] fame')—and as the arbiters of respectability, consequence, and
value ('For we're proud of you, old Mother, | The way you rule the
world, | The way you stand for truth and honest right').[1] Empire at once

---

[1] Wilfred Campbell, *The Poetical Works of Wilfred Campbell*, ed. W. J. Sykes (London:
Hodder & Stoughton, 1922), 113, 299–300.

reduced the colonists and colonized to positions of social neglibility, and yet trained these people to accept their connection with Empire as their only access to greatness. Contradictoriness was less a logical flaw than a social condition.

This condition does not coincide neatly with dates of political independence. Colonial attitudes sometimes persist long after national status is acquired (or reacquired), and independence movements frequently develop before colonial status is abandoned. The following table indicates the dates at which formal political independence was granted to or declared within former British colonies:

1776   the 13 American colonies
1867   Canada (federating the colonies of Upper and Lower Canada, Nova Scotia, and New Brunswick; other colonies—including Prince Edward Island, British Columbia, and Newfoundland—joined between 1870 and 1949)
1901   Australia (federating Queensland, New South Wales, Victoria, South Australia, Tasmania, and Western Australia, with Northern Territory transferred to the country in 1911)
1907   New Zealand
1910   South Africa (Union of South Africa, uniting the Cape of Good Hope Colony and Natal with the Boer Republics of Orange Free State and Natal)
1937   Irish Free State (→Eire→Irish Republic)
1947   India; Pakistan
1948   Burma (Myanmar); Ceylon (Sri Lanka)
1957   Ghana (uniting Gold Coast and Togoland); Malaya (→Federation of Malaysia 1963, with Sarawak and North Borneo)
1960   Cyprus; Nigeria
1961   Sierra Leone; Tanganyika (uniting with Zanzibar→Tanzania 1964)
1962   Jamaica; Trinidad and Tobago; Uganda; Western Samoa
1963   Kenya
1964   Malawi (Nyasaland); Malta; Zambia (Northern Rhodesia)
1965   The Gambia; Maldives; Singapore
1966   Barbados; Botswana (Bechuanaland); Guyana (British Guiana); Lesotho (Basutoland)
1968   Mauritius; Nauru; Swaziland
1970   Fiji; Tonga
1971   Bangladesh (East Pakistan)
1973   The Bahamas
1974   Grenada
1975   Papua New Guinea

| 1976 | Seychelles |
|---|---|
| 1978 | Dominica; Solomon Islands; Tuvalu (Ellice Is.) |
| 1979 | Kiribati (Gilbert Is.); St Lucia; St Vincent and The Grenadines; Zimbabwe (unilaterally as Southern Rhodesia 1965) |
| 1980 | Vanuatu (New Hebrides) |
| 1981 | Antigua and Barbuda; Belize (Br. Honduras) |
| 1983 | St Christopher (St Kitts) and Nevis |
| 1984 | Brunei |
| 1990 | Namibia (South West Africa) |

The sequence here (the settler colonies acquiring independence before the others) may be more important than the 'foundation dates'. But the table can mislead. Several societies had forms of self-government years before 'nationhood'; and even after 'independence', many social policies continued to be decided in Whitehall rather than in the new national capitals. New Zealand refused until 1947 to sign the 1931 Treaty of Westminster (which set up the Commonwealth), because the government of the day thought it would 'weaken the bonds of Empire'. Ireland and India were in many respects 'nations' before they became British colonies; Papua New Guinea, Bangladesh, Singapore, and Namibia asserted their independence respectively from Australia, Pakistan, the Malaysian Federation, and South Africa rather than from Britain; Canada, the United States, and Australia (all confederations of several separate colonies) did not acquire their present geographical limits until well into the twentieth century; many people in Ireland still claim Ulster as their territory; civil strife has divided Cyprus, Nigeria, the American colonies, and other societies; and the native peoples of northern North America deliberately employ the term 'First Nations' to describe themselves in the 1990s, reasserting their existence as independent societies prior to their role as colonized peoples.

This complexity emphasizes a further set of distinctions. To interpret 'colonial literatures' by relying on a binary opposition—whether 'colony vs. nation', 'colonizer vs. colonized', 'black vs. white', 'male vs. female', 'good vs. evil', 'Christian vs. "pagan" ', or 'written vs. oral'—would be simplistic. While all colonies suffer disparities of power, each colony separately experiences the particularities of history. Numbers, wealth, gender, class, education, custom—rehearsing social priorities can begin to sound like a litany of the obvious. Such differences, however, too often go unremarked, or disappear behind ahistorical generalizations; appreciating colonial literary sensibilities requires that they be taken into account. For example: New Zealand's colonial experience as a 'settler society' differs from Jamaica's experience as a 'plantation/slave society'; Jamaica's multiracial and politically resistant history differs from Barbuda's history as a slave nursery for Barbados's ruling families; Ghana's cultural history has been largely matriarchal, whereas neighbouring Nigeria's has been patriarchal; the Zulu were itinerant, the Haida long established in place, the Maori (displacing the Moa-hunters) relatively recent settlers themselves in 'Ao Tea Roa' when Europeans arrived in their midst; India's written history and the oral histories of black Australia long pre-date England's economic precedence and monarchical lines; Africans and Iroquois as well as Europeans bought and sold slaves; British women participated in the expansion of imperial authority overseas; and the role of educated Englishwomen, Irish and Cockney convicts, American whalers, Viceroys, Vicereines, dominies, traders, missionaries, Scots explorers, peasant farmers, and adventurers of various stripes in shaping the cultural mores of Upper Canada, Botany Bay, the Bay of Islands, Ootacamund, Hong Kong, Transvaal, and scores of other places hints at the way social distinctions deeply influence cultural behaviour.

The 'Colonist' (the person, usually European, who settles in the 'new' land, and who participates in the reshaping of its social mores) differs clearly from the 'Colonial' (i.e. the European temporarily resident in the new society, generally contemptuous of the life and customs observed, who remains tied to and is somehow identified with an administrative appointment abroad), though the latter can turn into the former. (A second use of the noun 'Colonial' applies to the child of the Colonist, who is generally dismissed as uncouth, especially by travellers from the Imperial Centre.) These types also have to be distinguished in theory both from the 'Colonizer' (the European power that asserts its precedence, and sometimes its ownership, over 'new' lands and ostensibly 'primitive' or 'savage' people) and from the 'Colonized' (the persons, generally non-European, who suffer this arrogation of authority). All four types, whatever separate combination of traits they displayed from colony to colony, participated in the articulation of 'colonial culture'—not just because their individual words subsequently became part of literary history, but also because the very fact that they occupied these roles had the effect of reconfirming the power of Empire, reiterating the subservience of Colony, fixing the relative status of individual people, and normalizing the terms of evaluation that effectively determined priorities and values.

The range of this essay is in consequence wide, having to take into account several centuries of colonial experience (from Robert Hayman's *Quodlibets* (1628) in Newfoundland to at least H. G. de Lisser's *The White Witch of Rosehall* (1929) in Jamaica), separate literary endeavours, and the disparate impact of time, place, custom, and social aspiration. Potentially it could look at the logbooks of travellers and explorers, at captivity narratives and official documents, at letters and domestic meditations, textbooks and work-songs, hymns and humour, speeches and sermons, manifestos and music-hall lyrics, as well as at conventional 'literary' genres. The focus, however, falls on writings of the eighteenth and nineteenth centuries. By the twentieth century, with the End of Empire *expected* (rather than just dimly *imagined*), the character of 'colonial' literature was changing; the native-born (not the imperial standard-bearers, and not the often uncertain settlers, though these categories sometimes blur) were beginning to set their own political and cultural rules.

## THE CONSTRUCTION OF 'LESSER'

Social histories variously describe the character and effects of European imperial expansion—isolating its assumptions (about wilderness, savagery, authority, civilization), its frequent ruthlessness (genocide, slavery), its occasional though not always sensitive concern for social welfare (educational programmes, the anti-slavery movement that deeply engaged the South African poet Thomas Pringle), and its growing faith in scientific rationalism. Behind European actions lay a desire for knowledge, and for the wealth and control that knowledge permitted. Often competitive (the European nations were primarily at war with each other in their quest for colonies), imperial actions thus had an economic base. Scientists charted land- and seascapes for military advantage; sea captains moved rabbits, breadfruit, and other plants and animals around the world, introducing predators and weeds to places where they had not been known, altering natural balances as well as trade routes; captains of industry (and the people who served them) displaced people, razed forests, and erased whole species, all for fashion and profit. Even the Christian missionaries were competitive, each sect seeking a greater number of conversions than the next; motivated by economic supremacy sometimes as much as by faith, they turned each converted territory into their own resource basin. The imperial enterprise, that is, turned 'other' places and 'other' peoples into commodities that would serve the needs of the imperial 'centre'. (Spanish colonial practice referred to the transport of slaves in terms of 'tonnage'.) This economic hierarchy supported a political hierarchy, one that assumed that the far-flung regions of Empire were intrinsically of 'lesser' importance; it also depended on the continuance of this relationship for its own power.

Why, then, if the inequalities in the relationship are so obvious, did the colonies permit imperial power to persist so long? Some of the answers to this question are obvious: unequal access to technology, the social power of the middlemen in the slave trade, the fact that some cultures (in North America, for example) were already in flux at the time of the European arrival. The question also ignores the fact that many slave revolts and other colonial dissatisfactions (the Eureka Stockade incident, the Easter Rising in Ireland, the 1837 rebellions in the Canadas, the Land Wars in New Zealand, and even the American Revolution) did indeed challenge the total authority of arbitrary rule. Military opposition did not, of course, always prove effective.

A less obvious means of ensuring that the status quo persisted lay in the way the trappings of authority made imperial judgements seem the norm of civilized behaviour. Architecture and fashion, for example—in the design of triumphal arches, ladies' dresses, and military uniforms—asserted power visually. Landscape painters also drew on conventional codes, representing the American wilderness as an expression of the European 'sublime' and Asian culture as 'pagan' and 'exotic'. Colonial writers, because their education trained them to Shakespeare, Milton, and the Classics (meaning those of Greece and Rome), absorbed the political assumptions of this tradition *even when the tradition somehow disregarded colonial realities or diminished colonial experience*. The language of colonial literature, that is, by mirroring the value systems of the imperial centre, tended to declare its own dependence. And while the vernacular accent and vocabulary of the colonies were despised (British travellers dismissed the local voice as a vulgar snuffle), the very fact of the dependency that characterized colonial *literary* language did not raise the reputation of colonial writers among those who regarded themselves as the Empire's élite—they continued to regard colonial talent as able mimicry. Instead, it reconfirmed for them the 'naturalness' of the hierarchy they espoused, one that gave them, rather than the colonists or the colonized, precedence and power.

The case of Francis Williams, the eighteenth-century Jamaican writer whom the Duke of Montagu sent to Cambridge, shows how closely politics and verbal deracination combined. When in 1759 Williams subsequently sought preference from General George Haldane, the governor of Jamaica, he sent his request in the form of a Latin ode; but for all his mastery of the forms of Western convention, Williams found that his race remained a social obstacle. Though his ode insists that the tribute to Haldane rises 'Not from the *skin*, but from the *heart*', it nevertheless admits to hesitation: 'Oh! *Muse* of blackest tint, why shrinks thy breast, | Why fears t'approach the *Caesar* of the *West*!' Williams then adds: 'Vade salutatum nec sit tibi causa pudoris, | Candida quod nigra corpora pelle geris!' In *A History of Jamaica* (1774), Edward Long translated these lines as 'Nor blush, altho' in garb funereal drest, | *Thy body's white, tho' clad in sable vest*'; Paula Burnett's retranslation in 1986 emphasizes the

Latin wordplay and the difference between the politics of celebration and the politics of dismissal: 'Go and greet him, nor let it be a source of shame to you that a black skin covers your fair body!'[2] The 200 years that separate Williams's writing from Burnett's revisionary literary history, however, told stories of persistent, debilitating stereotyping.

Half a dozen examples will illustrate the way the language of Empire functioned when portraying the colonies—even when an author's primary focus lay elsewhere. Shakespeare's Caliban, in *The Tempest* (*c.*1611), is characterized as a subhuman monster, a kind of plaything controlled by the magus-figure named Prospero; the central issues in this play involve the competing attractions of love and power, not colonial politics, yet the pseudo-tropical setting, in which a European intellect rules over an unreasoning native, has long been read as a paradigm of imperial relations. The motif of the castaway on the tropical island reiterates this paradigm in many subsequent English literary works also, Defoe's *Robinson Crusoe* (1719) being the foremost example. In this work, all power of design rests with the title figure, an Englishman who undertakes not only to devise ways of coping with his plight as the sole survivor of a shipwreck, but also to rule. This authority extends to the control he assumes over a black native whom he names 'Friday' *and takes on as his servant*: Crusoe *assumes* he has the right to name, the right to direct, the right to lead, *because he is European*—all 'others' by definition must defer in his mind to his version of civilization.

Some other eighteenth-century works did provide counter-examples, usually in satires of European excess. Yet even they sometimes extended the paradigm of power. In Voltaire's *Candide* (1759), one character, commenting caustically on the current war between England and France, asks what they are fighting for, and on perceiving that 'Canada' is the answer, dismisses it as a useless prize, merely 'quelques arpents de neige'. The notion of Canada being barren—'a few acres of snow'—persists as a stereotype of Empire. So with Jonathan Swift's Brobdingnag, set off the north-west coast of North America in *Gulliver's Travels* (1726). This land of giants is one of Swift's many satiric gibes against the exaggerations that travellers had been peddling as documentary observations, yet it has the simultaneous effect of reinscribing the colonized world as a place inhabited by the subhuman, non-human, savage, and surreal.

To find that nineteenth-century novel writers took up some of these stereotypes unquestioningly is scarcely surprising—they had by this time

---

[2]   Jean D'Costa and Barbara Lalla (eds.), *Voices in Exile: Jamaican Texts of the 18th and 19th Centuries* [Francis Williams, Michael Scott, and other writers] (Tuscaloosa: University of Alabama Press, 1989), 11; Paula Burnett (ed.), *The Penguin Book of Caribbean Verse in English* [Francis Williams, M. J. Chapman, and other writers, and examples of oral traditions] (Harmondsworth: Penguin, 1986), 101.

acquired the status of conventional iconography. A cult of the faraway exoticized Asia as romantic; New Zealand, as in Clough's long poem *The Bothie of Tober-na-Vuolich* (1848), served as a trope of closure ('They are married, and gone to New Zealand': the destination was equivalent to disappearance); Africa remained the 'dark continent' through to Conrad's *Heart of Darkness* (1902) and beyond; Australia, branded a convict colony, was regarded as uncouth, and when Dickens's character Magwitch, in *Great Expectations* (1860), is transported there, his reputation is sealed. The fact that the money Magwitch earns provides the central character, Pip, with the basis for his economic fortune does, however, suggest the ironic possibilities of colonial allegory. Charlotte Brontë's novel *Jane Eyre* (1847) furnishes a final illustration. The primary narrative tells of the title character's rise from orphanhood to ladyship, and of her moral worthiness as she resists temptation, learns from Nature, and coincidentally inherits the fortune her uncle has acquired in Madeira. Along the way, it transpires that one of the impediments to love is the fact that her would-be lover, Rochester, has a mad wife named Bertha Mason locked up in the attic of his estate. Because Bertha is characterized not only as mad but also as a Jamaican Creole, of 'mixed blood', the portrait illustrates the way the conventions of literary language drew on colonial references only to reassert English priorities. Brontë's adjectives in describing Bertha concoct a figure that is subhuman, subnormal, and evil—all taken unquestioningly as attributes of non-European savagery; Bertha is, *inter alia*, 'savage', 'ugly', 'discoloured', 'bad, mad, and embruted', 'monstrous', given to 'excesses', a maniac with 'purple face', 'bloated features', 'shaggy locks', a 'wild gaze', and 'tainted blood'— 'whether beast or human [one could not tell]'. The fact that she is also associated with the 'foul German spectre—the Vampyre' merely confirms her exclusion from the category 'human'. This persistent association between colony, savagery, wickedness, and non-human nature had the effect of morally justifying (to those who partook of Empire's fortunes) their economic intrusion into other parts of the world. That it should be unacceptable in the colonies, and that it should also, in the twentieth century, lead to such works as Jean Rhys's *Wide Sargasso Sea* (a reply to Brontë), George Lamming's *Water with Berries* (a coda to *The Tempest*), J. M. Coetzee's *Foe* (a revisionary look at Defoe), and various versions of Conrad (Patrick White's *Voss*, V. S. Naipaul's 'Conrad's Darkness', Timothy Findley's *Headhunter*), reveals one of the impulses behind literary post-colonialism.

Before it became widely 'unacceptable', however, this set of attitudes was widely regarded as received truth, not just among administrative authorities, but also among colonists and the colonized themselves. Colonial writers tended consequently to accept the social and aesthetic priorities of the 'parent' culture as their own standards and to emulate in art whatever fashion this parent culture had recently regarded as acceptable. Many colonial poets who were praised by their contemporaries—James Grainger, M. J. Chapman, Charles Harpur, Henry Kendall, Charles Sangster, Charles Heavysege—now seem, whatever their skill at crafting lines and images, to have been writing in the shadow of their European models. More extreme forms of imitation make the practice clear. The Scots dialect verses of John Barr of Craigielee distantly mirror Burns—'There's nae place like Otago yet, | There's nae wee beggar weans, | Or auld men shivering at our doors, | To beg for scraps or banes.'[3] The elevated language of J. Mackay mirrors James Thomson if not Sir John Denham—'My Doric reed for laurels would contend, | Where fam'd Quebec's aspiring heights ascend: | The native scenes that scatter'd round them lie, | Engage the mind, and charm the gazing eye; | Here, woods and waters, wilds and vales, conspire | To swell the cadence of the rustic lyre. | The lawns of Virgil, and his silvan shade, | Tho' in the poet's choicest colours clad, | Should here confess description more sublime, | Could my weak numbers emulate the clime.'[4] Barron Field, in 'The Kangaroo' (1819), attempted pastoral, with marsupials instead of sheep, the result being more comic, seemingly incongruous, than was probably intended. And the Canadian Oliver Goldsmith (grand-nephew of the author of *The Deserted Village*) drew deliberately on his more famous predecessor when writing *The Rising Village* (1825, rev. 1834), for a model, a muse, and the sanction of authority.

When John Talon Lesperance, in 'Empire First', wrote 'Britain bore us in her flank, | Britain nursed us at our birth, | Britain reared us to our rank |'Mid the nations of the earth. | Stand, Canadians, firmly stand, | Round the flag of Fatherland!',[5] he was sounding the sentiment that bound British colonies around the world into Empire, and using a form of discourse that perpetuated dependency. Indian-born Rudyard Kipling's 'The White Man's Burden' (1899, written to encourage the United States to take 'responsibility' in the Philippines and so gain the respect of its empire-building 'peers') sounded the other face of dependency. In so doing, he also gave imperialism its literary catch-phrase; in a language that now jars, the poem blithely assumes that European intervention was an unrequited *duty*, and also that the 'heavy harness' of colonial rule would serve a 'fluttered folk and wild—| Your new-caught, sullen peo-

---

[3] Robert Chapman and Jonathan Bennett (eds.), *An Anthology of New Zealand Verse* [John Barr, William Pember Reeves, and other writers] (Wellington: Oxford University Press, 1956), 1.

[4] Margaret Atwood (comp.), *The New Oxford Book of Canadian Verse in English* [Robert Hayman, Charles Sangster, and other writers] (Toronto: Oxford University Press, 1982), 7.

[5] Anthony Haslam (comp.), *Anthology of Empire* (London: Grayson & Grayson, 1932), 265.

ples, | Half devil and half child'.⁶ As late as 1983, writing about Barbados in 1950, George Lamming observed:

Today I shudder to think how [Britain] . . . could have achieved the miracle of being called Mother. It had made us pupils to its language and its institutions, baptized us in the same religion; schooled boys in the same game of cricket with its elaborate and meticulous etiquette of rivalry. Empire was not a very dirty word, and seemed to bear little relation to those forms of domination we now call imperialist.⁷

But related it was, as Lamming's *In the Castle of my Skin* (1970) took pains to reveal.

### GENDER AND ADVENTURE

Besides being the basis for a contrast with received civilization, the image of wilderness also encapsulated another set of social values. Exploration narratives, fanciful adventures, captivity narratives, and even some stories of settlement encouraged, among readers who stayed at home, a vicarious sense of the thrill of danger and conquest. Books designed for children—for boys especially—capitalized on the desert-island/ savage-jungle stereotype, as examples from J. R. Wyss's *Swiss Family Robinson* (1813) to Catharine Parr Traill's *Canadian Crusoes* (1852) to Kipling's *The Jungle Books* (1895–6) and *Kim* (1901) readily illustrate. The mid-nineteenth-century novels of Scots-born R. M. Ballantyne (who worked in Canada for the Hudson's Bay Company)—including *The Young Fur-Traders* (1856), *The Coral Island* (1858), and *The Gorilla Hunters* (1861)—suggest the degree to which the 'colonial wilderness' constituted for the European reader a fixed trope. Details of flora and fauna might vary from one setting to another, though (to judge from book illustrations) not with any necessary connection to empirical reality; but wilderness references were put to essentially interchangeable ends. Children's books almost uniformly coupled adventure with Christian piety; adventure 'among the savages' or in 'foreign' (and therefore conceptually dangerous) territory was construed as a moral trial as well as a physical test—from which boys emerged having somehow proved their manliness, and girls emerged espousing duty and faith. The wilderness thus became a social configuration, a kind of crucible of gender differentiation that preserved the status quo. Settlement narratives themselves (as in Lady Barker's books or Susanna Moodie's semi-novelistic *Roughing it in the Bush* (1852)) might suggest that women could acquire

⁶ Rudyard Kipling, *The Definitive Edition of Rudyard Kipling's Verse* [1885–1935] (1940; repr. London: Hodder & Stoughton, 1969), 323.
⁷ George Lamming, 'Introduction' (1983) to *In the Castle of my Skin* (1970; Ann Arbor: University of Michigan Press, 1991), p. xxxviii.

some degree of power and authority outside European custom. But the conventional images of penetrating-the-forest and subduing-the-savages, embraced so readily in popular romance, reiterated the sexual politics and social hierarchies of Adamic discourse.

These conventions reveal a paradox as well as melodramatic expectations and the obvious contradictions involving European gender inequities. The paradox involves the image of the adventurous man. Even when constructed conservatively, in the shape of a *Bildungsroman*, as in the widely read *The Man from Glengarry* (1901) and other 'muscular Christian' narratives by 'Ralph Connor' (the Revd Charles William Gordon), the adventurous man has to step outside his community to prove himself. The character of 'adventure' is such that—except when construed as an emotional fillip or an intellectual abstraction—it cannot take place inside the established world. But the stepping outside generally serves the established world's needs, by extending the community's power, by proving that the community's values are firm, and even by providing a social role for the potential community rebel. Outside the community, that is, the rebel becomes a 'hero', the adventurer is made 'nobler' by distance and discourse, and adventurous escapades perhaps even serve the more mundane ends of profit and command. The adventurer has consequently to be seen less as a character escaping from community than as the community's own construction. When characterized as a paradigm of virility, moreover, the adventure also serves to illustrate the conventional community's covert dependence on myths about its own invulnerability and the morality of violence.

The colonial male adventure novel, usually melodramatic and sentimental, is frequently cast as a historical romance. Nineteenth-century writers in Australia, Canada, and New Zealand—all to some degree influenced by the American writer James Fenimore Cooper's work, and the fashion for individualist adventure—used the form to celebrate the 'dauntless' actions of the few, but at the same time they demonstrate how the principle of rugged individuality is socially shaped by the growing nationalism of each separate colony. The stylistic construction of 'dauntlessness' served social ends; all manner of exile, warfare, anti-social attitude, and active intrusion into other people's cultures could linguistically be excused as 'self-reliance', and even praised. 'Mateship' in Australia and New Zealand—the interdependence of isolated men in 'frontier' territory: 'outback', 'bush', 'backblocks'—came by the 1890s, in the critical reaction to the stories of Henry Lawson and others, to be celebrated as the quintessence of their community's character. And when novelists turned to their community history, they looked for moments that the 'established' colony now regarded as turning points, using them as settings for 'heroic' and 'manly' tales of mayhem, plunder, deceit, and revenge.

For example, Major John Richardson's *Wacousta; or The Prophecy: A Tale of the Canadas* (1832) probes the war of 1812, finds honesty wanting among conventional English officers, and celebrates heroism only indirectly, in the title character, an Englishman who masquerades as an Indian in order to wreak havoc on usurpers and toadies and thus satisfy his own code of honour. Henry Butler Stoney's *Taranaki: A Tale of the War* (1861) romanticizes and denigrates the Maori—as 'cannibal' and 'foe'—in part to justify European claims to the land, which ostensibly lies 'waste' until European taste and investment reshape it. William Kirby's *The Golden Dog* (1877) and Sir Gilbert Parker's *The Seats of the Mighty* (1896) create revisionist versions of the *ancien régime* in Quebec, characterizing that earlier time as venal and corrupt, and depicting French society as one that was ripe for conquest by a more moral power. Richardson's sentences tend to periodic form, complexity taking precedence over directness; Kirby's metaphors tend to the military, shaping social relationships as intrinsically confrontative. For all four writers, social confrontation could be romanticized into historical inevitability, the linearity of plot serving a simplified version of social progress.

Australian examples extend this generalization. Marcus Clarke's *His Natural Life* (1870–2; rev. 1874) depicts life in the eighteenth-century penal settlements—criticizing the viciousness of the system and celebrating the heroic character of those whose misdeeds were minor and sufferings great. In the longer, earlier version of Clarke's novel, metaphors of alchemy construct a coherent subtext about the power of transformation, which permits problems to be resolved during an ultimate return to England; the consistency of imagery and the narrative organization shape an organically unified work, using subplots and patterns of contrast to build to a theatrical climax and closure. In the shorter version, overt melodrama rules the action and the hero dies in Australia; despite the sentimentality of this configuration, the sequence of events here perhaps expresses a shrewder sense of colonial realities (and colonial suspicions of English institutional justice) than does alchemical rehabilitation. In *Robbery under Arms* (1890), Rolf Boldrewood (Thomas Alexander Browne) raises another ambiguity; he celebrates the adventures of Captain Starlight, notorious bushranger (turning renegade into romantic hero), even as he has his central character, Dick Marston, openly moralize about the virtues of gentlemanliness and agricultural domesticity. The adventure model, it seems, carefully consigns rebelliousness to the past, apparently taming the intrinsic violence of individual action by making it appear to serve the working social values of the present. These values none the less remain coupled with the past; insofar as they reaffirm authority as a European male right, they are both hierarchical and exclusionary.

## DOMESTICITY AND THE STATE

The end of *Robbery under Arms* signals the way domesticity characteristically frames the adventure narrative. Dick Marston is released from custody, marries, and is off to a new life on a Queensland station which he's 'to manage and have a share in', and the last paragraph asserts: 'It freshens me up to think of making a start in a new country. It's a long way from where we were born and brought up; but all the better for that. . . . [I]n any part of Australia, once a chap shows that he's given up cross doings and means to go straight for the future, the people of the country will always lend him a helping hand, particularly if he's married to such a wife as Gracey.'[8] In James Tucker's *Ralph Rashleigh; or The Life of an Exile* (1844–5), yet another convict is reclaimed from his 'savage' life (this time associated directly with the Aborigines) when he meets a 'good woman' and becomes a station manager. The double message here is clear: freedom and power are interconnected; domesticity serves the state. This version of domesticity, however, retains and even reinscribes the social hierarchies of the past; the state preserves its own power, which is shared among a white male élite, by praising the status quo as 'stable', by granting limited opportunities to men it deems the 'right sort', and by elevating the home (called 'women's place') into a kind of rhetorical holy-of-holies for people it carefully excludes from public political life.

This paradigm is widespread through colonial literature, most obviously in the dominant metaphor used to describe Empire – colony relations, that of 'mother and daughter countries'. In practice, the term 'Mother Country' sanctified the centre of Empire as 'Home'; the term 'daughter country' perpetuated an image of dependency, especially when it is made clear that domestic convention regarded daughters as possessions, whose filial duty would take precedence over any 'unladylike' desire for independence. Men, however (Queen Victoria notwithstanding), governed the *institutions* that ran the Empire—the systems of Church, State, School, Court, and Company, over which women had little direct control—and paternalism governed race relations whenever ruthlessness did not. The numerous tales of family emigrations to the New World—a popular form of nineteenth-century quasi-travel narrative, including Alexander Harris's *The Emigrant Family* (1849), Henry Kingsley's *Geof-*

---

[8]   Rolf Boldrewood, *Rolf Boldrewood*, ed. Alan Brissenden [ *Robbery under Arms* and other writings] (St Lucia: University of Queensland Press, 1979), 413.

*frey Hamlyn* (1859), and Alexander Bathgate's *Waitaruna: A Story of New Zealand Life* (1881)—can be read in this context. They might praise the role of women as the nurturers of the new lives in the new colonies, the wellspring of both strength and gentleness, but they tended to restrict this role to domestic modelling; outside the home, boys learned 'mastery' from remodelling the wilderness and apparently reaffirming the state.

Frances Brooke's *The History of Emily Montague* (1769), the first English novel written in North America, demonstrates some of the assumptions behind this social paradigm. Set largely in the British garrison community outside Quebec, it portrays three sets of lovers who must variously come to terms with the social conventions governing marriage (free choice, parental demands, wealth, land, race, order, religion, and opportunity). While England affords opportunities only to those with property and education, Canada in some degree counters this paradigm—but not sufficiently for the lovers to settle there. Narrative as well as social convention intrudes; the sudden acquisition of wealth permits a return to England, the ownership of property, marriage, and a rise to propriety. One character then intones that by cultivating his own garden (Voltaire is never far from these pages) he is serving the state, for true self-love and social are the same. (The same argument was used to justify ownership of the sugar plantations in the West Indies.) What sets Brooke's epistolary novel apart from others at the time is the voice of a character named Bell Fermor, an intelligent observer of society who consciously uses a coquettish wit to puncture the pretentiousness of the would-be social mandarins. This counter-voice, ostensibly examining only the 'little commonwealth of woman',[9] undercuts the hierarchies that the male characters accept as universal truths; their simple definition of 'independence' as monetary freedom, for example, runs up against Bell's desire that women be both socially *and intellectually* independent. Yet for all its cautious criticism, the novel does not portray a society transformed. The state persists; imperial control over other races and places is never questioned; and (to use one of the book's controlling metaphors) masquerades go on.

Some nineteenth-century narratives did examine the covert relation between state and domestic models, either by exposing authority in the home (as in Rosanna Leprohon's *Antoinette de Mirecourt; or Secret Marrying and Secret Sorrowing* (1864), where a woman becomes a victim after her unauthorized choice of a husband) or by imagining the powers of a future state (as in Julius Vogel's *Anno Domini 2000; or Woman's Destiny*, 1889). Women writers in particular challenged the

---

[9] Frances Brooke, *The History of Emily Montague*, ed. Mary Jane Edwards (1769; Ottawa: Carleton University Press, 1985), 98.

status quo, sometimes as poets and novelists, often as journalists (Louisa Lawson, Catherine Helen Spence, Sara Jeannette Duncan). Ada Cambridge's poem 'Fallen' uses sentimental convention to attack social hypocrisy directly: specifically that of the 'prosperous matron' who condemns the 'fallen woman' but who, having married for money and position, is merely herself 'Wife by the law, but prostitute in deed, | In whose gross wedlock womanhood is slain'.[10] The journalists offered solutions to social inequities. Spence's essay 'Marriage Rights and Marriage Wrongs' argues in favour of easier divorce, on both humanitarian and social grounds ('Wife-desertion is a question which affects all the colonies, each one complaining that wives and families are deserted by their natural head and are made burdensome to the state'); by appealing, moreover, to 'true morality and social order' (the fundaments of the social contract that the status quo was widely believed to be upholding), Spence exposes the immorality of rigid laws and customary attitudes, especially those that found divorce and extramarital love more vicious than wife-beating and domestic enslavement.

But when Spence advanced similar proposals in fiction, her works were suppressed. *Handfasted* did not see print until 1984, ostensibly because it was 'too socialistic', but probably more because of its candid account of sexuality and its open critique of Presbyterianism. Written as a utopian traveller's tale, this novel tells of a young Australian who leaves Melbourne to visit the United States on his way to Europe; in an out-of-the-way corner he discovers an isolated colony where women's rights are equal to men's, a prospect made possible because the group's minister had died while they were emigrating from Scotland, and intelligent women rewrote the moral code. What possibly scandalized nineteenth-century Australian publishers most was the colony's belief in trial marriage, which permitted women to withdraw from a relationship without losing moral and social status. That the young Australian should agree to this custom is presented in the text as a moral breakthrough; that the novel should nevertheless circle back to marriage and Melbourne creates a narrative ambiguity that perhaps asks to be read as an ironic critique of a real society in which such social experiments were at best contentious. Here, however, as with Duncan's fiction set in India (such as *The Simple Adventures of a Memsahib* (1893)), irony is itself a problematic technique; it demonstrates the narrative's awareness of the limitations in the attitudes it explicates, but at the same time it appears to perpetuate the very system of social exclusions that it seeks to reform.

[10] Leonie Kramer and Adrian Mitchell (eds.), *The Oxford Anthology of Australian Literature* [Barron Field, Charles Harpur, Henry Kendall, Marcus Clarke, and other writers] (Melbourne: Oxford University Press, 1985), 79.

Many women who opposed the domestic models that the increasingly nationalist colonies were using to configure state structure were censored before their writings appeared in print. (Barbara Baynton's story 'The Chosen Vessel' was truncated by its first editor, who by emphasizing the story's bush setting managed to shift its focus away from its implicit exposé of male violence towards women.) Other women began writing using male pseudonyms: Duncan wrote as 'Garth Grafton', Olive Schreiner as 'Ralph Iron'. Schreiner's identity was soon revealed, however; and her allegories about art, science, the cruelty of conventional men, and the difficulty of committing oneself to truth won her a wide readership—especially in *The Story of an African Farm* (1883), where the central character Lyndall rejects the usual forms of social discourse, and chooses to have a child but not to marry.

This novel, together with Schreiner's attack on Cecil Rhodes in *Trooper Peter Halket of Mashonaland* (1897), and her championing of women's rights in *Woman and Labour* (1911), signalled new directions for colonial writing; the avant-garde of the new century was egalitarian, anti-imperialist, and possibly in equal measure idealistic and disillusioned. For until the First World War, Empire continued to command conventional enthusiasm, and a work such as William Pember Reeves's 'A Colonist in his Garden' is in many respects typical of the temper of the age. In this poem, a settler resists (as Reeves did not) the blandishments of a friend that call him to return to 'home' and England; the 'colonist' declares, by way of reply,

> Here am I rooted. Firm and fast
> We men take root who face the blast,
>    When to the desert come,
> We stand where none before have stood
> And braving tempest, drought and flood,
>    Fight Nature for a home.[11]

'Desert', 'tempest', 'fight', 'blast': the language is that of the conventional adventure tale, trial being the man's proof of his own worth. For the time, it was a functional proof. For later readers, the obvious biases intrude: 'history' begins in New Zealand only when the settler arrives, 'nature' consists only of the English plants the settler imports, and the colonist's prize exhibit and possession ('could I rear in England's air | A sweeter English rose') is his daughter. Reeves's use of the Adamic, English garden as a *civilized replacement for wilderness* reaffirms, without irony, the convention in colonial writing that locates a domestic morality at the heart of the state structure.

---

[11] Chapman and Bennett (eds.), *New Zealand Verse*, 35.

FORMS OF SUBVERSION

The English word 'colony' derives from the Latin word 'colonus', meaning 'farmer', which underscores why the land carried so much symbolic weight in colonial literature. Tilling the land—which for settlers meant *owning property*: status and independence—reiterated the imperial design of 'cultivating' the wilderness. Yet not all colonial writing happily reconfirmed convention; many writers resisted the status quo, asserting the validity and separate nature of colonial perspectives. Some writers openly criticized received standards and political 'norms'; others tried through artistic practice to counter the values that stereotypes and established techniques persistently, if often unconsciously, purveyed.

Colonists and the colonized both asked to be heard, using subversive irony, local speech sounds, and alternative genres as modes of protest as well as techniques of expression. Irony (as in James De Mille's mock utopia *A Strange Manuscript Found in a Copper Cylinder* (1888) ) could question the conventions of literary taste as well as the philosophical presumptions of science and religion; oral literary forms (speeches, songs) began to attract attention; journalism emerged as a forceful *literary* medium of social reform; and by the end of the century, Lawson, Baynton, D. C. Scott, and others were skilfully using the sketch and short story to articulate colonial perspectives (Katherine Mansfield was less than a decade away). Epic aspiration and Latin pastoral allusion did not disappear from colonial literature as the vernacular came into prominence; nor did all colonial expressions receive equal measures of approval. Letters, diaries, and autobiographical memoirs—forms that women writers often used—were commonly dismissed as 'non-literary'; documenting gender as well as genre discrimination, they left subsequent generations of critics to consider the implications of the hierarchies of form.

The politics of all these gestures was seldom widely recognized; the Imperial Establishment, when they thought about colonial art at all, regarded vernacular speech as dialectal aberration, empirical reference as exotic local colour, and alternative modes as aesthetic failures. Yet the various forms of the vernacular suggest the broad literary range of social protest, as in the multitude of folk-songs and work-songs that survive from the lives of Atlantic fishermen, Caribbean cane-workers, and Australian transports and drovers: 'I's the B'y that Builds the Boat', 'Mary Ann', 'Guinea Corn', 'Sangaree Kill de Captain', 'Hail South Australia', 'The Female Transport'. Such sources, coupled with the popularity of the 1890s music-hall, subsequently encouraged 'folk *writing*'—as in the poems of Lawson, Banjo Paterson, Robert Service, and Johnny Burke— and these in turn, most especially in Australia, served the political cause of 1890s nationalism.

Earlier, and with deliberate literary intent, Judge Thomas Chandler Haliburton's *The Clockmaker* (1836), and other anecdotes involving a Yankee clock pedlar named Sam Slick, used the vernacular to argue that Bluenose (i.e. Nova Scotian) economic practices needed reforming. But Haliburton approved Sam's vernacular *energy* (an alternative voice), not his *republicanism* (an alternative politics): the two forms of irony make Haliburton's conservatism clear. His narrator, a 'squire', ironizes about Sam's uncouthness, but because the squire is so resistant to change, he is himself also the object of irony; the one technique assumes the validity of current social exclusiveness, the other probes the arbitrariness of unexamined convention.

More rebelliously (in less democratic, mid-eighteenth-century Newfoundland), Donncha Ruah MacConmara used a verse variant of interlinear glossing to attack rather than just to dispute authority; lines in English that praised 'Royal George' and his power were followed by lines in Irish Gaelic that (translated) said, 'may I see the brute defeated'.[12] As well as emulate, the local voice could undercut.

But because colonial experience was wide-ranging, any account of the emergence of a 'national'—or a 'post-colonial'—literature has to acknowledge at once the impact of convention, the impulse to reform, and the consequences of formal choice. Neither vernacular writing nor received literary language alone can adequately characterize this body of literature. And just as emulation did not always lead to acceptance, so resistance did not always result directly in social action or take expected literary forms. In Caribbean culture, for example, Creole speech—as in two graces, spoken by the cane-workers, that were first recorded in the eighteenth and nineteenth centuries—tells more profoundly of social inequity than pastoral ever could. The first precedes a meal of rats: 'Massa, bless this little infreshment. May it tick to me ribs as burr grass to cuntung coat.' The second expresses the uncertainty of daily survival even after slavery has been abolished: 'Tank you, me fader for all me na swallow | Hope me may lib, fe nyam smo' to-morrow.'[13] For all the intricacy of established literary fashion, these two graces express, with simple eloquence, the kind of life that colonial literature seldom exposed—but that colonialism repeatedly constructed, in the hunger for land and the hope of glory.

---

[12] *Atlantic Provinces Literature Colloquium Papers* [essays by Cyril Byrne *et al.*, on early Newfoundland and Maritime poetry and journalism] (Saint John: Atlantic Canada Institute, 1977), 25.
[13] D'Costa and Lalla (eds.), *Voices in Exile*, 9, 128.

# CHAPTER SEVEN

# 'Forging the Conscience of Their Race': Nationalist Writers

## C. L. INNES

The literature produced as part of a cultural nationalist project is a literature produced in opposition to the narratives and representations which deny dignity and autonomy to those who have been colonized. But this opposition is addressed not just to the colonizing power, nor even primarily to it, but to the people of the emerging nation, and seeks to engage them in their own project of self-definition. This essay sets out to explore some aspects of the construction of a national literature in those countries which have been defined by European powers as culturally lacking and uncivilized, where the claim of an *absence* of culture has been taken as the justification for the imposition of the colonizer's government and culture. My discussion will focus on comparisons between Irish, Australian, and West African writing, as a means of exploring the similarities and differences between nationalist texts produced in a variety of cultural, ethnic, and historical contexts.

There are, of course, significant differences between the experiences of the Irish, Australians, and West Africans as colonized subjects. Ireland's propinquity to England resulted in a wave of settlements from its neighbour, beginning with the Norman barons in the eleventh century, followed by Henry II's claim to rule Ireland, and continuing through Elizabethan and Cromwellian settlements in the sixteenth and seventeenth centuries. Christianity took hold as early as the fifth century, and long coexisted with traditional Brehon law and custom. With the coming of the Reformation and the Church of England's break from Rome, and the promulgation of a whole series of laws barring native Irish and then Catholics from participation in the political, economic, and social life of the nation, Catholicism became for many Irish (and English) identified with Irish nationalism and was seen as quite compatible with the restoration of Gaelic customs. Nevertheless many of those descended from the Protestant settler populations, Anglo-Irish men and women such as Lady Gregory, William Butler Yeats, and John Millington Synge, took leading parts in the political and cultural movements which flourished in the late nineteenth and early twentieth centuries and which were concerned with establishing and authenticating Irish independence. And Irish independence was fought for and achieved, at least partially, between 1916 and 1923 when the British Empire was at its height (or perhaps one should say its depth), an empire which often drew on the services of Anglo-Irishmen such as Sir William Gregory, Lady Gregory's husband (who served as governor of Sri Lanka and Egypt). Australia, on the other hand, was not claimed and settled by the English until 1788, and was at first regarded primarily as a convict rather than a plantation settlement. The indigenous peoples of Australia were treated with even greater brutality than the native Irish, their presence on the continent and in the consciousness of the settlers almost obliterated (except, significantly, in the place names which were retained), for the first 150 years of white settlement. A nationalism which affirmed realism and stoicism and which abjured romanticism of the kind espoused by Yeats became focused in the decade preceding the creation of Australia as a federal nation in 1901. In the late 1920s and again in the late 1960s, however, new cultural nationalist movements began to appropriate and then recognize Aboriginal culture as fundamental to the definition of Australian culture. In the mean time, the Aboriginal peoples of Australia have increasingly asserted the right to define their own national narrative.

In contrast to these two settler colonies, Nigeria and Ghana, after experiencing long histories of trading contacts, especially slave trading, involving Danish, Dutch, Portuguese, French, and English merchants and militia, were not formally colonized until the late nineteenth century, and it is only during the nineteenth century that Christianity makes a significant impact. West Africa's distance from England, the colour, appearance, and customs of its peoples, the comparatively short period of political governance and interaction, made it easier for the English to exoticize those areas, and see them as wholly mysterious and fearful. The Second World War, with the social and economic changes it brought and the rhetoric of freedom and democracy which the Allied Powers employed to maintain morale, contributed to the rapid disintegration of the British Empire. Ireland had gained its independence in 1923, and left the Commonwealth in 1949. Australia and Canada claimed separate citizenship in 1946. India became an independent state in 1947. African and Caribbean states also claimed the right to self-government, and in 1957 Ghana was the first to achieve it under the leadership of Kwame Nkrumah and his appeal to Pan-Africanism. Nigeria followed suit in 1960, as did the majority of African and Caribbean nations in the subsequent five years. The move towards the assertion of political independence was accompanied by an extraordinary efflorescence of literary creation and cultural assertion in these nations.

Given the historical and cultural differences between their societies, it is perhaps surprising that so many of the self-definitions proclaimed by cultural nationalists in Ireland, Australia, and West Africa appear to be so similar. All claimed to be more humane, more in tune with the elemental and natural, more vital and less alienated than the Englishman or European, whose culture was denounced as mechanistic, artificial, and decadent. African, Australian, and Gaelic cultures were defined as collective or democratic, expressive of the people as a whole; the metropolitan English artistic tradition was contrasted as élitist, self-absorbed, isolated, and emasculated. The printed word and privately read book were linked to the European tradition; African, Australian, and Gaelic cultures were considered most authentic when associated with songs, ballads, anecdotes, oral culture, and the spoken word. These similarities in definition are all the more unexpected when one considers that each group was generally concerned with expressing the uniqueness of its culture, emphasizing those elements which set it apart from all others and hence made it a cohesive and separate whole—a distinctively national culture.

One explanation for these similarities of definition may be that these groups of nationalists were caught up in a similar dialectic, wherein the metropolitan imperial power categorizes all 'other' groups in opposition to its own self-image. Long before Edward Said published *Orientalism*, Frantz Fanon had described (in *The Wretched of the Earth*) the colonial world as a Manichaean world, in which the world of the native is the negation of the world of the settler. Within this opposition there are differences of degree depending on the historical and political context as well as the attitudes of individual speakers; that is, the native may be categorized as brute or vermin at worst, or as childlike and effeminate at best, but the sets of oppositions remain fairly constant. A letter written in 1861 by the novelist and reformer Charles Kingsley to his wife about what he had seen in Ireland illustrates the near equation between Irish and African natives, and equally recalls comments made by missionaries and cattle station owners about Australian Aborigines in their 'care':

But I am haunted by the human chimpanzees I saw along that hundred miles of horrible country. I don't believe they are our fault. I believe there are not only more of them than of old, but that they are happier, better, more comfortably fed and lodged under our rule than ever they were. But to see white chimpanzees is dreadful; if they were black, one would not feel it so much, but their skins, except where tanned by exposure, are as white as ours.[1]

Another trope which recurs again and again in colonialist discourse represents the natives as endearingly childlike or feminine, and hence in

[1]   Quoted by L. P. Curtis, *Anglo-Saxons and Celts* (Bridgeport, Conn.: Conference on British Studies, 1968), p. 6.

need of paternal or husbandly masculine governance. The image of the colonial relationship in terms of a family was a common one, and worked in terms of both parent – child, and husband – wife relationships, as they were defined in the nineteenth century.

In response to dismissal of 'native culture' by the colonizers, many cultural nationalists tended to assert the existence of a culture which was the antithesis of the colonial one—and hence either antagonistic to or complementary to it. What is striking and paradoxical about the antithesis proclaimed by some nationalists is that it so frequently derives from and affirms the antithetical images already developed by the colonizer in order to justify his presence. Instead of denying the distinctions made by the colonizers in order to justify their presence, and insisting that the Celt, Australian, or African is as capable of reason and self-discipline as the Englishman, many cultural nationalists celebrated the very characteristics for which they were disparaged—emotionalism, irrationality, primitiveness. Thus Yeats qualified the dichotomy between Anglo-Saxon rationality and industry and Celtic sentimentality, femininity, and eagerness 'to rebel against the despotism of fact' set up by Matthew Arnold in his lectures on Celtic literature, by arguing that the Celtic touch related to primeval spirituality untouched by English rationality and materialism; he did not challenge the dichotomy itself. Senghor, the spokesman for 'Negritude' and later President of Senegal, proclaimed that 'emotion is completely Negro, as reason is Greek' and went on to define the essential characteristics of Negro literature as 'rhythm, emotion and humour'—characteristics which sound all too similar to those expected of the stage Negro minstrel. Where the colonizer has contemptuously dismissed the native as belonging to the natural rather than the human world, cultural nationalists affirmed their peoples' 'closeness to nature', and declared their culture essentially agrarian or peasant in contrast to the urban and mechanistic civilization of the colonizer. Where the colonizer insisted that the native had no history, and had been left out of its linear progression, cultural nationalists pointed to an unchanging tradition, a timelessness, or a circular history which would reinstall the pre-colonial past. Where the colonizer celebrated his literature, his written records, as a mark of his superior and developing civilization, the colonized intellectual emphasized oral traditions, which were claimed to *preserve* the past, and celebrated the language and voice of the non-literate 'folk'.

Having defined their culture in these terms, those nationalist writers who expressed themselves in European languages and literary forms found themselves in a peculiar position, for they were almost inevitably to some degree shaped by European culture. Senghor was educated from the age of 6 entirely in French, became a Catholic, wrote his dissertation on Baudelaire, and, when he returned to predominantly Muslim Senegal in 1947, had spent more of his life in France than in Africa. Both Achebe and Soyinka were the children of Christian converts and catechists, and graduated from university after studying a very English canon. Yeats was educated for at least half of the time in England, and his strongest early influences were the English Romantic poets Shelley and Byron. All four wrote mainly in the language of the colonizing country, rather than Wolof, Igbo, Yoruba, or Gaelic, the language of the cultures they celebrate. For most of the early Australian nationalists, English was their first language, and English literature and culture the tradition in which they were educated.

Despite their contact with the metropolitan culture and nineteenth-century Romanticism, however, that emphasis on the agrarian world and closeness to nature is no mere Romantic hangover on the part of nationalist writers, for what is being expressed in their works is not merely a generalized relationship between man and nature, but rather a relationship between a particular group of people and a particular geographical area. The claim being made in nationalist literature is that *the people and the land belong to each other*. The culture of the colonizer is not only alienated in general, but alien to that particular area; it does not belong *there*. The unity between people and place is marked in Synge's writings on the Aran Islands and in his plays; it is also a central feature of the Australian nationalist idealization of the 'bush man' and later of Aboriginal culture, but it is even more marked in Achebe's novels, such as *Things Fall Apart* and *Arrow of God*, or Soyinka's plays and poems. In each case, the proverbs and analogies and images which create the world of Pegeen Flaherty or Coonardoo or Okonkwo, the people, their way of life, their mode of thought, their language and land are all seen as organically interrelated. Particularly in African novels, descriptions of the landscapes *as such* are rare; there is no distanced eye, but an insistence that the land and the consciousness of the narrator or the characters are completely integrated.

One other similarity between a number of nationalist literatures is the recurrence of plots which involve conflict between fathers and sons. (Australian literature provides an exception which I will discuss later.) The father–son conflict is central to Synge's *Playboy of the Western World* and to Achebe's *Things Fall Apart* as well as his three other novels written before 1966. Such a conflict is also either explicit in other works, such as Yeats's *Baile's Strand* and all of Joyce, or implicit in much other writing where a father figure is opposed by a representative of the younger generation, as in almost all of Synge's other plays or Soyinka's *Lion and the Jewel* and *Kongi's Harvest* or Okara's *The Voice*. Antagonism between fathers and sons is, of course, a common theme in all literature, not just that which is written in a cultural nationalist context, but within that context it takes on a number of additional weightings. In addition to those I have suggested already, there is the resistance to the patriarchal authority of the colonizer, and also the resistance to the weight and authority of particular literary fathers. Harold Bloom has written about the anxiety of influence with regard to Yeats's rewriting of Shelley, but gives almost no attention to the ways in which that and later rewriting interacts with his rejection of Anglo-Saxon influence and his concern with asserting a voice which will be not only distinctively his own but also distinctively Irish. Achebe tells us he began writing in reaction to English writers such as Conrad and Joyce Cary, and his first four novels can be read in part as rewritings of Cary's four African novels. We have the additional irony, of course, that for Achebe Yeats is also a literary father, and his first novel, titled *Things Fall Apart* from the first line of Yeats's poem, 'The Second Coming', reworks the implications of Yeats's vision of history.

The father–son conflict in nationalist literature is also complicated in interesting ways by its relation to a myth of the motherland. Senghor and other Senegalese poets as well as many black South African writers assert their loyalty to Mother Africa, who is also portrayed as the embodiment of African tradition, of the true African self. Even writers like Soyinka and Achebe who parody or attack such mythologies often do so with some ambivalence, or betray their influence in other ways. Senghor is the best known and most prolix of francophone African poets who frequently return to the trope of Africa as mother and mistress, and Achebe parodies his imagery and style in Kul Max's invocation to the Motherland in *A Man of the People*. But this trope appears frequently also in anglophone poetry, fiction, and drama, from the poetry of Nigeria's Christopher Okigbo and its invocation to Mother Idoto, to the recurring figure of Mammy Water as a bewitching seducer and image of the nation and nature in the writings of Okigbo's fellow Nigerian Wole Soyinka. The Mammy Water figure frequently appears in the novels of the Ghanaian writers Ayi Kwei Armah and Kofi Awoonor.

However, this image of the motherland as nurturing mother and sensual bride is by no means limited to African writing (or Caribbean, where women are frequently linked to the fruits and contours of the Caribbean islands). One of the most familiar nationalist poems for Irish readers is James Clarence Mangan's 'Dark Rosaleen', in which the allegorical significance of Rosaleen as colonized Ireland is foregrounded. Mangan bases his nineteenth-century version on an earlier Gaelic love poem. William Butler Yeats's early nationalist poetry was strongly influenced by Mangan's, and he drew on Mangan's reworking of other Irish vision poems for 'Red Hanrahan's Song about Ireland', first published in 1894. With its refrain revering 'Cathleen, the daughter of Houlihan', this poem shares with other nationalist poetry not only its invocation of a feminized symbol of the nation, but also, with the reference to Maeve, legendary Queen of Connaught, whose burial place was said to be on top of Mount Knocknarea, its invocation of a pre-colonial past, a Celtic mythology which precedes English settlement, but survives buried in the hearts of true Irishmen and in the archaeology of the land. Yet another link between land and women whose names become linked with it is suggested in the reference to Clooth-na-Bare, the pool in which the 'Woman of Beare' or 'the old woman of Ireland', said by some to be the mother of the Celtic gods, had drowned herself. Characteristic of Yeats's poetry too is this insistence on attaching the old Irish names to the landscape, in a land which had been remapped and renamed during the nineteenth century by English cartographers. Like many of his poems 'Red Hanrahan's Song' is very specifically local in its naming and in its descriptions of nature; this is the landscape of Sligo that is being named and described; its significance is personal as well as national, particular as well as symbolic.

Yeats's invocation of landscape and of Celtic mythology is a means of laying claim to the land, and asserting the existence of a distinctively non-Anglo-Saxon culture, as well as an implicit appeal to other Irishmen to revive the ideal of the nation. It is an ideal and an appeal which evades other and more divisive identities, such as class, religion, and 'race'. As in their manifesto for the Irish Literary Theatre, Yeats, Lady Gregory and Edward Martyn hoped that their work would be 'outside all the political questions that divide us'.[2] The appeal to the Celtic legendary past, the invocation of a landscape which is peopled only by mythological figures, bypasses a long history of colonization, the creation of the Protestant landlord class to which Yeats aspired, and the deep divisions between tenants and landlords, Catholics and Protestants. The nationalist play *Cathleen ni Houlihan*, written by Yeats and Lady Gregory and first performed in 1902, seemed to succeed powerfully in its twofold aim of invoking the past and appealing for Irishmen to participate in the violent and 'terrible beauty' which might create the new nation.

As Edward Said has pointed out, the recurring invocation of violence in Yeats's poetry is not untypical of nationalist literature, and parallels Fanon's counter-colonial narrative and analysis which endorses the violent uprooting of the colonized psyche from colonial oppression.[3] Like Fanon, Yeats was unable to envision a new Irish society after liberation; his poetry is caught up in the task of romanticized struggle, while the future, as in 'The Second Coming', holds only violence and disorder,

[2] Lady Gregory, *Our Irish Theatre* (New York: Capricorn Books, 1965), 8–9.
[3] Edward Said, *Culture and Imperialism* (London: Chatto & Windus, 1993), 282–3.

mere anarchy. Increasingly, his poetry reacts against his sense of his own exclusion from that imagined community appealed to in the Irish Literary Theatre manifesto; 'that uncorrupted and imaginative audience trained to listen by its passion for oratory', the 'ancient idealism' invoked in 'Red Hanrahan's Song', seemed to recede into the past. Yeats turns then to the task of haranguing the nation that has betrayed that ancient idealism:

> What need you, being come to sense,
> But fumble in a greasy till
> And add the halfpence to the pence
> And prayer to shivering prayer, until
> You have dried the marrow from the bone?
> Romantic Ireland's dead and gone,
> It's with O'Leary in the grave.
>
> ('September, 1913')

Yeats's antagonism to the middle class as epitomizing all that is antipathetic to the ideal nation is shared by almost all nationalist writers. Yet, when the 1916 Rising proved that 'Romantic Ireland' was not dead and gone, Yeats responded to the violence of both sides with a poem, 'Easter 1916', which was personal rather than public in its ambivalent reaction to the 'terrible beauty' born in that action. Moreover the features of the landscape, 'the living stream', 'the birds that range from cloud to tumbling cloud', now do not embody history and the past, but are in opposition to it. Published privately at first, and circulated only to close friends several months after the execution of the leaders of the rebellion, 'Easter 1916' reveals Yeats questioning not only his own previously confident sense of the nation, but also his role as national poet, no longer one who inspires or prophesies action, but one who simply records and names:

> ... our part
> To murmur name upon name,
> As a mother names her child
> When sleep at last has come
> On limbs that had run wild.

Here and in Yeats's later poems, the world and names of Celtic myth and legend are replaced by names drawn from history and his own biography—Parnell, Casement, Swift and Burke, Lady Gregory, Synge, his relatives and acquaintances become the figures in a defiantly Anglo-Irish narrative; the 'Big House' becomes the symbol of order and culture with which he seeks to counteract what he saw as the disorder, philistinism, and materialism of the new Irish state. To the very end, he wanted to believe that Irish poets had a duty to help shape the nation:

> Irish poets, learn your trade,
> Sing whatever is well made,
>
> . . .
>
> Cast your mind on other days
> That we in coming days may be
> Still the indomitable Irishry.
>> ('Under Ben Bulben')

Although Yeats enlisted Synge and Lady Gregory in his own enterprise ('We three alone in modern times had brought | Everything down to that sole test again, | Dream of the noble and the beggar man'), Synge and Lady Gregory had rather different tests to establish a truly Irish art. Synge abjured what he termed an 'unmodern, ideal breesy [*sic*], spring-dayish, Cuchulainoid National Theatre', and sang the living peasantry, rather than the 'hard-riding country gentleman' or lords and ladies of the past. Whereas Yeats's play, *Deirdre*, emphasizes her queenly nobility, Synge turns Deirdre into a country girl who speaks in the idiom of the folk. Yeats asserts his identity with the land by naming and describing it in a language which is highly poetic and only slightly inflected from metropolitan English; Synge insists on the hardship of rural life, while celebrating the vitality of rural Irish speech, and insisting on the close connection between Irish consciousness and the land from which they wrestle a living (a project continued in very different ways by later poets such as Patrick Kavanagh and Seamus Heaney).

The interaction between Irish and Australian nationalism is a subject worth exploring, but it is not the task of this essay. Suffice it to mention that Charles Gavin Duffy, the founder of the Young Irelander paper the *Nation*, emigrated to Australia and was Prime Minister of Victoria (1871–2). After his return to Europe in 1880, he was made President of the Irish Literary Society founded in 1892 by Yeats and others. The Australian bushranger folk hero Ned Kelly was the son of Irish immigrants. Kelly's laconic comment, 'Such is life,' when he was sentenced to death (by Irish immigrant judge Redmond Barry), was taken as the title for a novel by Joseph Furphy, whose parents came to Australia from Ireland in 1841. Furphy's novel was published by the nationalist magazine, the *Bulletin*, in 1903 and has in later years been seen as one of the seminal works in the creation of a 'truly Australian' literature.

In form and genre, *Such is Life* perhaps has more in common with Melville's *Moby Dick* or even James Joyce's *Ulysses* than with the Australian novels which preceded it. Nevertheless, what critics and reviewers commented on when it was first published was not the oddity of its form, its episodic and encyclopedic nature, and its rejection of the conventions of the genre, but its truth to what was judged to be 'the Australian experience'. Furphy's own succinct description of the book,

'Temper, democratic; bias, offensively Australian',[4] was well phrased to appeal to the editor of the *Bulletin* and the ideology of its readers. A. G. Stephens praised the novel for its 'accurate representations of our character and customs, life and scenery', while other reviewers followed suit in stressing the documentary value, the truth to Australian pastoral life, rather than the experimental form.[5] As John Barnes points out, *Such is Life* is 'an attempt to represent life without giving it a recognisable novelistic shape'.[6] More than that, it deliberately rejects stereotypical and exoticized colonial Australian novels such as Rolf Boldrewood's *Robbery under Arms* or Henry Kingsley's *Geoff Hamlyn* with their 'outlawed bushrangers; the lurking blackfellows; the squatter's lovely Diana-daughter, awaiting the well-bred greenhorn'.[7] Furphy refuses to be 'the novelist who brings forth out of his imagination the very thing required by the exigencies of the story', for 'such is not life'.[8]

Furphy's belief that fiction which is to be 'Australian' and 'democratic' must eschew established conventions of plot and character was shared by other writers promoted by the *Bulletin* in stories designed as sketches of Australian life and character, episodic and anecdotal in form and style. Like Furphy, Lawson writes about the men who know the land: shearers, drovers, and those struggling to make a bare living from small holdings in a hostile and often barren land. Lawson's identification of the Australian character with the qualities which are demanded by day-to-day endurance, the heroism of the struggle to wrest a living from a meagre land, his skill at crafting a language and form which suggest the voice and idiom of such men, has some analogies with Synge's representation of the Aran Islanders and the poor tenants and farmers of Wicklow and the west coast of Ireland. But there are also significant differences. While Synge generally focuses on a community which has deep ties with the landscape it inhabits, Lawson's and Furphy's characters are typically lone men (and occasionally lone women) who are suspicious or resentful of communal or family ties. The landscape they inhabit is not only hostile or barren, but alien. And perhaps most strikingly different from Irish or African cultural nationalism is the absence of the past (and with it the absence of fathers) in Australian literature of this period. We are very rarely given a family history for any of these characters: they come into being and exist in an unchanging present, and whatever changes they experience occur in space, in change of location—which is nevertheless always a similar location—rather than in time. Writers of this period

---

[4] *Portable Australian Authors: Joseph Furphy*, ed. John Barnes (Brisbane: University of Queensland Press, 1981), p. xv.

[5] John Barnes, 'Introduction', in *Joseph Furphy*, p. xv.

[6] Ibid. p. xvii.

[7] *Such is Life*, ed. Barnes, 271.

[8] Ibid. 269.

eschew myth, legend, history, the depths that belong to romantic nationalism. Their project is Whitmanesque, and their characters and the anecdotes they narrate are metonymic rather than symbolic.

Closely related to the particular socialist nationalism of the 1890s in Australia, and the dream of a new beginning where a working man's democracy might be established, the literature of this period also expresses the fact that most of the writers are first-generation immigrants, for whom the Australian landscape is alien, unconnected to any personal history. This is a world in which community is yet to be created, out of isolated individuals, not a world where community is to be restored. Here the ethos of 'mateship', of two or three equals sharing their thoughts and their goods, replaces the hierarchical communities of aristocrats, saints, and peasants, of romantic heroes and beautiful women, which are invoked in Irish nationalist literature. It is also primarily a world of men, where women are valued (as in Lawson's 'The Drover's Wife' or in Furphy's women characters disguised as men) insofar as they can do the work of men and not succumb to 'feminine' weaknesses.

Despite the fact that the native habitat of more than two-thirds of all Australians in the 1890s and throughout the twentieth century was one of the large urban areas on the coast, and although most of the authors lived in the cities of Sydney or Melbourne, the literary ballads written by Henry Lawson, Banjo Paterson, and Adam Lindsay Gordon celebrate the lone man in the 'outback', the stock man, the man from Snowy River, the drover, the shearer. Such characters, and the ballads that affirm them, become the basis for later nationalist definitions. Thus the historians C. E. W. Bean and Russel Ward both see the ballad and the pastoral world as representing the ideal expression of the Australian type. Bean, writing in 1907, declared that the bush had 'hammered out of the old stock a new man',[9] ready to serve the Empire and prove Australia's worth. Ward drew on the ballad tradition for more radical purposes, to argue a socialist and working-class narrative of Australian history.

The ideal Australian type was not only masculine but white; a focus on the man of the bush as the essential Australian marginalized women while almost completely eradicating Aborigines and other Australians who were not of Anglo-Saxon stock. (Even the large Irish population was generally ignored.) Similarly, the insistence on the Australian as an existential being, living in a present untrammelled by a past, also encouraged the pretence that Australia was an empty continent without a history of conquest and dispossession. Indeed, this aversion of the eyes from the past perhaps betrayed an uneasy conscience about the disgraceful treatment of Aborigines and the occupation of their land. Publicly,

---

[9] Richard White, *Inventing Australia* (Sydney: Allen & Unwin, 1981), 126.

however, Aborigines were claimed to be a dying race, who could play no part in Australia's future. There was in the late nineteenth and early twentieth centuries an almost hysterical racism regarding Chinese and other non-white peoples, as expressed in the *Bulletin* in 1887:

All white men who come to these shores—with a clean record—and who leave behind them the memory of the class-distinctions and the religious differences in the old world . . . are Australian. In this regard all men who leave the tyrant-ridden lands of Europe for freedom of speech and personal liberty are Australian before they set foot on the ship which brings them hither . . . . No nigger, no Chinaman, no lascar, no kanaka, no purveyor of cheap coloured labour is an Australian.[10]

This insistence on the white male worker in the outback, and on mateship, has dominated one important strand of Australian literature and literary criticism. Nevertheless, it was contested at the time and in later years by a number of women writers. Barbara Baynton, whose stories were also published in the *Bulletin*, portrays the vulnerability of women in the bush, and paints a harsh and damning picture of the consequences of the emphasis on masculinity and male comradeship. The title character in 'Squeaker's Mate' is not a man but a woman, who has carried the burden of work on the small holding she shares, and who is abandoned by her feckless male partner when a tree falls on her and breaks her back. In 'Billy Skywonkie' Baynton narrates the tragedy of a young half-Chinese housekeeper who is scorned and rejected by the men she has been sent to work for. Christina Stead's first novel, *Seven Poor Men of Sydney*, foregrounds the tragedy of women who can find neither useful work nor intellectual comradeship in a city and a capitalist system which also distorts all relationships. In Henry Handel Richardson's fiction, it is the women who sustain the family and the community and the egos of their men. Katharine Susannah Prichard's novels include working women as well as men, and a number of significant Aboriginal characters who are given sympathetic and respectful treatment. Prichard's fifth novel, *Coonardoo*, illustrates not only her sympathy for the Aboriginal peoples who first inhabited Australia, and her dismay at the ways in which white settlers have treated them, but also a great deal of ambivalence about the role and place of Aborigines in a developing Australian society. *Coonardoo* might well be seen as a precursor of the 'Jindyworobak' movement, described by one critic as 'the most passionate and romantic outpouring of Australian nationalism'.[11] Led by the poet Rex Ingamells, the Jindyworobaks sought to draw upon Aboriginal

[10] Cited by White, ibid. 81.
[11] John McLaren, *Australian Literature: An Historical Introduction* (Melbourne: Longman, 1989), 121.

myths and legends as a means of revisioning an indigenous and non-European relationship to the land. Similarly the opening paragraphs of *Coonardoo* seek to represent an Aboriginal response to a particular landscape:

Coonardoo was singing. Sitting under dark bushes overhung with curdy white blossom, she clicked two small sticks together, singing:

> 'Iowera chinima poodinya,
> Iowera jinner mulbeena . . .'

Over and over again, in a thin reedy voice, away at the back of her head, the melody flowed like water running over smooth pebbles in a dry creek bed.[12]

The song, the language, the voice, and the character all blend into and become one with the character and the land, the melody like water, the words rattling together like the smooth pebbles and the sticks. Throughout the novel, the analogy between Coonardoo and the land is insistent, and Coonardoo is also the embodiment of her people. One can read this novel as an allegory of white settlement, moving from the mystical and communal world of the Aborigines living in harmony with the land, to a feudal relationship between the first white settlers, embodied in the person of the matriarch Mrs Bessie, who is both mother and father to the Aborigines who gladly serve her. But her son's puritanism and his wife's concern to preserve class distinctions and relationships destroy that feudal relationship, and ultimately both Coonardoo and the land are degraded and ruined. Throughout the novel, Coonardoo (named after the deep well near which she was born) is also linked to female sexuality and fertility, and a feminine principle which is seen to belong to the Aborigines and the land generally, while Hugh (referred to always by the Aborigines as 'You', and thus always 'Other') clings to ideals of masculinity nourished by Homer and his boarding school. Their son, we are told, 'looked . . . with the eyes of his aboriginal intuition, instinctive wisdom, his white man's intelligence, reasoning' (p. 133).

Prichard's portrayal of the Aborigines as essentially feminine, instinctive, and intuitive in their closeness to nature is as deeply problematic as her constant underscoring of Coonardoo's devotion to Mrs Bessie and Hugh, a devotion shared by the other Aborigines on the station, who never question the sovereignty of the white man or woman. In recent years, Aboriginal writers themselves have retold the national narrative in very different terms. Sally Morgan's *My Place*[13] is set in the same territory as *Coonardoo*, but reveals the suffering, the anger, the amazement and contempt of Aborigines for the white men and women who dispossessed

---

[12] *Coonardoo* (1929; Sydney: Angus & Robertson, 1975).
[13] London: Virago, 1988.

while claiming to care for them. Mudrooroo Narogin (Colin Johnson) in his third novel, *Doctor Wooreddy's Prescription for Enduring the End of the World*,[14] focuses, like Chinua Achebe in his first novel, on the first violent coming of the white man and the physical and cultural resistance of the indigenous people.

As a nationalist writer, Chinua Achebe has more in common with Mudrooroo and Synge than with Prichard or Yeats. Like Synge's, Achebe's work moves away from the cultural nationalism of his predecessors, in this case the Negritude movement with its implication of a 'glorious technicolour past'.[15] The declaration in *Things Fall Apart* that 'among the Ibo the art of conversation is regarded very highly, and proverbs are the palm-oil with which words are eaten'[16] parallels in its sentiments as well as its analogy of words to food Synge's belief, expressed in the preface to *The Playboy of the Western World*, that 'In countries where the imagination of the people, and the language they use, is rich and living, it is possible for a writer to be rich and copious in his words, and at the same time to give the reality which is the root of all poetry, in a comprehensive and natural form . . . In a good play every speech should be as fully flavoured as a nut or apple, and such speeches cannot be written by anyone who works among people who have shut their lips on poetry.'[17]

Unlike Yeats and Senghor or Lawson, who create the writer as solitary protagonist, or whose ballads, fiction, and drama stage heroes and heroines in isolation, Synge and Achebe seek to recreate a community. Thus the opening paragraphs of Achebe's seminal novel *Things Fall Apart* proclaim its departure from European novels which assume that the artist's integrity rests in his separation from the values of his society:

Okonkwo was well known throughout the nine villages and even beyond. His fame rested on solid personal achievements. As a young man of eighteen he had brought honour to his village by throwing Amalinze the Cat. Amalinze was the great wrestler who for seven years was unbeaten, from Umuofia to Mbaino. He was called the cat because his back would never touch the earth. It was this man that Okonkwo threw in a fight which the old men agreed was one of the fiercest since the founder of their town engaged a spirit of the wild for seven days and seven nights.

[14] South Yarra: Hyland House, 1983.
[15] 'We cannot pretend that our past was one long technicolour idyll. We have to admit that like other people's pasts ours had its good as well as its bad sides.' Chinua Achebe, 'The Role of the Writer in the New Nation', *Nigeria Magazine*, 81 (1964), p. 161.
[16] *Things Fall Apart* (London: Heinemann Educational Books, 1976), 5. Further references to this edition will be included in the text.
[17] J. M. Synge, *Collected Works*, iv: *Plays*, Book II, ed. Ann Saddlemyer (London: Oxford University Press, 1968), 53–4.

The drums beat and the flutes sang and the spectators held their breath. Amalinze was a wily craftsman, but Okonkwo was as slippery as a fish in water. Every nerve and every muscle stood out of their arms, on their backs and their thighs, and one almost heard them stretching to breaking point. In the end Okonkwo threw the cat.

That was many years ago, twenty or more, and during this time Okonkwo's fame had grown like a bushfire in the harmattan. (p. 1)

The narrative voice in these opening sections, and throughout much of the novel, emulates the voice of the oral story-teller, merging with the voices of the village elders, 'the old men' who remember the legendary founder of their town. It assumes a world which is harmonious and unified, in which values are shared (that fame should rest on personal achievements and that such achievements should bring honour to the village as a whole), a world which is firmly centred in Umuofia, to which 'the world beyond' is marginal. It is not a world which has to be placed and described for the outside reader; instead the implicit audience is a village audience, a part of the community, to whom the story-teller is attuned, supplying details as they are needed. Past and present are intertwined, and the story moves not in a linear fashion, but constantly backwards and forwards in time. The wrestling match is brought alive in the presence of the implicit audience, as the story of Okonkwo is brought from the end of the nineteenth century to live in the mid-twentieth century for the reader.

Like Yeats, Achebe invokes and asserts the continuity of myth and legend in the face of the colonizer's narrative which denies that History belongs to Africa or Ireland prior to his coming, insisting that they have experienced only 'an unbroken cycle of clannish brawls and idolatry', as Benjamin Disraeli described the Irish experience.[18] Like Yeats and Synge, Achebe celebrates the culture of a peasant community, removed from urban and Anglo-Saxon influence. Achebe shares with Synge above all an appreciation for the drama, played out within and against the social, religious, and economic foundations which both unite and constrain the individuals within that society, and the language which uniquely expresses that community. He also shares with Synge the sense of English as an alien language, which must be re-formed, through idiom and imagery, to suggest the consciousness of Irish or Igbo speakers. The frequent use of proverbs and similes such as the comparison of Okonkwo's rapid fame to 'a bushfire in the harmattan' suggest the inextricable relationship between the Igbos and their land.

Synge and Achebe both seek to express difference between an Irish or Igbo community and an English one through a literary version of a

[18] Quoted by Curtis, *Anglo-Saxons and Celts*, 84.

specifically national idiom and speech. Achebe goes further than Synge, however, in calling to the reader's attention the existence of the Igbo language and its inclusion of non-European concepts, such as *chi, ndichie*, and *agbala*, which English can never quite encompass. In this and many other ways, the issue of language is foregrounded in the novel, so that the English language is seen to be not only inadequate, but indeed at times to deny Igbo (and African) perceptions and dignity. Thus, the missionary Mr Smith, who succeeds the more tolerant—and thus appropriately named—Mr Brown,

saw things as black and white. And black was evil. He saw the world as a battleground in which the children of light were locked in mortal conflict with the sons of darkness. He spoke in his sermons about sheep and goats and about wheat and tares. He believed in slaying the prophets of Baal. (p. 164)

Not only the connotations of black and white, but the Manichaean world-view which insists on totalizing distinctions between 'children of light and sons of darkness', are anathema to members of a black African community which, according to Achebe, affirms the values of tolerance and the belief that 'wherever something stands, something else also stands'.[19] It is this language and the culture that it embodies that is replaced at the end of the novel, as the District Commissioner meditates upon the book he plans to write:

The story of this man who had killed a messenger and hanged himself would make interesting reading. One would almost write a whole chapter on him. Perhaps not a whole chapter, but a reasonable paragraph, at any rate. There was so much else to include, and one must be firm in cutting out details. He had already chosen the title of the book, after much thought: *The Pacification of the Tribes of the Lower Niger*. (pp. 148–9)

This final paragraph marks the end of one narrative and the beginning of another, the colonialist narrative, which will marginalize the story of Okonkwo to one paragraph, and submerge in abstractions and generalizations (about 'pacification', 'Africa', and 'the tribes of the Lower Niger') the specificity and the details of the Igbos' own story. Moreover, as the emphasis on paragraphs, chapters, and titles makes clear, written narrative will supplant oral narrative, replacing an immediate community of listeners with a distant readership, seeking to celebrate and to further European conquest. And yet, like Cathleen ni Houlihan, the story of Okonkwo, the culture of his community has survived; the language and written culture of the colonizer is used to affirm that the District Commissioner's book, itself now reduced to one paragraph, will be

[19] Chinua Achebe, *Beware Soul Brother and Other Poems* (London: Heinemann Educational Books, 1971), 66.

overwhelmed by 'the story of this man who had killed a messenger and hanged himself'.

Despite his awareness of English as a language which is often at odds with and inadequate to the expression of Igbo culture, and despite his use of Igbo for some of his own poetry, Achebe has maintained that the evidence of the poetry, prose, and drama of Okigbo, Soyinka, and others demonstrates that English can 'carry the weight of their African experience'.[20] Moreover, it is precisely because of his commitment to Nigeria as a nation, for which English is the only common language, that Achebe chooses to write in that language. The Kenyan novelist and dramatist Ngugi wa Thiong'o, on the other hand, after his fifth novel, *Petals of Blood* (1977), ceased writing in English, except for critical essays, and turned to Gikūyū, his mother tongue, as the medium for drama and a new prose form developed from oral story-telling. His reasons for rejecting English and taking up Gikūyū are set out in the series of essays gathered in *Decolonizing the Mind*, where he rejects the language of the colonizer as 'the most powerful vehicle through which [the colonizer's] power fascinated and held the soul prisoner. The bullet was the means of physical subjugation. Language was the means of spiritual subjugation'.[21] It carried with it the cultural assumptions of the imperial power and also encouraged a total rupture between the domestic and agrarian world of the African child and his school environment, eventually divorcing the English-educated African writer from his own roots and from the majority of his countrymen. Moreover, Ngugi argued, it is the duty of the African writer to contribute to the development of his own indigenous language, and to its enrichment rather than its decline. As a committed Marxist, Ngugi's choice of Gikūyū also entails his choice of audience, and his concern to reach and influence the group he believes most likely to bring about change, the workers and peasants, for whom the English language and the genre of the English novel are alien.

The argument concerning the viability or desirability of English as the medium for expression of a national culture also has a long history in Ireland, and is perhaps less complicated than the African debate because the choice lies between just two languages, Irish and English, whereas in India, Nigeria, or Kenya, there exist within each nation a number of indigenous languages and traditions. Increasingly during the nineteenth century, Irish, almost in proportion to the degree to which schooling in English diminished its daily use, became not merely a means of recovering texts and folk experience from a distant Celtic past, but a badge of nationalist commitment. Douglas Hyde, in his speech to an 1892 meeting

---

[20] Chinua Achebe, *Morning Yet on Creation Day* (London: Heinemann Educational Books, 1975), 62.
[21] *Decolonizing the Mind* (London: James Currey, 1986), 9.

of the Irish Literary Society on 'The Necessity for De-Anglicising Ireland',[22] urged the revival of the Gaelic language as a means of healing the schizophrenic mentality developed by fighting England while embracing her language and culture. He became President of the Gaelic League, one of whose chief aims was the revival of Gaelic as a national tongue, and himself wrote both poetry and drama in Gaelic. Yeats's counter-argument in a letter responding to Hyde's speech was a pragmatic one: he believed that the Gaelic language was fast dying out and that the nationalists lacked the men or the money to revive it. But Yeats felt that it would be possible to 'build up a national tradition, a national literature which [would] be none the less Irish in spirit for being English in language,' and went on to declare, 'When we remember the majesty of Cuchulain and the beauty of sorrowing Deirdre, we should not forget that it is that majesty and that beauty which is immortal, and not the perishing tongue which first told of them'.[23] Forty years later, the critic Daniel Corkery argued that Irish literature must be defined first of all as literature written in the Irish language. Although Irish is now the national language in the Republic of Ireland, the debate about the provenance of literature written in English continues.

Despite the foregrounding of the issue of language within nationalist drama, fiction, and poetry, and in nationalist rhetoric, writing in indigenous languages has rarely received attention from contemporary critics and theorists. It is commonly and implicitly assumed that generalizations about the nature of national or post-colonial literatures can be made on the basis of the texts written in English (or other European languages). This assumption has been vigorously questioned by Aijaz Ahmad, first in the pages of *Social Text* and then more fully in his book *In Theory*.[24] Ahmad disputes not only the assumption that it is not necessary even to acknowledge literature in written languages other than English or French, and the consequently very limited understanding of the variety of discourses, nationalist and non-nationalist, produced in any one country, but also the homogenized view of a 'Third World' which he finds typical of 'black' and 'Third World' studies. His essay is particularly addressed to Fredric Jameson's influential argument that all 'Third World' literature can be read as national allegory, drawing upon one short story by a Chinese writer and one novella by an African writer to prove his assertion.[25] As Ahmad points out, the whole concept of 'Third World'

[22] Repr. in Mark Storey (ed.), *Poetry and Ireland since 1800: A Source Book* (London: Routledge, 1988), 78–84.

[23] W. B. Yeats, *Essays and Introductions* (London: Macmillan, 1970), 255/6.

[24] Aijaz Ahmad, *Social Text*, 17 (Fall 1987); *In Theory* (London: Verso, 1992).

[25] Fredric Jameson, 'Third-World Literature in the Era of Multinational Capitalism', *Social Text*, 15 (Fall 1986), 65–88.

current in American and European academic institutions is 'a polemical one, with no theoretical status whatever' (p. 96), and part of my own project in bringing together the comparisons of Irish, Australian, and West African literary nationalism has been to move away from the frequent assumption that the categories of colour and the categories commonly applied to 'Third World' culture overlap. Jameson's patronizing view that Third World literature struggling out of the colonial experience typically offers literature in the realist mode and lacks 'the sophisticated pleasures' offered by modernist writers such as Proust and Joyce ignores the colonial experience of Ireland and Joyce's concern to 'create the conscience of his race' as well as the quality and quantity of non-realist texts which have emerged from the South American, African, and Indian subcontinents in the last forty years and which have impinged even upon English and American readers. In the case of Ireland, it is arguable that it is the writing in the realist mode which is least likely to be concerned with nationality, while Irish writing in English, when it is concerned with speaking to and for the nation, betrays the ambivalences of class, history, and language and identity which make it more akin to modernist and post-modernist writing in England and North America. But Yeats and Joyce have now so long been incorporated into the English literary canon that their identities as Irishmen are often marginalized by critics; they are read as embattled individuals with a special relationship to Ireland. Achebe and Soyinka, and perhaps Narayan, on the other hand, are read as representatives of their race, who must, willy-nilly, speak for the nation as a whole.

We should be clear that many, probably most, literary texts written in English by African, Indian, or Irish authors are not written as national allegories, nor need they be read as such. We should also be clear that a great deal of written and oral literature in emerging nations eschews European languages and concerns itself with matters other than the past or future of the nation as a whole. Equally, plenty of literature and orature in indigenous languages is concerned with national issues, although this is not necessarily the same as constituting national allegory. (And despite Benedict Anderson's claim that national identity is dependent upon literacy, the Irish, South African, Ghanaian experiences demonstrate the importance of oral poetry, ballads, and drama in the formation of a national identity.) Allegory is a form chosen by Yeats, Prichard, Sembene Ousmane, Armah and Ngugi, among others, to represent their nation's experience; other nationalist writers, such as Synge, Lawson, Achebe, and Soyinka, may occasionally use figures, especially female figures who are metaphorical or symbolic, but more typically the story they tell and their characters are metonymic rather than allegorical. They narrate or dramatize events and stories which are local and specific to Igbo or Yoruba history, but which may be multiplied or enlarged to represent the stories of the colonial encounter in many other parts of Ireland, Australia, Nigeria, or Africa.

PART IV

# POST-COLONIALISM AND ITS DISCONTENTS

CHAPTER EIGHT

# Plato's Cave: Educational and Critical Practices

## HELEN TIFFIN

In *Images in Print* (1988) Ruby King and Mike Morrissey note that although some countries of the Commonwealth Caribbean have been independent for twenty-five years, many aspects of colonialism persist in general ideas about education in syllabuses and curricula, and in text-book choices and contents. Their study, and more general ones such as Philip G. Altbach's 'Education and Neocolonialism' (1971), direct attention to the potency of colonialist histories of education not just in the Caribbean but across all post-colonized cultures; to the interactions between oral and 'literate' cultures; and to the entire history of publishing and distribution both in and about colonized and formerly colonized cultures.

In 1995 at least three Australian television commercials depended for their success on the broad public knowledge of the basic terms of Daniel Defoe's eighteenth-century novel *Robinson Crusoe*. The assumption is that the colonial tropes of that work remain so pervasive and powerful in English-speaking cultures that they may be readily drawn on by contemporary commercial interests. In *The Hot Zone* the American journalist Richard Preston invokes and quotes from *Heart of Darkness* to reinforce the tropes naturalized throughout the English-speaking world in Conrad's widely read and widely taught classic. The 'savagery' coming 'Out of Africa' was now a 'flesh-eating' viral disease whose terrifying contagion is easily spread, in the era of airplane travel, to all areas of the world, even, the author portentously tells us, to the (neo-imperial) heartland of Washington.[1]

I begin with these instances to suggest the ways in which European texts and Anglo-European educational systems maintain their authority and power throughout the post-colonized world. My focus in this essay is thus on two apparently different yet related topics: the role of education, specifically literary education in colonial, post-colonial, and

[1] Richard Preston, *The Hot Zone* (New York: Doubleday, 1994).

neo-colonized cultures, and post-colonial *representations* of this literary education and its formative and persisting roles in colonization.

Texts like *Robinson Crusoe* and *Heart of Darkness* retain their efficacy because, as the British realized, their appeal is to 'the heart'. Where history and maths curricula also serve to interpellate the colonized within a European episteme, the added power of literary texts is conferred by affective (metaphoric/symbolic) use of language, and through subject matter in conjunction with explicit literary critical claims of 'universality'. This affective force of the colonizer's language is attested by a number of writers including Derek Walcott:

> I who am poisoned with the blood of both,
> Where shall I turn, divided to the vein?
> I who have cursed
> The drunken officer of British rule, how choose
> Between this Africa and the English tongue I love?
> Betray them both, or give back what they give?[2]

Language and literary education in post-colonial cultures are sites of radical ambivalence whose continuing power necessitates interrogation and dismantling, reconsideration, rereading, and rewriting.

In *Masks of Conquest: Literary Study and British Rule in India* Gauri Viswanathan demonstrated the ways in which the British in formulating education policies in nineteenth-century India used literature and 'literary criticism' as a means of colonialist control. Not only English literature and literary criticism but the exclusive teaching of other subjects in English in Indian education programmes ensured widespread Anglo-interpellation. While the most famous document establishing this policy was Thomas B. Macaulay's 1835 Indian Education Minute similar policies were in place in the rest of Britain's Empire. In the Caribbean, the slave trade and plantation economies had virtually eradicated the mother languages of Africa—or rather, partially eradicated, since African survivals were and are to be found in popular speech, dance, song and folk culture. However, by the twentieth century,

> the education system inherited from the colonial power was one in which English, in addition to being a subject to be taught, *was the sole medium by which literacy was acquired* as well as the sole medium of instruction. The assumption underlying this language education policy was that those who entered the education system were, in fact, native speakers of English, English-lexicon Creole being no more than a form of 'broken English' which had to be corrected by the education system.[3]

---

[2] Derek Walcott, 'A Far Cry from Africa', in *Collected Poems* (New York: Farrar, Straus, & Giroux, 1986), 18.

[3] Hubert Devonish, *Language and Liberation: Creole Language Politics in the Caribbean* (London: Karia, 1986), 102.

The legacy for contemporary Caribbean societies was, as Allsopp claimed in 1972, that

it imposed British English as the desirable standard in all matters of Anglophone Caribbean language (not just syntax, but actually pronunciation and vocabulary); it also instilled a sense of apology in all Caribbean speakers of English for every aspect of their local English that differentiated it from British English.[4]

Devonish's observation that 'the very use of a language in the education process, as a medium for acquiring literacy establishes the validity of the language in the eyes of the pupils as well as the society at large'[5] attests to the fulfilment of one of the aims of educators in the previous century as outlined in a Circular Dispatch enclosing a suggested 1847 scheme for industrial and normal schools in the colonies. This purpose was 'to diffuse a grammatical knowledge of the English language as the most important agent of civilization for the coloured population'.[6]

Thus colonial education—in the language 'English' and in its specific studies of the literature of England—in the English Caribbean (as in India and colonies elsewhere) was designed for, and continued to be promulgated in the service of, colonialist control. It stressed the 'universal'/imperial at the expense of the 'local'; it fostered and validated the centrality of and belief in the excellence of all things English and instilled its pan-colonial companion, the 'cultural cringe'; and since its aim was a social control whose effective mechanism was the spread of English values, it focused on the language, religion, and, in particular, the literary culture of England.

These general educational principles are not unrelated to a more particular consideration, for they affected not just the place of literature within colonial curricula, but the specific literary 'models' available to colonized cultures. Literary texts encountered in the processes of formal education have potent and long-lasting effects, especially those which form part of the primary curriculum. When coupled with an important learning technique prevalent in primary schools up to a generation or so ago (i.e. the learning of set pieces 'by heart'),[7] the emotional, as well as the intellectual impact afforded a strong and subtle mechanism of Anglo-interpellation. To learn 'by heart' is to absorb into the very processes of one's being the material so taught; to absorb that text as part of the emotional core of one's nature. Like the use of the English language, learning by heart is one of the fundamental processes through which are produced 'persons', in the language of Macaulay's Minute, 'Indian in blood and in colour, but English in taste, in opinions, in morals and in

---

[4] Quoted ibid. 108.    [5] Ibid. 119.
[6] Shirley Gordon, *A Century of West Indian Education* (London: Longman, 1963), 58.
[7] See ibid. 44.

intellect'. And it is in the primary and tertiary sectors in particular that literary works are likely to be most influential—in the first because of the more widespread nature of primary education; in the second, because local literati and intellectuals with a tertiary education generally have a direct influence on policies or disseminate ideas which have a significant influence on secondary curricula.

The Bible provided the early basis for learning to read in pre- and post-emancipation non-denominational Caribbean schools. Increasingly however, English literature replaced the Bible as raw material for learning the skills of reading and writing. An 1870 *Circular from the Board of Education* prescribes 'Reading aloud a passage from some English prose author and also a passage from some English poet'.[8]

Amongst the conclusions and recommendations of the 1940–2 West India Royal Commission was that 'the literary curriculum in the primary schools requires to be simplified and brought more into relation with the environment of the children'. The Commission members also noted that 'although much thought has recently been expended on this matter, and some developments have taken place, curricula are still out of touch with the needs and interests of the bulk of the population. There is too great a stress on purely literary work, and on rote as against training in clear speech and thought.' Consequently their recommendations were for 'the revision and simplification of the cultural curriculum, concentrating on clear and connected speech and thought, and giving subjects where possible a West Indian background rather than an English one'. They further recommended that history and geography be taught 'with special reference to the West Indies, and radiating from there', and the use of 'local topography and historical monuments'. Most significantly, perhaps, they argued for the lessening of the dominance of Cambridge 'by abolishing the Junior Cambridge Examination which is used in the West Indies for a purpose for which it is not intended in England, and which is not taken in English schools maintained or aided from public funds'.

But such attempts to alter the biases and prejudices inculcated through the education system during the previous century now met with local resistance. Ten years later, the 1952 Commission found that 'Book learning' still held the keys to settled employment in government service and to the 'learned professions', and was normally preferred to a more practical type of education. The 1960s saw the last fully administered O level exam from Cambridge, but only in the 1980s was the Junior Cambridge Certificate exam replaced by a locally administered one (the Caribbean Examinations Certificate), and in the 1990s Cambridge still controlled the senior literary examination in secondary schools, even

[8] Gordon, 201.

though the curriculum for both O and A levels now had a substantial West Indian component. (The Trinidadian novelist V. S. Naipaul in *Miguel Street* satirized this persisting Anglo-orientation and domination through Elias' struggles to please 'Mr Cambridge'.)

Some of the most influential teaching texts throughout the Caribbean (and in other of Britain's colonies) were the *Royal Readers* and/or the *Irish Readers* and their descendants. Used throughout the Empire, the effect of these texts, and their role in education generally and in literary education in particular, was potent. *Readers* (or versions of them) were the basic texts in most primary schools throughout Britain's former Empire at least till the 1950s, and to the 1960s at some levels. Their replacement by texts such as *Nelson's West Indian Readers* in the early 1970s signalled localization of much of the older ethnographic, economic, and agricultural material, but the literary orientation remained generally English.

In the first series of *Royal Readers* (also published by Nelson), used throughout Caribbean schools from the early part of the century until the 1960s, are to be found sections headed 'Useful Knowledge'. As with many lessons in these *Readers* a series of catechistic questions were appended to the *West Indian Readers*:

*Question*: Into how many seasons is the year divided?
*Answer*: Four: Spring, Summer, Autumn, Winter.[9]

In this way not only the English seasons but English domestic animals, and the English 'House', were rendered normative and authoritative. As V. S. Naipaul and other post-colonial writers and commentators have noted, the total environment—social, climatic, economic—of the colonial child was thus seen at best as a degenerate rendition and at worst as a shameful aberration of that imperial norm. The Nigerian novelist Chinua Achebe has recounted the story of the schoolchild who found the *harmattan* 'shameful' because it was not one of the English seasons.[10] In this direct transfer of English material to colonial contexts no concessions were made to the local readership. The *Royal Readers* said the coffee plant 'is a shrub that resembles the laurel' and 'two kinds of tea are imported into this country'.[11] Empire and Crown loyalty are prominent in 'About Kings and Queens'. Caribbean (and Australian and South African) children learned:

Queen Elizabeth's time is not her own. She cannot always be seeking to please herself; for God has given her a great empire to rule over. The Bible tells us to

---

[9] Capt. O. Cutteridge, *Nelson's West Indian Readers Book I* (London: Nelson, 1971), 92.
[10] Chinua Achebe, 'The Novelist as Teacher', *Morning Yet on Creation Day* (Garden City, NY: Doubleday, 1975), 71.
[11] Capt. O. Cutteridge, *Royal Readers*, First Series (London: Nelson, 1952), 126.

honour those who rule over us; therefore it is our duty to obey the laws of our country.
*Questions*: What are Kings and Queens?
Who rules over the British Commonwealth and Empire?
Why is the Queen's time not her own?
What are we taught in the Bible?[12]

Even though Captain J. O. Cutteridge in *Nelson's West Indian Readers* supplied 'a long-felt want—viz., that of local text books specially prepared for West Indian schools', the colonialist educational legacy was still apparent. 'It has been my endeavour', Cutteridge writes in his prefatory note, 'to include local names and terms whenever possible, as my experience has been that the pupils have great difficulty in spelling common words which they seldom if ever see in print.' Coffee is now localized as a Jamaican product not an 'import'; kings and queens have gone; the animals, insects, plants, and crops (nature study and agricultural products) are localized, and the folk-tales of Grimm and Aesop (Aesop's tales still assumed to be Greek rather than African in origin) are now accompanied by Creole ones. Nevertheless, 'Poetry for Reading and Recitation' remains almost exclusively English and English oriented—Swift, Alfred Lord Tennyson, Robert Louis Stevenson, Kingsley, Keats, and others of less canonical stature are included. In all of the poems—poems for learning by heart—English and 'white' are inevitably normative, from Kingsley's

> I once had a sweet little doll, dears
> The prettiest doll in the world,
> Her cheeks were so red and so white dears,
> And her hair was so charmingly curled[13]

to the 'gift' of a 'sunny day '—a wonderful exception in England, but not of course in the Caribbean or Queensland. The ultimate effect of such colonialist literary education is that, as Leigh Dale notes in the Australian instance, 'England is constructed as *text* and is therefore inviolable; Australia is constructed as *context* and is therefore ultimately irrelevant.'[14]

The power of such primary *Readers*, and the practice of reciting poetry (or catechistic answers on prose pieces) by heart, is and has been interpellative to a degree difficult to underestimate. Both the pedagogy of recitation and the relevance of English material and English norms to the West Indian context are satirized by the Mighty Sparrow in one of his calypsos, 'Dan is the Man in the Van', which singles out J. O. Cutteridge, to whom V. S. Naipaul's Mr Biswas also has a particular antipathy.

---

[12] Ibid. 117–18.     [13] Cutteridge, *West Indian Readers*, 57.
[14] Leigh Dale, 'Courting Captivity: The Teaching of English Literature and the Inculcation of Englishness in Australian Universities' (Ph. D. thesis, University of Queensland, 1993).

Well into the 1970s, curricula of the English Department(s) of the University of the West Indies and Guyana, like most post-colonial universities in both the colonies of occupation and settler-invader colonies, were still dominated by the study of the works of Shakespeare, Spenser, Johnson, Donne, Herbert, Dryden, Pope, Swift, Johnson, Keats, Eliot, Defoe, Fielding, Emily Brontë, Dickens, George Eliot, in spite of the inclusion of some local writing. A survey of courses and papers to the present suggests that while there have been radical changes (in proportion of local and other to English material, and the inclusion of many courses on the national or regional literatures and a more significant structural placement of them), students entering the university from high schools do so in the Caribbean, for instance, through an 'English' exam paper still controlled from Cambridge.

The situation in the Caribbean can be read as broadly symptomatic of that in both the major colonies of occupation—India and the African countries—and the settler-invader colonies which had similar primary and tertiary educational policies and histories. The *Queensland School Readers*, also descendants of the *Royal* and *Irish Readers*, were used (as in the Caribbean) until the 1960s, and, as in Barbados, they remained popular with an older generation well after their official displacement. (These *Readers* were reprinted in the late 1980s in both Barbados and Queensland and sold out immediately to parents who planned to use them to give their children a 'genuine' education at home.) Thus although curricula have changed, at primary, tertiary, and secondary levels, the effects of the dominance of British literary texts and cultural values remain pervasive and powerful.

These effects have been charted and assessed not just by educators themselves, but by creative artists throughout the former Empire. Writing of tertiary education in Australia the poet Les Murray has noted that a 'major' in English at an Australian university produced 'minor Englishmen', and a more general effect of both literary education and the fetishization of the imperial centre has been commented on by the Australian novelist Christopher Koch:

The society that had produced us, so far away from what it saw as the centre of civilisation, made us rather like the prisoners in Plato's cave. To guess what that centre was like, that centre 12,000 miles away for which we yearned, we must study shadows on the wall, as our parents and grandparents had done.[15]

Magda, the protagonist of South African novelist J. M. Coetzee's *In the Heart of the Country*, reproduces in her account the ways in which a settler-invader colony education elided destructive imperial and local

[15] C. J. Koch, 'Literature and Cultural Identity', *Tasmanian Review*, 4 (1980), 2.

white involvement in conquest and colonization. Things 'just happen'; no one is actually responsible:

This is not Hendrick's home. No one is ancestral to the stone desert . . . Hendrick's forebears in the older days crisscrossed the desert with their flocks and their chattels, heading from A to B or from X to Y, sniffing for water, abandoning stragglers, making forced marches. Then one day fences began to go up . . . Men on horseback rode up and from shadowed faces issued invitations to stop and settle . . . Fascinating, this colonial history . . . There is another great moment in colonial history: the first merino is lifted from shipboard, with block and tackle, in a canvas waistband, bleating with terror, unaware that this is the promised land where it will browse generation after generation on the nutritious scrub and provide the economic lease for the presence of my father and myself . . . [16]

George Lamming in *In the Castle of my Skin* details the ways in which colonial and post-colonial education systems in the Caribbean deliberately repressed slave history and thus the ancestral origins of contemporary Afro-Caribbeans, while Margaret Atwood in *Cat's Eye* shows how imperial/colonial and post-colonial education reproduced those stereotypes which had enabled and facilitated European conquest and colonization of other parts of the globe, and which were then (re)presented to school pupils as axiomatic through authoritative *Readers*.

'The sun never sets on the British Empire,' says Miss Lumley, tapping the roll-down map with her long wooden pointer. In countries that are not the British Empire, they cut out children's tongues, especially those of boys. Before the British Empire there were no railroads or postal services in India, and Africa was full of tribal warfare, with spears, and had no proper clothing. The Indians in Canada did not have the wheel or telephones, and ate the hearts of their enemies in the heathenish belief that it would give them courage. The British Empire changed all that. It brought in electric lights.[17]

Twentieth-century responses to colonialist education at all levels have come both from post-colonial educators and from creative writers who were themselves 'products' of this education. This response, as in the case of Derek Walcott, was a necessarily ambivalent one. British literature became a loved literature, but one whose colonialist purpose and effects were necessarily disturbing. Like Walcott, Koch, and Murray, post-colonial writers have frequently acknowledged—with ambivalent emotions—the influence of this Anglo-literary education on their societies and on their own lives and work:

Caliban received not just words, but language as symbolic interpretation, as instrument of exploring consciousness. Once he had accepted language as such,

---

[16] J. M. Coetzee, *In the Heart of the Country* (Harmondsworth: Penguin, 1976), 18–19.
[17] Margaret Atwood, *Cat's Eye* (Toronto: McClelland & Stewart, 1988), 79.

the future of his development, however independent it was, would always be in some way inextricably tied up with that pioneering aspect of Prospero.[18]

It is thus the investigation of the ambiguous 'gifts' of colonial education systems, and, in particular, literary education, with which writers throughout the post-colonial world have been and continue to be engaged.

Erna Brodber's novel *Myal* (1988) is a profound meditation on colonialist education and potential modes of decolonization. Set in Jamaica, *Myal* has a complex plot, both strands of which are concerned with 'spirit thievery' and the strategies whereby 'illegal' and profoundly destructive representational capture and confinement might be undone. The protagonist Ella O'Grady (whose mixed blood is itself metonymic of the effects of Anglo-education on black Jamaicans, 'divided to the vein' by that ambiguous gift of the English language) is introduced as the reciter ('by heart') of a poem by Kipling. Speaking as if she were of the imperial party (and not the subjectified colonials the poem represents) Ella enjoins the Jamaican primary school class to

> Take up the whiteman's burden
> Send forth the best ye breed
> Go bind your sons to exile
> To serve your captive's need
> To wait in heavy harness
> On filtered folk and wild
> Your new caught sullen peoples
> Half devil and half child.[19]

Symptomatically, Ella *lives* in the world of the English books she has been taught and has read (and the poems she recites), and not in her Jamaican Grove Town. As a teenager she is eventually taken to the United States, where she meets Selwyn Langley, the man who will administer a cruel but vital lesson in representational aggression and imperialist interpellation. Eager to move from his family's patent medicine business to stage production and direction, he extracts and transforms Ella's Jamaican memories, 'distilling' them into a classic 'coon show'. Langley, pleased with his production, triumphantly presents these grossly racist representations to Ella on opening night. Where Ella had not apprehended the profound effects of British textual representations, Langley's (re)production of Jamaicans literally brings the dis-ease of imperialist stereotyping home. Ella begins to suffer from an apparently incurable abdominal swelling and is taken back to the Caribbean. She has as yet no way of analysing the two forms of 'spirit thievery' that have

[18] George E. Kent, 'A Conversation with George Lamming', *Black World*, 22/5 (1973), 88–9.
[19] Erna Brodber, *Myal* (London: New Beacon, 1988), 6.

occurred and which Langley's 'patent medicine' is powerless to cure. But back in Jamaica, Ella ('the little cat choked on foreign') is finally restored through the ministrations of Mass Cyrus and the processes of communal healing (Myalism).

Still, Ella's cure is not quite complete. For this to be effected she must return to the source of original infection, the school, and to the texts she was taught there. Ella has recovered sufficiently to become a teacher, and finds she is constrained by the primary syllabus to teach the stories of Mr Joe's Farm. On this farm the animals are protected and well cared for, but they have no freedom or autonomy, no way of relating to the world except through the benevolent rule of Mr Joe. A number of the animals decide to rebel and set off to make their own way in the outside world. One by one, however, they find they cannot fend for themselves, and like naughty children, they return, chastened, to Mr Joe's forgivingly adult care and attention. Since this story is on the primary school syllabus Ella is constrained to teach it. She risks dismissal (and replacement by a compliant teacher) and/or disadvantages the children who will be examined on it if she refuses. So in conjunction with other members of the Grove Town community Ella adopts the following strategy: she will teach the text, but she will teach it against the grain, situating it historically and politically, critiquing and interrogating the parable of colonial obedience it was designed to inculcate. Ella, the once proud re-presenter of Kipling's poem thus comes not only to interrogate the practices of a colonialist literary education, but to do so through the very texts which deliberately (and sometimes adventitiously) produce(d) obedient colonial subjects.

*Myal* is both an enjoyable novel and an educational text, one which offers a theory of post-colonized literary teaching which is inextricably interwoven with a politics of demystification of literary representation in what Sara Suleri has termed 'context[s] of colonial exchange'.[20] It thus insists on situating the text culturally, politically, and institutionally; in particular, in terms of its imperial production and colonial consumption. It insists on the importance of texts, specifically literary texts, in sponsoring colonialist subjectification and creating obedient subjects who 'consent' in their own colonization. And it suggests ways in which the same texts might be presented and taught differently so that their potency is harnessed to a project of *de-* rather than *re-*colonization. Moreover *Myal*, like many post-colonial novels, raises the issue of the fetishization of education and hence of the Anglo-canonical in colonized communities—even in those classes/groups who have not themselves had access to education. Most important of all, perhaps, *Myal* demonstrates

---

[20]   Sara Suleri, *The Rhetoric of English India* (Chicago: University of Chicago Press, 1992), 2.

the ways in which bodies are constituted, dis-eased, and reconstructed through representation.

Such affective inculcation and the variety of post-colonial responses to it are not confined to 'high' cultures, nor do they inevitably take a serious form. The Mighty Sparrow's calypso 'Dan is the Man in the Van' stresses both the persistence and the irrelevance of the texts taught to primary school children:

> According to the education you get when you small
> You'll grow up with true ambition and respect from one an all
> But in my days in school they teach me like a fool
> The things they teach me I should be a block-headed mule.
> . . .
> The poems and the lessons they write and send from England
> Impress me they were trying to cultivate comedians
> Comic books made more sense
> You know it was fictitious without pretence
> But like Cutteridge wanted to keep us in ignorance.[21]

As well as interrogating curricula, texts, and the educational processes of Anglo-cultural inculcation, post-colonial writers often have singled out for scrutiny a particular text (or texts) from the English canon and rewritten its terms from the local, post-colonial perspective. This counter-discursive strategy interrogates not just the Anglo-canonical texts themselves, but the whole of the discursive field within which they were instantiated as authoritative, as part of colonial and post-colonial interpretative frameworks.

In 'The Other Question' Homi Bhabha argues that a primary strategy of colonialist discourse is the circulation of the stereotype, which, through its repetitive 'fixity', renders the colonized 'knowable and visible'. Anti-colonial discourses have thus focused on exposing the *effectivity* of the stereotype, on destabilizing its apparent 'fixity', and on unmasking the imperialist anxieties which underlie and energize its still efficacious repetitions. But to 'judge the stereotyped image on the basis of a prior political normativity is to dismiss it, not to displace it, which is only possible by engaging with its *effectivity*; with the repertoire of positions of power and resistance, domination and dependence that constructs the colonial subject (both colonisers and colonized)'.[22]

In *Moses Ascending* and *Moses Migrating* the Trinidadian novelist Samuel Selvon recirculates and reanimates racist and colonialist clichés

---

[21] The Mighty Sparrow [Francisco Slinger], 'Dan is the Man', in Stewart Brown, Mervyn Morris, and Gordon Rohlehr (eds.), *Voiceprint: An Anthology of Oral and Related Poetry from the Caribbean* (Kingston: Longman, 1989), 129–30.
[22] Homi Bhabha, *The Location of Culture* (London: Routledge, 1994), 67.

and stereotypes, interrogating and destabilizing them through partial, ironic, and/or incomplete inversions of the binary codes which are foundational to both the production and the persisting potency of such stereotypic figurations. In unmasking and dismantling stereotypes of both colonizers and colonized, frequently by 'collapsing' one into the other, Selvon relies primarily on his (re)figuration of the Moses of his earlier *The Lonely Londoners* as an almost absurdly interpellated colonial subject, 'obedient' (to use Pêcheux's term) to the point of caricature. The ironic distance between Selvon and Moses is far greater in the two later works than it is in *The Lonely Londoners*, and both texts focus more on an investigation of colonial and post-colonial subjectivities than on presenting a 'realist' account of West Indian experiences in London or English travellers in Trinidad.

In colonialist discourse the potency of the stereotype depends not just on its fixity and its endless repetition but on the binaristic codifications that serve as its inescapable foundations. Such rigidly maintained binaries as colonizer/colonized; master/slave; white/black; 'European'/'native' are, of course, also hierarchized. 'Obedient' colonial subjects like Moses represent the fulfilment of colonialist desire; they are products of an apparently perfected imperialism which, to borrow again from Macaulay's Minute, has produced '[Indians] in blood and in colour, but English in taste, in opinions, in morals and in intellect'.[23]

But this 'perfected' colonial subjectivity is inherently destabilizing of those very hierarchized binaries upon which the ideology of Empire and colonial governance rests, since paradoxically such 'ideal' subjects necessarily annihilate those very divisions by which their subjectivity is constituted. Moses' taste(s), opinions, morals, intellect (and, one might add, affiliations and loyalties) are, he believes, white and English. But, Afro-Trinidadian in 'blood and colour', Moses' Anglo-affiliative speech and behaviour occasionally produce a degree of self-mockery and constantly attract the derision of others—West Indians and Britons alike. It is not only through Moses' split colonial subjectivity, however, that Selvon interrogates stereotypes and their binary bases. In both *Moses Ascending* and *Moses Migrating* comedy, irony, and subversion are enacted through a series of narrative inversions, intertextural and historical ironies, which unsettle stereotypical figurations and the hierarchies which provide their foundation. These inversions are never fixed or completed but produce further inversions and upsets which energize more vortices of spiralling instabilities.

In *Moses Ascending* the black poverty-stricken foreign 'migrant' (who is not quite 'foreign' and has come 'home' to the motherland; and is thus

---

[23] Samuel Selvon, *Moses Ascending* (London: Davis-Poynter, 1975), 37.

not really a 'migrant' either) becomes landlord and resident, owner of a 'great house' in London, renting rooms to other Commonwealth 'migrants'. Man Friday thus becomes Crusoe, inverting those paradigmatic stereotypes which were reflected in and widely disseminated through Defoe's influential 1719 work. Landlord Moses takes on, as helper/servant, the illiterate English Bob from the 'Black Country' of the white heartland (the Midlands) of England. (Moses resolves, like Crusoe, 'to teach' Bob the Bible when he 'have the time'.) Inversions of the roles of master and servant; white and black; colonizer and colonized here serve to denaturalize the stereotypes and their hierarchization; to expose their constructedness, their *interested* representational foundations.

These counter-discursive responses make the plays, novels, poems of many prominent post-colonial writers an inherent part of the project of post-colonial literary *theory* as well. Indeed much that is significant in post-colonial literary theory has occurred and is occurring through such creative intertextual dialogue.

But when creative writers of the formerly colonized cultures began to 'write back' to this history of literary education/cultural interpellation, a major movement within Anglo-European (and United States) tertiary institutional cultures began the processes of a more unambiguous reinvestiture of that authority in metropolitan epistemology through the academies. While 'post-colonial' and generally counter-canonical courses of various kinds have multiplied within English departments, this increasing pluralism has not displaced the emphasis on British literature; in many cases the effect of apparently radical challenges to the canon has been, paradoxically, a reinforcing of the status and fetishization of the Anglo-canonical. Any teaching of post-colonial literatures (and literary theory) in the academy is thus obliged to address the issue of literary teaching as a whole, of structural placement within departments and particularly the relationship between British literature and other literatures in English.

The intersection of post-colonialism and contemporary Euro-American literary theories, particularly those which might be broadly designated 'post-structuralist', is important here. For all its apparently radical critique and destabilizing implications, Euro-American post-structuralist theory has reinforced the centrality of the English literary canon within the academy. This has occurred for a number of reasons. First, where post-colonial, Marxist, and feminist theory had begun to destabilize the naturalized centrality of British literature courses (usually still being taught in New Critical mode), post-structuralism facilitated new and revivifying ways of reading and teaching canonical works without disturbing their status. 'The Body in Shakespeare' or 'Shakespeare's Representations of Women' still fetishize the study of Shakespeare, without questioning *why* Shakespeare or Milton may still be accorded separate courses while all of Australian, Caribbean, Indian and African literature, might be compressed into a similar time frame. Secondly, the fetishization of European theory itself as a sort of universal intelligence test within the discipline has reinstated Europe as originator of normative modes of thought, at the precise moment when post-colonial analyses—creative and critical—were exposing its earlier techniques of appropriative ideational control.

Paradoxically, this new hegemony contradicts the relativities and attention to difference which the theories imply. Ironically, it is the post-colonized cultures which have proved most susceptible to what Simon During has termed 'import rhetoric'.[24] Thirdly, the attractions of contemporary literary theories, where they *are* associated with potentially radical challenges to an Anglo-core curriculum, have tended to isolate theoretical study from analysis of the literary text, leaving the literary ground in English departments to the English 'core' texts while those students with philosophical (rather than literary) inclinations do contemporary theory courses where literary texts studied or used as illustrative material tend to be Anglo-conservative: Shakespeare, Milton, the Romantics, George Eliot.

Contemporary Euro-American literary theory, which could have been the Trojan Horse in Anglo-centred departments, has instead smuggled in a revivification of the English canon. In its frequent conjunction with post-colonial theory, post-structuralism offers a great deal; but it can prove a dangerous travelling companion. A genuinely post-colonial literary theory would be wary of (while utilizing) this potential, aware of the dangers incurred in accepting this 'ambiguous gift'.

Around this persisting (and sometimes newly invigorated) English core curriculum 'radical' courses of various kinds have proliferated. Many contemporary English departments are genuinely pluralist in their content, teaching methods, and political and philosophical underpinnings. While this seems an ideal and harmonious arrangement, such pluralism never forces staff or students to confront the crucial questions of what they teach and why they teach (or read) it (let alone how). Since a major issue for any post-colonial theory is current institutional placement and the history of colonialist education, the *relationship* between post-colonial courses and English canonical ones within an 'English' department becomes a crucial theoretical and political issue. But rarely are English literary texts studied in a genuine conjunction with post-colonial ones.

The key concepts here are 'colonialism' and 'literary studies'. What has come to be included in the field of the 'post-colonial' has broadened to a

---

[24] Simon During, 'Postmodernism or Postcolonialism?', *Landfall*, 39/3 (Sept. 1985), 369.

point where the term has become inefficaciously synonymous with all forms of oppression and/or resistances to it. Where almost any marginalization and anti-oppressive gesture can be discussed under the rubric of the post-colonial, political purchase is necessarily lost, and the discipline is in danger of losing its historical base and its theoretical coherence. It is a term that has been almost promiscuously adopted by and across a vast range of areas. Stephen Slemon notes,

'Post-colonialism,' as it is now used in various fields, describes a remarkably heterogeneous set of subject positions, professional fields, and critical enterprises. It has been used as a way of ordering a critique of totalizing forms of Western historicism; as a port manteau term for a retooled notion of 'Class', as a subset of both post-modernism and post-structuralism (and conversely, as the condition from which those two structures of cultural logic and cultural critique themselves are seen to emerge); as the name for a condition of nativist longing in post-independence national groupings; as a cultural marker of non-residency for a Third World intellectual cadre; as the inevitable underside of a fractured and ambivalent discourse of colonialist power; as an oppositional 'reading practice'; and—and this was my first encounter with the term—as the name for a category of 'literary' activity which sprang from a new and welcome political energy going on within what used to be called 'Commonwealth' literary studies.[25]

Such a proliferation has generated heated debate over terminology, often at the expense of substance; it has often sponsored ahistorical and acultural approaches which reify 'marginality' and a sometimes naïvely self-defeating identity politics within a fashionable rhetoric of undifferentiated and unsituated anti-oppressive gestures. Paradoxically such politically debilitating moves have also frequently sponsored unrealistic demands that the discipline cure all the ills of a post-colonized world.

Both as a foundation for an academic discipline and in the interest of a retention of political efficacy, the use of the term is best restricted to the legacies of and responses to European imperialism and colonialism. While everything from the moment of invasion to the present in such areas is included in the field of the 'post-colonial', the particularities of time and place within this broader categorization are crucial. Post-colonial theory and post-colonial literary studies are inescapably embedded in the transplanted language (English), in English literary culture, and in the vastly differing cultures of the colonized. Moreover, differences in time as well as place generate(d) radically different responses to invasion and colonization, just as British strategies and policies also differed in various colonized cultures at different times. The term 'post-colonial' in most of the post-colonized world is generally used to cover the processes of British (and European) territorial conquests; the

---

[25] Stephen Slemon, 'The Scramble for Post-colonialism', in Chris Tiffin and Alan Lawson (eds.), *De-scribing Empire: Post-colonialism and Textuality* (London: Routledge, 1994), 16.

various institutions of British and European colonialisms; and, most import-antly, the differing *responses* to such incursions and their contemporary colonial legacies in pre- and post-independence nations and communities.

The term post-colonial is not synonymous with the term 'post-inde-pendence'. For all the difficulties raised by 'post-colonial' (as a category applied to literary studies), it has proved more resilient than such possible alternatives as 'new literatures' or 'world literatures (in English)' or 'Commonwealth literatures' because it implies the *persistence* of colonial legacies in post-independence cultures, not their disappearance or erasure. Moreover the term stresses the inescapable historical grounding in the practices and institutions of British imperialism and colonialism and the responses to and legacies of this history across a variety of widely dispersed and vastly divergent cultures. Such legacies—for example, the use of the English language; legal codes; educational practices; philosophical and interpretative frameworks—frequently persist in formerly colonized cultures long after independence has been achieved. In many cases they persist, in widely variant and/or culturally hybridized and syncretic forms, in the present. The 'post' in the 'post-colonial', then, to borrow Terry Eagleton's terms in relation to Romanticism, is not 'confidently posterior' to an epoch, but rather a 'product' of it.[26]

Two years before the publication of Said's *Orientalism* in 1978, Robert T. Robertson, a New Zealander working at the University of Texas, argued that the discipline of post-colonial/Commonwealth literary studies was already constituted as a separate field. The moment of 'critical mass' as he noted, must 'differ for each proto-discipline as it emerges from the parent-body of study', but the 'phenomena' which mark the moment are identifiable:

The institution of undergraduate courses, the narrowing of graduate seminar topics, the increase in library holdings, checklists of theses and dissertations, the placing of graduated students in colleges . . . A separate section in the PMLA bibliography and the MLA annual meeting, independent organisation, conferen-ces and journals.[27]

By 1976 such symptomatic 'phenomena' were already evidenced in a number of academies in the United States as well as in Britain and other countries throughout the English-speaking world. The journal *World Literature Written in English* (and its precursor the *CBL Newsletter*) had begun in the 1960s and was regularly appearing by 1971; a division of MLA (ethnocentrically entitled 'World Literatures in English outside the United States and Britain') was already in existence. In England the

---

[26] Terry Eagleton, *Literary Theory: An Introduction* (Oxford: Blackwell, 1983), 18.
[27] Robert T. Robertson, 'Harvesters in May: Commonwealth Literary Studies 1970–1980', *Commonwealth*, 2 (1976), 18.

*Journal of Commonwealth Literature* had begun in 1966 and the third major journal devoted exclusively to theory and criticism of post-colonial literatures (*Kunapipi*) was ready to begin publication in late 1978.

We need to be aware of the two major streams of study through the chiasmus of which the contemporary field of post-colonial comparative and theoretical studies is constituted, and understand the reasons behind the current amnesia in relation to the extensive work already done by 1978. This 'amnesia' is in part occasioned by the ways in which the entry of a post-structuralist approach into a discipline originally constituted as 'Commonwealth' literary studies resulted in the dismissal of much earlier foundational work as untheorized and thus non-existent. Contemporary post-colonial studies, however, represent the intersection of Common-wealth literary studies and what is usually now referred to as 'colonial discourse theory'. As Peter Hulme notes in his essay 'Subversive Archipe-lagoes', colonial discourse is 'a formulation of recent currency which can perhaps be best understood as designating a conceptual area first marked out by Edward Said's *Orientalism*', though, as Hulme goes on to note, 'much of the work in the area published after *Orientalism* obviously had its genesis long before'. Edward Said's 1978 work is foundational in the development of colonial discourse theory and is crucial to it because of the assurance with which it conjoined two apparently alien spheres: an intellectual realm called, by way of shorthand, 'post-structuralism', infa-mous for its often rebarbative and hermetic vocabulary, but with a developing reputation in the 1970s for the rhetorical power of its textual readings, and a 'real' world of domination and exploitation, usually analysed by a Marxism hostile to post-structuralism's epistemological scepticism.[28] It is important to note, however, that in *Orientalism* Said is not concerned with 'Commonwealth' writing. His focus was necessarily on the European documents of capture, colonization, and containment, and this concern remains characteristic of colonial(ist) discourse theory.

The foundational moment for the Commonwealth/post-colonial line is more dispersed, though it is often traced to the Leeds Conference of 1964, the proceedings of which were published in 1965.[29] Like *Oriental-ism*, which established future developmental lines for colonial discourse theory, the papers delivered at the Leeds Conference, in particular D. E. S. Maxwell's 'Landscape and Theme', set some of the terms that would dominate Commonwealth post-colonial criticism and theory for the next decade. But much that happened at Leeds had already been determined

[28] Peter Hulme, 'Subversive Archipelagoes: Colonial Discourse and the Break-up of Con-tinental Theory', *Disposite*, 14 (Autumn 1989), 3, 3–4.

[29] John Press (ed.), *The Commonwealth Pen: Unity and Diversity in a Common Culture* (London: Heinemann, 1965).

by the growth of nationalist (literary) movements in Commonwealth countries, a growth based on an understanding of the uses of English literature as a means of colonialist control throughout Britain's former Empire. In the 1960s the initiation of American literature courses in a number of Commonwealth universities, together with the rise of nationalist cultural sentiment, necessarily interrogated and destabilized not just the (till then) unquestioned centrality of British literature in English department curricula, but the grounds on which much of that study was based, particularly the notion of 'literary universality'. The Leeds Conference and the 1960s questioning of such Anglocentric assumptions could themselves also be traced to a history of colonial (and racial) resistance and critique of which the Negritude movement of the 1930s and 1940s is a prominent example. This movement also forms part of the genealogy of Said's *Orientalism*.

There is some similarity of origins but an initial separation of the two 'streams' which comprise contemporary post-colonial literary studies, even though after the late 1970s these become increasingly difficult to disentangle. Colonial discourse genealogy is more generally embedded in Continental philosophy and in Euro-Marxist political theory, while Commonwealth post-colonialism, at least till the 1980s, remained more deeply grounded in and focused on colonial and nationalist critiques, in literary production and consumption, and in Anglo-Commonwealth pedagogic practice. Where colonial discourse theory was dominated by philosopher-theorists, Commonwealth post-colonialism was grounded in colonial literary practices, with an emphasis on the role of the creative writer as well as those of the critic and theorist. Much of the literary writing produced in English-speaking colonies this century has in both its content and its cultural deployment functioned as both colonialist critique and post-colonial (counter-colonial) literary theory. Decolonizing theoretical work often exclusively attributed to a post-Orientalist colonial discourse *theory* was already being done by post-colonial creative writers (such as Raja Rao in *Kanthapura*) from the 1930s onward. Commonwealth post-colonial critics, less engaged by Continental philosophies, initially concentrated their energies on rendering this important creative writing visible within a discipline of literary studies whose assumptions, bases, and power were deeply (and almost exclusively) invested in the literatures of the United Kingdom.

In fighting for the recognition of post-colonial Commonwealth writing within academies whose roots and continuing power depended on the persisting cultural and/or political centrality of the imperium, and in a discipline whose manner and subject matter were the focal signs and symbols of that power—British *literature* and its teaching constantly reified, replayed and reinvested the colonial relation—nationalist critics were forced to conduct their guerrilla war on Anglo-critical turf. In so doing they initially adopted the tenets of New Criticism, reading post-colonial texts within a Euro-modernist framework, but one whose increasing and inevitable erosion was ensured by the anti-colonial (and anti-modernist) pressures of the literary texts themselves. Forced from this New Critical hermeticism, Commonwealth post-colonialism increasingly took on the cast of what would become its developing 'sister' stream.

The histories of these two streams have left slightly different legacies. Commonwealth post-colonialism remains primarily committed to the literary text even though it has increasingly turned as well to imperial documents and the discourse of Empire, and it has remained, following the Leeds Conference, both nation-based and determinedly comparative in its practice. Tending increasingly during the 1970s to the *anti*-colonial, it challenged the centrality of English values and the English canon, and raised the important issue of the continuing interpellative effects of English literary education. Such anti-colonialist arguments were necessarily accompanied by calls for the institutional introduction of national or regional literatures. In terms of future debate within the field, it retained its historical basis in the institutions and practices of British colonialism (and resistance to these), continuing to include study of the settler-invader colonies as crucial for the understanding of imperialism, resistance, and the post-colonial.

The post-structuralist/post-colonial or colonial discourse theory stream, by contrast, with its basis in European philosophy and politics, has been less interested in contemporary writing by the formerly colonized and the politics of anti-colonial pedagogy within the academies. It has been considerably less focused on creative writing (with the exception of British imperial works). Above all perhaps, on the basis of its philosophical groundings, it has rejected the national as a kind of 'false consciousness', thereby bringing it into conflict with its sister stream, much of whose important early anti-colonial work was necessarily grounded in the national as a counter to both pre- and post-independence Anglo-interpellation. As colonial discourse theory gained influence in United States academies it became imbricated with certain forms of identity politics, rendering it prone to reject outright the inclusion of the settler-invader colonies within the ambit of the post-colonial. Colonial discourse theory has tended to dismiss its sister stream as 'undertheorized', and has been suspicious of the older 'Commonwealth' connection with its potential for imperial sentimentality. It has justified its lack of attention to and/or dismissal of the post-1950s creative work of post-colonial writers on the grounds of their interpellation by (and thus collusion with) a Euro-modernist project, and on the basis of an objection to the often determinedly 'realist' texts produced in post-colonized societies.

Nevertheless, in spite of these differences in bases of the field of study and in their broadly differing trajectories, by the late 1970s the two streams became increasingly difficult to disentangle, meeting both in Ashcroft, Griffiths, and Tiffin's *The Empire Writes Back* (1989) (which though coming from the Commonwealth post-colonial stream is deeply influenced by colonial discourse theory), and in Edward Said's *Culture and Imperialism* (1992), which, in contrast to his earlier *Orientalism*, provides an extensive account of the work of contemporary post-colonial writers (including settler-invader writers) and, like the earlier Commonwealth post-colonial stream, reads these texts as resistant. Significantly, while both streams, by the 1970s, were underpinned by implicit (or explicit) Manichaean or binarist paradigms of colonizer versus colonized, or discursive 'capture' of the colonized subject within Euro-representation, both had, by the late 1980s, begun to reject those models in favour of the exploration of hybridity, creolization, complicity, syncretism, and liminality.

These struggles within the academy over both terminology and the constitution of the field form an essential part of that continuing trajectory comprised by the inextricably interwoven arenas of colonialism, education, and literary production and consumption. While the most cogent and brilliant critiques of that complex history have come from the post-colonial writers themselves, they have, ironically, even tragically, lost out, at the neo-imperial academic 'centres', to Anglo-European philosopher critics. It is difficult not to see that at the point where, as W. J. T. Mitchell has noted,[30] post-colonial writers were becoming the most prominent in the world, the powerful academies shifted ground away from the literary text and creative writing to critique, commentary, and philosophy, thereby reinstating the (neo)imperial authority of the Anglo-European. Paradoxically the anti-canonical, anti-national, anti-literary philosophies of post-structuralism have occluded the reading of post-colonial *writers* at the very moment of fetishizing European- and United States-based 'post-colonial' literary critics.

A decolonizing of literary curricula then would seem to imply a process similar to that adumbrated in Brodber's *Myal* and practised in those works which rewrite canonical English literary texts: an interrogation of those profoundly affective English works—their contents as well as their conditions of consumption and production—and a radical rereading of their terms, not so much 'against the grain' as within their historical and

---

[30] W. J. T. Mitchell, 'Postcolonial Culture, Postimperial Criticism', *Transition*, 56 (1992), 12.

geographical situation(s)—demystifying (while still acknowledging) their power in the contemporary world. And it would take account both of the history of the discipline and of the (often contradictory) neo-colonial shifts within the Academy, treating both the literatures themselves and the ways in which they are institutionally framed and interpreted.

# CHAPTER NINE

# The Post-colonial Project: Critical Approaches and Problems

GARETH GRIFFITHS

Although the primary focus of this volume is on the recent literature that emerged in countries subjected to colonization by English-speaking peoples, criticism of this terrain has various aims of which the comparative study in and between these literatures is not always primary. The study of post-coloniality has recently moved away from earlier literary models towards models of discourse analysis and textuality, in which the literary text is seen as only one kind of document in the larger archive (the total body of material by which we designate and investigate an event or cultural phenomenon) of the post-colonial. Nevertheless the literary text, and the emergence of literatures in English in post-colonial countries, even in these readings, continue to be viewed as crucial evidence, since writing, literacy, and the control of literary representations are vital in determining how the colonizers and colonized viewed each other, and how the colonized established or renewed their claims to a separate and distinctive cultural identity.

While the study of these literatures pre-dates the interest in critical theory within the Anglo-American academy, recent definitions of our field have become deeply involved in and related to theory. Edward Said is influential in having shifted assumptions from those held by such traditional humanist critics as Joseph Jones, J. P. Matthews, or William Walsh to current colonialist discourse theories.[1] Post-colonialism, however, did not begin with Said's work. If the term is understood to include the whole range of attempts to recover or develop the distinctive modes of representation of societies on which colonization has had a decisive impact then that enterprise pre-dates Said by many decades. It would need to include the long and distinguished range of nineteenth- and early twentieth-century writers and commentators as diverse as Greece Chunder Dutt, J. E. Casely Hayford, C. L. R. James, and Marcus Clarke

---

[1] Edward Said, *Orientalism* (New York: Pantheon, 1978); Joseph Jones, *Terranglia* (New York: Twayne, 1965); J. P. Matthews, *Tradition in Exile* (Toronto: University of Toronto Press, 1962); William Walsh, *A Manifold Voice* (London: Chatto & Windus, 1970).

in cultures as different as India, Africa, the West Indies, and Australia. Such recent figures as E. K. Brathwaite, Chinua Achebe, Ngugi wa Thiong'o, and Raja Rao, also, prior to the publication of Said's *Orient-alism*, had discussed such issues as the creolization of culture, universalism, language and culture, and cross-cultural recovery and the suppression of indigenous traditions.

The range of work and politics represented by such writers indicates how vital it is to see the effects of colonialism as beginning (at least potentially) to create conditions for appropriation and resistance from the moment of its impact, and to recognize how superficial the exigencies of political change and independence may have been in bringing the need for resistance and change to a satisfactory conclusion. Crucial as national independence has been to recuperation, it is not in itself a guarantee of the end of external manipulation and control at the level of politics, economics, or culture. Said's role was developing a bridge between early accounts of these issues and the language and concerns of contemporary European theory. He was the catalyst not of post-colonial critical theory, but of colonial discourse theory as found subsequently in the work of Spivak and Bhabha.[2] Said's own work, however, especially since *The World, the Text, and the Critic* (1983), displays a broader ideological interest that sits uneasily in the company of some of those he has influenced.

Said's concern is the relationship between textual representations and social practice. His influential analysis of the emergence in European thought of the concept of the Orient and the mode of knowledge ('orientalism') to which it gave rise in *Orientalism* provided a model for considering how peoples and cultures could be partly coerced and partly persuaded into defining themselves by the stereotypes offered by a dominant alien culture. Said insisted that knowledge and power always exist in a close relationship, and applied this Foucauldian conjunction to an analysis of European imperialism's control of the world it discovered during its phase of colonial expansionism. Combining this theory with the Self/Other dichotomy, whose roots were in Hegelian thought as developed by Jean-Paul Sartre, Said argued that colonialism created non-mutual and hierarchic relations in which the colonizer was always and inescapably the Self to the marginalized Other of the colonized. By 'knowing' the Other the colonizer asserted his right to determine what that Other could or should be. In other words the colonized could be literally moulded into whatever best served the economic and political purposes of the colonizer.

---

[2] Gayatri Chakravorty Spivak, *In Other Worlds* (New York: Methuen, 1987); Homi K. Bhabha, *The Location of Culture* (London: Routledge, 1994).

The written text, both official and literary, was a central tool in this process, becoming, as Homi Bhabha subsequently has characterized it, 'a sign of wonder' whose power far outstripped its objective content.[3] The indigenous culture which continued in invaded cultures to exist alongside this new construction was not expunged by this process, but it was metaphorically 'silenced', in so far as its voice ceased to be heard in the arenas of power, and its values ceased to be privileged or even recognized in the new hierarchy of control except under such labels as the exotic or the traditional, concepts which were viewed as opposed to the more dynamic formulations of the pragmatic and the modern. Modernization became synonymous with the promotion of the cultural values of the colonizer, and the development of so-called civilization.

Said shows, too, how this process is represented as an act of philanthropic generosity, part of a process of bringing the 'native' out of darkness into light. The linkages between cultural control, forms of knowledge, and the actual practices of colonial officials, merchants, and missionaries formed a complex nexus; they constituted a powerful and irresistible force. Indigenous cultures and languages continued to exist, though with an increasing tendency to generate new hybrid forms within the colonized culture, usually in modes which reinforced their subordinate position in the newly emerging power structures.

Although the use of terms like post-colonial to investigate a very wide range of social practices stems from Said's work, it could be argued that he privileges the literary text in a way that his mentor, the French theorist Michel Foucault, would never have approved. This misreading of Foucault has made Said interesting to literary scholars, and accounts for the importance of his work in establishing many recent accounts of literary activity in the post-colonial world. Such broadening of the field from the exclusively literary model implicit in Commonwealth literature or the new literatures in English to the new post-colonial discourse theory carries, however, its own potential for confusion. The resulting diversity of purpose is the subject of Stephen Slemon's excellent essay 'The Scramble for Post-colonialism' (1994), which warns of the danger of institutionalizing the field in a contest for the territory of the post-colonial. There is also considerable danger involved in the appropriation of the literary and cultural output of the post-colonial societies around the world to the Euro-American critical industry. As several critics have noted[4] this might be seen to replicate the colonial relationship whereby the colonies produced the raw material (the literary text) and

---

[3] Homi K. Bhabha, 'Signs Taken for Wonders: Questions of Ambivalence and Authority under a Tree outside Delhi', *Critical Inquiry*, 12/1 (Autumn 1985), 144–65.

[4] W. J. T. Mitchell, 'Postcolonial Culture, Postimperial Criticism', *Transition*, 56 (1992), 11.

the metropolitan societies added the value (critical judgement, evaluation, and commentary) and, of course, took most of the profit.

In recent constructions of the post-colonial, particularly in America, the interest in writing from regions other than England and America which characterized earlier approaches has shifted to an essentially philosophical concern with issues of marginality, subalterneity, and agency. In addition, the term 'post-colonial' in America has become locked in an internecine struggle with older traditions of radical theorizing of alter-native oppositions in the sociological and political science tradition of Third World studies and anti-imperialist studies. Unfortunately, the result of these shifts in concern has sometimes been once again to marginalize or ignore the creative and critical writing which has emerged from the post-colonial world itself. The debate within the American academy is increasingly one between scholars ignorant of and often quite uninterested in the actual writers of Nigeria, Kenya, India, or Malaysia, let alone countries such as New Zealand, Australia, and Canada. The power and size of the American academy acts as a vortex into which the specific claims of cultural difference that are so vital to the post-colonial societies themselves are sucked. While there are important ways in which American society itself can be understood as being a society shaped by the colonial experience, and ways in which it has constructed itself with internal imperialism, which have marginalized its own minorities, such concerns should complement rather than displace the interest in writing from other post-colonial societies. It is arguable that the intellectual isolationism which often characterizes American intellectual discourses needs such openness to other voices as Americans confront the fact, as Europeans have had to do before them, that they are not the world. Finally, the diffusion of the term 'post-colonial' in recent accounts to refer to any kind of marginality at all, either directly or by loose association with the interests of other marginalized groups, has tended to leach out its specific political valency and its central, defining concern with the historic reality of colonization. Interest has shifted from the direct, conflicting, concerns of post-colonial societies to the more general theoretical models underlying the specific events and processes with which post-colonial societies have to deal. This has been the simultaneous cause and product of the increasing tendency to privilege criticism produced in the metropolitan centres over that produced in post-colonial societies themselves. The study of post-colonial societies and texts has been recruited to the politics of the metropolitan academies. As a result, although it is easy to obtain the writings of colonial discourse theorists, since they appear in highly promoted international publications, critical material by even leading and well established post-colonial writers and critics such as E. K. Brathwaite,

U. R. Ananthamurthy, Emmanuel Obiechina, Dennis Lee, and Judith Wright is either unavailable or unknown to the participants in many contemporary discussions or ignored.

More recently, though, the problem has arisen that with the realization of the danger that post-colonial theory may act as a globalizing international force to wipe out local differences and concerns, an opposite and equally different reaction has developed in the form of a resurgence of atavistic, essentialist nativist theories. This has been especially so in post-colonial societies facing communalist tendencies, such as India or Malaysia, where it is possible to construct a pre-colonial myth to serve as a focus for a modern nation-state from the indigenous social and cultural forms. The recent upsurge of such regressive nativisms is different from the earlier critical nationalism which characterized the period of national liberation struggles as found in the work of writers such as Fanon, Cabral, or C. L. R. James. Such theorists were acutely aware of the problems implicit in nationalism as well as its benefits, and stressed the need to maintain a social critique which focused on issues of class, race, religion, and gender as factors in social discrimination within the newly emergent nation. They understood that a national state might be a tool in the hands of a national bourgeoisie still firmly under neo-colonial control, yet representing itself as the natural and historically legitimized government of the people.

Constructions of pre-colonial society are at best mythic and at worst deliberative fictions of the new ruling élite. Even the continuing cultures in the indigenous languages have been subject to profound modifications and hybridizations, in their ready and wholesale adoption of such forms of European literature as the novel and short story, as well as in the fact that the markets and readerships of such literature overlap and influence each other. In countries such as India, where there are many substantial literatures in the indigenous languages, writing in contemporary Kannada, Malayalam, or Bengali shows the influence of Western literary forms and concerns alongside, or admixed with, the indigenous. In Nigeria oral performative traditions survive in a variety of modes, from traditional forms and social contexts to hybridized forms, such as the Yoruba popular music theatre of Ladipo and Ogunde, and now in television serials and soap operas. In South Africa traditional Zulu praise songs were adapted at ANC rallies in the struggle against apartheid. The denial of the possibility of using colonial languages to represent post-colonial experiences is a simplistic assertion of authenticity often made alongside dubious claims concerning the ways in which culture is inscribed in language. It assumes that cultures in the contemporary world which continue to function in pre-colonial indigenous languages have not themselves been subject to colonial hybridization and that colonial languages were not available for resistance or opposition. While it is true that in some societies English and French may not be accessible to the mass of the people, the choice of a specific language for cultural renewal may serve to delegitimize other language groups in that community and exclude them from participation as equals in the new state. Post-colonial or new literatures are the result of fusions.

The nature of 'nationalist' constructions, which can never be either absolute or more than a specific 'national narrative' constructed in and for the purposes of the present, is shown clearly through the more problematic condition of invader-settler societies such as Canada, Australia, and New Zealand, where the mythic nature of the authentic is much more readily discerned. For this and other reasons the study of settler colonies has continuing importance in defining post-colonial studies. Unfortunately, because the simplistic construction of resistance as overt opposition has been dominant in most debates, these issues have not been given the attention they deserve and recent discourse theory critics continue to focus attention almost exclusively on the colonies of invasion, notably India. For all its political flaws the older models of new literatures and Commonwealth literatures at least had the virtue of encouraging comparative work across and between the different colonial situations leading to a broader and more effective analysis of how colonial power actually worked and continues to work in the world.

Although some recent nativist criticisms promulgate the idea that there is a simple alternative to the complex intercultural processes post-colonial theory has sought to address, others are more complex, forceful, and substantial, such as Aijaz Ahmad's (1992) criticism of Said and Fredric Jameson. For Ahmad Said's major flaw lies in his reconciliation of Foucauldian theories of discursive regimes (the practices of specific historical eras or epistemes, as Foucault terms them, dominated by specific discourses or ways of structuring representation) with the humanist tradition of a seamless, continuous history of European thought in which Said argues anti-Orientalist features can be discerned from the Greeks to the present. For Ahmad this is to take on board the myth of a single unfolding history which, as a Marxist, he resists, preferring to see the humanist vision of a homogeneous European history as an elision or collapsing together of a series of very different periods with radically different economic and social structures at their base.

More significantly, Ahmad suggests that the presentation of a unified European episteme linking the Ancient, medieval, and post-Renaissance periods to the modern world is exacerbated by the tendency in Said's work to present this myth of European culture (and the texts through which he constructs it) as the sole influence on the formation of the excluded cultures (those which, Said argues, the practice of that dominant

European textual realm effectively Orientalizes, that is, renders as the denigrated Other to the European Self). As Ahmad notes, if one steps out of the Euro-American traditions, one is struck by the fact that neither the architecture of *Orientalism* nor the kind of knowledge the book generally represents has any room in it for criticisms of colonial cultural domination of the kind that have been available in Latin America and even India, on an expanding scale, since the late nineteenth century.[5]

This tendency, further exacerbated by the narrow focus of recent theory, means that many texts which continue to be produced in the colonized cultures in the indigenous languages, as well as those produced in the language of the colonizer, are not considered as formative. In his earlier, and more sympathetic, analysis of the American Marxist Fredric Jameson's discussion of Third World writing and the construction of a 'national allegory', Ahmad in a similar vein argues that Jameson's view is also limited by its selection only of those texts which support the perception that all writing in the 'Third World' was engaged in a process of active resistance to colonial formulation, engaged that is in the construction of a counter-colonial national allegory. Using the example of Urdu literature (the literature of the area currently occupied by Pakistan, and the language of the ruling culture of much of northern India during and after the Moghul period from the sixteenth century to the nineteenth century) the latter part of the essay details the tendency in much of that literature to concern itself with problems which Ahmad characterizes as '[not] in any direct or exclusive way about the experience of colonialism and imperialism', such as the clash between the desire for modernization and the wish to maintain traditional values, for example in the issue of how to promote the education of women without losing the ideals of traditional Muslim womanhood.[6]

Ahmad makes an important point through this specific example. Analyses which develop a simple binary of them/us or colonizer/colonized, may have a double effect: first, they may refuse to permit and recognize the complexities of the ongoing processes within those societies. (Ahmad as a Marxist is thinking specifically of class divisions, but the point need not be limited to this specific view and can be seen to have a wider validity.) Secondly, they encourage the perception and promulgation of simplistic, nativist views of the post-colonial cultural past as primal, innocent, and pure. As Ahmad puts it, 'The typical Urdu writer has had a peculiar vision, in which he or she has never been able to construct fixed boundaries between the criminalities of the colonizer and the brutalities of all those indigenous people who have had power in our own society. We have had our own hysterias here and there—far too many, in

5 A. Ahmad, *In Theory: Classes, Nations, Literatures* (London: Verso, 1992), 174.
6 Ibid. 118.

fact—but there has never been a sustained, powerful myth of a primal innocence, when it comes to the colonial encounter.'[7]

Much hangs on the phrase used in the earlier quotation 'not in a direct way', since, clearly, at a far from superficial level the clashes which Ahmad details within Urdu-speaking society in India during the nineteenth and early twentieth centuries could be argued to have been an indirect result of the colonial process. The issue of modernization and of education for women, for example, which Ahmad cites, is a clear example of the kind of hybridization of the 'indigenous culture' which follows from the historical impact of Europe.

Ahmad represents a sophisticated version of the notion that contemporary criticism privileges European textuality and the colonial period over the continuity of the pre-colonial and the cultural diversity of the post-colonial world. It is a warning which has been echoed by other critics from post-colonial societies, especially those who have not relocated to the metropolitan universities. Formulations of study of such cultures which concentrate on English-language texts are, from this perspective, seen as distorting the reality of these societies' self-representations by excluding the texts which continue to be produced in the indigenous languages; or, at the very least, by privileging those produced in English and, it is sometimes asserted, directed at the outside world as much as to the audience of the post-colonial world itself. While this may be true, it is difficult to see how it can be addressed effectively without a recognition that the process reflects the international control of the production of literary and, indeed, other (mass media, electronic information, etc.) texts in the late twentieth century. The sociology of such control needs study and analysis.

Oddly enough, though, the overall result of the invasion of the study of post-colonial writings by theory has not been to add texts from indigenous languages to the body of material generally studied in Western institutions. Rather the number of works studied has diminished even from the already limited representativeness constituted by the body of writing in English from these societies to a few favoured canonical English texts, such as those by Rushdie, whose form favours current methodologies.

Ahmad's own analysis, for example, is primarily concerned with an internal dispute within Western cultures between the post-structuralist-inspired discourse theorists and those theorists who desire a continuing (Marxist) materialist analysis of social processes in post-colonial societies. Ahmad's position is limited by this dispute between Marxism and post-structuralism. This dispute takes precedence over the recuperation

---

[7] Ibid.

of the Urdu texts he discusses, which become ammunition in this essentially Euro-American critical debate.

One of the most telling moments in his criticism of Said is when, in attempting to place Said's essay 'Figures, Confrontations, Transfigurations', Ahmad launches an attack on the Association for Commonwealth Literature and Language Studies, at whose conference Said's paper was originally presented: 'such Associations . . . are usually very conservative and mindless affairs'.[8] In making this blanket assertion Ahmad is unwittingly dismissing the work of important post-colonial writers and critics as diverse as Ama Ata Aidoo, Wilson Harris, Carolyn Cooper, Ketu Katrak, Gabriel Okara, Simon Gikandi, Helen Tiffin, Diana Brydon and others, all of whom presented papers at the same conference. For many of the delegates the most radical keynote address was not that of Said, but that of the Guyanese novelist Wilson Harris. As the editor of the published proceedings, Anna Rutherford, put it in her introduction:

The theme of closure, the dangers posed by the demand for heterogeneity and the hegemonic idea of national purity, has from the beginning been a constant in the work of Wilson Harris. 'Concepts of invariant identity,' argues Harris, 'function in the modern world as a block imperative at the heart of cultural politics. The oppressor makes this his or her banner. The oppressed follow suit. *Such is the tautology of power*.' Instead of these 'invariant identities' he proposes a syncretic identity, made up of all the cultures and races which have taken part in the history of a particular place. . . . he believes in 'the essential heterogeneity of being' and rejoices in 'the ecstasy of complex counterpoint between partial origins'. (Compare Said's statement that he did not believe 'that global and contrapuntal analysis' could be modelled on the notion of a symphony; 'rather we have to do with atonal ensembles'.)[9]

Given then that Ahmad claims to speak 'for' the post-colonial world against the metropolitan it is significant that he himself restricts his vision of that world so drastically. He shares with those figures he criticizes a blindness to the significance of work done outside the frame of contemporary literary theory as it is constituted by the debates of the European and American academy. He ignores Harris, or, for that matter, such writers as Wole Soyinka, Brathwaite, and Lee.

Jameson's, Said's, and Ahmad's shared myopia with regard to the great diversity and variety of critical and creative writing which constitutes post-colonial literatures and theory in English is only a small part of the larger and more significant shift which has resulted from this uneasy alliance of post-colonial theory and contemporary European critical

---

[8] A. Ahmad, 202.
[9] A. Rutherford (ed.), *From Commonwealth to Post-colonial* (Sydney: Dangaroo, 1992), pp. vii–viii.

discourse. The most damaging result of this has been a gross neglect of the contribution made by the literary texts of the post-colonial world themselves to the theorization of the issues of post-colonialism. Many critics from these societies have long argued that such texts are themselves the main sources for the development of literary theory, where that is conceived of as the articulate response of people to their cultural and political situation rather than as more narrowly defined by contemporary critical accounts which equate literary theory with a specific and historically limited concern with the crisis of European philosophy and linguistic theory, or, as in Ahmad's case, with the struggle of late twentieth-century Marxism to assert its continuing relevance in the contemporary world. Texts such as West Indian writer Jamaica Kincaid's *A Small Place* (1989), the preface to Raja Rao's novel *Kanthapura* (1937), or numerous other examples, such as the poetry and essays of post-colonial writers as diverse as Robert Kroetsch, Judith Wright, or Derek Walcott, arise out of and articulate the experience of the post-colonial world. The negative impact of the dismissal of this kind of personal and direct response on the assessment of the ability of the societies of the post-colonial world to represent themselves and analyse their condition has been eloquently summed up by Barbara Christian in her article 'The Race for Theory' which, published as it was in the leading American journal *Cultural Critique*, effectively takes the fight to the heart of the opposing camp.

People of color have always theorized—but in forms quite different from the Western form of abstract logic. And I am inclined to say that our theorizing (and I intentionally use the verb rather than the noun) is often in narrative forms, in the stories we create, in riddles and proverbs, in the play with language, since dynamic rather than fixed ideas seem more to our liking. . . . My folk, in other words, have always been a race for theory—though more in the form of the hieroglyph, a written figure which is both sensual and abstract, both beautiful and communicative. Among the folk who speak in muted tones are people of color, feminists, radical critics, creative writers, who have struggled for much longer than a decade to make their voices, their various voices, heard, and for whom literature is not an occasion for discourse among critics but is necessary nourishment for their people.[10]

Although there is nothing to prevent post-colonial critics from appropriating European theory as they have appropriated its literary genres and practices to their own purposes, it is important to recognize that contemporary literary theory has a base in a specific cultural and institutional power structure, largely still located in Europe and America. It carries with it the philosophical and cultural preoccupations of those

[10] Barbara Christian, 'The Race for Theory', *Cultural Critique*, 6 (1987), 51–63.

structures, not all of which will be either relevant or friendly to the endeavours of the people and texts it claims to serve. Otherwise the danger exists of the study of post-colonial literatures becoming a colonizer in its turn, merely another mode of appropriation of the cultures of the post-colonial world. Ahmad's intervention, for example, while recognizing some of this danger becomes entwined in the coils of the problem it seeks to address and expose.

The polarization of recent post-colonial critical debates into pro- or anti-theory has too often ignored the contribution of those critics who have sought to take on board the more useful insights of contemporary theory, but who have also striven to resist incorporation into a new universalist paradigm under some generic label such as post-structuralism or post-modernism. Critics such as Diana Brydon in Canada and Helen Tiffin in Australia pioneered such an approach in essays that have been mostly ignored by recent colonialist discourse theorists and their opponents. These essays were significant in that, coming as they did from people who had a commitment to the writing of the new post-colonial societies, often having been graduate students of the pioneers of Commonwealth literature, they brought to their critical endeavours a broad familiarity with the actual texts of a range of new literatures in English. In this respect they contrast strongly with more recent critics whose generalizations often show a lamentable ignorance of the variety and range of work which characterize post-colonial writing in English, and which draw their examples from only the narrowest of literary perspectives. In 'Landscape and Authenticity' (1981) Brydon explored the complex of responses which allow the formation of a new vision of a country or landscape to come into being. Her essay resists simple nativist reversions even as it struggles with the problem of defining the authentic in a context whose references are 'always outside and always already there' (to appropriate a pertinent phrase of Louis Althusser). The reference to Althusser is appropriate, since Brydon has also produced a fascinating argument on the nature of such post-colonial critical appropriations of European high theory in her essay ' "The Thematic Ancestor": Joseph Conrad, Patrick White and Margaret Atwood' (1984). Helen Tiffin's essay 'Commonwealth Literature and Comparative Methodology' (1984) was one of the earliest attempts to argue for the need to theorize the study of this field in a consistent and effective way and not simply conceive of the new literatures as works to be tagged on to the study of English in the old, humanist mode of earlier critics such as William Walsh. Tiffin's 'Comparative Literature and Post-colonial Counter-discourse' (1987) sought to appropriate the idea of a counter-discourse, that resistance which is both contained within and yet subversive of the dominant discourse which defines it.

Brydon and Tiffin are from settler colonies, Canada and Australia respectively. Stephen Slemon, also a Canadian, has argued that some of the most direct articulations of that ambivalence which colonialist discourse theorists such as Homi Bhabha have claimed is at the heart of the colonial experience for both colonizer and colonized can be found in writing from former settler colonies.[11]

Slemon argues that resistance may be more complex than overt opposition, and that the urge to limit study to texts which embody overt opposition may lead to misunderstanding the complicated nature of colonization, and the degree to which it involves a mutual interactive and transformative relationship between colonizer and colonized, a relationship which cannot be avoided in the study of texts from settler colony societies where the subject may often be both oppressor (with respect to the indigene) and oppressed (with respect to the metropolitan colonizing culture).

Settler colony cultures also raise the issue of the difficulties involved in claims to an authentic indigeneity, when writers whose cultural ancestry is hybridized speak on behalf of an unproblematic and pure indigeneity. Leaving aside the issue of legitimacy, and how that is constituted in such claims, what such texts and writers do is to highlight the inadequacy of the idea of cultural purity which underpins claims to authenticity and legitimacy. The concept of purity is at the heart of the binary structures of colonization (black/white, civilized/native); it is transferred to the oppositional mode only at the great risk of replicating the very divisions it seeks to address.

The future study of the new literatures appears assured as it is difficult to see how a canon can be restored in a form which excludes such literatures, their concerns, and the theoretical problems they raise. Nevertheless, the theory of the construction of the field, as it has developed in recent years, has had both a positive and a negative effect. It has been positive in recognizing that merely accreting literatures and literary texts onto a unified model of English studies, even one which accepts a plurality of differences, does not ensure a genuine equality of cultures and of diverse reading and speaking positions.[12] Such formulations overcome the limitations of the more simplistic kind of liberal pluralism which underpinned the earlier models of the field.

The institutional power of post-colonial discourse theory has, however, privileged the views of metropolitan academics over the actual

---

[11] Stephen Slemon, 'The Scramble for Post-colonialism', in Chris Tiffin and Alan Lawson (eds.), *De-scribing Empire* (London: Routledge, 1994), 15–32; Homi Bhabha, 'Of Mimicry and Man: The Ambivalence of Colonial Discourse', *October*, 28 (Spring 1984), 125–33.

[12] Homi Bhabha, 'The Commitment to Theory', *New Formations*, 5 (1988), 5–23; Slemon, 'The Scramble for Post-colonialism', 15–32.

concerns of the societies on whose behalf it claims to speak. It has also had a negative effect in that as with many other developments in the general field of literary theory there has been a tendency to substitute philosophical and critical issues for the exegesis and analysis of the literary texts themselves. This has been doubly unfortunate in a field where the literary text has been a prime site in which to articulate such vital issues as language change and linguistic variance, cultural representation and culture clash, and issues of value construction and transformation.[13]

The future seems to require that the insights of recent theory be applied in the study of specific local traditions and to comparisons that can be discerned in and between them. How are modern post-colonial texts and the societies they seek to represent, despite their many differences, illuminated by their shared experience in colonization and later? Such shared experience does not imply a historically seamless process without radical differences. The comparison across a range of periods and of the societies on which European colonization impacted can lead, however, to new insights about the modes of representation that developed in post-colonial societies. But as Ahmed has warned, the focus of colonialism and post-colonialism may risk ignoring the continuing pre-colonial and internal preoccupations of societies. Studies which examine varying cultural inheritances are urgently needed, and these challenge us to cross the barriers set up by institutions which resist the kind of integrated study needed to link the varying traditions of the modern post-colonial inheritance. The pioneer work of scholars such as Janheinz Jahn and Albert Gérard in the study of the new literatures of Africa in their full cultural context has not been followed up by later scholars, daunted perhaps by their scope.[14]

In addition, recent theory needs to be balanced by more historical and sociological study, concentrating on the issue of who controlled and controls the production and consumption of the literary text; this affects the degree to which the colonial subject is silenced with at least as much force as the philosophic and linguistic issues which have exercised recent criticism. There has been no real follow-up from the pioneer work of Lefevere, Kotei, and Altbach.[15]

---

[13] Bill Ashcroft, Helen Tiffin, and Gareth Griffiths, *The Empire Writes Back* (London: Routledge, 1989).

[14] Janheinz Jahn, *Muntu* (New York: Grove Press, 1961); id., *A History of Neo-African Literatures* (London: Faber, 1968); Albert S. Gérard, *African Language Literatures* (Harlow: Longman, 1981).

[15] A. Lefevere, 'Interface: Some Thoughts on the Historiography of African Literature Written in English', in D. Riemenschneider (ed.), *The History and Historiography of Commonwealth Literature* (Tübingen: Gunter Narr Verlag, 1983), 99–107; S. I. A. Kotei, *The Book Today in Africa* (Paris: Unesco, 1981); P. Altbach, 'Literary Colonialism: Books in the Third World', *Harvard Educational Review*, 15/2 (May 1975), 226–36.

The interest in theories of the new literatures in English or post-colonial literatures has initiated an irresistible impulse towards consolidating the field by exploring these initiatives and their effect on older historical and critical traditions. The task ahead is an effective pedagogy for introducing the study of these complex interactions into the undergraduate curriculum and the development of sociologies of individual post-colonial literatures sufficiently detailed to be useful and yet illuminated by a comparativist awareness of differences and similarities across the great range and variety of post-colonial experience.

# CHAPTER TEN

# Post-colonial Critical Theories

STEPHEN SLEMON

What is post-colonial theory? What are its foundational assumptions and its critical methods? And what does it have to say to a student of the 'new', or 'Commonwealth', or 'post-colonial' literatures in English?

I begin with these perfectly reasonable questions because each one of them is just about impossible to answer. This is unsurprising—if we were to ask the same questions of 'feminist theory', for example, or to seek solid definitions for concepts such as 'allegory', or 'modernism', or 'multi culturalism' or 'queer studies', we would find that whatever the field or object of study, scholarly discussion is rarely unified when it comes to the methods and goals of critical analysis, let alone the political outcomes such analysis attempts to bring about. The field of post-colonial theory is in this way no different from most critical fields in the humanities. Problems of definition, object, motive, ground, and constituency are, however, exacerbated within the field of post-colonial critical theory. Probably no term within literary and critical studies is so hotly contested at present as is the term 'post-colonial'; probably no area of study is so thoroughly riven with disciplinary self-doubt and mutual suspicion.

For some commentators this lack of consensus and clarity is what is wrong with the field—listen to Russell Jacoby, a US-based academic Marxist, concluding his provocative article entitled 'Marginal Returns':

Post-colonial theory is all over the map. Of course, it is supposed to be. . . . The field is inchoate and can move in any number of directions. Nevertheless, the preliminary report is not positive. While post-colonial studies claims to be subversive and profound, the politics tends to be banal; the language jargonized; the radical one-upmanship infantile; the self-obsession tiresome; and the theory bloated.[1]

For others this lack of obvious clarity in post-colonial theory—the fluidity, the ambivalences, the theoretical anti-authoritarianism in the writing—is what is genuinely enabling about the field. Homi K. Bhabha,

---

[1] Russell Jacoby, 'Marginal Returns: The Trouble with Post-colonial Theory', *Lingua Franca* (Sept.–Oct. 1995), 37.

for example—whose remarkable contributions to post-colonial theory have been berated and celebrated in equal measure—argues that new forms of social collectivity have emerged in the contemporary post-colonial world, and these new forms require new ways of describing them. 'The post-colonial perspective', he writes,

forces us to rethink the profound limitations of a consensual and collusive 'liberal' sense of cultural community. It insists that cultural and political identity are constructed through a process of alterity. Questions of race and cultural difference overlay issues of sexuality and gender and overdetermine the social alliances of class and democratic socialism. The time for 'assimilating' minorities to holistic and organic notions of cultural value has dramatically passed. The very language of cultural community needs to be rethought from a post-colonial perspective.[2]

Regardless of where one stands on the question, there is no single post-colonial theory, and no one critic can possibly represent, or speak for, the post-colonial critical field. And so despite my pluralizing gesture in the title of this chapter, the following discussion of post-colonial critical theories is necessarily doomed at the level of comprehensiveness and coherence. What follows is about how I understand some aspects of some post-colonial critical and theoretical positions— for and against— in what is a complex and rapidly changing field of intellectual contestation and disciplinary debate.

## POST-COLONIALISM AND ITS TERMS

One of the most vexed areas of debate within the field of post-colonial theory has to do with the term 'post-colonial' itself. The debate lies in two parts: debates about the 'post', and debates about 'colonialism'.

'Colonialism' comes under debate because the word is already predicated within a concept of 'imperialism', a concept that is itself predicated within larger theories of global politics and which changes radically according to the specifics of those larger theories. Wolfgang Mommsen tells us that 'the original meaning of "imperialism" was not the direct or indirect domination of colonial or dependent territories by a modern industrial state, but rather the personal sovereignty of a powerful ruler over numerous territories, whether in Europe or overseas'.[3] For Vladimir Lenin, on the other hand, imperialism meant a late stage in European

---

[2] Homi K. Bhabha, 'Post-colonial Criticism', in Stephen Grenblatt and Giles Gunn (eds.), *Redrawing the Boundaries: The Transformation of English and American Literary Studies* (New York: MLA, 1992), 441.

[3] Wolfgang J. Mommsen, *Theories of Imperialism*, trans. P. S. Falla (Chicago: University of Chicago Press, 1977), 3.

capitalist expansion, a stage in which capital accumulates domestically, profit-taking slows, and so Europe seeks out foreign markets and foreign sources of labour.[4] Neither of these meanings lines up neatly with the general meaning of imperialism that predominates in literary critical discussions of the European empires—Edward Said, for example, uses imperialism to mean 'the practice, the theory, and the attitudes of a dominating metropolitan centre ruling a distant territory'.[5] Whatever they actually mean by the term, however, post-colonial theorists in the humanities—if not always their colleagues in the social and political sciences, for Marx did not use the word[6]—generally think of imperialism as constituting the larger political force that drives specific acts of colonialism (the direct rule of a nation or people by another nation or people) or colonization (the establishment of settler colonies in foreign lands). But without a specific theory of how imperialism drives these acts, it remains unclear how 'colonialism' operates politically, economically, and culturally, and how 'colonialism' and 'colonization' are related.

This slippage in the concept of the 'colonial' and its cognates becomes a problem when the 'post' part of the 'post-colonial' is brought into the equation. According to some theorists, after sustained anti-colonial struggle finally brings about national or 'flag independence' in colonial locations through a process of political decolonization, a new kind of state formation comes into being. (Bill New's chapter in this volume provides a useful chart of the moment of formal independence for Britain's former colonies.) This new formation is the post-colonial state, or the 'post-colony': a state thought to be at least institutionally free of foreign control, and one now possessing a greater measure of political autonomy than it did under colonialism.[7] Since most, but not all, of Europe's formal colonies have by now achieved political independence, the world itself, to some commentators, has shifted into a 'post-colonial condition'. Here, post-colonial nation-states develop new forms of international relations and self-constitution as they proceed. And the one-way traffic of imperial centre to colonial periphery is reformulated as a genuine circulation of peoples, so that members of various cultural and national backgrounds, ethnicities, religions, and languages move more freely across international borders than they used to, in the process developing new structures for group identification and collectivity.

[4] Anthony Brewer, *Marxist Theories of Imperialism: A Critical Survey* (2nd edn., New York: Routledge, 1987), 7 ff.; Kofi Buenor Hadjor, *The Penguin Dictionary of Third World Terms* (London: Penguin, 1992), 150.

[5] Edward Said, *Culture and Imperialism* (London: Chatto & Windus, 1993), 9.

[6] Brewer, *Marxist Theories*, 25.

[7] Hadjor, *Dictionary*, 250–1.

The problem with the thesis of autonomous state 'post-colonialism', however, is that the achievement of flag independence, or formal decolonization, may do nothing about the economic domination that continues after Empire: at the level of real politics in the 'post-colonial' nation, some argue, nothing has really changed. To describe this political condition in which the old regulatory practices of direct colonialism are continued by new forms of foreign domination—the manipulation of national economies through the production and administration of 'Third World debt', for example—Kwame Nkrumah, the first President of independent Ghana, coined the term 'neo-colonialism'. 'The essence of neo-colonialism', wrote Nkrumah, 'is that the State which is subject to it is, in theory, independent and has all the outward trappings of international sovereignty. In reality its economic system and thus its political policy is directed from the outside.'[8]

The concept of a 'post-colonial condition', then, is already a little different from the notion of a 'post-colonial state' or nation, for the first describes a global situation (which may or may not be distributed equally across different nations and cultural groups) while the second refers to the political status of independent former-colonies of the European empires. This second term, however, begs the question of the difference between, on the one hand, 'white' or 'invader-settler' 'post-colonial' nations like Australia, Canada, New Zealand, or South Africa and, on the other hand, 'Third-World' 'post-colonial' nations like Ghana, Pakistan, Vanuatu, or Barbados. On a crude scale that ranges from 'oppressor' to 'oppressed' within contemporary neo-colonial international relations, the political location of such nations may differ foundationally, and this raises a question as to whether both kinds of ex-colonial states ought to be thought of equally as 'post-colonial nations'. Further, the terms of nation and nationhood themselves are inherently monolithic ones, and they conceal important differences between constituent groups within the 'post-colonial' nation. White settler 'Canadians', to give one example, may be differently located within 'post-colonialism' from the aboriginal or First Nations 'Canadians' whose land they retain—the question of land-claims and 'native' resistance is an enduring one, and many people in both communities consider 'Native Canadians' to remain under a condition of political colonialism in their own 'post-colonial' country. To give another example: some 'Melanesian' Fijian citizens understand their claim to political control in Fiji as constitutionally prior to the claims of those 'Indian' Fijian peoples brought over by British colonizers as indentured plantation labourers in the nineteenth century. Both groups in Fiji have legitimate grounds for understanding themselves

---

[8] Ibid. 215.

historically as 'colonized' peoples under British colonialism, and for now thinking of themselves as post-colonial citizens of an independent Fiji, but the question of whether both groups have an equal constitutional claim to the category of Fijian citizenship was the subject of a political coup in 1989, and it remains unresolved. Of course, categories such as 'native', 'settler', 'Melanesian', 'white', 'Canadian', and so on—as is always the case with the homogenizing nomenclature of race, class, gender, nation, sexual orientation, and the like—themselves conceal forms of division within groups, they conceal intersection lines and cross-over points between groups, they say nothing about the social processes that construct these groups in specific places at specific times, and they ignore the social forces that fuse different constituencies and individuals into social groups.

The term 'post-colonial' or 'post-colonialism', therefore, has to be seen as problematized at the outset by lack of consensus on what it is that makes the term 'colonial' meaningful—that is, by a lack of consensus over how 'colonialism' is structured within a concept of 'imperialism'— and by a lack of consensus over what it might mean to be 'post' the 'colonial' moment. If neo-colonial relations still prevail between and within modern nations, if the 'practices, theories and attitudes of dominating metropolitan centres' (to re-employ Said's words) remain in place after European colonialism has formally ended, then at some level contemporary 'post-colonialisms', however they are conceived, must take place within a structure of contemporary and continuing imperial relations. For many commentators, this means that a critical practice that calls itself 'post-colonial' must necessarily be confused about its political theory and compromised in its political aims. Here is how Anne McClintock puts the case:

[T]he term post-colonial . . . is haunted by the very figure of linear development that it sets out to dismantle. Metaphorically, the term post-colonialism marks history as a series of stages along an epochal road from 'the precolonial,' to 'the colonial', to 'the post-colonial'—an unbidden, if disavowed, commitment to linear time and the idea of development. . . . Metaphorically poised on the border between old and new, end and beginning, the term heralds the end of a world era but by invoking the very same trope of linear progress which animates that era. . . . If post-colonial *theory* has sought to challenge the grand march of Western historicism and its entourage of binaries (self–other, metropolis–colony, centre–periphery, etc.), the *term* post-colonialism nonetheless reorients the globe once more around a single, binary opposition: colonial-post-colonial . . . [I]t does not distinguish between the beneficiaries of colonialism (the ex-colonizers) and the casualties of colonialism (the ex-colonized). The post-colonial scene occurs in an entranced suspension of history, as if the definitive historical events have preceded our time and are not now in the making. . . . [T]he singularity of the term effects a recentering of global history around the single rubric of European time. Colonialism returns at the moment of its disappearance.[9]

A number of concepts from political and critical theory are being run together under the name of the 'post-colonial'—if not by individual post-colonial theorists, then at least within the general field of post-colonial critical studies. One is a temporal concept about the decolonized nation-state, confused about its relation to neo-colonialism and imperialism. Another is a geopolitical concept of contemporary group identity, confused about what kinds of national or cultural groups deserve inclusion. A third is a sociological concept about global cultural conditions and experiences, confused about its constituency and about its relation to concepts of race, class, gender, ethnicity, and the like. At some point, therefore, most participants in the field of 'post-colonial critical theory' find it necessary to position their own work in relation to some other critical theory, or methodology, or social object, or political goal. While 'feminist theorists', for example, may generally understand themselves to be working in the interests of feminism (though not necessarily 'for women'), few 'post-colonial theorists' will understand their work as operating specifically in the interests of 'post-colonialism' itself. 'Post-colonialism' is a portmanteau word—an umbrella thrown up over many heads, against a great deal of rain. Confusion necessarily abounds in the area.

The result of this confusion is disciplinary anxiety, and one of the most salient features of post-colonial critical discussion is the ubiquity of debate over the extent to which any given post-colonial theory or critical practice really is opposed to colonialism. The passage I have just quoted from McClintock discusses how an unintended 'colonialism' crops up in critical post-colonialism. The term 'post-colonial', McClintock is arguing, is by definition intimately connected with the great progress myths that promulgated and sustained European empire-building, and with the assumptions about history, culture, and human development that underwrote those myths. Observations of this kind about the unintended political consequences of a great many critical positions that take place under the post-colonial umbrella are very common in contemporary critical debate—Vijay Mishra and Bob Hodge use the term 'complicit postcolonialism'[10] to identify such compromised critical positions and social locations—and, as I have tried to suggest, the structure of disciplinary anxiety that produces such commentary comes about because the discipline of post-colonial studies houses so many different kinds of theoretical and critical work, and such a wide range of assumptions

[9] Anne McClintock, *Imperial Leather: Race, Gender and Sexuality in the Colonial Contest* (New York: Routledge, 1995), 10–11.

[10] Vijay Mishra and Bob Hodge. 'What is Post(-)colonialism?' *Textual Practice*, 5/3 (Dec. 1991), 407.

about what the terms of post-colonial criticism actually mean. And so: theorists who consider themselves part of the field of post-colonial studies may understand themselves to be working towards a description of imperial or colonizing cultures and their literatures at different moments, for example, or towards a description of specific colonized or 'post-colony' cultures and their literatures, or towards a description of specific minority groups and individuals variously located within and across colonial or post-colonial cultures, or towards a description of what a comparative study of specific post-colonial conditions in specific locations should look like , or towards a description of a global condition of post-coloniality . . . the list goes on.

Obviously, these many 'post-colonial' projects will assume no common object of description, let alone a common theoretical or critical methodology. And just as obviously, these descriptive enterprises will not be grounded in a common political goal—indeed, much post-colonial critical work carries no political commitment whatsoever. As for those post-colonial critics and theorists who do avow a political motive to their work, they may understand their scholarship to be aligned with a nationalist or pan-nationalist form of anti-colonialism, or with a group-based anti-nationalist form of post-colonialism, or with a decolonizing enterprise pitched at the level of cultural representations, or with a specific form of anti-imperialist social theory—again, the possibilities for understanding political goal and constituency within post-colonial studies are extremely multiple and diverse. Needless to say, a political commitment to social change in the contemporary world assumes no monadic theory of anti-imperialism or decolonization or 'post-colonialism', and even if it did it would not necessarily find its way to a common critical methodology.

The noisy, and often remarkably angry, debates over the uses and abuses of 'post-colonial critical theory', therefore, come about partly because of conceptual confluence in the discipline, partly because of confusion over the role of social and political theory in the field. But they also come about because many different social constituencies take up a position within post-colonial critical theory—and against it. In what follows, I want to identify just a few of the disciplinary roads that run into the post-colonial traffic jam, but again: these are only a few of the roads that interest me, and the commentary of a single traveller through a given landscape is never the same thing as a map.

A YELP AT THE ENGLISH FLAG

My title here is taken from the depressingly famous opening stanza to Rudyard Kipling's poem 'The English Flag', which reads:

Winds of the world, give answer! They are whimpering to and fro—
And what should they know of England who only England know?—
The poor little street-bred people that vapour and fume and brag,
They are lifting their heads in the stillness to yelp at the English Flag!

One of the earliest, and still one of the most substantial, disciplinary
'yelps' in the area of post-colonial studies took place under the mantle of
'Commonwealth Literature Studies', a name now widely ridiculed within
critical commentary but one which, as I read it, had much to do with
bringing post-colonial studies into being as a discipline, and which
continues to play a role in shaping theoretical debate within the field.

Commonwealth Literary Studies date formally from the mid-1960s
though obviously there were a number of comparative studies between
the various Commonwealth national literatures before this time.[11] Part of
what brought this field into being was pure instrumentality: a number of
young writers and critics from Commonwealth nations happened to be
in England at this time, many of them on Commonwealth academic
scholarships, and they came together at a conference for literary study
(the first conference of the Association for Commonwealth Literature
and Language Studies) at Leeds. Unsurprisingly, these diverse participants found much to talk about, and one of their common concerns was
the maniacal Anglocentrism that dominated English department curricula and canons in their home countries and throughout the English-speaking world. If they agreed on nothing else, they shared a desire to
introduce creative works from the 'Commonwealth' or 'new' literatures
onto English department syllabuses, and one of the strategies they employed for doing this involved a yoking together of the various Commonwealth literatures, whatever their differences, under terms that seemed to
afford them a similarity and thus make them a coherent field. The reason
for this was obvious: in a climate in which non-British and non-American
literary texts could wilfully be ignored by departments of English in
colonial and post-colonial universities, the collectivizing of those many
literary texts under the banner of 'Commonwealth Literary Studies'
constituted a powerful argument against the dominant view that very
little literary activity actually took place outside the USA and the UK, and
that what few texts there were 'out there' weren't very good.

In retrospect, this collectivizing strategy must be seen as a monument-
ally effective one. Courses in Commonwealth literature came into being,
though of course not everywhere, and a series of scholarly books and
articles appeared, each of them offering various ways of advancing the
march of Commonwealth difference onto the unfeatured fields of literary

---

[11] See Hena Maes-Jelinek, Kirsten Holst Petersen, and Anna Rutherford, *A Shaping of
Connections* (Sydney: Dangaroo Press, 1989), 1–83.

Englishness. This strategy, needless to say, tended to shade much of the field construction of Commonwealth literary studies towards patterns of similarity across the various Commonwealth national literatures, sometimes at the expense of an articulation of the many differences between these literatures. 'The search for identity', 'a coming of age', 'the absence of sentimentality'—these were just some of the early avowals of thematic and modal patterns of similarity across Commonwealth national literatures, but behind each of them was the idea that such a pattern could provide a useful location for comparing the Commonwealth national literatures with one another. Few critics within post-colonial studies would now employ these specific patterns as grounds for comparison—thematic criticism, generally, has shifted from the centre of literary critical methodology—but as Commonwealth studies has more recently moved into a 'post-colonial' phase, new comparative principles have come forward in their place, and these principles for comparative analysis continue to excite debate within the field. I want to discuss two of them.

The first of these principles for reading post-colonial literatures has to do with the representational contract of 'realism'. Much can be said about how realism works contractually between text and reader, but one of the common arguments—possibly a prejudice, and certainly an argument that needs to be theorized—is that at some level at least, realist writing is tied to a naturalizing drive in language. This, if true, constitutes a problem for post-colonial writing, for one of the most insistent concerns of post-colonialism is the locating of English language-use in a history of imperial expansion. If language carries a naturalizing drive, one must remember where that language, that notion of the natural, is coming from, and question whose interests it is serving. As Derek Walcott puts it:

> This is my ocean, but it is speaking
> another language . . .
> I resist the return
> of this brightening noun.[12]

For some post-colonial thinkers, the imperial imposition of European language on non-European peoples binds post-colonial peoples to a uninterruptable condition of ironic relations with the world. Others assert that cultural continuities and exchanges consistently take place 'under Western eyes', even if the imperial reader does not notice them. One of the most interesting post-colonial theorists to engage with the realist contract in language is the Guyanese novelist, poet, and critic

[12] Derek Walcott, 'Midsummer', in *Collected Poems: 1948–1984* (New York: Farrar, Straus, & Giroux, 1986), 496.

Wilson Harris. For Harris, realism is nothing less than 'a negation of the complexity of language' in post-colonial times, for it cultivates an addiction to 'normality' in meaning—ethnographic positivism in the first world, protest realism in the third.[13] But Harris does not believe that post-colonial writing can simply step away from contractual realism, nor does he believe that a simple anti-realist approach to either reading or writing will lead anywhere but to cognitive scepticism—itself a kind of post-modern realism, in Harris's view, and one that cannot commit to principles of global change. The kind of literary practice Harris advocates, therefore, is one that fractures inherited representational conventions— the 'block imprints' of imperial history—and thus activates a 'ceaseless dialogue' between adversarial cultures and their orders of 'meaning'.[14]

At heart, those post-colonial critical theorists who attempt to ground the representational contract of literary realism to the modality of language diffusion under Empire are attempting to figure out how literary writing might contribute to a way out of the disempowering cognitive legacies of imperialism—to use the phrase of Ngugi wa Thiong'o, they are attempting to examine post-colonial writing at the level of literary mode in the hopes of making a contribution to the general project of 'decolonizing the mind'. This does not mean such critics believe that all genuinely useful post-colonial literary writing is somehow non- or anti-realist, but for many participants in post-colonial critical debates, an overarching attention to non-realist writing implicitly devalues realist post-colonial textual practice, and there is at present a great deal of debate in the field over which audiences prefer which kinds of literary texts, and why. One of the many counter-arguments to a post-colonial critical interest in non-realist literary writing is that First World reading tastes, fashioned as they are by the glitzy depthlessness of post-modernist performativity, actually programme the production of much post-colonial writing, and that 'post-colonial' novels such as Salman Rushdie's *Midnight's Children* or Ben Okri's *The Famished Road*, for example, function far more as baubles for the bored infants of contemporary modernity than as epistemological interventions into the colonizing mind.

A second principle for theorizing post-colonial texts is the principle of reading for 'resistance'. Such a practice is so ubiquitous in post-colonial criticism as to make a general description of it impossible, but one of the most sustained engagements with the concept is advanced by Bill

---

[13] Wilson Harris, 'A Note on Zulfikar Ghose's "Nature Strategies" ', *Review of Contemporary Fiction*, 9/2 (Summer 1989), 181.

[14] Wilson Harris, *The Womb of Space* (Westport, Conn.: Greenwood, 1983), 185; pp. xviii–xx.

Ashcroft, Gareth Griffiths, and Helen Tiffin in their influential *The Empire Writes Back*. They begin with the proposition that 'language is a medium of power':[15] this means, they argue, that post-colonial literary language has to 'seize the language of the [imperial] centre and [re-place] it in a discourse fully adapted to the colonized place'. This, they suggest, happens first by an 'abrogation' or refusal of the normative standards of the imperial culture—the standards of 'correct' grammar, syntax, and pronunciation, for example—and then by an 'appropriation' of the colonizer's language, appropriately adapted, to the cultural and political ends of the colonized. They discuss many strategies by which they see this broad structure of literary resistance taking place in post-colonial writing: sometimes it involves figuring literary silence (as in Lewis Nkosi's *Mating Birds*), for example; sometimes it involves the exorbitant rewriting of canonical literary texts from the other side of the colonial divide (as in the case of Timothy Findley's *Not Wanted on the Voyage*, Jean Rhys's *Wide Sargasso Sea*, or J. M. Coetzee's *Foe*); and sometimes it involves portraying the distortions that occur in colonized cultures when imperial languages have *not* successfully been abrogated and appropriated (as in V. S. Naipaul's *The Mimic Men*).[16]

Needless to say, this general tactic of reading for resistance comes in for much the same kind of debate within post-colonial criticism as does the tactic of reading against the contract of realism. Ashcroft, Griffiths, and Tiffin have a theory of literary resistance that has to do with an inevitable hybridization within, and 'continuity of preoccupations' between, those cultures 'affected by the imperial process' (p. 2)—a theory that is grounded in the Commonwealth studies strategy of collectivized literary intervention into the Anglocentric, English-department monologue. Since no text has been as influential as theirs has in advancing the claims of Commonwealth or post-colonial literary studies to a place at the table, *The Empire Writes Back* itself has to be seen as the primary factor in bringing about a disciplinary moment in which this specific part of its own argument is no longer as necessary as it once was, for the location of non-British, non-American literary writing in most departments of English has somewhat changed. Each of its three authors has subsequently refined his or her theory of post-colonial literary resistance in other published work. The question remains open, however, exactly how textual resistance ought to be theorized. Some critics have shifted to discourse-based models of power, grounded in the archaeological theories of Michel Foucault and mediated through Richard Terdiman's powerful thesis of literary textual repetition as a provisional and precari-

---

[15]  Bill Ashcroft *et al.*, *The Empire Writes Back* (London: Routledge, 1989), see 38–77.
[16]  Ibid.; see 83–8 for Nkosi, 88–91 for Naipaul, and 97–104 for Findley, Rhys, and Coetzee.

ous 'counter-discourse'.[17] Other critics have turned to a culturalist model of resistance, where opposition to power is seen to be so thoroughly infused into the everyday experience of an oppressed people that resistance becomes an inherent aesthetic and finds its way into everything.[18] Still other critics have turned to psychoanalytic theory and the concept of 'colonialist disavowal', with a view to identifying how colonial power itself enables forms of 'native resistance' through differential repetitions (for example, in 'mimicry')—repetitions that become resistances because they have the power to effect social transformations.[19]

### HISTORY IN THE WIND

I began the previous section of this chapter with what I understand to be one of the foundational currents in the making of contemporary post-colonial critical theory. This section concerns another of those foundational currents, and to introduce it I will turn to the Uruguayan writer Eduardo Galeano's *Memory of Fire: Genesis*, a narrative that retells the Spanish conquest of South and Central America through a poetic, fragmented rewriting of original historical sources. Notice what Galeano focuses upon in telling of the slaughter of the people of Quetzaltenango in 1524:

The poet will speak of Pedro de Alvarado and of those who came with him to teach fear. . . . The children, seated in a circle around the poet, will ask: 'And all this you saw? You heard?'
'Yes.'
'You were here?' the children will ask.
'No. None of our people who were here have survived.'
And he will teach them to smell history in the wind, to touch it in stones polished by the river, and to recognize its taste by chewing certain herbs, without hurry, as one chews on sadness.[20]

Why should Galeano figure the remembering of colonial history, at its most brutal and abject, in a language of smell, touch, and taste? There are many answers, but the one I want to develop here has to do with the problem of rethinking the category of history itself from the perspective of post-colonial critical theory.

[17] Helen Tiffin, 'Post-colonial Literatures and Counter-discourse', *Kunapipi*, 9/3 (1987), 17–34.
[18] Selwyn R. Cudjoe, *Resistance and Caribbean Literature* (Athens, Oh.: Ohio University Press, 1980); Barbara Harlow, *Resistance Literature* (New York: Methuen, 1987).
[19] Homi K. Bhabha, 'Signs Taken for Wonders: Questions of Ambivalence and Authority under a Tree outside Delhi, May 1817', *Critical Inquiry*, 12/1 (1985), 144–65.
[20] Eduardo Galeano, *Memory of Fire: Genesis*, trans. Cedric Belfrage (New York: Pantheon, 1985), 77.

Robert Young's important survey *White Mythologies: Writing History and the West* identifies the construction of history and historiography as the central problematic in the fashioning of a modern Eurocentric worldview. At the centre of this problematic, Young argues, is Hegelian historicism, which 'articulates a philosophical structure of the appropriation of the other as a form of knowledge' and then presupposes a 'dialectic of the same and the other' to posit a single, unifying 'governing structure of self-realization in all historical process'.[21] Such a description works when all forms of historical oppression can be subsumed under a centralizing category of oppression—gender and race as a subset of class, for example—but the problem with any single-motor theory of historical process, as Young sees it, is that 'the dialectical structure of oppositional politics no longer works for the micro-politics of the post-war period in the West' (p. 5). Indeed, from the perspective of the colonized, any unitary notion of human 'progress' or 'development' may be seen to carry with it the appalling risk of justifying the 'White Man's Burden' of globalizing enlightenment—a risk that as some see it Karl Marx himself gave substance to in his writings on English colonialism in India. 'We must not forget', wrote Marx in 1853,

that the idyllic village communities, inoffensive though they may appear, had always been the solid foundation of Oriental despotism, that they restrained the human mind within the smallest possible compass, making it the unresisting tool of superstition, enslaving it beneath traditional rules, depriving it of all grandeur and historical energies. . . . We must not forget that this undignified, stagnatory, and vegetative life, that this passive sort of existence evoked . . . wild, aimless, unbounded forces of destruction, and rendered murder itself a religious rite in Hindustan. We must not forget . . . [the] brutalizing worship of nature, exhibiting its degradation in the fact that man, the sovereign of nature, fell down on his knees in adoration of Hanuman, the monkey, and Sabbala, the cow.

England, it is true, in causing a social revolution in Hindustan, was actuated only by the vilest interests, and was stupid in her manner of enforcing them. But that is not the question. The question is, can mankind fulfill its destiny without a fundamental revolution in the social state of Asia? If not, whatever may have been the crimes of England she was the unconscious tool of history in bringing about that revolution.[22]

What is post-colonial theory to do with such a statement, especially when it is made by the social theorist who stands at the headwaters of anti-capitalism and hence anti-colonialism? Aijaz Ahmad, in a spirited chapter on 'Marx on India', argues that although Marx's writing is

---

[21] Robert Young, *White Mythologies: Writing History and the West* (New York: Routledge, 1990), 3–4.

[22] *Marx/Engels: The First Indian War of Independence 1857–1859* (Moscow: Progress Publishers, 1959), 16–17.

'contaminated in several places with the usual banalities of nineteenth-century Eurocentrism', Marx never argued that resistance to European colonialism was misdirected: his 'systematic, universal history of all modes of production' may be 'flawed', notes Ahmad, but nevertheless it is 'brilliant' and empowering.[23]

Other theorists, however, have turned away from the central thesis of unitary historicism in order to come at the question of history—and histories—very differently, and this area of post-colonial theory has been at the centre of a great deal of contemporary critical debate. One branch of this turn from Eurocentric historicism is occupied by a coherent group of scholars who have come to be known as the 'subaltern studies' collective. Taking their name from Antonio Gramsci's 'subaltern'—as Robert Young explains, a name for subordinate individuals and groups 'who do not possess a general "class consciousness" ' (p. 160)—the subaltern studies historians not only seek to identify the modes of domination that make subalterns subordinate to power, but also seek an understanding of subaltern peoples as 'subjects of their own histories'.[24] To do so, writes Veena Das, the subaltern historians focus on 'the historical moment of rebellion' effected by subordinated, colonized people, with a view to discovering the specific nature of the 'oppressive contract' those people were 'compelled to make with the modern institutions of domination' (p. 314). 'What is important', Das continues, 'is that the subjects of this power are not treated as passive beings'—as they are, for example, in Marx's description, quoted above—'but are rather shown at the moments in which they try to defy this alienating power' (p. 314).

This sounds a little like 'reading for resistance' as I described it in the preceding section, but the central difference here is that the documents the subaltern historians consider in arriving at their sense of the past are not those texts produced by oppressed figures— in most instances, such texts simply do not exist—but rather are the bureaucratic reports, the legal proceedings, the formal and informal administrative documentation produced by the colonizers. This already tells us something about what it must mean to have been subaltern, notes Das: it implies that 'the moment of rebellion is also the moment of failure or defeat' (p. 315). This in turn produces the theory that subaltern peoples under colonialism are neither fully subjected to power nor fully agential, in the sense of having full self-knowledge, and will, and purpose—they somehow live out their lives between these two concepts of social subjectivity, and the historian's job is to describe that social location. The subaltern, notes

[23] Aijaz Ahmad, *In Theory* (London: Verso, 1992), 229.

[24] Veena Das, 'Subaltern as Perspective', in Ranajit Guha (ed.), *Subaltern Studies VI: Writings in South Asian History and Society* (New Delhi: Oxford University Press, 1989), 312.

Partha Chatterjee, 'is a contradictory unity of two aspects: in one, the peasant is subordinate, where he accepts the immediate reality of power relations that dominate and exploit him; in the other, he denies those conditions of subordination and asserts his autonomy'.[25]

The subaltern studies collective thus attempts to shift the project of history-writing away from a form of representation that unhesitatingly places Europe at the centre of theoretical knowledge. But needless to say, not all groups and individuals within colonized cultures are subalterns, and so subaltern historical studies—even if they avoid Eurocentric historicism—can never amount to a 'complete' historical description. And, as the brilliant theorist Gayatri Chakravorty Spivak notes in a now-famous essay entitled 'Can the Subaltern Speak?', subaltern historiography may not fully have considered the representational predication of the historical subject it seeks to retrieve from Eurocentrism. 'The object of the group's investigation', writes Spivak,

is itself defined as a difference from the elite. It is towards this structure that the research is oriented. . . . What taxonomy can fix such a space? Whether or not they themselves perceive it [i.e. the subaltern historians] . . . their text articulates the difficult task of rewriting its own conditions of impossibility as the conditions of its possibility.[26]

Clearly, the project of understanding the colonized peoples as genuinely historical subjects, as subjects of their own histories, and not as passive figures in the burgeoning history of others, is of paramount importance to the field of post-colonial theory. But Spivak's argument raises a problem of seemingly insuperable difficulty: how do we retrieve a sense of colonized peoples as subjects of their own history when our understanding of those subjects and their histories depends upon colonial texts? Spivak's answer is that we cannot: 'the subaltern cannot speak,' she concludes. 'Representation has not withered away' (p. 308). To act outside a knowledge of the impossibility of historical retrieval, she continues, is to encounter the 'danger of appropriating the other by assimilation' (p. 308). And to do that would reinstall the Hegelian dialectic of Eurocentric historicism. And so Spivak counsels the critic to develop 'a historical critique of our own position as the investigating person. . . . [T]hen you are indeed taking a risk . . . and can hope to be judged with respect.'[27]

[25] Partha Chatterjee, *The Nation and its Fragments: Colonial and Post-colonial Histories* (Princeton: Princeton University Press, 1993), 167.
[26] Gayatri Chakravorty Spivak, 'Can the Subaltern Speak?' in Cary Nelson and Lawrence Grossbert (eds.), *Marxism and the Interpretation of Culture* (Urbana: University of Illinois Press, 1988), 286.
[27] Gayatri Chakravorty Spivak, *The Post-colonial Critic: Interviews, Strategies, Dialogues*, ed. Sarah Harasym (New York: Routledge, 1990), 62–3.

With a view to developing such a historical critique of the imperializing prerogatives of Western modernity itself, a very diverse group of 'post-colonial' scholars has attempted to negotiate another way of challenging Eurocentric historicism—this is the branch of post-colonial critical theory known as 'colonial discourse analysis'. This group takes its cue from Michel Foucault's dismissal of a Marxist theory of ideology in favour of a notion of 'discourse': at heart, a notion that considers social subjects, social consciousness, to be formed not through ideologies that have their base in economic or class relations but through a form of power that circulates in and around the social fabric, framing social subjects through strategies of regulation and exclusion, and constructing forms of 'knowledge' which make possible that which can be said and that which cannot.[28] The problem with Western historicism, for Foucault, is that it overlooks these processes of social formation.

The ur-text of colonial discourse analysis is Edward Said's *Orientalism*, which provides a Foucauldian reading of those British and French scholarly treatises on, and fantastic projections onto, 'the Orient' in the eighteenth and nineteenth centuries. In *Orientalism*, Said argues that although there indeed were and are peoples who actually live in a space Europe knows as 'the Orient', this space was in fact never anything other than an 'idea', 'a creation with no corresponding reality'.[29] What brought that purely conceptual space into being, argues Said, is a European 'style of thought based on an ontological and epistemological distinction' made between 'the Orient' and 'the Occident' (p. 2). Said's name for that 'style of thought' is Orientalism.

Orientalism, in short, is a Foucauldian 'discourse', and by showing how such a discourse worked in a particular location and at a particular time, Said's book made possible the critical idea that colonial relations in general might be interwoven with—produced by and productive of—a 'colonial discourse' that one could analyse through textuality. One of the most able practitioners of colonial discourse analysis is Peter Hulme, who defines 'colonial discourse' as 'an ensemble of linguistically based practices unified by their common deployment in the management of colonial relations'.[30] Hulme's book *Colonial Encounters* locates the workings of colonial discourses in a variety of historical contexts—one of his chapters, for example, considers the extent to which one can employ a 'symptomatic' reading to make a colonialist document disclose more than its writer himself knows about the rules and regulations that

---

[28] Michel Foucault, *The Archaeology of Knowledge*, trans. A. M. Sheridan (London: Tavistock, 1972), 21–39.

[29] Edward Said, *Orientalism* (New York: Pantheon, 1978), 5.

[30] Peter Hulme, *Colonial Encounters: Europe and the Native Caribbean 1492–1797* (New York: Routledge, 1986), 2.

make possible European 'knowledges' of itself and its others. Specifically, Hulme considers Columbus' journal of his voyage to the New World, and he meditates on the hidden discursive rules and regulations that might have been in effect when Columbus historically 'mishears' an Arawak word for 'Carib' as 'caniba' or 'cannibal'—a word Columbus understands to mean 'a subject of the Great Khan', and thus a word that confirms his belief that he has found a sea-route to Asia. Interestingly, this discursively manufactured mishearing precipitates the noun 'cannibal' into European language, but Hulme's greater point is that the discursive regulations that to some extent govern Columbus' understanding are productive of a specifically colonial discourse that regulates not only how Europe understands its Others but also, foundationally, how European 'sovereign' subjects understand themselves. Instead of reinstalling a pure historicist notion of a single motor to human history, therefore, one that turns in Europe, Hulme's colonial discourse analysis presents the central argument that Western self-constitution is dependent, at least at a minimal level, on the actual historical acts and practices of its Others. Whereas for Said there is no necessary 'other' figure in that style of European thought that constructs the 'Orient' and thus the 'Self', for Hulme some 'other' at least has to speak—if only to be misheard. Such a formulation, of course, is a long way from a notion of full subaltern agency under colonial relations, but at least it begins to unsettle the historicist dialectic by asserting a minimal condition of contingency—if not actual negotiation—in the making of a historical European self.

Hulme's employment of the concept of 'colonial discourse' is always highly specific to a particular moment and location in history, but not all practitioners of colonial discourse analysis have been as careful as Hulme has been, and several commentators have worried about the currency of the notion that a single 'colonial discourse' regulates all colonial relations between European colonizers and non-European colonized peoples, in all places, and at all times. Other commentators have worried that the concept of colonial discourse, or Orientalism, although capable of describing specific Eurocentric formations, can actually become a 'prisonhouse' for non-Western readers who seek a more enabling understanding of themselves within contemporary political relations, and a more enabling understanding of their culture under colonial management, than such a model of critical analysis can ever afford.[31] Colonial discourse analysis, despite its compelling recognition that colonial discourses circulate around both colonizing and colonized subjectivities, cannot substan-

---

[31] Zakia Pathak, Saswsati Sengupta, and Sharmila Purkayastha, 'The Prisonhouse of Orientalism', *Textual Practice*, 5/2 (June 1991), 195–218.

tially address the question of what a lived historical reality under colonialism might look like for non-European subjects, and the challenge remains for post-colonial critical theory to attempt to navigate between the Scylla of Eurocentric self-critique at the expense of a history of others, and the Charybdis of nativist historical recuperation at the expense of a theory of representation.

There are a number of remarkably promising responses to this challenge in theory, but the approach I want to conclude with is one taken by Homi K. Bhabha in an article entitled 'In a Spirit of Calm Violence'. Bhabha's essay addresses one of the most stereotypically charged narratives in British colonialism, the so-called 'Indian Mutiny', and specifically, it focuses on British historical descriptions of how, at a moment of political panic before the sepoy rebellion began, Indian people 'from village to village' and from hand to hand, 'passed a mysterious token', a chapatti.[32] What interests Bhabha about this historical collective act of chapatti-passing is that it is simply not clear in the documents what self-knowledge and purpose—what social and historical agency—such an act posits for the colonial subjects who participated in it. The British seemed to believe that most of the participants understood the message of the chapatti to be 'a signal of warning and preparation'—this is the form of 'Orientalism' that claims the capacity to know the colonial Other, and the thesis of historical agency that individual subjects act with genuine self-knowledge and will. But the British also thought that some of the participants in the collective act of chapatti-passing acted out of 'common superstition', and that others participated 'in the belief that it would carry off . . . disease', and that others yet passed on the chapattis despite their horrified suspicions that the British had infiltrated 'bone dust' into the chapattis as a way of violating Indian religious protocols and thus producing defiled colonial subjects more capable of being Christianized (p. 333). Clearly, Bhabha argues, a single, individualized notion of historical agency for either the British colonizers or the chapatti-passing colonized will not account for this collective and mystifying historical act.

Bhabha at once recognizes that the panic associated with the act of chapatti-passing, though projected squarely onto 'native custom and ethnic particularity' by the British, had as much to do with panic among the British bureaucrats in 1857 as it did among the Indian peasants (p. 335). This means that the historical agency behind the act of chapatti-passing cannot purely be thought of as simple subaltern agency, even if a collective one—the episode of chapatti-passing must be seen to have

---

[32] Homi K. Bhabha, 'In a Spirit of Calm Violence', in Gyan Prakash (ed.), *After Colonialism: Imperial and Post-colonial Displacements* (Princeton: Princeton University Press, 1995), 333.

taken place within 'too much meaning and a certain meaninglessness' (p. 334). Whatever it is that produces this specific historical act, it cannot be conceptualized as any kind of a single motor. Having broadened the field of historical agency to include a remarkably wide range of disunified participants, conceptualized spatially—various forms of self-knowledge, kinship patterns, superstitions, various kinds of panics on the part of both British and Indian peoples—Bhabha then effects a form of theoretical 'strong reading' on Foucault himself by pointing out that, in addition to all these spatial displacements of historical agency, a Foucauldian position also requires that one takes seriously the claim that historical moments are also temporally contingent: a point Foucault himself makes but then 'massively' forgets (p. 327). This means for Bhabha that a theory of historical agency behind this act of chapatti-passing needs to be relocated into a 'space for a new discursive temporality' (p. 327)—a space that includes subsequent meditations and panics on the part of colonized and colonizing peoples from every location, and that also includes the scholarly reconstructions of contemporary theorists and historians. It is this space, Bhabha argues—temporally discontinuous and spatially disunified—that provides a place for the contemporary theorist or historian to begin to formulate a critical understanding of the disparate and differential social processes 'by which marginalized or insurgent subjects create a collective agency' under colonial relations.

This specific manoeuvre of Bhabha's represents a specific historical enactment of his general critical project, which he elsewhere describes as an attempt to pose the question of 'solidarity and community from the interstitial perspective' of post-colonialism itself.[33] Bhabha attempts to shift our theoretical concern away from the monolithic building blocks of culture—nation, race, class, colonizer, colonized— towards a reading of the 'in-between' spaces, the spaces in excess of the sum of the parts of social and cultural differences (p. 2). In doing so he can be seen to be aligning his critical method with the demand now being made by all kinds of 'in-between' groups in the contemporary post-colonial world— diasporic and minority communities, migrant individuals and groups, aboriginal communities, disidentified social collectivities of all descriptions—that social and critical theory must discover new and articulate ways to come to terms with their experiences, past and present, that it must do so in a way that avoids appropriating those experiences into someone else's story, and that it must learn how to articulate a politics of cultural, or racial, or religious, or sexual differences without simply celebrating plurality at the expense of a cognizant description of social power and the differences it makes.

---

[33] Homi K. Bhabha, *The Location of Culture* (London: Routledge, 1994), 3.

Few critical practices can actually accomplish what contemporary circumstances rightfully require, although they certainly need to try. As post-colonial theories attempt to come to terms with the massive complexifications of what Cornell West calls 'the new cultural politics of difference',[34] they too become massively complexified, both in argument and in critical language. This complexification itself is the object of perhaps the most vociferous debate going on within the field. At their best, post-colonial theoretical complexities constitute exacting intellectual responses to heartfelt social demands. At their worst, they respond to the dismayingly insular and rarefied protocols of academic critical language itself. It is at least one measure of the precarious conditionality of post-colonial theory at this present moment that these necessary theoretical complexifications take place at a time when university-based scholarship slips further and further away from the notion of public intellectual engagement, and when more and more of those social citizens outside the university find themselves desperate for participation in social and public debate. The intellectual challenge for post-colonial critical theory is to attempt to come to know the story of colonial and neo-colonial engagements in all their complexity, and to find ways to represent those engagements in a language that can build cross-disciplinary, cross-community, cross-cultural alliances for the historical production of genuine social change. This is how I read Eduardo Galeano's message about the poet of the conquest, who seeks out history in the stones in the river, who teaches history in the smell of the wind.

[34] Cornell West, *Keeping Faith: Philosophy and Race in America* (New York: Routledge, 1993), 3–32.

PART V

# BRANCHES, SITUATIONS, AND DIFFERENCES

# CHAPTER ELEVEN

# Exiles and Expatriates

CHELVA KANAGANAYAKAM

In the half-life, half-light of alien tongues,
In the uncanny fluency of the other's tongues
We relive the past in rituals of revival
Unravelling memories in slow time; gathering the present.
                    (Abena P. A. Busia, 'Migrations')

In an article entitled 'Night on the Parapet,' written soon after the
publication of his memoirs, Roy Heath speaks candidly about the effect
of his exile in England on his sensibility, and the reasons for his decision
to confine his fiction to Guyana, a country he left almost forty years ago.[1]
England for him is an unwelcoming society, and he chooses to return the
compliment by excluding it from his fiction. In fact his memoirs, titled
*Shadows round the Moon*, end with his departure from Guyana in 1951,
at the age of 24. He adds in his essay that if he were to write the second
volume of his memoirs, it would not be a labour of love, presumably
because it would deal with his life in England. In many ways Heath's
work serves as a paradigm for the literature of exile in its thematic
preoccupations and its propensity to place remembered realities above
immediate, referential ones. It jettisons even the lives of the migrant
community for an ethos whose everyday concerns are relatively distant
from the author's life. That he and dozens of other post-colonial writers
continue to write about the land they left rather the one in which they
live problematizes the experience of exile and creates the distinctive
texture of this corpus.

   Some years ago, Andrew Gurr wrote *Writers in Exile*, a work that
looks at the literature of marginalization in modern literature, in which
he deals with a wide spectrum of writers, with particular emphasis on
James Joyce, Ngugi wa Thiong'o, V. S. Naipaul, and Katherine Mansfield. The theoretical assumptions that underpin his argument are at once
the strength and weakness of the work. Says Gurr: 'An artist born in a

---

[1] Roy Heath, 'Night Rain on the Parapet', *Guardian*, 17 May 1990, p. 21.

colony is made conscious of the culturally subservient status of his home and is forced to go into exile in the metropolis as a means of compensating for that sense of cultural subservience.' And having moved into exile, the preoccupation of the writer is to create a fictive version of home, one which entails a return to childhood and a concern with stasis: 'the exile is still more deliberately concerned to identify or even create a stasis, because home is a static concept rooted in the unalterable circumstances of childhood'.[2] These assertions, despite their validity in certain writers, raise more questions than they answer, but Gurr is in fact right in pointing to dualities that characterize expatriate writing.

Gurr's argument is based on a straightforward binary, with the metropolis being identified as the centre of power and artistic refinement and the margin or colony as a somewhat philistine environment. The exile, in this scheme, is the outsider, who must achieve solitude and distance in order to write. Such a frame permits a cohesive stance for the book, and is, in some cases, accurate in its description, even if Ngugi is clearly a difficult writer to fit into the category. The reality, however, is that the phenomenon of exile and expatriation, particularly for post-colonial writers, is a lot more complex. Even fundamental definitions of exile, expatriate, refugee, and immigrant have now become increasingly problematic. How, for instance, does one classify David Malouf, who divides his time between Australia and Italy? For writers like him, as Aamer Hussein points out, 'the term *expatriate* is notional or nonsensical in its literal sense for much of the year'.[3] Or Vikram Seth who lived in England and the United States and has now made India his home? Dennis Brutus and Satendra Nandan, on the other hand, are political exiles who cannot live in South Africa and Fiji respectively. And that is probably true of Salman Rushdie, whose situation is even more complex. How does one describe Zulfikar Ghose, who grew up in Bombay and left India after the partition, unable to live in what he perceived to be an increasingly hostile environment, and who must now, with a British passport and permanent residence in the States, call himself an Indo-Pakistani? Archie Weller's collection of short stories entitled *Going Home* is about the identity of home in an oppressive climate, and is very much the work of an outsider although it would not fit into the traditional taxonomy of exile or expatriate literature.

One cannot gloss over or underestimate the differences among exile, expatriate, and refugee although convenience dictates that they be seen together as one corpus. The sensibility that informs these conditions

[2] Andrew Gurr, *Writers in Exile: The Identity of Home in Modern Literature* (Brighton: Harvester Press, 1981) 8, 23–4.

[3] Aamer Hussein, 'The Echoing of Quiet Voices', in Mimi Chan and Roy Harris (eds.), *Asian Voices in English* (Hong Kong: Hong Kong University Press, 1991), 105.

results in very different thematic preoccupations. About expatriation Hussein comments: 'it implies neither a forced eviction from one's motherland, nor a deliberate rejection; there are no connotations of permanent or obligatory leavetaking. There is, instead, a tremendous inherent privilege in the term, a mobility of mind if not always of matter, to which we as writers should lay claim: a doubling instead of a split.'[4] In an essay entitled 'Homing in on the Pigeon', Nuruddin Farah speaks specifically about the politics of the refugee experience and its effect on writing. For the refugee the notion of home brings to mind disintegration rather than nostalgia. As he puts it, 'one sees more refugees fleeing as empires disintegrate, as more and more of these empires kill the idea that had been their country, the hypothesis that had been their home'.[5] In practice, however, the distinction is difficult to maintain, and the argument of the present essay is that the literature of marginalization, despite its multiplicity, defines a space that can be distinguished from the literature of 'stay at home' (Gurr's phrase) writers.

Texts that deal with the pain of having to live on the fringes of another society are in some ways easier to classify and group. Moyez Vassanji's *No New Land*, Sam Selvon's *Moses Ascending*, Timothy Mo's *Sour Sweet*, Zulfikar Ghose's early poetry, Hanif Kureishi's *The Buddha of Suburbia*, V. S. Naipaul's *The Enigma of Arrival*, to name a few, present fewer theoretical problems, although the works in themselves may be remarkably complex. The consciousness that informs such texts is predominantly one of alienation. As Arnold Itwaru puts it: 'To be in exile is considerably more than being in another country. It is to live with myself knowing my estrangement. It is to know that I do not belong here.'[6] Granted the obvious differences between the Toronto of Vassanji and the London of Mo, the issues explored in the two novels are strikingly similar. The texts recall Busia's lament of being 'stranded on the shores of saxon seas'.[7] They are often concerned with the outer reaches of the immigrant experience, the point at which it intersects with the larger community and causes discrimination and cultural conflict. More problematic are those that dwell on the past in ways that compel an inquiry into the space of exile.

Naipaul's *The Enigma of Arrival* is a good place to begin a discussion, for the novel is at once a tribute to the land he has adopted and a moving statement about the land which he cannot call home. On the one hand, the celebratory tone reinforces Gurr's notion of superiority associated

[4] Ibid. 102.

[5] Nuruddin Farah, 'Homing in on the Pigeon', *Brick*, 48 (Spring 1994), 7.

[6] Arnold Itwaru, 'Exile and Commemoration', in Frank Birbalsingh (ed.), *Indenture and Exile: The Indo-Caribbean Experience* (Toronto: *Toronto South Asia Review*, 1989), 202.

[7] Abena P. A. Busia, *Testimonies of Exile* (Trenton, NJ: Africa World Press, 1990), 5.

with the metropolis. It parallels, for example, Patrick White's sense of alienation in Greece, about which he writes eloquently: 'even the most genuine Hellenophile accepts automatically the vaguely comic role of Levantine beachcomber. He does not belong, the natives seem to say, not without affection; it is sad for him, but he is nothing.'[8] But more to the point is the final section of the novel that deals with the death of the author's sister Sati, with the loss of tradition, the visit to the cemetery, and with the pathetic mimicry of a dimly remembered tradition that stresses the rootlessness of a whole community. Naipaul does not write with the conviction of an Edward Brathwaite or Derek Walcott. For him, the Caribbean continues to be a place that denies him a sense of identity. The entire section could hardly have been written by an insider. The sense of disillusionment that underpins the section is in fact the consciousness of exile. The novel mediates between a sense of tradition linked with the English countryside and the decadence and rootlessness of Trinidad society. The pervasive sense of death is a reflection of the author's own crisis at being denied a central and nurturing tradition. About this dichotomy Meira Chand has said: 'Tradition nurtures, it offers the consistency of a bloodline, a springboard for evolution, growth and experimentation . . . The expatriate writer has forsaken all this. He has been cut off from his own tradition and culture, from osmosis and introspection, and from his own context within it. How he deals with this trauma, this crisis of identity, is perhaps the greatest problem confronting him in his situation.'[9] Naipaul's characteristic attitude is one of denunciation and satire, which contrasts with the deep-seated empathy of other authors.

In marked contrast to this sense of deracination is the work of Roy Heath, whose realism and graphic sense of the life of Guyana produce a very different sense of locale and texture. His vision is the opposite of Naipaul. He sees myths, customs, and rituals that are peculiar to the Caribbean and the landscape of Guyana. It is possible to argue that his writing negates the experience of exile, since he hardly ever goes beyond the boundaries of Guyana. And yet his writing is a blend of realism, myth, and fantasy, all combined in a manner that, for the most part, preserves the illusion of referentiality. His protagonists are often outsiders, on the fringes of society, straddling a world of reality and fantasy. Thus in *Kwaku*, the movement of Kwaku from C Village to New Amsterdam is in fact a transition from a sense of community to one of dislocation and marginalization. The subversion of mimesis alerts the reader to the consciousness of exile that frames the work.

[8] Patrick White, *Patrick White Speaks* (London: Jonathan Cape, 1990), 14.
[9] Meira Chand, 'The Experience of Writing in an Expatriate Situation', in Chan and Harris, *Asian Voices in English*, 51.

Heath preserves a strong sense of realism, but the realism is of a particular kind, one that oscillates between fact and fantasy. The factual creates the referential surface while the fantasy explores the hidden depths of exile. He insists, however, that his consciousness was formed in Guyana and that becomes the source of all his writing. The implicit nostalgia that permeates his writing confirms Gurr's argument about the incessant sense of loss and the desire for a version of home. Heath's work can hardly be exhausted at that level, but it is important to remember that having lived in Guyana and left at a particular stage in that country's history gives his writing a particular perspective. His Guyana is neither referential nor static; it celebrates without naïve romanticization, and it asserts the centrality of a culture while projecting the life of the marginalized. Politics is never absent from his writing, but the political upheavals of post-colonial Guyana are not his major concern. Between Naipaul and Heath, both resident in Britain, there are major differences and these indicate the complexity of expatriation and exile. Strangely enough, Wilson Harris, another writer from Guyana, writes with a very different focus and employs a distinctly experimental narrative mode. A lot more 'difficult' than Heath, Harris dislocates the premises of realism as he charts, for instance in *The Palace of the Peacock*, a mythic journey into the hinterland, in search of Mariella, who is both a woman and a place. For him the novel of consolidation—the referential work created in the manner of the nineteenth-century British novel—is hardly adequate to express his vision. In fact he comments in his critical writing that the foregrounding of realism, which has been the concern of his contemporaries, is inherently flawed. A strong sense of social ethos is less his concern than a need to deconstruct a complex history in order to forge a sense of identity. In *The Palace of the Peacock*, the contemporary situation of Guyana is less a concern than the layers of conquest, guilt, and complicity that make up the fabric of the country. His mode, to use David Lodge's term, is a metaphoric one, in which the realism gives way to a more allusive, associative process of suggestive resonance. Thus even descriptive passages take on a significance that can only be understood in relation to a complex and often harsh history.

That Harris and Heath, both contemporaries from the same country, write in two very different ways serves to complicate rather than resolve the issue of expatriate writing. Different as they are, they both occupy that cusp created by the intersection of two cultures, which one identifies as the space of exile. The notion of occupying a cusp is central to expatriate writing which, curiously enough, establishes its own centrality while locating itself on the margins of two cultures. For the most part it disregards its own migrant community, which might have been its logical choice, to assert its autonomy from and its dependence on the cultures of 'home' and 'exile'.

The realities of home are a concern for all post-colonial writers, but the idea of home is of particular concern to exiles and expatriates. Such binary formulations that deconstruct 'home' are not always easy to defend, but they are in fact useful in establishing tentative boundaries for exilic writing. For writers who have not chosen to leave, the epistemology of home is hardly ever problematic. Social and political conditions are of immediate concern, and they write about them with anger, cynicism, indignation, or love. For Catherine Lim, the idea of Singapore is not problematic, although the country could well be a source of numerous contradictions. Her ironies are directed at what she sees as inconsistencies in the social fabric. This would be equally true of, say, R. K. Narayan, who speaks of his Malgudi with hardly any ontological uncertainty. The decision not to leave does not make the perspective of a writer stronger or weaker, but it certainly makes it different.

The exception to this relation between author and place would be those who feel a sense of persecution in their own countries and who consider themselves to be exiles despite their decision not to leave the country. Jean Arasanayagam from Sri Lanka, for instance, would be a case in point, whose status as a Burgher and whose marriage to a Tamil have consistently caused a sense of alienation. She speaks repeatedly of the predicament of exile. The same could be said of, say, Maori writers in New Zealand or Aboriginal writers in Australia. Here again, the experience is one of injustice, of oppression rather than homelessness. Hence the main thrust of such work is on social and political circumstances that result in discrimination and alienation. Interestingly, another Burgher, Michael Ondaatje, who left Sri Lanka several years ago, writes very differently and serves as a useful point of comparison with Jean Arasanayagam. The politics of the country hardly ever concerns him deeply, which is understandable given the number of years that he has been away. But home is an insistent presence, as he demonstrates very clearly in his one work that deals entirely with Sri Lanka, namely *Running in the Family*. Particularly when the conscious mind loses control, and the delicate balance (symbolized by balancing a glass of wine on his forehead) fails, then home becomes a compulsion. And he writes about home with nostalgia, with longing, and with a historical consciousness. *Running in the Family* has met with a mixed reception, and understandably so, for it combines brilliant prose and a well-crafted collage with accounts that are close to essentialist pronouncements. The perspective de-emphasizes immediate political and social realities for one that is both more personal and historical. The perspective is not that of an outsider, not that of Forster's *A Passage to India*, but something more intimate and yet distanced.

Ondaatje is enigmatic in more ways than one, for all his other works avoid direct reference to Sri Lanka. And yet it could be argued that he never really stops writing about the country or his own predicament as an expatriate writer. *The Skin of a Lion* and *The English Patient* are about outsiders, about those for whom identity is elusive and home remains a site of conflict and uncertainty. Here again one encounters the concern with allegory in those who seek to establish a niche that transcends marginalization.

When the circumstances that occasion exile are political, the literature is immediately recognizable in its subject matter. Dennis Brutus focuses almost entirely on the repressive politics of South Africa in *A Simple Lust*. Curiously enough, such literature is often not very different from literature produced by local writers, particularly after a change in the government or in defiance of censorship. A strong sense of referentiality pervades the work of political exiles. Thus Satendra Nandan's *The Wounded Sea* is an impassioned statement about the coup in Fiji that not only ousted a legally constituted government but also threw into uncertainty the future of the large number of Indians in the country. Combined with a genuine love for the country and the way of life it symbolized is an unmistakable indignation, a sense of outrage. Such works are often subject to censorship within and are more typically the work of exiled authors. Theirs is the literature of resistance, with a clearly identifiable political agenda.

For those who left voluntarily, but with a sense of dissatisfaction—the expatriates—the writing is often more difficult to define. They remain outsiders, for the conditions that alienated them do not always change, and their memory creates images that are divorced from immediate realities, thus creating a more fluid space. And it leads to a very different kind of writing. The opposites are best seen, for instance, in the work of Salman Rushdie and Vikram Seth, both successful and very accomplished but also very different. When *Midnight's Children* came out in 1981, it seemed all but impossible for subsequent writers to go back to the referential mode of Mulk Raj Anand, Kamala Markandaya and Khushwant Singh. And yet, ten years later, Seth writes a decidedly referential work, traditional in its linearity, unpretentious in its subject matter, and conventional in its prose. It is a work that grows out of the sensibility of an insider. While Rushdie's work is concerned with history, historiography, and the collapse of identity, Seth's concern in *A Suitable Boy* is with consolidation of family, community, and the nation.

Rushdie's *Midnight's Children* and *Shame* are intermittently realistic, but predominantly counter-realistic in their mode. Particularly in the latter, the narrator speaks about the novel that could have been written from a different perspective. When the narrator of *Shame* claims that realism can break a writer's heart, he or she is in fact speaking about a particular kind of writer. Seth is comfortable in his realism, whereas Rushdie could not have been. The metafictional comments in his works are a constant reminder of the problems faced by the writer who would rather not look in the direction of home but who cannot turn his gaze away either. As Arnold Itwaru rightly maintains: 'But this sense of estrangement goes further. It touches upon the very notion of home, the lands and places of our birth. For that land, there, that region, lives in us as memory and dream, as nostalgia, romance of reflection, that which defines us as different, that to which we *think* we belong but no longer do.'[10]

It is thus not surprising that Rushdie's work, and quite often the work of exiled writers, is not realistic. The premisses of realism, which have to do with consolidation or metonymy, are inadequate to express the voice of the periphery, of a vision shaped by two ontologies. Hence the counter-realism, the fantasy, and the magic realism to straddle the worlds of the referential and the speculative. Rushdie's *Shame* is about the politics of Pakistan, but it is also about religion, and history and gender and colonialism. They form a peculiar mosaic that needs to be captured in a particular form. In fact the pages of realism that are woven into the novel constitute a salutary reminder of what the novel could have become had it been written differently.

Such generalizations are sometimes negated by exilic literature. Rohinton Mistry's *Such a Long Journey* is the notable but somewhat uneven work of an expatriate writer. Decidedly a referential work, the novel deals with the Parsi community in Bombay, and their struggle to maintain a sense of identity in a predominantly Hindu environment. Its careful sense of realism is hardly different from, say, that of Mulk Raj Anand. What makes it an unusual novel, however, is its sense of liminality, its depiction of the pressure among the marginalized to succeed, the constant sense of being beleaguered, and the sense of the tragic. Since works about the Parsis are relatively few, comparisons are limited. But if one were to see this work against Bapsi Sidhwa's *The Crow Eaters*, the differences would be obvious. *The Crow Eaters* comes across more as the work of an insider, and the texture and tone of the work hardly stress liminality. Mistry foregrounds the sense of periphery, but attempts to create the illusion of an insider novel.

The exilic literature of Zulfikar Ghose, although distinctly unlike that of Heath, is in many ways equally paradigmatic. Having lost a sense of national identity after the partition, he left India, and his fiction, which

[10]   Itwaru, 'Exile', 203.

often deals with locales totally unconnected with India, is still about the home he left. But it does not impose a stasis, a sense of order on what is perceived to be chaotic. In fact when such an attempt is made, as in *The Murder of Aziz Khan*, the impact is much smaller than that of his subsequent works. Realism, particularly of a tendentious kind, is not his objective. As he comments in *The Art of Writing Fiction*: 'A group of novels by South African writers, for example, makes for a semester's package tour of racial guilt, moral outrage and historical enlightenment, and the eager economy class students, who are more anxious about their grades than about their culture, don't even realise that the ride they're being taken on has nothing to do with literature.'[11] Interestingly, the politics of a country which caused the author's own displacement does not figure prominently in his writing.

In a significant essay entitled 'Going Home', Ghose speaks about the complexities of perception that surround the experience of exile. Having visited a museum in Peshawar—one is reminded that Peshawar was once the capital of the Kanishka kingdom—the writer adds:

At the Peshawar Museum I was struck by the power of the incomplete statue of the fasting Buddha to fix the itinerant self in a timeless and bodiless space. The missing parts of the statue appear to have a vital presence: the starved, absent organs—shrunk, withered, annihilated—throb bloodily in the imagination; that which is not there startles the mind with the certainty of its being; it is an image of amazing contradictions, and illustrates the essential ambiguity of all perception: reality can be composed of absent things, the unseen blazes in our minds with a shocking vividness.[12]

Given the circumstances of Ghose's displacement, and the arbitrary political decisions that shape national identities, it is hardly surprising that the author's mind focuses on the idea of palimpsest, on the layers of history and the processes of historiography rather than the actual social and political conditions. The two are not mutually exclusive, but the exile or expatriate is often distanced spatially and temporally, and that changes authorial perspective. Fixity, for the exile, is hardly ever possible. It is important to note that Ghose's novel *The Triple Mirror of the Self*, which, after three decades of writing, goes back to India, does so in a manner that is counter-realistic, tentative, and allegorical. The insistent presence of magic realism in the novel is a reminder of how the novel that insists on realism is less convincing as a statement about the predicament of exile than one which parades its experiment.

The complexity of exile is the concern of Michelle Cliff's novel *No Telephone to Heaven*, whose title encapsulates the sense of ontological

---

[11] Zulfikar Ghose, *The Art of Creating Fiction* (London: Macmillan, 1991), 58–9.
[12] Zulfikar Ghose, 'Going Home', *Toronto South Asian Review*, 9/2 (1991), 15.

uncertainty that accompanies expatriation. It is significant that the novel begins and ends with the notion of camouflage, for this idea includes the oppressor and oppressed and accommodates a wide spectrum of meanings. The novel begins with a visual sense of camouflage, and as it progresses it becomes increasingly clear that the trope is hardly simple. From getting by in an alien culture to ambushing foreign industrialists in one's own country, camouflage becomes a central strategy of subversion, escape, and attack. In fact it becomes a reality in itself. Ghose's short story entitled 'Arrival in India' is also about camouflage, about that particularly deceptive quality that makes immigrant writing about a sensibility rather than a place. Both referential and allegorical, the story, set in eleventh-century Spain, traces the journey of a young man called Jose Abbado Mejid, who flees the country to avoid religious persecution. Not until his arrival in India does he reveal that his real name is Yusuf Abdul Majeed. No sooner does he proclaim his Muslim identity than he is confronted by three hostile Hindus, and suppressing his impulse to shout 'India' he yells 'Hindustan'. The richly textured story is a reminder of the perspective of immigrant writing. To miss this is also to miss the centrality of this genre.

The writer as social critic is nothing unusual. What distinguishes the exile is the questioning of fundamental assumptions that concern ontology, of time-honoured traditions. The dilemma of being bound to the world-view that one is born into but also being able to transcend its constraints is the perspective afforded by the cusp of exile. And that could involve the political, the social or the personal and sexual. Hence the particular force of one of the most unusual of contemporary writers, namely, Suniti Namjoshi. Her own statements attest to the Indianness of her world, one which shapes so much of her writing. Her *Conversations of Cow*, for instance, is decidedly Indian, with the cow Bhadravati, a curious amalgam of Parvati and Pathini, very much tying into the sexual politics of the work. A lesbian cow who is also sometimes Baddy and at others an anonymous B, being in love with Suniti and exploring the multiple identities that she is forced to adopt or live with is a fundamental statement about gender and patriarchy. It is not surprising that Diane McGifford, writing about Namjoshi, finds her work too individualistic to be conveniently lumped together with the rest of the Indian diaspora. Says McGifford: 'Again the themes one tends to associate with the writings of the diaspora—a sense of cultural and social isolation and alienation, the shock and violence of racism, yearnings for the homeland, the difference between expectation and reality—are absent.'[13]

---

[13] Diane McGifford, 'Suniti Namjoshi', in Emmanuel S. Nelson (ed.), *Writers of the Indian Diaspora: A Bio-bibliographical Critical Sourcebook* (Westport, Conn.: Greenwood Press, 1993), 293.

However, Namjoshi's world is clearly about the cusp—neither West nor East. As she says:

> In the West I burn;
> here,
> when my wings give out
> I cannot breathe.[14]

Her entire corpus—except perhaps her early work that deals with the death of her father—is an attack on what she calls the 'Principle of Corroborative Reality', which strengthens and upholds a male-centred consciousness. In more straightforward terms, she wonders: 'as a creature, a lesbian creature, how do I deal with all the other creatures who have their own identities, or perhaps I mean their own identifications'?[15]

Interestingly enough, her reference to India, or to other referential realities, is minimal. Her sense of the ironic finds its mode in the fabulist, as birds, animals, witches, and goddesses populate her world. Her mode is anecdotal, minimalist, and often open-ended. Nourished and oppressed by two traditions, she finds herself unable to participate in the conflict between centre and margin, between colonizer and colonized. In fact, one of her principal strategies is to avoid the creation of a character within a recognizable ethos, for to do so would be to recapitulate the paradigms of patriarchy. The conflict as well as the dilemma comes across in her poems:

> And there is only a man-made language
> with its logic
> of need and greed,
> doom, dearth, despair.
> But in spite of a hurtful history
> Shall we speak of a hurtful history
> Where women may walk freely
> in the still, breathable air?[16]

Her form suggests her quest for new meaning. Science fiction, fantasy, magic realism, fable, and mimesis merge to form curious combinations in her work. At times her work is all but inaccessible, and she is aware of the dangers of mixing modes and genres. Speaking about mathematics, she claims that 'jumping systems is disastrous. You get absurd results, because the axioms are different. In literature, on the other hand, some of the best results are obtained by using several systems simultaneously, though you have to be very clear about what you are doing.'[17] It is significant that she is acutely aware of the particular configuration of gender relations in India. She claims that caste, class, and family work in

---

[14] Suniti Namjoshi, *Because of India* (London: Onlywomen Press, 1989), 118.
[15] Ibid. 84.    [16] Ibid. 123.    [17] Ibid. 104.

unison to oppress women in the country. And yet her work eschews the social and cultural dimension in favour of less determinate worlds. Her concern is inclusive, but her project gives the impression of being personal.

In marked contrast to Namjoshi is Dambudzo Marechera, whose concern is less with the personal than with the public and the political. Very much an expatriate and exile, the Zimbabwe he left was distressingly colonial, and the one he returned to repressive and neo-colonial. He writes about a wide range of subjects, but his focus, in one form or another, is the nation. Even the most intensely personal is transformed into the public and merges with the national. And that creates an interesting scenario, for some of the major works published in recent years in Zimbabwe have been concerned with the political and the national. Stanley Samkange, Wilson Katiyo, Stanley Nyamfukudza and Shimmer Chinodya, for instance, have all dealt with nationalist concerns. Even a work like *Nervous Conditions*, despite its preoccupation with issues of gender, is equally concerned with colonialism.

At its most obvious, Marechera's work is fragmented, discontinuous, contradictory, and experimental. And he jealously guards his artistic freedom by calling himself the *doppelgänger* that African writing had not encountered. Rather than be identified within narrow boundaries, he claims a universalist stance and insists that either one is a writer or one is not. Such disclaimers notwithstanding, he remains very much a writer obsessively concerned with the nation. His theme is 'nationism' (to use Satendra Nandan's term) rather than nationalism. The uncritical celebration of a nationalist ideology that one encounters in Samkange is hardly ever present in Marechera. His concern is with the manner in which the nation as an entity has been created. In short his process is one of active deconstruction of nationalist and essentialist myths, as in the beginning of *Black Sunlight*, where the confrontation between the black chief and the white anthropologist begins to take on binary configurations. The historical, political, mythical, and sexual clash as a fragmented but accurate sense of the nation begins to emerge. Even the syntax echoes this struggle as fragments struggle to emerge as complete sentences. His stance, despite all the multiplicity of his work, is not ambivalent. But he sees the birth pangs of Zimbabwe as a series of narratives rather than as one overarching one. Seemingly minor, disconnected episodes project the nation as it is perceived by different consciousnesses, and in the process a more composite picture begins to emerge.

Marechera's situation is a curious one in that in the last years of his short life he actually lived in the country that spurned him. And yet he remained very much a homeless outsider, typing out his work in parks and temporary shelters. Shaped and guided by a consciousness that was very much his own, his nationism was at odds with the prevailing nationalism. The space he inhabits is enigmatic, often problematic, but it remains the authentic voice of exile.

To be an expatriate or an exile is not to inhabit a void. It is not, as Gurr maintains, to choose the artistic freedom and anonymity afforded by the metropolis. It is, rather, to be granted a special insight, a vision not available to the insider. What Farah has to say about the refugee is equally true of the whole corpus of exiles and their works: 'Indeed, somewhere between fleeing and arriving, a refugee is born, who lives in a country too amorphous to be favoured with a name but which, for the sake of convenience, we may label as one delivered out of the womb of sublime hope, a country whose language is imbued with the rhetoric of future visions.'[18]

[18] Farah, 'Homing in on the Pigeon', 5.

# CHAPTER TWELVE

# Diasporas and Multiculturalism

## VICTOR J. RAMRAJ

In international English literature (or specifically that component of it with Commonwealth origins), there are two bodies of writing that could be designated as diasporic. The first comes from the descendants of peoples uprooted from their homelands in the eighteenth and nineteenth centuries and transported from one region of the globe to another to serve British economic needs: Africans as slaves to the West Indies, and Indians, Chinese, and Portuguese as indentured labourers to such corners of the Empire as the West Indies, Fiji, and Mauritius. The second is by those from English-speaking regions of the Indian subcontinent, Asia, Africa, and the diasporic communities of the West Indies and Fiji, who for economic, political, cultural, and familial or personal reasons left their homelands for London, England, which many, as citizens of the Empire, considered their capital, and for North America and Australia, continents that long had provided living space for peoples from over-crowded Europe; since the 1980s, the second generation of immigrants in Britain has added a new dimension to this second constituent of diasporic writing. Yet another dimension is to be found in the works of individuals like Jean Rhys, born of Welsh parents in Dominica, who spent her childhood in the West Indies, to which (like Phyllis Shand Allfrey) she remained imaginatively attached after she returned to Europe at the age of 17.

In contemporary literature, the term diasporic writing has come to be associated with works produced by globally dispersed minority communities that have common ancestral homelands. Their relationship with the homeland does not necessarily involve, as in the original Jewish conception of the term, commitment to 'the maintenance or restoration of their homeland', which is 'their true ideal home . . . the place to which they or their descendants would (or should) eventually return'.[1] Stuart Hall underscores this point in his study of the Afro-Caribbean diaspora: 'diaspora does not refer us to those scattered tribes whose identity can

---

[1] William Safran, 'Diasporas in Modern Societies: Myth of Homeland and Return', *Diaspora: A Journal of Transnational Studies*, 1 (1991), 84.

only be secured in relation to some sacred homeland to which they must at all costs return.'[2]

V. S. Naipaul tells of his father hiding from his parents at the docks in Trinidad, not wanting to return to India on a repatriation ship; he hid until 'his mother changed her mind about the trip back to India'.[3] In *A House for Mr Biswas*, the narrator mentions some old Indians (brought to the West Indies with the promise of repatriation at the end of their indenture) who chatted nostalgically about returning to India but like Naipaul's father and grandfather would not avail themselves of the opportunity to do so. As Naipaul observes in *An Area of Darkness*, they knew that for them their journey to Trinidad 'had been final'.[4] Historical documents support Naipaul's observation. In *A History of Indians in Guyana*, Dwarka Nath shows that many Indians chose grants of land in Guyana in lieu of their rights to return passages. As early as 1843, of 396 who landed in Guyana, 236 returned home; while 62 remained in Guyana (98 died during the five-year indenture, 1838–43). By 1957, when the Indian population in Guyana was 250,000, chartering ships to repatriate Guyanese Indians was discontinued because of the negligible number of repatriation rights claimants.

Yet though diasporans may not want actually to return home, wherever the dispersal has left them they retain a conscious or subconscious attachment to traditions, customs, values, religions, and languages of the ancestral home. Hall notes that for most diasporans the return to the homeland is metaphorical, existing in what Edward Said perceives as the 'imaginative geography and history' and Benedict Anderson calls the 'imagined community'.[5] Naipaul initially tells us that though as a youth he was ignorant of the rituals and ceremonies of his people, and though he did not understand their language, he felt that he had 'received a certain supporting philosophy'.[6] In *India: A Million Mutinies Now*, he observes that he has succeeded in 'abolishing the darkness that separated [him] from [his] ancestral past'.[7] Hall, referring to the Afro-Caribbean experience, makes a similar observation: for Afro-Caribbeans, Africa 'is the great aporia . . . which lies at the centre of [their] cultural identity and gives it a meaning which, until recently, it lacked'.[8] He suggests that what these Afro-Caribbeans yearn for is not an Africa that belongs to a

[2] Stuart Hall, 'Cultural Identity and Diaspora', in Patrick Williams and Laura Chrisman (eds.), *Colonial Discourse and Post-colonial Theory: A Reader* (New York: Columbia University Press, 1994), 401.

[3] V. S. Naipaul, *Finding the Centre: Two Narratives* (London: André Deutsch, 1984), 62.

[4] V. S. Naipaul, *An Area of Darkness* (London: André Deutsch, 1964), 31.

[5] Anderson quoted by Hall, 'Cultural Identity', 399.

[6] Naipaul, *Area of Darkness*, 35.

[7] V. S. Naipaul, *India: A Million Mutinies Now* (New York: Viking, 1991), 516.

[8] Hall, 'Cultural Identity', 394.

past 'unchanged by four hundred years of displacement, dismemberment, transportation' but one whose meaning is constantly being 'deferred' by 'politics, memory and desire'.[9] This attachment to the homeland appears in accounts of the actual or imaginative journeys to Africa undertaken by Edward Brathwaite, O. R. Dathorne, Claire Harris, M. Nourbese Philip, Walter Rodney, Denis Williams, and many other Afro-Caribbean writers and scholars. The last line of Derek Walcott's 'A Far Cry from Africa' is a declaration of diasporic attachment to Africa—an Africa not temporally or spatially specified: 'How can I turn from Africa and live?'

The common homeland and the common experience of displacement by slavery (in the case of Africans) and by indenture (in the case of Indians) and colonization have established strong ties among the scattered communities. Naipaul makes this point about diasporic communities in *India: A Million Mutinies Now*: cut off from the people they found themselves among and cut off from India itself by distance, diasporic Indians 'developed something they would never have known in India: a sense of belonging to an Indian community'.[10] Though linked by shared homelands and shared history of uprooting, these diasporic communities are not monolithic or homogeneous entities; they are richly diverse communities. Their diversity may originate in the first instance in different attitudes and values prevalent in their homelands and subsequently in the different political and cultural histories of their host societies. Such regions as the Indian subcontinent and Africa, for instance, are vast regions with many different customs, languages, religions, and political entities. The way of life of the Janglee Indians in Sonny Ladoo's *Yesterdays* is different from that of the Indians in V. S. Naipaul's or Sam Selvon's novels. The Indo-Fijians' political, economic, and cultural restrained relationship with the indigenous Fijians differs from the Indo-Trinidadians' easy association with Afro-Trinidadians, with whom they share a diasporic history. And Trinidad with two dominant peoples has developed a cultural, economic, and political identity that sets it apart from, say, Jamaica or Barbados, islands populated predominantly by descendants of Africans.

Diasporic writings are invariably concerned with the individual's or community's attachment to the centrifugal homeland. But this attachment is countered by a yearning for a sense of belonging to the current place of abode. Caught psychically between two worlds, diasporans are, to use Victor Turner's terms, 'transitional-being[s]' or 'liminal *persona[e]*',[11] that is, they are in the process of moving from one cultural state of existence to another. In this state of transition, some respond

---

[9] Hall, 399.   [10] Naipaul, *Million Mutinies*, 7.
[11] Victor Turner, 'Betwixt and Between: The Liminal Period in *Rites de Passage*', in *The Forest of Symbols: Aspects of Ndembu Ritual* (Ithaca, NY: Cornell University Press, 1967), 95.

ambivalently to their dual, often antithetical, cultures or societies. Some attempt to assimilate and integrate. For others the liminal or transitional state is too prolonged or too excruciating to cope with and they may withdraw to their ancestral identity or homeland, which, as Mordecai Richler's protagonist observes of his Montreal Jewish community of the 1960s in *St. Urbain's Horseman*, is both a cage and a haven.

The attachment to the ancestral homeland varies considerably among the diasporans and is inversely proportional to the degree individuals and communities are induced to or are willing to assimilate or integrate with their new environment, or remain wedded to ancestral customs, traditions, languages, and religions. Those tending towards assimilation are less concerned with sustaining ancestral ties than with coming to terms with their new environment and acquiring a new identity. Writers like Bharati Mukherjee expect the assimilation to be mutual. To achieve this mutuality requires, as Homi K. Bhabha indicates in his theoretical study of the modern nation, a 'cultural liminality—*within the nation*', not just in the immigrant community. Referring to the national memory, he says: 'Being obliged to forget becomes the basis for remembering the nation, peopling it anew, imagining the possibility of other contending and liberating forms of cultural identity.'[12]

The conflict between traditionalists and assimilationists in diasporic communities is a recurring theme in diasporic writings. Many of the Indo-Caribbean writers depict rural communities that were able to retain their cultures and traditions in the face of imperial cultural and educational assaults against them. V. S. Naipaul's short story 'A Christmas Story' depicts the conflict between two brothers, one who has become a Christian and is Westernized and the other who remains a Hindu with strong attachment to India and the Hindu way of life. The Hindu brother mocks his Westernized sibling, who experiences tormenting ambivalence towards his adopted religion and his inherited culture. In *A House for Mr Biswas*, while Mr Biswas attempts to adjust to the Creole world in the urban environment of Port of Spain, the Tulsis isolate and insulate themselves in their culturally impregnable home, Hanuman House, known as the White Fortress.

Ismith Khan similarly focuses on the Hindu adaptation to Western life and the conflict between the traditionalists and the assimilationists. In *The Jumbie Bird*, Khan traces in paradigmatic fashion the generational progression of a diasporic Indian family, the Khans, towards accommodating themselves to their new environment. The grandfather, Kale Khan, is culturally alienated in Trinidad and yearns to return to India. His son is in a liminal state: he knows India is not his home but he cannot

[12] Homi K. Bhabha, 'Dissemination: Time Narrative, and the Margins of the Modern Nation', in Homi K. Bhabha (ed.), *Nation and Narration* (London: Routledge, 1990), 299, 311.

claim to be at home in Trinidad. He truly is caught between two worlds, one dead, the other powerless to be born. His grandson accepts Trinidad as his home at the expense of losing his Indian identity. Khan suggests that the grandson's assimilationist approach is perhaps more acceptable than the grandfather's longing for a homeland no longer to be accessed readily; but he cautions against cultural self-loathing of those who unquestioningly adopt the ways of the host society. Selvon's 'Turning Christian' is also about the struggle between the convert to Christianity and the Hindu traditionalist. In this story (which constitutes an early section of Selvon's unfinished novel), two Indian friends fall out because one wants his son to become a Christian. Sonny Ladoo's *Yesterdays* examines (in a scatological, harshly satirical style that contrasts with Selvon's genial comedy) a similar situation of a father sending his son off to a Christian school to improve his prospects in his impoverished village. But when the boy is pressured into converting to Christianity by his Canadian Presbyterian teachers, he is flogged by his father, who wants him to remain a Hindu.

Sudesh Mishra of the Fijian diasporic Indian community also addresses in his poetry the conflicts and tensions diasporans face in connecting with Christianity and Western values. In 'Mt. Abu: St. Xavier's Church', an ambivalent visitor to India (an Indo-Fijian no doubt) with 'many axes to grind' wonders whether he should be concerned that an Anglican church will crumble away if not funded by the rajah. He asks 'What | Perverted sense, what religious romance | Gave rise to this house—while in Calcutta | They sold you, Father, across the water?' The conflict with Christianity evident in Mishra's poem is not a recurring aspect of Indo-Fijian literature; the Indo-Fijians were not as subjected to Christian missionaries as were the Indo-West Indians. Raymond Pillai mentions an Indo-Fijian couple's squabble over Christmas celebration in his story 'The Celebration', but he focuses on the marriage problems of the couple rather than on the cultural conflicts raised in Naipaul's 'A Christmas Story'.

The Indo-Fijian diasporic community has a different socio-cultural history from its Indo-Caribbean counterpart. The primary difference is that while assimilation with the Creole culture was generated in the Caribbean, the Indo-Fijian culture developed apart from the indigenous Fijians, who, as Ahmed Ali notes,[13] reacted to the Indo-Fijian as an interloper and usurper (as indeed was the initial response of the Afro-Caribbeans to the Indian indentured labourers). Yet another difference was that the Indo-Caribbeans looked to London as their cultural centre, to which many travelled to be educated; they consequently were affected

[13] Ahmed Ali, 'Indians in Fiji: An Interpretation', in Subramani (ed.), *The Indo-Fijian Experience* (St Lucia: University of Queensland Press, 1980), 4.

by and found themselves engaged in examining their relationship with the imperial culture. The Indo-Fijians were less tied to the imperial cultural centre and were left more on their own culturally. The Indo-Fijian literary community is much smaller and has a more recent history than that of the Indo-Caribbeans; as Satendra Nandan says as late as 1993, 'Fiji is an unwritten world'.[14] But like their Indo-Caribbean counterparts, Indo-Fijian writers like Nandan, Subramani, and Pillai exhibit a psychic attachment to the motherland India, though they do not necessarily want to return there. And they share a similar displacement and exploitation by imperial forces.

Subramani acknowledges that though the contact with India in recent years is 'mainly through Bombay movies, visiting cultural troupes, and occasional package tours to holy places', he agrees with Ali that India remains 'an important emotion' and 'a symbol of home' for Indo-Fijians.[15] In one of his short stories, Subramani has his young protagonist seek refuge from his brutal, menacing life in the Fijian Indian barracks in a cave symbolically called the 'Kailas' (Home of Shiva). Many of Subramani's early stories are about the brutal lives of the indentured labourers and of the *girmit* man (the term for the indentured contract or agreement).[16] Subramani describes the squalid lives of these labourers in a land where they are set apart from the indigenous inhabitants and their imperial masters. 'Sautu' is a poignant portrayal of the physical and mental deterioration of a lonely *girmit* man. This and other Subramani stories of indenture have an Indo-Caribbean parallel in Sonny Ladoo's *No Pain Like this Body*, one of the few Indo-Caribbean works to focus on the indenture experience, an aspect of the Indian diaspora that so far has preoccupied Indo-Fijian writers more than Indo-Caribbean writers. In his later stories collected in *The Fantasy Eaters*, Subramani focuses on Indo-Fijians who are in a characteristic diasporic liminal state, caught between attachment to their homeland to which they do not belong and their adopted home where they remain marginalized. Many of Pillai's stories in *The Celebration* advocate that the diasporic Indian community should be prepared to modify and adapt their traditions and customs according to modern Western (rather than indigenous Fijian) thoughts and practices.

Allusions to Indian languages and literature recur more in Indo-Fijian than in Indo-Caribbean writing and demonstrate in this regard a stronger tie to India in Fiji than in Trinidad or Guyana. Compared with

[14] Satendra Nandan, 'Return to a Certain Darkness', in Victor J. Ramraj (ed.), *Concert of Voices* (Peterborough: Broadview Press, 1995), 318.
[15] Subramani (ed.), *The Indo-Fijian Experience*, pp. xi, x.
[16] Vijay Mishra, 'Indo-Fijian Fiction and the *Girmit* Ideology', in Subramani (ed.), *The Indo-Fijian Experience*, 171–83; id., 'The Girmit Ideology Revisited: Fiji Indian Literature', in Emmanuel S. Nelson (ed.), *Reworlding* (New York: Greenwood Press, 1992), 1–12.

Indo-Caribbean writings, Indo-Fijian include far more Hindi words and phrases, references to Indian myths, gods and goddesses, and religious rites and rituals. In Nandan's *Voices in the River*, several poems in fact are rendered in Hindi. Perhaps the Caribbean writer who comes closest to these Fijian writers in his allusions to Indian literature and mythology is Sasenarine Persaud, an Indo-Guyanese immigrant in Canada. He contends that Indo-Caribbean writers should not allude to local and metropolitan literatures and mythologies to the exclusion of Indian.

The Fijian coup of 1987 saw the beginnings of another phase of the Indo-Fijian diaspora. In the 1980s, Ali remarked that the indentured labourers had left India to escape a heritage of uncertainty and insecurity, but now in a land where they are marginalized by the indigenous Fijians, the contemporary Indo-Fijians have inherited 'the same legacy . . . that was their fathers' '.[17] Ali's comment aptly conveys the diasporic situation of those who remained in Fiji after the 1987 coup and those like Pillai and Nandan, who fled the islands exiling themselves, Pillai in New Zealand and Nandan in Australia. In his account of his brief visit to Fiji in 1993, Nandan regrets that he no longer is at home in Fiji. He describes the Indo-Fijians still resident there as 'landless . . . countryless . . . the invisible people of Fiji, the outsiders within'.[18]

While V. S. Naipaul, Selvon, Khan, Ladoo, and other Indo-Caribbean writers focus on Hindus adapting to the Creole world around them, many Afro-West Indian writers are concerned with retrieving their African culture, which slavery and colonialism sought to deny them. But the writers approach this attachment differently. Edward Kamau Brathwaite focuses on discovering and resuscitating his African roots. Derek Walcott, of black and white ancestry, emphasizes his in-between state. Initially, he is troubled by ambivalence—'Where shall I turn,' he asks, 'divided to the vein . . . how choose | Between this Africa and the English tongue I love?'[19]—but in his later poems, he responds to the binary opposites as complementary rather than oppositional. Towards the end of his epic poem *Omeros* he recurringly demonstrates the complementarity of opposites through a host of images and allusions. In *Other Leopards*, set in Africa, the Guyanese writer Denis Williams takes yet a different approach: he has his protagonist, who is at home in neither Africa nor Britain, strip himself naked in the wilds, an allegory of his rejecting both his British and African education and culture, neither of which he finds fulfilling, and returning to an elemental state in the hope of making a fresh start. Williams himself, uncomfortable in Europe and

[17] Ali, 'Indians in Fiji: An Interpretation', 24.
[18] Nandan, 'Return', 314.
[19] Derek Walcott, 'A Far Cry from Africa', in *In a Green Night* (London: Jonathan Cape, 1962), 19–20.

Africa, eventually returned to his own 'primordial world', the hinterland of Guyana, where for a period of seven years (1968–74) he wrote and painted, read no books, and tried to free himself of his 'anxieties'.[20] Claire Harris, who left Trinidad for Canada in 1966, accepts Africa as an indelible part of her psyche but she regrets that she will be 'forever oyibo [foreigner]' in Africa. She would like to 'throw her heart across alien centuries | and slavery' but admits sadly: 'I dream in another tongue | I cannot.'[21]

Many of the second generation of immigrant writers, who were born or grew up in Britain, see themselves as belonging to minority communities. They do not consider themselves exiles, like the early immigrants, whose experiences are recorded in such works as Zulfikar Ghose's *The Confessions of a Native Alien*, George Lamming's *The Emigrants* and *The Pleasures of Exile*, Kamala Markandaya's *The Nowhere Man*, V. S. Naipaul's *The Mimic Men*, and Sam Selvon's *The Lonely Londoners* and *Moses Migrating*. They are conscious, however, of the reluctance by many to accommodate their presence in a country that passed the 1971 Immigration Act restricting immigration to Britain. Like other diasporic peoples the intensity of their attachment to their parents' homeland varies—in some it is a peripheral concern; in others it induces intense ambivalence.

Caryl Phillips, who was taken to Britain from St Kitts when he was just a few weeks old, is aware of his (and his parents') double diasporic condition. His first two novels, *The Final Passage* and *A State of Independence*, are about the second diaspora, that is, his parents' generation's immigration to Britain. In *The Final Passage*, the female protagonist tries to escape an unhappy life in her Caribbean island by journeying to Britain with her husband and baby. Forced into an even unhappier life as the victim of racism, poverty, and domestic and personal disappointments in the West Indian immigrant community of London, she plans at the end of the novel to return to her Caribbean home. In *A State of Independence*, the male protagonist Bertram discovers that it is difficult to go home again. After twenty unfulfilling years in Britain, he escapes to his West Indian island only to feel unwelcome. His mother and his former lover, whom he ignored while in Britain, are indifferent to his return. One of his contemporaries, now a minister in the government, interprets his reappearance on the island as opportunistic rather than patriotic and advises him to repair to England where he and other 'English West Indians' belong. Bertram, however, considers himself to have been a victim of colonization as a youth on his island and as an

---

[20] Victor J. Ramraj, 'Denis Williams', in Daryl Cumber Dance (ed.), *Fifty Caribbean Writers: A Bio-bibliographical Critical Sourcebook* (New York: Greenwood Press, 1986), 484.

[21] Claire Harris, *Travelling to Find a Remedy* (Fredericton: Goose Lane, 1986), 26.

immigrant in Britain; he tells his mother that whatever business he invests in it must not make him 'dependent upon the white man'.[22] Though Phillips recognizes that he is to some extent agent of his personal failures—Bertram admits that he has been a selfish wastrel—he depicts Bertram as a colonial caught up in a world that he could not control: 'England', he says, 'just take me over.' At the end of the novel, Phillips suggests that though the island has been and will be at the mercy of imperial and neo-imperial forces (through the image of an islander attaching wires to telegraph poles that will bring the first cable television pictures to the island from the United States), the individual can survive and find fulfilment by performing little acts of personal kindness; Bertram's concluding thoughts are about 'how he might help his mother'.[23]

Phillips's later novels, *Cambridge* and *Crossing the River*, encompass the epic theme of the Afro-Caribbean (and the African American) diaspora since the beginning of the slave trade. While *Cambridge* is restricted to the eighteenth century, *Crossing the River* ranges over 250 years, beginning with an African father selling his three children into slavery and concluding with his descendants' diasporic lives in the mid-twentieth century. Phillips uses multiple voices to relate the history of this diaspora, voices from both sides of the hegemonic divide. In *Cambridge*, for instance, the two dominant voices are those of Emily, an absentee West Indian plantation-owner's daughter, who is exposed to the realities of slavery on a visit to her father's plantation, and of Cambridge (or Olumide), a West African slave, who is taken to Britain as a house-servant and eventually, after journeying to Africa as a missionary, is captured and taken to the West Indies, where he dies on the gallows. Phillips's use of multiple often antithetical voices points up his complex, ironical vision of the black diaspora. He does confront the horrors of slavery and he does recognize the brutality of the agents of slavery, but his purpose in these novels is less to blame or protest than to provide psychological insights into those involved on both sides of the institution of slavery. Of his tone and attitude in his portrayal of the past and present diasporic African communities' relationship with the African homeland, Phillips says: 'I wanted to make an affirmative connection, not a connection based upon exploitation or suffering or misery, but a connection based on a kind of survival.'[24] This, Phillips believes, is what binds the diasporic communities to each other and to Africa, not a romantic yearning for a return to an ever-receding African homeland; African diasporic communities, then, should establish roots wherever they find themselves.

---

[22] Caryl Phillips, *A State of Independence* (London: Faber, 1986), 136, 50.
[23] Ibid. 85, 158.
[24] Caryl Phillips, 'Interview', *Ariel*, 25/4 (Oct. 1994), 93.

As Phillips and other second-generation writers show, however, establishing roots and attempting to adjust to the dominant society are not free of conflicts, tensions, and ambivalences. Fred D'Aguiar, who was born in London and spent part of his childhood in Guyana, exhibits such responses to Britain in his poem 'Home'. Returning to London after a trip abroad, D'Aguiar 'resigns himself to the usual inquisition' at Heathrow and to a cab driver who 'rounds on Asians'. Yet in spite of his chilly reception, he declares his love for London: 'Grey light and close skies I love you.' However, in 'Notting Hill', he cautions that the diasporan must 'sort out the sting | from the honey'. D'Aguiar's collections of poems, *Mama Dot* and *Airy Hall*, demonstrate his deep imaginative and psychic attachment to Guyana, the setting of many of his childhood experiences.

David Dabydeen is another second-generation writer who grew up in both Guyana and London. The poems in his first collection, *Slave Song*, written in both Standard English and Guyanese Creole, are powerful evocations of the lives of the Indo- and Afro-West Indians during and after slavery and indenture. In his second volume, *Coolie Odyssey*, Dabydeen seeks almost reverentially to rediscover his ancestry as he relates the epic journey of the Indo-Guyanese people from India to Guyana and then, for many, to Britain. His first novel is an account of this second diaspora to Britain. Brought to London as a boy from Guyana, the narrator experiences recurring feelings of homelessness, alienation, and self-hatred when confronted with white racism. He learns of the racial and ethnic divisions in the various diasporic communities among the Hindus and Muslims and the Indo- and Afro-West Indians but also of their shared lot as immigrants. Believing that he and other diasporans should not be invisible (a characteristic of the liminal persona, according to Turner[25]) in Britain, Dabydeen, in his preface to *Black Presence in English Literature*, a collection of essays compiled and edited by him, agitates for the integration of black studies in the British educational curricula.

Pauline Melville, who grew up in Britain and Guyana, depicts in her stories collected in *Shape-Shifter* the in-between, liminal state of the West Indian second-generation immigrants who are of Britain yet apart from it, who yearn to escape to their West Indian homes but once there want to return to Britain. Her diasporans, some of mixed blood, are caught between two allegiances, two countries, two landscapes. Many try to turn their fractured psyches to their advantage, coping with their environment by constantly modifying and shifting their identities. Mutations, transformations, and impersonations are recurring motifs in Melville's

---

[25] See Turner, 'Betwixt and Between'.

stories. In 'The Truth is in the Clothes', the narrator endorses the Greek philosopher Heraclitus' theory that the world is alive only when it is in a constant state of change, perpetually moving between opposites. Several of her stories set in London portray diasporic protagonists from the West Indies and elsewhere as victims of prejudice; afflicted by poverty and unemployment, many turn to crime. Melville views them sympathetically, as she does the Scottish protagonist in 'McGregor's Journey' who tries futilely to separate himself from British imperial exploitation, of which he is as much a victim as are the diasporans who rebuff him.

Though Hanif Kureishi, born in England of an Indian father and a British mother, claims that unlike his father he is not 'caught between two cultures' and insists that he is British and 'can make it in Britain',[26] his work focuses on the Asian immigrant experience in London, which he chooses to see inclusively as an aspect of the contemporary urban experience. In his novel *The Buddha of Suburbia*, as in his films *My Beautiful Laundrette* and *Sammy and Rosie Get Laid*, he shows that issues of politics, sex, and class transcend ethnic and racial divides. The Asians are not the only ones marginalized; so too are the less fortunate whites, who in fact are often aided by economically prosperous Asians. In his portraits of some of his Asian characters in London, he addresses problems of acculturation. However, at the end of *The Buddha of Suburbia*, he lets the protagonist return from a trip to the United States with his belief intact that he is British, despite his divided nature and the efforts of others to deny him this identity.

Timothy Mo—the son of an English mother and a Cantonese father—who grew up in Hong Kong and went to Britain when he was 10 years old, examines in his novel *Sour Sweet* the adjustment of the Chens, a Chinese immigrant family, to life in Britain. The opening of the novel depicts them in a liminal state: they had been living in Britain for four years, 'which was long enough to have lost their place in the society from which they had emigrated but not long enough to feel comfortable in the new'.[27] Like Ismith Khan in his depiction of the Khans' responses to Trinidad in The *Jumbie Bird*, Mo examines paradigmatically the Chens' different responses to their adopted home. The husband perceives himself as an interloper in Britain and adamantly adheres to his ancestral way of life, which further alienates him from his new home. He is linked with a secret criminal organization, the Triads, which is wedded to the 'old and true way'.[28] His sister-in-law abandons tradition and readily assimilates into the new culture. His wife Lily, the central figure in the novel, tries to find the point of 'equilibrium' between her two cultures,

---

[26] Hanif Kureishi, 'Interview', with Marcia Pally, *Film Comment*, 22 (Sept.–Oct. 1986), 53.
[27] Timothy Mo, *Sour Sweet* (London: Abacus, 1982), 1.
[28] Ibid. 71.

between her husband's and her sister's response, and to balance yin with yang—an aspiration similar to that of Walcott's speaker in *Omeros*, who strives to show the complementarity of his antithetical cultures. Initially, Lily is as inflexible as her husband. At the end of the novel, she abandons his rigid adherence to ancestral ways but does not espouse her sister's easy assimilationist ways. She modifies her views on her own terms, which categorically exclude abandoning her heritage or her attachment to her homeland. The novel concludes with her recognition that her young son, Man Kee, must be exposed to both Western and Chinese cultures. The hope that he will begin with a new, clean slate recalls Williams's for his protagonist at the end of *Other Leopards*: 'Man Kee, happy child, was getting a fresh start. He had no history, no heritage to live up to, no goal to fulfill, no ancient burden to carry.'[29]

In the 1970s, Canada and the United States opened their doors more widely to immigrants from the developing regions, and these countries replaced Britain as the destination of English-speaking immigrants. North America had long attracted immigrants from the West Indies. In the 1910s, Claude McKay (of Jamaica) and Eric Waldron (of Guyana) had migrated to New York and wrote about their experiences there and in their homelands. And in the 1950s, while many of their compatriots immigrated to London, Ismith Khan went to the United States and Austin Clarke (of Barbados) to Canada. Since the 1970s, however, the number of writers who have immigrated to North America has increased substantially. A current bibliography of writing by West Indian Canadians, which three decades ago listed just the name of Austin Clarke (whose novels provide takes and retakes of the experiences of Barbadian immigrants in Toronto), now includes such names as Neil Bissoondath, Dionne Brand, Cyril Dabydeen, Kwame Dawes, Claire Harris, Arnold Itwaru, Sasenarine Persaud, M. Nourbese Philip, and Nigel Thomas.

In 1971 Canada adopted a policy of multiculturalism and in 1988 passed the Canadian Multiculturalism Act which 'recognizes the importance of preserving and enhancing the multicultural heritage of Canadians'.[30] Though the policy proclaims Canada's official liberal stand on immigration, several immigrant writers complain that it keeps immigrant writers out of the mainstream. Neil Bissoondath equates state-sanctioned multiculturalism with a mild form of apartheid,[31] and M. Nourbese Philip regards it as a political weapon intended to neutralize and diffuse a potentially explosive situation.

[29] Ibid. 278, 111.
[30] Canadian Multiculturalism Act, in *Statutes of Canada*, vol. i. (Ottawa: Queen's Printers, 1989), 835.
[31] Neil Bissoondath, *Selling Illusions: The Cult of Multiculturalism in Canada* (Toronto: Penguin, 1994), 142.

Despite their shared opposition to this policy, these two writers reflect an antithetical attitude towards their adopted society: Bissoondath, who moved to Canada from Trinidad in 1973, argues for mutual assimilation and integration; Philip insists on retaining cultural distinctness. Though Bissoondath is aware of the distinctness of immigrant experiences, he does not want to be shoved into an ethnic ghetto. In his fiction, he transcends ethnic barriers and writes of the immigrant experience of individuals other than West Indians. In fact, in many of his stories in *Digging up the Mountain* and *On the Eve of Uncertain Tomorrows*, he deliberately refrains from establishing the ethnic or national identity of his characters. This arguably encourages readers to acknowledge that the experiences of his characters are not nationally and ethnically exclusive; however, a problem with this technique is that lack of particulars tends at times—when Bissoondath is in unfamiliar territory and his writing becomes too studied—to work against the authenticity of his characters, narratives, and settings. Despite his advocacy of acculturation, Bissoondath's stories are seldom about the excitement and energy of new beginnings. His immigrants are marginalized, unanchored, and insecure. The aged protagonist of 'Security', who fled to Toronto to escape the racial and political turmoil on his West Indian island, spends 'endless stretches of being alone'.[32] In his novel *A Casual Brutality*, Bissoondath describes as 'a melancholy epic' the East Indians' journey from India to Trinidad 150 years ago. The protagonist links himself with an old Guyanese immigrant in Canada for whom 'home' was 'a word alien to him, a word without meaning' and he sees his own flight to Canada in terms of his diasporic people's placelessness: 'What began so long ago as a flight from a dusty and decrepit village in India brings me now on a jet [to Canada].'[33]

Though Philip agrees with Dionne Brand, another Trinidadian Canadian, that the Canadian and West Indian societies are 'not that far apart' in that both were colonies of Britain (though one was settled and the other invaded), she detects a divisive racism in Canada which makes communion with the dominant society difficult. Coming from the Afro-West Indian diasporic community where her African identity was eroded by the dominant British culture and education, she wants now as a double diasporan in Canada to preserve her identity as a black West Indian with African ancestry. When this is threatened or exposes her to racism she becomes confrontational. She accepts that as an Afro-West Indian she has a dual cultural identity, but she and Brand are less inclined than Caryl Phillips to understand the psychology that could sanction an

---

[32] Neil Bissoondath, *On the Eve of Uncertain Tomorrows* (Toronto: Macmillan, 1990), 87.
[33] Neil Bissoondath, *A Casual Brutality* (Toronto: Macmillan, 1988), 233, 377.

institution like slavery, electing to protest, at times as militant political activists, the past and present abuses of blacks by the imperial and the dominant.

Brand is one of the diasporans in Canada who share Philip's concern with preserving her distinct Afro-West Indian identity and resisting assimilation. Others lean towards Bissoondath's assimilationist approach, some with major modifications and emphases. Michael Ondaatje, who moved to Britain from Sri Lanka at the age of 9 in 1952 and then to Canada in 1962, contends in *Secular Love* that all Canadians (and Australians, other than the Aboriginals) are immigrants; he therefore is no less at home in Canada than any other Canadian whatever his or her ethnic or national background. He writes about the North American folk hero Billy the Kid (in *The Collected Works of Billy the Kid*) as well as about immigrant workers who contributed to the building of Toronto (in *In the Skin of a Lion*) and about his parents' generation in Sri Lanka (in *Running in the Family*).

Aware of the problems faced by immigrants in Canada, which he believes 'still is a xenophobic place', Cyril Dabydeen (born in Guyana) nevertheless responds to his immigration to Canada in 1970 not as a dislocation but as an adventure, as a chance to start afresh. However, as his volume of selected poems *Coastland* and his collection of short stories *Still Close to the Island* show, he retains an attachment to his Guyanese homeland. Dabydeen's fellow Guyanese Arnold Itwaru looks back in anger at the history of colonial exploitation in Guyana in his novel *Shanti*, but in his exploration of the immigrant experience his tone is different: he is dismayed by the prejudice and intolerance that force individuals and peoples to go their 'separate ways'.[34]

Rohinton Mistry, who immigrated to Canada in 1975 from India, focuses on the Parsi community of Bombay—which perhaps could be seen as a diasporic community that migrated to India in the eighth century—in his novel *Such a Long Journey* and his collection of short stories *Tales from Firozsha Baag*. In stories like 'Swimming Lessons', Mistry, who accepts the concept of 'universalities' in human experience, depicts a young Parsi immigrant's recognition of the commonness of the experiences of his neighbours in Toronto, who are not much different from the Parsis of the Firozsha Baag. In 'Squatter', another Parsi in Canada who is unable to adjust to life, noting only the differences between his adopted and his ancestral home, elects to return to Bombay. Mistry underscores personal and individual characteristics which account for the immigrants' varied responses to the difficulties of living in a new land and coping with a dominant culture. M. G. Vassanji, who

[34] Arnold Itwaru, *Entombed Survivals* (Toronto: Williams-Wallace, 1987), 18.

was born in Kenya, lived in Tanzania, and moved to Canada in 1978, traces in *The Gunny Sack* the history of the Indian community in East Africa and their eventual dispersal to Britain and North America following the racial conflicts in the 1970s. In *No New Land*, he portrays the Indo-East African immigrants' difficulties with prejudice as they try to adjust to life in Toronto. In both works, Vassanji sanctions efforts at assimilation and syncretism on the part of the diasporic community.

Bharati Mukherjee was born in Calcutta and resided in Canada from 1966 until 1978, when, disillusioned with Canada (where she felt marginalized by racism and came to see herself as an 'invisible woman'),[35] she immigrated to the United States. Mukherjee makes a distinction between expatriation and immigration, claiming that in Canada she is forever the expatriate, the temporary dweller, whereas in the United States she is an immigrant and is allowed the 'exuberance of immigration'.[36] The diasporic consciousness (of Indian as well as of other diasporic peoples from such regions as the West Indies, Vietnam, Lebanon, Sri Lanka, and Italy) preoccupies Mukherjee. But what she emphasizes is not so much the nostalgic yearning for the homeland but the exuberance of immigration, which fosters new beginnings. She is aware of the challenges and difficulties immigrants face but feels that these are exacerbated if they are constantly vacillating between two worlds, as she depicts in the stories of the aptly titled collection *Middlemen and Other Stories*. Mukherjee has declared that she is for mutual assimilation and acculturation of the dominant and the immigrant communities, seeing the process as 'a two-way metamorphosis'[37] and advocating what she calls 'mongrelization' of peoples and cultures.[38]

Categorizing a body of writing as diasporic raises the question of its relationship to such counterparts as immigrant writing or exile and expatriate writing. Diasporic writing has affinities with, but stands apart from, both. It diverges from immigrant writing in its preoccupation with the attachment to the homeland; immigrant writing does not ignore this but focuses more on the current experiences in the adopted home. (In a broader—perhaps meaningless—sense immigrant writing could refer to any work whatever the topic by an immigrant.) Exile and expatriate writing is more immersed in the situation at home and the circumstances that prolong the individual's exile or expatriation than with the *émigré*'s or *émigré* community's relationship with the dominant society. Diasporic

[35] Bharati Mukherjee, 'Invisible Woman', *Saturday Night*, 96 (Mar. 1981), 36.

[36] Bharati Mukherjee, *Darkness* (New York: Penguin, 1985), 3.

[37] Patricia Holt, 'Mukherjee's Vision of America', *San Francisco Sunday Examiner and Chronicle*, 17 Feb. 1991, p. 2.

[38] Bharati Mukherjee, Plenary Lecture, Canadian Association of American Studies Conference, Ottawa, 4 Nov. 1994.

writing then is about or by peoples who are linked by common histories of uprooting and dispersal, common homelands, and common cultural heritages, but it develops different cultural and historical identities depending on the political and cultural particularities of the dominant society. And even within a particular region there are likely to be differences among the traditionalists, the assimilationists, and the inte-grationists. Some focus on the negative aspects of their status, on their marginality and the destruction of their cultures; others see the positive aspects, agreeing that, in both individuals and nations, the liminal process results in '[u]ndoing, dissolution, decomposition [which] are accompanied by processes of growth, transformation, and the reformulation of old elements in new patterns'.[39] Given its historical and cultural dualities, conflicts, contradictions, and ambivalences, writing designated as diasporic has an inherent complexity, which is amplified when—as in literature at large—the writer's personal experiences are brought into the equation.

[39] Turner, 'Betwixt and Between', 99.

# CHAPTER THIRTEEN

# Post-colonial Women Writers and Feminisms

KETU H. KATRAK

This essay undertakes a literary discussion of selected post-colonial women writers in English and a theoretical exploration of Third World feminisms. (I use post-colonial and Third World interchangeably. Although problematic for their negative connotations, they are useful as political categories that can assert solidarity.) Writers and theorists cover a range of issues that share a concern with gender as it relates integrally to race, class, sexuality, and culture. I include writers from areas of the world that experienced varying periods of British colonization—India; the African nations of Nigeria, Ghana, Kenya, among others; and the Caribbean nations of Jamaica, Barbados, Trinidad, among others. This vast and diverse geographical arena includes peoples of various religions, cultures, and languages as different as Hindi, Gujarati, Tamil (India), Igbo, Yoruba, KiSwahili, Shona (Africa), and varieties of Caribbean creoles. A study that focuses only on English-language post-colonial writers involves some loss, even distortion in terms of the complex reality of linguistic situations in post-colonial areas.

Even as they use English (learned in colonial schools, and which has the advantage of being a world language), post-colonial women writers explore their own cultural specificities in their literary work—for example, Botswanan/South African Bessie Head's representations of exile, displacement, and home in her novels and short stories; Nigerian Buchi Emecheta's exploration of Igbo culture and traditions of bride-price and polygamy in her novels; Ghanaian Ama Ata Aidoo's portrayal of her society transitioning from traditional, rural mores to modern influences evident in Western medicine and education; Indian Anita Desai's inclusion of Hindu and Muslim traditions of female socialization, wifehood, motherhood in her novels; Jamaican Olive Senior's representation of class and colour hierarchies in her poems and short stories.

Post-colonial writing in English is fairly new, post-1960s when most African and Caribbean nations became independent. The recentness of these English-language traditions must be distinguished from the much

longer cultural heritages of these areas, and even ancient literary traditions in certain Indian and African indigenous languages. Although male
writers like Chinua Achebe and Wole Soyinka in Nigeria, George Lamming in Barbados, Roger Mais in Jamaica came to prominence first,
women writers like Flora Nwapa in Nigeria and Anita Desai in India,
whose careers span over three decades, were also writing at the time.
Only recently have women writers been recognized in their full right as
literary creators worthy of serious study. As Lloyd W. Brown remarks,
'Western male Africanists have contributed heavily to an old boy network of African studies in which the African woman simply does not
exist as a serious or significant writer.'[1] In *Ngambika: Studies of Women
in African Literature*, Carole Boyce Davies asserts the need for serious
re-evaluations of women writers who have often been dismissed casually
by a male literary establishment. Boyce Davies cites Flora Nwapa's
recuperation in critical work by Lloyd Brown, and Naana Banyima-
Horne (in Davies's collection). Constructive criticism according to
Davies can enable women writers to move beyond the image of woman-
asvictim, and to transform voicelessness into speech.

One promising factor that corrects women writers' exclusions and
erasures is the wealth and variety of their writing that emerged in the
1980s and 1990s. Whereas, even two decades previously, a mere handful
of post-colonial women writers were known (and available in print),
such as South African Nadine Gordimer, or Dominican Jean Rhys, today
there are several who are worthy of serious critical attention—Tsitsi
Dangarembga (Zimbabwe), Bessie Head (Botswana/South Africa), Ellen
Kuzwayo, Miriam Tlali (South Africa), Buchi Emecheta, Flora Nwapa
(Nigeria), Ama Ata Aidoo, Efua Sutherland (Ghana), Micere Mugo
(Kenya), Kamala Markandaya, Anita Desai, Nayantara Sahgal, Shashi
Deshpande, Eunice de Souza, Kamala Das (India), Lorna Goodison, Erna
Brodber, Olive Senior (Jamaica), Merle Hodge (Trinidad).

The many cultures that the post-colonial field covers have complex oral
traditions that have undergone varieties of transformations through a
colonial, print-dominated tendency. Many pre-colonial African cultures
were predominantly oral, and the colonizer's racist superiority assumed
that since these languages were not written, they did not exist. Along
with erasure of language went devastating denials of culture and identity.
African feminist criticism, remarks Boyce Davies in her introduction to
*Ngambika*, develops the tools of 'an African Female Aesthetic' where
oral literatures are recuperated and re-evaluated, where the modes and
forms of creative expression are constructively criticized. Boyce Davies
cites 'the inclusion of small talk' as an important literary tool rather than

---

[1] Lloyd W. Brown, *Women Writers in Black Africa* (Westport, Conn.: Greenwood Press,
1981), 5.

a weakness in the writing as judged by certain Euro-American standards of narrative excellence.

Today, women writers work in a variety of literary genres—short story, drama, poetry, essay, life story/testimony, and the novel—that are often inspired by and rooted in a writer's own indigenous oral and folk traditions (as in Africa and the Caribbean), as well as literary traditions in other languages (in India). Aidoo's collection of short stories *No Sweetness Here* is rooted in oral story-telling traditions. As she remarks in an interview, 'we cannot assume that all literature should be written. One doesn't have to be so patronizing about oral literature . . . The art of the speaking voice can be brought back so easily.'[2] Similarly, *Lionheart Gal: Life Stories of Jamaican Women* combines oral and written forms—the written stories are based on oral testimony and interviews transcribed into print. Among written forms, the novel is the most favoured among writers in English. This has much to do with publishing and market-place realities. After all, written forms in English are fairly recent and are conditioned by marketing forces which often commodify women writers doubly (race and gender) to their detriment in dictating what themes will be desirable.

African, Indian, and Caribbean women writers in English cover a range of issues that share a concern with gender—how their female protagonist's self and sexuality are constructed and controlled by indigenous patriarchies and British colonial practices. Further, they show how patriarchy and colonialism collude to worsen women's predicament. Although women writers do not romanticize a pre-colonial past, they are well aware of how indigenous and colonial patriarchies collude as represented in Zimbabwean Tsitsi Dangarembga's complex and noteworthy first novel, *Nervous Conditions*. Even as patriarchy is critiqued, Third World theorists reveal the historical and cultural specificities of patriarchy as in Hazel Carby's essay 'White Woman Listen! Black Feminism and the Boundaries of Sisterhood.'

Women writers share specific gender concerns in terms of how social and cultural factors appear from a female point of view. Their literary works imaginatively explore several conflicts between tradition (social custom, religion) and modernization. Ama Ata Aidoo's short stories *No Sweetness Here* portray female protagonists caught in the restrictive and contradictory demands of traditional mores and Western norms introduced by colonialism. Head's short story 'Life' and Aidoo's 'In the Cutting of a Drink' and 'Two Sisters' portray women's limited work options as prostitutes in newly formed urban areas. Kamala Markandaya's *Nectar in a Sieve* presents the complex financial and emotional

---

[2] Cosmo Pieterse and Dennis Duerdin (eds.), *African Writers Talking* (New York: Africana Publishing, 1972), 23–4.

repercussions on a rural farming community when a tannery is opened in the village.

Women writers explore the contradictory benefits of a colonialist educational system that was fundamentally gendered in that it maintained traditional hierarchies intact. English education often renders educated women into outsiders in their own communities as represented in Dangarembga's *Nervous Conditions*. In general, female education, governed by Victorian ideology and Christian missionary zeal, was aimed at producing women as good wives and mothers. English education often fostered a denial and denigration of indigenous history. Racist images of self-deprecation were compounded for women through a forced repression of their sexuality as illustrated in Jamaican Olive Senior's poem 'Colonial Girl's School':

> Borrowed images
> willed our skins pale
> muffled our laughter
> lowered our voices
> let out our hems
> dekinked our hair
> denied our sex in gym tunics and bloomers
> harnessed our voices to madrigals
> and genteel airs
> yoked our minds to declensions in Latin
> and the language of
> Shakespeare.
>   Told us nothing about ourselves
>   There was nothing about us at all.[3]

The poem takes on that sad refrain with variations: 'There was nothing left of ourselves . . . Feeling nothing about ourselves | There was nothing about us at all.' Senior testifies to the denials of histories, traditions, and cultures of colonized peoples who had to learn British history, British geography, British songs.

A poem by Eunice de Souza, 'Sweet Sixteen', evokes a female persona's experiences at a Catholic School where repressions and denials of sexuality could lead to disastrous ignorance about one's female body:

> Well, you can't say
> they didn't try,
> Mamas never mentioned menses.
> A nun screamed: You vulgar girl
> don't say brassiers
> say bracelets . . .

[3] Olive Senior, *Talking of Trees* (Kingston: Calabash Press, 1985), 26.

The preacher thundered:
Never go with a man alone.
Never alone
and if you're engaged
only passionless kisses.
At sixteen, Phoebe asked me:
Can it happen when you're in a dance hall
I mean, you know what
getting *preggers* and all that, *when*
you're dancing? I, sixteen, assured her
you could.[4]

Post-colonial women writers share many of the concerns of their male counterparts especially a history of colonialism and continuing imperialistic controls of ex-colonies. In literary representations of 'the personal as political', post-colonial women writers explore the personal dimensions of history rather than overt concerns with political leadership and nation-states as in the work of their male counterparts. This does not make women writers' concerns any less political; rather, from a feminist standpoint of recognizing the personal, even the intimate and bodily as part of a broader socio-political context, post-colonial women writers enable a reconceptualization of politics as in Head's short stories *The Collector of Treasures*.

Women writers demystify accepted and oppressive aspects of 'cultural tradition' that legitimize certain cruel practices such as genital mutilation (in some African societies), or dowry-related murders (in India). They also challenge a commonly held male notion that, given the high status that mothers have especially in Africa and India, women are already liberated, and have no need of 'feminism', which is dismissed as 'Western' and hence irrelevant for post-colonial societies. Women writers deromanticize male writers' portrayals of woman as goddess, earth-mother, supreme being who is revered for her mysterious powers of fertility. Such glorification mystifies the realities of incessant child-bearing, of survival within poverty-ridden conditions, and of women's actual lack of social and political power.

Women writers are concerned with the many aspects of female sexuality: joys and burdens of motherhood as in Emecheta's *The Joys of Motherhood*; the social censures of infertility as in Aidoo's *Anowa*; family bonds as wife or as single woman in Desai's *Clear Light of Day* and *Games at Twilight*, and in Markandaya's *Nectar in a Sieve*. Polygamy, monogamy, and changing roles from traditional wifehood to working mother are portrayed in Aidoo's novel *Changes*. Issues of female fertility take on different ramifications in a Caribbean context as

---

[4] Eunice de Souza, *Fix* (Bombay: Newground, 1979), 12.

rendered in the Jamaican working-class women's group Sistren. Several of their stories in *Lionheart Gal* portray the women's ignorance of their female bodies, and non-responsible 'baby-fathers' as they are called, who impregnate and then abandon the mothers. Olive Senior's *Working Miracles: Women's Lives in the English-Speaking Caribbean* presents interviews with women and women's groups, along with historical and sociological material on issues such as 'The Concept of Motherhood', 'Family and Household', 'Education and Gender-Role Stereotyping'. This text is a fine example of Senior's creative and activist roles, of her commitment to working towards social change and a better future for her community.

## POST-COLONIAL FEMINISMS

The interdisciplinary approach so important in women's studies is useful in scholarly and theoretical discussions of post-colonial feminisms. Third World feminists such as Christine Obbo, Filomena Steady, Molara Ogundipe Leslie (Africa), Kumari Jayawardena (Sri Lanka), Chandra Mohanty, Vibhuti Patel, Madhu Kishwar (India), Peggy Antrobus, Caro-lyn Cooper, Carole Boyce Davies (Caribbean) among others have made important theoretical contributions. Post-colonial feminisms also draw upon theorists like Edward Said, as well as progressive Western scholars like Barbara Harlow, Michele Barrett, Hazel Carby, among others. Recent work of feminist historiographers and sociologists who revise colonial versions of women's history, as in Lata Mani's essay on *sati* (widow-burning) in the Indian context, is useful. Mani systematically analyses nineteenth-century British documents on 'eradicating *sati*' and demonstrates that the British, far from their claim of liberating women from this barbaric custom, used women as the *ground* on which debates about tradition took place. They did not wish to jeopardize the power structure of the Brahmins (highest caste), even if that involved life and death issues for women.[5]

Post-colonial societies present more serious challenges than First World societies for academic feminism and women's movements because often women are literally facing life and death issues, such as dowry murders in India, and the resurgence of *sati*. It is important to lessen the gap between feminist theory and activism, to make post-colonial feminist criticism respond to and recognize issues that concern women's movements in the Third World.

[5] Lata Mani, 'Contentious Traditions: The Debate on "Sati" in Colonial India', in Kumkum Sangari and Sudesh Vaid (eds.), *Recasting Women: Essays in Colonial History* (New Delhi: Kali for Women, 1989), 88–126.

Whereas feminist figures and practices have long and significant her-stories in post-colonial areas, the articulation of feminism as a discipline is more recent. The issue of naming is a crucial starting-point for the delineation of feminisms as relevant for African, Indian, or Caribbean women. What then are the parameters of Third World feminism and how can theorists and activists participate, even collaborate in forging definitions and charting out boundaries for feminist agendas? As we redefine feminisms, we need to be vigilant and sensitive to the different historical, social, cultural conditions that women face. Achola Pala's essay on 'Women and Development' presents an important cautionary tale about an anthropologist who goes into an African village with a set of predetermined questions, and goes about gathering those data, remaining deaf to the issues that the women there want to talk about, such as their basic need for clean drinking water!

Today, it is commonly accepted that feminisms are historically, culturally, and geographically specific. This does not eliminate hegemonic tendencies in certain schools of feminism that continue to be universalist, perhaps not overtly, but subtly, and hence more dangerously, and in spite of the challenges of black and Third World feminist theorists. To respect various cultures and voices and to hear their perspectives and needs, are still uphill struggles. As Achebe points out aptly and with characteristically biting irony in his essay 'Impediments to Dialogue':

No definition of partnership can evade the notion of equality. And equality is the one thing which Europeans are conspicuously incapable of extending to others, especially Africans . . . a British governor of Rhodesia in the 1950s defined the partnership between black and white in his territory, apparently without intending any sarcasm, as the partnership between the horse and its rider!

My sense of the situation tells me that in more or less polite formulations that was, and is, the fundamental attitude of Europe to Africa. Even the enunciation of the metaphor in human/animal terms is neither new nor accidental . . . For centuries Europe has chosen the beastly alternative which automatically has ruled out the possibility of a dialogue. You may talk to a horse but you don't wait for a reply![6]

Olive Senior's poem 'Letter from the Lesser World' echoes the rifts in dialogue between the privileged and the under-privileged of the world, differences rooted in economic disparities and in different values:

> Friend of the cellophane world . . .
> Do not
> O do not say
> it is the sea only

---

[6] Chinua Achebe, 'Impediments to Dialogue between North and South', in *Hopes and Impediments: Selected Essays 1965–87* (New York: Anchor, 1988), 23.

that divides us . . .
that you understand
You do not understand . . .
Friend,
you do not understand
sickle cell anaemia
or sleeping on pavements
as we cannot understand
Baseball Season
—or Fall
We do not need
interstellar leaps
we want to shorten
distances between hospitals.

And in another poem, 'Reaching my Station', Senior echoes a similar sentiment:

But mothers know the starkness
of these times: guns easier
to obtain than milk. The moon's
been conquered, the hospital
not yet—it's just as far
and alien.[7]

Senior's poems evoke issues relevant for Third World feminism, namely, the interlocking forces of race, sex, class, along with colour, nation, culture. For Third World peoples with histories of colonial domination, race is an important category. I do not wish to privilege it, nor to reify race and subsume it into the category of culture. Racism along with sexism are important analytic categories within Third World feminisms, as are also the intersecting categories of class, colour, nation, without which one cannot undertake a satisfactory analysis of Third World women.

In their essay 'Challenging Imperial Feminism' Valerie Amos and Pratibha Parmar critique the 'political limitations of Euro-American feminism' which does not pay adequate attention to race, and when it does make black women visible, it does that in problematic and distorted ways: 'What forms of contemporary feminist and socialist theories share is an inability to adequately deal with the contradictions inherent in gender and class relations within the context of a racist society. "Race and sex are social realities which at particular historical moments structure class relations in as much as class relations structure them." ' Amos and Parmar caution against a sentimental 'sisterhood' of women on an

---

[7] Senior, *Talking of Trees*, 47–8, 77.

essentialized biological commonality, and they also warn against 'the idealization and culturalism of anthropological works' that regard 'others' as 'exotic subjects'.[8]

Amos and Parmar, as does Carby, enable a rethinking of certain familiar territories of patriarchal oppression. When contextualized, an analysis of patriarchy includes differences in economic class and education levels, racism and exploitations within the household and in society. The domestic, familial arena is the most legitimized space for male domination even when, or particularly when, the male faces racism outside the home.

We live 'in a world with powerful histories of resistance and revolution in daily life' notes Chandra Mohanty in her excellent introduction to *Third World Women and the Politics of Feminism*. Mohanty 'suggest[s] significant questions and directions for feminist analysis in the 1990s— an analysis which is made possible by the precise challenges posed by "race" and postcolonial studies to the second wave of white Western feminisms'. Mohanty believes 'that these challenges suggest new questions for feminist historiography and epistemology, as well as point toward necessary reconceptualizations of ideas of resistance, community, and agency in daily life'. Mohanty does not 'posit any homogenous configuration of third world women who form communities because they share a "gender" or a "race" or a "nation" '. (5) Her essay 'Under Western Eyes' demonstrates the problems in associating 'third world women' with images of 'underdevelopment, oppressive traditions, high illiteracy, rural and urban poverty, religious fanaticism', and other stereotypical concepts. Mohanty suggests a useful direction in stating that any 'definitions, descriptions, and interpretations of third world women's engagement with feminism must necessarily be simultaneously historically specific and dynamic, not frozen in time in the form of a spectacle'. Just as there is no single, homogeneous category of 'western women', similarly, there is no 'automatic unitary group' of 'third world women. . . . It is third world women's oppositional political relation to sexist, racist, and imperialist structures that constitutes our potential commonality.'[9]

What Mohanty discusses theoretically, namely, Third World feminist politics that analyses gender as connected integrally to race, class, culture, is represented fictionally in Zimbabwean Dangarembga's *Nervous Conditions*. This novel presents an intricate fictional rendition of the interlocking forces of traditional patriarchy, sexual, racial, and class

[8] Valerie Amos and Pratibha Parmar, 'Challenging Imperial Feminism', *Feminist Review*, 17 (Autumn 1984), 3–20.

[9] Chandra Mohanty *et al.* (eds.), *Third World Women and the Politics of Feminism* (Bloomington: Indiana University Press, 1990), 3, 5, 6, 7.

oppressions as they play out on the site of Nyasha's female body. She is uprooted as a child and taken to England by her parents. Upon her return, she has 'forgotten' her mother tongue Shona. It becomes increasingly difficult for Nyasha to belong within the constraints of traditional patriarchal norms embodied in and enforced by her father Babamukuru. His attempts to have a 'traditional' daughter, obedient to his will, backfire in the terrible dramas around food as Nyasha becomes bulimic and attempts to take control of her life. She literally vomits out what Babamukuru and, by extension, what the colonial schools have fed her. By the end of the novel, her life hangs in the balance.

In this discussion of post-colonial feminisms, it is important to recognize not only theorists but post-colonial women writers' and activists' articulations on this subject from their creative and experiential perspectives. Statements made by writers like Ama Ata Aidoo, Eunice de Souza, Olive Senior, Erna Brodber among others in essays and interviews provide significant insights on issues of language, culture, and feminism. Although their discussions of culture, politics, women's issues are not collected in entire volumes, they are available none the less in interviews, essays and various comments. Let me cite from Buchi Emecheta's essay 'Feminism with a Small "f"!'

Being a woman, and Africa born, I see things through an African woman's eyes. I chronicle the little happenings in the lives of the African women I know. I did not know that by doing so I was going to be called a feminist. But if I am now a feminist then I am an African feminist with a small f. In my books I write about families because I still believe in families. I write about women who try very hard to hold their family together until it becomes absolutely impossible. I have no sympathy for a woman who deserts her children, neither do I have sympathy for a woman who insists on staying in a marriage with a brute of a man, simply to be respectable. I want very much to further the education of women in Africa . . . It is true that if one educates a woman, one educates a community, whereas if one educates a man, one educates a man. I do occasionally write about wars and the nuclear holocaust but again in such books I turn to write about the life and experiences of women living under such conditions.[10]

Indeed, it is sad when any discussion of women's issues is dismissed as 'feminism equals Westernism hence not relevant for post-colonial women'. This debate evokes the very power in naming a phenomenon or a field of study—as in naming feminism as an academic discipline and its visibility in academia, so also, more recently, in naming post-colonial theory. While I acknowledge the problems, even backlashes that are part of institutionalizing any field of study, I also recognize the very power of

---

[10] Buchi Emecheta, 'Feminism with a small "f"!', in Kirsten H. Petersen (ed.), *Criticism and Ideology: Second African Writers' Conference* [Stockholm, 1986] (Uppsala: Scandinavian Institute of African Studies, 1988), 175.

naming. Even as feminism in Western locales contends with contemporary attacks on its perceived power, Western feminist theory has a vocabulary and a system of ideas to contend with such attacks. Without a name, it is that much more difficult to contend with attacks and, as the following discussion in the African context reveals, when the 'feminist flag' is raised, it can be shot down since feminism can be dismissed as 'Western' and hence irrelevant for post-colonial societies. The need then is highly significant for women writers to define feminism for their own purposes, and to identify a set of issues that demonstrate the relevance of feminism for their societies. The following discussion about feminism in the African context carries resonances, albeit with important cultural differences, for other post-colonial areas.

At a symposium on African literature, male writers like Taban lo Liyong spoke about feminism as a declared war by African women against African men: 'I think I should appeal to us to keep the African household intact at the end of the day otherwise we may have our younger sisters going off and joining in dances in Lapland which concern the people of Lapland only.'[11] African women writers Aidoo (Ghana), Lauretta Ngcobo, Miriam Tlali (South Africa) present at this meeting make significant responses. Aidoo's impassioned response urges the audience 'not to over-sentimentalize anything'.

Anytime it is suggested that somehow one is important we hear that feminism is something that has been imported into Africa to ruin nice relationships between African women and African men. To try to remind ourselves and our brothers and lovers and husbands and colleagues that we also exist should not be taken as something foreign, as something bad. African women struggling both on behalf of themselves and on behalf of the wider community is very much part of our heritage. It is not new and I really refuse to be told I am learning feminism from abroad, from Lapland. Africa has produced a much more concrete tradition of strong women fighters than most other societies. So, when we say that, we are refusing to be overlooked. We are only acting today as daughters and grand-daughters of women who always refused to keep quiet. We haven't learnt this from anybody abroad.[12]

Miriam Tlali remarks that 'there is a definite fear of feminism in the African men, especially in South Africa ... Anytime you ask him to do something, to go and fetch the child today, or something like that he says, "Look, you are already a feminist." You are a white woman and a feminist. It is thrown into your face in the same way in which Communist is thrown into the face of the blacks in South Africa.'[13]

Lauretta Ngcobo echoes the need for African women to assert their notion of feminism, not as a monolithic concept borrowed from the

    [11] Taban lo Liyong, ibid. 183.    [12] Aidoo, ibid. 183.    [13] Tlali, ibid. 185.

West, but as redefined and articulated by them for their particular concerns. She notes that the feminist movement in the West has often 'restrict[ed] itself to a certain class' and has excluded working-class women, and, in certain cases, men. Such exclusions would not work in African societies where women and men have endured racism, colonialism, and continuing imperialism. Hence, feminist theorizing in the African context needs to include working-class women and supportive men. Along with her critique of the feminist movement in the West, Ngcobo acknowledges that there is much to learn from the limitations and exclusions of Western feminist definitions. One can redefine and transform its concepts as relevant to one's own history and culture.

Carol Boyce Davies in her introduction to *Ngambika: Studies of Women in African Literature* notes that 'African feminism is a hybrid of sorts, which seeks to combine African concerns with feminist concerns', a sort of 'balancing' act where women's own issues along with a 'common struggle with African men' against imperialism are important. Boyce Davies acknowledges the 'inequities and limits' within traditional, often feudal societies, and she cites Molara Ogundipe Leslie's important point, namely, a struggle against women's own internalized oppressions: 'Women are shackled by their own negative self-image, by centuries of the interiorization of the ideologies of patriarchy and gender hierarchy.'[14]

Even as one acknowledges the necessity of solidarity among Third World men and women, and not a separatist feminist movement, it is crucial not to romanticize this solidarity. For Third World women, feminist struggles aim for the full dignity of women along with men. Filomena Steady's articulation that 'African feminism combines racial, sexual, class, and cultural dimensions of oppression to produce a more inclusive brand of feminism through which women are viewed first and foremost as human, rather than sexual beings' mystifies the specifically sexual aspects of women's oppressions. What Steady terms 'Humanistic Feminism' can ignore the specific sexual, racial, and other power dynamics that underlie unequal gender relations. Despite these problems, Steady's essay is useful in placing African women's situation within their own history, and in discussing how the colonial encounter generally worsened women's predicaments, for instance, 'the disintegration of self-provisioning agricultural systems, through the introduction of commercial agricultural and exploitative wage employment'.[15]

---

[14] Davies citing Molara, in Carol Boyce Davies and Anne Adams Graves (eds.), *Ngambika: Studies of Women in African Literature* (Trenton: Africa World Press, 1986), 8.

[15] Filomena Steady, 'African Feminism: A Worldwide Perspective', in Rosalyn Terborg-Penn *et al.* (eds.), *Women in Africa and the African Diaspora* (Washington: Howard University Press, 1989), 10.

In the work of African women writers like Flora Nwapa, Emecheta, Aidoo, Head, the transition from a rural to an urban economy is often painfully rendered in its impact on female protagonists. The constraints of wage-earning, and the need for money in a city, become urgent realities for Emecheta's Nnu Ego in *The Joys of Motherhood*. She has to feed her children single-handedly since her husband has gone to fight on the British side during the Second World War. Nnu Ego does not understand anything of these politics. She has some vague notion that the 'British own Nigeria' but beyond that all her physical energy and mental resources are consumed in a bitter struggle for survival. In rural Ibuza where she comes from she would face back-breaking farm work, but perhaps she would not face the kinds of isolation and starvation that she does in the city. The stark and painful self-reliance that faces Nnu Ego in the city contrasts vividly with communal support in a rural setting. However, Emecheta does not romanticize either urban individualism or rural communalism. These themes of how women are caught in societies making a transition from rural to urban, from traditional values to more Westernized norms, from a traditional private and public life that becomes rigidly compartmentalized with Victorian attitudes of a woman's place in the home, are represented also in Attia Hosain's *Sunlight on a Broken Column*, Anita Desai's *Games at Twilight*, Emecheta's *The Bride-Price* and *The Slave Girl*, Flora Nwapa's *Efuru*, and Aidoo's *No Sweetness Here*.

Male migrations often necessitated female-headed households, leading to what Steady terms the 'survival strategies' and 'strong bonds among female kin'. In Head's title story, 'The Collector of Treasures', she traces 'two kinds of men' in African society; one is the irresponsible kind who live near the animal level, breed children, and abandon mother and child. The other kind is described as 'a poem of tenderness'. The narrator traces three historical time periods that influenced male gender roles.

First, traditional patriarchal prerogatives that often considered women to be inferior; second, colonialism and wage-economy which necessitated male migrations especially true in the front-line states of Southern Africa where men were absent from their families for long periods of time. Third, African independence which seemed merely one more affliction on top of the afflictions that had visited this man's life. Independence suddenly and dramatically changed the pattern of colonial subservience. More jobs became available . . . It provided that first occasion for family life of a new order. Men and women, in order to survive, had to turn inwards to their own resources. It was the man who arrived at this turning point, a broken wreck with no inner resources at all.[16]

---

[16] Bessie Head, *The Collector of Treasures* (London: Heinemann, 1977), 92.

In the Caribbean context, economic hardships often necessitate migrations. Whereas men have more options in terms of leaving the country and going abroad, women mostly migrate internally, from rural to urban areas in search of work in order to feed their children. This leads to a cycle of poverty, of women's dependency on men, trading sex for food, and finding themselves in violent situations. As several Sistren stories in *Lionheart Gal* portray, women accept abusive relationships with men often out of desperation for food for their children.

Since Third World women's struggles often revolve around basic survival, the issue of economic necessity is raised as another strategy to make women's issues and feminist concerns secondary to economic, development issues. This false dichotomy between economic and feminist struggles does immense disservice to women's struggles for social change. Just as one regards racism and sexism as interlocking and not separate or hierarchized categories of analysis, so one needs to bring together the economic and sexual. Imperialism, economic and cultural, along with personal exploitations in the family and workplace are not separate categories that overtly and covertly endorse fundamental sexual inequalities. A politics of female sexuality must be analysed within a framework of imperialism and not separate from it. Women writers' portrayal of prostitution, of matters of fertility and infertility, are often rendered as part of 'cultural tradition'. Breaking tradition often entails severe costs for women.

Controls of fertility are validated under the auspices of 'tradition'. When the African American Eulalie and the Ghanaian Ato in Aidoo's drama *Dilemma of a Ghost* decide to practise birth control, their family and rural community assume the worst—barrenness. They wonder 'if the stranger-woman is barren', or is she 'pregnant with a machine child'? Young Eulalie is outside tradition anyway with her life-style of 'buying cigarettes, drinks . . . and machines'. Finally, when Ato tells his mother Esi the truth, she is astounded to learn that 'human beings [can decide] when they must have children'. She admonishes her son for not explaining this 'modern' option to the family: 'Why did you not tell us that you and your wife are gods and you can create your own children when you want them? . . . You do not even tell us about anything and we assemble our medicines together. While all the time your wife laughs at us because we do not understand such things.'[17]

Post-colonial women writers have made most significant literary contributions in their explorations of issues of culture, language, sexuality. They constitute an integral part of the post-colonial literary tradition. Their representations of the deeply personal, even intimate

[17] Ama Ata Aidoo, *The Dilemma of a Ghost* (London: Longman, 1965), 49.

issues facing their protagonists in their novels, poems, short stories are historicized within their particular socio-political milieux. African, Indian, Caribbean women writers enrich and illuminate any serious study of contemporary literature.

# CHAPTER FOURTEEN

# Paper Tracks: Indigenous Literatures in Canada, Australia, and New Zealand

### ADAM SHOEMAKER

In recent years, the indigenous peoples of Canada, Australia and New Zealand have demanded and received an unprecedented level of media and political attention, both within their respective borders and overseas. One important contributing factor was the global focus on Fourth World issues established by the International Year of World Indigenous People in 1993.

Of course, many other groups unfurled their flags during that special year as well: the rainforest tribes of Brazil; the Ainu of Japan; the Sami of Lapland; indigenous Fijians and Peruvians. All of these peoples initiated agendas for change in their respective nations throughout 1993; agendas which were founded upon cultural pride and distinctiveness. At the same time, it is possible to trace this process through the creative expressions of such nations within nations. Whether it is via painting, sculpture, music, dance, drama, or literature, indigenous ideologies find their voice through an enormous range of cultural productions. The visual, performing, and literary arts are vital to the identity of native minority groups, no matter what continent or hemisphere they may live in.

Of all of these art-forms, one of the most fascinating is indigenous writing. Such literature mediates between dominant and subordinate national traditions, male and female viewpoints, autochthonous and external issues as well as between minority languages and English and does so with vibrancy, humour, and political engagement.

In this connection, the example of Canada, Australia, and New Zealand is relevant. These three advanced Western nations share a colonial legacy, an official use of English, and a plethora of cultural, economic, diplomatic, and governmental ties. Their populations are predominantly Caucasian and, at the same time, all three are officially multicultural democracies. Most important to this argument, all three have deep, significant, and unresolved relationships with their indigenous peoples;

relationships which are becoming more urgent and pressing with each day that passes.

For, even without the United Nations-nominated special year, indigenous issues have been thrust into the popular consciousness as never before in these three Commonwealth nations. Constitutional debates have been crucial. The saga of the ill-fated Meech Lake Accord in Canada in 1990, the aftermath of the Australian High Court's 1992 decision in the Mabo case, and some of the most fervent Waitangi Day protests ever to take place in New Zealand have ensured that the legal, political, and cultural implications of all of these events would reverberate for at least the next generation. If there is a post-colonial moment at which indigenous voices can no longer be silenced, it has occurred in all three countries since 1990.

But these national debates over what is called aboriginal rights are only one dimension of indigenous ideologies; one which is expressed in fairly rigid and conventionally defined political terms. When that expression becomes fluid, creative, and unconventional, the domain being contested (and the strategies for its contestation) becomes extremely challenging though no less political or controversial. The prime example of this capacity is native or indigenous literature, both in English and in original or tribal languages.

For Canadian Indians, the Métis and the Inuit; for Australian Aborigines and Torres Strait Islanders; for New Zealand Maori the past has been one of violence, of dispossession, of death at foreign hands. Indigenous writers reflect these trials of invasion—for how could they ignore such issues?—with more passion and persuasiveness than many government inquiries or Royal Commissions. Such books provide an unparalleled view of indigenous histories as lived experiences; therefore, the flesh-and-blood genre of historical and family realism is very strong in all three countries. Largely for this reason, autobiographical and semi-autobiographical prose was prominent in the indigenous writing of all three nations up to the 1970s and, to this day, the life story remains one of the most popular formats of publication for native authors.

With few exceptions, it is mainly since 1970 that the fictional equivalent of this self-exploration has taken place. There has been a rapid development of what could be termed *indigenous creative writing*, one which parallels in an intriguing way the explosion of interest in native art on the part of non-aboriginal people. While the ambit and restrictiveness of the term creative writing is itself problematic—for almost all of this creative inscription is founded upon a powerful oral tradition—it is a useful shorthand for the type of narratives most frequently published, viewed, and read in the non-native world: the novel, the short story, poetry, and drama.

The paradox is that, as a non-aboriginal critic, I am inevitably trying to formulate a methodology for classifying native works, while being fully aware of the Eurocentric bias which this implies. A partial solution to this conundrum is an international, comparative one: instead of setting aboriginal texts against others from the European traditions of Canada, Australia, and New Zealand, here I propose to contrast such works with those by indigenous authors from the other two nations. If one requires any justification for this method, it is that the cross-border comparisons of aboriginal literatures demonstrate striking similarities of concern, timing, theme, and execution, even though the authors have almost always had little or no direct contact with each other. Despite the strength of the nation-state, native writing demonstrates an uncannily powerful sense of pan-aboriginality which, if anything, is increasing. Finally, if this essay enters into the paradox of subsuming indigenous literatures into imposed categories, it does so because no brief survey can possibly do justice to the full complexity of indigenous verbal art.

When aboriginal authors write, they provide far more than a recapitulation of the past from the indigenous point of view, as important as this might be. For, if one adopts a perspective in which history becomes solely a narrative of victimization, native peoples lose the all-important element of agency. Whether it is a Haida, Pitjantjatjara, or South Island Maori story which is being related, the resilience of tribal groups is absolutely central to the consciousness of the story-teller. All of the major aboriginal novelists in Canada (Jeannette Armstrong and Thomas King), in New Zealand (Witi Ihimaera, Patricia Grace, Keri Hulme, and Alan Duff), and in Australia (Archie Weller, Sam Watson, and Mudrooroo) explore these notions of pride and survival. Rather than simply lamenting the crimes of the past, indigenous writers deal with them in their own fashion satirically, symbolically, sometimes militantly but always in a way which demonstrates pride in their singular heritage.

Native publications thus defy simple categorizations. Though they are variously labelled by critics as protest writing, minority literature, and work from the Fourth World, it is just as possible to discover indigenous stories which are cultural celebrations and read like narratives of the dominant majority. Where one expects seriousness and sorrow, one often finds humour and wit; where one expects realism and naturalism, one often finds magic realism and the supernatural. In all three nations, indigenous writing defies non-aboriginal expectations, just as native authors have broached Western styles and genres in radical literary experiments. I will try to explore some of the ways in which those experiments have burst upon the post-colonial literary scene, from the earliest published examples of native writing until the present day.

I hope to answer several specific questions. First, is the rapid growth of aboriginal writing in Canada, Australia, and New Zealand over the past twenty years directly linked with the recent prominence of native affairs on the political agenda? Next, does an increased awareness and appreciation of indigenous authors, especially playwrights and novelists, indicate a change in dominant attitudes towards aboriginality, or literature or both? For example, when the prominent indigenous Australian novelist Mudrooroo was asked why the last three decades have seen the creation of a space for aboriginal writing he replied: 'Because . . . of postmodernism: the European monoculture has collapsed.'[1] However, other native authors believe that they and their people have *created* the space and forged the opportunity for their words to be heard, through continued activism, cultivation of the media, and insistent lobbying of government.

The issue of the role of publishers is also crucial here: have they made it possible for aboriginal writing to become known both domestically and internationally, or have they seized upon a commercial opportunity to generate sales? Clearly, this is not a simple matter, but one case suffices to illustrate the point. The only novel by an indigenous author to win the prestigious Booker McConnell Prize is Keri Hulme's *the bone people*, which was given the award in 1985. It has sold over half a million copies world-wide. Yet, after a ten-year gestation period (and five rejections from commercial publishers) Hulme's manuscript was first released in 1983 by an alternative women's press in New Zealand, the Spiral Collective.

Printed in a cheap, paper-bound edition of 2,000 copies, its runaway success in New Zealand caught many critics by surprise and rapidly led to its global distribution by Hodder & Stoughton. However, it is possible that Hulme's novel might never have been published at all had its author not received the support of a women's collective at that crucial stage. And it is as true in Canada and Australia as in New Zealand that many examples of indigenous literature were first released like *the bone people* by small, independent publishers who were motivated by a combination of bravery and commitment. What is equally certain is that now the climate has altered radically; if anything, in the 1990s commercial publishers were competing with each other for manuscripts by native authors especially in the case of novels and anthologies.

Therefore, concentrating upon the recent spate of anthologies of indigenous literature in all three nations, I intend to theorize here about why they have been produced and, more importantly, what the circumstances of their production signify. Finally, I hope to investigate what this

---

[1] Quoted in Adam Shoemaker, *Mudrooroo: A Critical Study* (Sydney: Collins/Angus & Robertson, 1993), 165.

process of anthologizing means for the self-definition of indigenous people whether it is termed Indianness, Aboriginality, or Maoridom.

The difficulty is that so little is really known about the cause and effect of the indigenous writing phenomenon and whether a linear model is even appropriate to the discussion. The investigation then becomes a sequence of further questions, some of which may appear circular and self-reflexive, but all of which are pertinent. For example, is aboriginal literature a new academic industry? Is it a means of liberation for native people or is it more a preoccupation of white academic theoreticians? Or is it, above all, a form of cultural expression which expresses indigenous ideology in a unique way? I hope to address these issues here, and to explore why in a very real sense these paper tracks of indigeneity are always mobile ones. In fact, in the case of aboriginal writers, the marks on the paper are almost always travelling, altering, on the move.

Of course, this begs one final question: why focus upon native authors, instead of lawyers, health-workers, or other spokespeople? There are a number of answers to this; including the fact that for good or ill aboriginal writers and their works are one of the clearest manifestations of the process whereby native peoples have achieved so-called mainstream recognition. One of the most significant breakthroughs in this area has undoubtedly occurred in indigenous theatre over the past two decades.

For example, in the 1970s and 1980s, native dramatists such as the New Zealander Harry Dansey, the Australians Robert Merritt and Jack Davis, and the Canadian Tomson Highway all received enthusiastic reviews for their inaugural works. Dansey's *Te Raukura: The Feathers of the Albatross* (1972) with its symbolic opposition between Maori pacifism and aggression was one of the most overtly powerful and political New Zealand dramas to be staged during that decade. In this, the first published play by a Maori dramatist, Dansey presented a highly allegorical, epic vision of the Taranaki wars and offered the audience the choice between a Christian solution to contemporary New Zealand racial violence and the outright rejection of this spiritual resolution. Despite its equivocal ending, the production of *Te Raukura* is still noted with pride by Maori authors. For example, in the introduction to *He Reo Hou* (1991), the first published collection of Maori drama, Roma Potiki observes:

Harry Dansey's *Te Raukura* . . . was one of the first to receive wide coverage on stage, radio and television as well as touring extensively . . . Without the first wave of playwrights, who continue to challenge us and write for a Maori audience, we could not have had the second wave of Maori writing or performance.[2]

---

[2] Roma Potiki, introduction, in Simon Garrett (ed.), *He Reo Hou: 5 Plays by Maori Playwrights* (Wellington: Playmarket, 1991), 9, 11.

Merritt's *The Cake Man* was first performed in 1974, the same year that *Te Raukura* was published. While the core of the drama was a poignant evocation of the trials of New South Wales reserve life for Aborigines in the 1950s, the play is leavened by humour as much as it is marked by pathos. At the close of the action the ironically named protagonist Sweet William is arrested by the Sydney police simply because he is standing at the door of a pub when a brawl takes place inside. However, this seemingly pessimistic ending is offset by dream-sequences which bracket the drama, and give a legendary dimension to the apparently simple story. Clearly, *The Cake Man* is a play which travels well: it enjoyed a two-week, sell-out season at the Festival of World Theatre in Denver, Colorado in 1982 and has been continuously in print since 1978.

Although Merritt's was the first black Australian play to be published, it is Jack Davis who is undoubtedly the most significant Aboriginal dramatist to date. His theatrical début, *Kullark* (1979), was written to be a highly ironic counterpoint to the sesquicentenary of the British occupation of Western Australia. Davis certainly achieved his aim in a play which set historical and contemporary scenes in telling parallel; he then followed this achievement with a string of successful productions throughout the 1980s, the best known of which are *The Dreamers* (1983), *No Sugar* (1985), and *Barungin (Smell the Wind)* (1988). *No Sugar* itself went on to be presented at the World Theatre Festival held in conjunction with World Expo 86 in Vancouver and was also re-mounted for a short season at the Riverside Studios in London in 1988.

In the same year that Davis toured *No Sugar* to Canada, a major native breakthrough on the Canadian stage was also imminent: the first mainstream production of Tomson Highway's *The Rez Sisters* (1986). Probably the single most important play by an indigenous Canadian, *The Rez Sisters* was set on the fictional Wasaychigan Hill Indian Reserve on Manitoulin Island, Ontario. In style, it was (like Davis's *The Dreamers*) simultaneously naturalistic and surrealistic; in content, it was outrageously funny as well as enormously moving. Highway portrayed the rez (or reservation) as a cool place, where seven native women vie to win the biggest bingo game in the world by travelling all the way to Toronto, only to find that much more is being gambled than money. Such was the play's success that, in addition to a full Canadian tour in 1988, it was performed on the main stage of the Edinburgh Festival later in the same year.

Dansey, Davis, and Highway all used the stage to great effect to communicate their indigenous message to the wider non-aboriginal society. Notably, these early playwrights were all men, which raises some pointed questions about the power structures of the theatre (both indigenous and non-indigenous) in all three nations. That said, it clearly was because of the work of these three playwrights that native drama first gained popular recognition and an international voice, as far afield as Perth, Wellington, Sydney, London, Vancouver, and Edinburgh.

Since that time, female indigenous playwrights in New Zealand have more than redressed the balance. It is significant to note that the first Maori play to be performed outside that country and the first such play by a woman was Rena Owen's prison drama for two actors *Te Awa i Tahuti*, which enjoyed a successful London tour in 1987. In addition, by far the most prolific Maori dramatist has been Renée, who has had at least seven separate productions mounted in New Zealand since her first play, *Asking For It*, was performed in Kaikohe in 1983. However, in Canada and Australia, the majority of published aboriginal plays are still written by males, such as the Canadian Drew Hayden Taylor (*The Bootlegger Blues* (1990) and *Someday* (1991) ) and the Australians Bob Maza (*The Keepers* (1988) ), Richard Walley (*Coordah* (1987)), and Jimmie Chi (*Bran Nue Dae* (1987)). Clearly, the masculine/feminine dynamic of indigenous theatre in these three nations merits further examination.

It is probably impossible to define the complex interrelationship between written texts by indigenous authors and larger socio-political events. However, since 1970, a pattern seems to have emerged in all three countries. It is that major social upheavals involving native people have been accompanied by an explosion in literary production. This happens for a wide variety of reasons: international media exposure, political crisis points, government funding for special projects, changing school syllabuses, the readiness of publishers to test and develop markets, and, above all, the ever-present talent of indigenous writers. The interplay of these factors is fascinating. They can be observed peaking in importance at various times over the past twenty-five years: in New Zealand, during the lead-up and the aftermath to the passage of the Treaty of Waitangi Act in 1975; in Australia, during and following the Commonwealth Games of 1982 and the Bicentenary of 1988; in Canada, in the environment of the Oka confrontation in Quebec in 1990.

It is fascinating that what began in New Zealand as an apparently superficial gesture towards Maori autonomy had far-reaching political and artistic effects. In response to continuous demands by Maori activists in the early 1970s for greater legal self-determination, the Treaty of Waitangi Act established for the first time the Waitangi Tribunal, a body whose true importance and power was not revealed for over a decade. As Paul Havemann explains:

The Act was passed, despite widespread ambivalence, under the advocacy of Labour's Minister of Maori Affairs, Matiu Rata, a Maori. There appears to have been little inkling or intention that it would lead to an irreversible revolution in constitutional discourse . . . Judging by how the Tribunal was set up originally, it must have been conceived of as a way merely to placate Maori and to provide some cathartic moments.

However, Havemann adds: 'During the 1980s the Tribunal became the engine room of the Maori Constitutional Revolution.'[3]

Events which ultimately led to the Act accelerated throughout the early 1970s. There was a rapid increase in Maori demonstrations, sit-ins, blockades, and Waitangi Day protests during the period and this was just one index of the burgeoning Maori cultural renaissance. This activity reached its apex in 1975 when the Maori Land March took place throughout the length of the North Island. It is no coincidence that the same period saw a flowering of Maori literature in English. In just six years (from 1972 to 1978) Maori authors achieved many publishing milestones beginning with Witi Ihimaera's *Pounamu, Pounamu* (1972) and *Tangi* (1973); respectively, the first collection of short stories and the first novel to be written by a Maori author. This was soon followed by Dansey's *Te Raukura* and the signal achievements of Patricia Grace, whose inaugural collection of short stories, *Waiariki*, appeared in 1975. With *Waiariki* and her début novel *Mutuwhenua* (1978) Grace became both the first Maori woman to publish a book of short fiction and also the first female Maori novelist. And, in the same year, Vernice Wineera Pere published *Mahanga*, the inaugural collection of verse by a Maori woman.

The clustering of these titles and genres and their appearance within such a short period of time points to the fact that the desire to express Maoridom through literature and the means to achieve this end both surfaced at a specific socio-political moment in recent New Zealand history. The same pattern repeats itself in Australia and Canada. In the former, Colin Johnson (now Mudrooroo)'s début novel *Wild Cat Falling* was released by Angus & Robertson in 1965, just a few months after a different publisher (the Jacaranda Press) had launched Kath Walker (Oodgeroo)'s inaugural collection of poetry *We Are Going*. Both achieved commercial success: Oodgeroo's collection was so popular that it was reprinted seven times in seven months and individual poems (such as 'We Are Going') are frequently anthologized, while Mudrooroo's novel has been continuously in print since its release. Significantly, both books also appeared during a period in which the debate over Aboriginal civil rights which culminated with the Australian Federal Referendum of 1967 had an extremely high profile.

[3] Paul Havemann, 'What's in the Treaty? Constitutionalizing Maori Rights in Aotearoa/New Zealand, 1975–1993', in Kayleen Hazlehurst (ed.), *Legal Pluralism and the Colonial Legacy* (Aldershot: Avebury, 1995), 88, 90.

One striking Canadian example of the coalescence of protest and publication is the fact that in one year, 1990, five separate collections of Native literature were released and a further one was commissioned. This flourish of literary activity occurred in the wake of the most dramatic Native Canadian protest of the twentieth century: the two-month blockade of the Mercier Bridge in southern Quebec by the Mohawk Band. Spanning the summer months of July–August 1990, the protest was in retaliation for provincial police incursions into the sovereign Mohawk settlement near Oka, Quebec and the proposed extension of a local golf course into Mohawk sacred sites. The provincial police action resulted in the accidental shooting of a police officer and ultimately led to the calling-up of the Canadian army, a decision which dismayed many citizens of the country, aboriginal and non-aboriginal alike.

This is not to say that literature is written on the barricades, nor that it could not appear without such specific and violent catalysts. However, it is undeniable that there has been a close relationship between public manifestations of indigeneity and the form of political expression reflected in native literatures. At the same time, it is not true to say that all aboriginal authors are recognized activists, nor do they all write occasional poems in the wake of a demonstration or a death in custody. For example, probably the best-known Maori novelist Keri Hulme lives a solitary, almost reclusive life, and has very little overt involvement in the Maori political movement. Yet, no one could deny the fiercely proud sense of indigenous identity which is embedded in her work and words. Hulme is the author of two books of poetry (*The Silences Between: Moeraki Conversations* (1982) and *Lost Possessions* (1985)) as well as short fiction (*Te Kaihau/The Windeater* (1986)) although she is still undoubtedly best known for *the bone people*. Her best-selling novel is imbued with the language and spirituality of her indigenous forebears; the same consciousness informs the dialogue (which is replete with Maori terms) and the characterization of the book. However, the trajectory of *the bone people* towards the discovery of the moral or immoral centre of the protagonist, Kerewin Holmes, is not just one of indigeneity. Instead, it is towards a new connection with all of the constituent elements of New Zealand culture. The novel, then, comprises a circus of disparate images; as Mark Williams has put it:

Her own language spills from a hectic word hoard of Anglo-Saxonisms, Latinate words, the specialised terminologies of medicine, pharmacopoeias, floral taxonomies, craft-derived terms, especially nautical and carpentering expressions.[4]

---

[4] Mark Williams, *Leaving the Highway: Six Contemporary New Zealand Novelists* (Auckland: Auckland University Press, 1990), 88.

All of this eclecticism is mediated through the legendary world of dreams, the motivation for which the author explains as follows:

There is one especial aspect of my Maori heritage which I take gleeful and joyous pride in and that is its amazing rich mythology—but I equally take pride in the Celtic and Norse mythology which is also mine by heritage.[5]

Undoubtedly, an emphasis upon the uniqueness of Maori spirituality is one of the distinguishing characteristics of much recent indigenous fiction in New Zealand. All of the major Maori novelists who began publishing in the 1970s and 1980s, Witi Ihimaera, Patricia Grace, and Hulme, emphasize a connection between the physical and the metaphysical via Maori magic and religion. As early as 1977, Ihimaera's story 'The Greenstone Patu', published in the collection *The New Net Goes Fishing*, in which a traditional Maori weapon is called into life through incantation, is invested with what Ken Arvidson calls extreme animism.[6] This strong emphasis upon sacred objects as a key to Maori knowledge, power, and prescience is a theme which is reiterated in the novels of Grace (to a minor degree in *Mutuwhenua* (1978) but very prominently in her major work, *Potiki* (1986)), for which she won the fiction section of the New Zealand book awards. In what is one of the most perceptive brief surveys of contemporary Maori writing in English, Arvidson notes that 'It is undoubtedly one of the purposes of this kind of writing, perhaps the major purpose, to assert the survival of Maori spirituality and to stress its difference from the Judaeo-Christian tradition.'[7]

The most prolific male Maori author, Ihimaera, returns to a similar theme throughout his work, in which both sacred places and things are inspired with the breath of Maori beliefs in order to define both their power and their distinctiveness. At times the stylistic representation of this tendency can overbalance into an excess of romanticism, as in the author's juvenile novel *The Whale Rider* (1987) 'Once, he had a golden master who had wooed him with flute song. Then his master had used a conch shell to bray his commands to the whale over long distances. As their communication grew so did their understanding and love of each other.'[8] On the other hand, in his major novel *The Matriarch* (1986) Ihimaera gives this animism a far greater focus, strength, and persuasiveness:

[5] Quoted in Sue Kedgley (ed.), *Our Own Country: Leading New Zealand Women Writers Talk about their Writing and their Lives* (Auckland: Penguin Books, 1989), 104.

[6] Ken Arvidson, 'Aspects of Contemporary Maori Writing in English', in Graham McGregor and Mark Williams (eds.), *Dirty Silence: Aspects of Language and Literature in New Zealand* (Auckland: Oxford University Press, 1991), 121.

[7] Arvidson, 'Aspects', 125.

[8] Witi Ihimaera, *The Whale Rider* (Auckland: Heinemann, 1987), 24.

She felt the elements coming alive, the long silent dynamo of creation beginning to hum. The earth, breathing. The sky taking the form of a giant tattooed god. The forces of life, animate and inanimate, stirring in the wind and flooding through a widening cleft of light.[9]

In *The Matriarch*, Ihimaera invests in spirituality, but it is spirituality with a political edge: the shaman meets the activist.

This approach to indigenous culture is reproduced in a remarkably similar fashion in Australia, exemplified by the work of Mudrooroo. For example, in his *Master of the Ghost Dreaming* the female character Ludgee recaptures her spiritual energy in a talismanic way:

The female power surged within her; ancestors were connected in an unbroken line. The grid of the Female Dreaming flowed with energy. She dived into the water in a quick flowing motion which took her under and under . . . She was free in her tradition.[10]

The emphasis upon secret knowledge, the power of the Dreaming, and the so-called clever man is reiterated throughout Aboriginal Australian works. Mudrooroo's *Long Live Sandawara* provides another clear example of this concentration upon the so-called *maban*:

Then from out of the darkness, from the direction of the pool a strange but familiar humming begins to murmur. It rises and rises until it is a roar . . . The men collect at the water's edge and nearby they see a soft rainbow light pulsating without strength from a dark figure . . . A lightning flash strikes a tree right next to where Sandawara is sitting and fire runs down the trunk. In amazement and fear they seem to see a huge serpent wrapped about the body of their leader. It writhes about his body.[11]

In the same vein of masculinist magical realism is Sam Watson's novel *The Kadaitcha Sung*. Here, the entire narrative is suffused with images of punishment for spiritual sins, for the Kadaitcha men are black Australian executioners, messengers of death:

A light flashed and he saw blue flames dancing through the wood. A yellow smoke reached out to embrace him. He closed his eyes and fought the fear that tried to claim him. As a mortal he must be hardened within the eternal flame before he could be initiated into the clan of the Kadaitcha. So be it! He was ready for death if death it was to be.[12]

As all of these extracts reveal, native authors believe that an exploration of traditional religious beliefs is an essential underpinning for their

[9] Witi Ihimaera, *The Matriarch* (Auckland: Heinemann, 1986), 108.
[10] Mudrooroo Narogin, *Master of the Ghost Dreaming* (Sydney: Angus & Robertson, 1991), 59.
[11] Mudrooroo Narogin, *Long Live Sandawara* (Melbourne: Hyland House, 1979), 82.
[12] Sam Watson, *The Kadaitcha Sung* (Ringwood: Penguin, 1990), 30.

verbal art. However, this phenomenon should not be considered solely on the level of content: it is not just the writings which reflect this preoccupation but the writers themselves. Put another way, Maori, Aboriginal, and Indian authors introduce a crucial element of spirituality into their *attitude* towards writing, not just towards the product of that craft.

Jeannette Armstrong, the author of *Slash* (1985), the first novel by a Native Canadian woman, expresses her beliefs as follows:

I did prepare myself in the Indian way for this novel. I asked for the guidance to write it. And I fasted for the guidance to write it. I didn't decide, I'm gonna write this! I didn't just decide that I know everything. I asked for help and assistance, through the same process from the Okanagan.[13]

The result was an internationally acclaimed book which focused upon the ideological development of the protagonist Thomas Kelasket as he becomes increasingly involved in the North American First Nations movement. Armstrong's comments are reminiscent of those of Hulme, who noted that *the bone people* was launched in a very Maori fashion; as she added: 'In fact no other book of fiction in New Zealand had been launched that way. I think that the spiritual input from the Maori side was an enormous contribution and is maybe the reason for its great success.'[14]

What, then, does this mean? I believe these comments illustrate that many native writers perceive themselves as being far more concerned and involved with the *process* of story-telling rather than just with the *content* of the tale. This also underlines the primacy of the oral tradition in such works, for it is seen as the wellspring and the model for such literature.

However, I should emphasize that this is not just a matter of freezing oral material in written form. As the leading Australian critic Stephen Muecke has argued, native cultures are anything but pre-literate.[15] This is as odious a term as pre-Columbian or pre-historical, and carries with it all sorts of incorrect connotations of inferiority and the need for progress towards improvement. Rather, the First Nations of Canada, New Zealand, and Australia were *profoundly* literate in the sense that body painting, inscription, mapping, and caring for land were all forms of reading the country as long as reading is understood in a larger, semiotic sense. Clearly, indigenous reading of this sort involved nothing like stasis—quite the opposite. It was as true for the Indians and Inuit as

[13] Quoted in Hartmut Lutz, *Contemporary Challenges: Conversations with Canadian Native Authors* (Saskatoon: Fifth House, 1991), 20.

[14] Quoted in Kedgley (ed.), *Our Own Country*, 97.

[15] Stephen Muecke, *Textual Spaces: Aboriginality and Cultural Studies* (Kensington: New South Wales University Press, 1992), 164–78.

for the Maori and the Aborigines that movement through one's country now reproduced via the paper tracks of literature was an essential element of survival and of care. Muecke describes it this way:

To know this country is to walk around it along tracks put down by the ancestors, participating in ceremony; for the arts are performed, repeated arts, not unique creations. The texts collected in one's travels *are* the travelling, the landscape is always in the process of being constructed, and authority is constantly deferred because one has to engage with so many people. All those responsibilities (towards the land) can't stop you from getting any work done; they are the work getting done.[16]

One of the other insights communicated by indigenous authors, such as the Native Canadian novelist, poet, and anthologist Thomas King, is that in Indian works preoccupations with right and wrong, good and evil are often supplanted by the indigenous concern for harmonious balance. As one of the most popular native writers in Canada (and, along with Mudrooroo, one of the foremost indigenous literary critics) King has explored the dimensions of that balancing act in all of his work, which is marked by subtlety, intelligence, and wry irony. As simple a sentence as the following taken from his first novel, the award-winning *Medicine River* (1990), displays all of these features:

After a six-year courtship and a four-month pregnancy, Jonnie Prettywoman and Cecil Broadman got married. Cecil's parents were Catholic in a reasonable sort of way and were pleased that the ceremony was performed before they had to make plans for the baptism.[17]

While one might feel that the Indianness of this passage is not immediately obvious, it is typical of a novel in which the cross-cultural position of Native Canadians is mediated through formal institutions such as organized religion. The understated humour of the passage is also typical, not only of King's prose, but of that of many other indigenous authors in all three nations. Such an approach is striking because First Nations writers so frequently use laughter to offset pain, to celebrate their communities, and to act as a cultural marker distinguishing them from non-natives. In his novel *Green Grass, Running Water* (1994) as well as in his collection of short fiction *One Good Story, That One* (1993) King continues this pattern of gently satirizing both non-aboriginal and Canadian Indian culture from within, whether it is on the basketball court, in a steakhouse, or on the highway. Throughout, the traditional trickster figure of North American native mythology is as prominent in his books as in the plays of Tomson Highway, the novels of Mudrooroo, or the wild characters of Keri Hulme.

---

[16] Ibid. 178.    [17] Thomas King, *Medicine River* (Markham: Viking, 1990), 88.

A similar preoccupation with balance is often expressed by indigenous authors, artists, and performers on the other side of the Pacific; the Aboriginal singer, songwriter, and poet Mandawuy Yunupingu puts it like this:

> You see that old man taught me things I should know
> From the memories of the past
> And the situation is the bottom line between illusion and reality
> We have always thought of making things right
> It's a big proposition from the Yolngu of this Earth
> How about you come too
> This is my kind of life
> This a Yolngu Yolngu way of life.[18]

Yunupingu establishes a point which even those who are opposed to indigenous rights have to accept. It is that native people do have a world-view which differs dramatically from that of the majority cultures of Canada, Australia, and New Zealand. This is not a matter of roman-ticizing aboriginal races or depicting them as indigenous philosophers operating on an ethereal plane but it *is* a matter of recognizing that attitudes towards central concerns such as land are vastly different. As a corrective to this bias, some researchers have sought to compile collec-tions of interviews with indigenous authors, in order to counteract the tyranny of second-hand information and bigotry.

Of course, even this technique has its drawbacks, since it centres upon the *moment* at which information is collected, opinions are received, and in anthropological terms field work is completed. Given that this is the starting-point in a process which often leads to publication under the name of the interviewer, it is no wonder that native people are now becoming far more wary of such approaches, and are more likely to question the credentials and the purpose of those researchers who ap-proach them for assistance. It is ironic that, in a book which is so conscious of the perils of appropriation the German interviewer Hartmut Lutz is able to have the following exchange with the Canadian Indian story-teller Lenore Keeshig-Tobias:

HL: 'It's true! And it's not just the sort of national resources that are out there, but now it's Native people becoming a natural resource!'
LKT: 'Yes, right. Exactly, exactly! They have our land, and now they want our stories, our voices, too. And I say, No!'

To his credit, Lutz is perceptive enough to realize that such comments could also apply to him, so he asks, What do you say about non-native people taking an interest in native literature? People like me, cruising

---

[18] 'My Kind of Life', on Yothu Yindi, *Tribal Voice* (Sydney: Mushroom Records, 1991).

through Canada, meeting with native writers and presses? Keeshig-Tobias's response is a classic combination of diplomacy and directness: 'Well, it depends. I think I always give people the benefit of a doubt, first. And if you prove yourself to be (*LAUGHS*) an arsehole, I'll tell you!'[19]

In Australia, Kevin Gilbert cites a different sort of potential exploitation. In the introduction to his 1988 anthology of Aboriginal and Torres Strait Islander poetry *Inside Black Australia*, he decries what he sees as the increasing tendency of non-Aborigines to obtain university degrees on the backs of the blacks: 'A whole new education industry has arisen in the academic area, where it would appear that every student is doing his or her PhD English thesis on Aboriginal Literature.'[20] While Gilbert may exaggerate the extent of research (and appropriation) in the field, his comment does challenge all students of indigenous writing: if aboriginal peoples do own such writing how is this to be expressed? This is the gauntlet thrown down by indigenous authors and why their writings are inescapably political. More than anything else, native writers are establishing an independent cultural space for their peoples. However, at the same time, such work cannot be dismissed solely as the literature of a minority or of the margin. In a very real sense, as the Native Canadian poet, playwright, and anthologist Daniel David Moses has put it, it is central to our understanding of what written communication is all about. When asked if there was a threat that native literature could be swamped by the mainstream, he replied: 'My image of that mainstream is that it is pretty wide but it's spiritually shallow. I don't think we are worried about being subsumed. If we become part of that mainstream we're going to be the deep currents.'[21]

The Western Australian Aboriginal elder Paddy Roe puts it in a similar way:

> all the top, top soil
> in this country
> this belongs to the
> this belongs to the government
> government got the place
> and er, government
> we only gotta find little places for ourselves, to live
> but the bottom part of the soil again
> THIS belongs to the tribal people
> because the LAW is there.[22]

[19] Lutz, *Contemporary Challenges*, 82.
[20] Kevin Gilbert (ed.), *Inside Black Australia: An Anthology of Aboriginal Poetry* (Ringwood: Penguin, 1988), p. xvi.
[21] Daniel David Moses and Terry Goldie (eds.), *An Anthology of Canadian Native Literature in English* (Toronto: Oxford University Press, 1992), p. xiv.
[22] Quoted in Muecke, *Textual Spaces*, 171.

In New Zealand, the editors of the massive six-volume anthology of contemporary Maori literature *Te Ao Marama* treat the matter slightly differently, but the essential core of indigenous strength is undeniably clear. According to Witi Ihimaera, Haare Williams, Irihapeti Ramsden, and D. S. Long:

> In the 1990s we may have come to a crossroads, of a literature of Maori writing and a literature of race relations, of a literature of the past and a literature of the present and future, and of a Maori response and an individual response . . . But Maori writers need to keep regarding the world as Maori, and not Pakeha. There is no reason why the world should cease being Maori for, say, a Maori in Sydney.[23]

So, the challenge remains: how can one disseminate the words of native peoples in a way which does do justice to their intentions? Many different approaches have been tried. In the 1960s the Australian novelist Dame Mary Durack edited and introduced the then Colin Johnson's novel *Wild Cat Falling* in as maternalistic a fashion as anything in Canada's Indian Act of the same era—and certainly in as patronizing a way as Noel Hilliard treated the theme of Maori urban debauchery in his 1960 novel *Maori Girl*. In the 1970s the course of developments in Australia and Canada diverged from that of New Zealand. While in Auckland the first works of Ihimaera and Grace were being printed, in the other two nations publishers were still largely fixated on the life-story genre: Maria Campbell's *Halfbreed* (1973) and Charles Perkins's *A Bastard Like Me* (1975) are prominent examples (and even their titles are remarkably similar). Despite the example of Maori literary achievements in New Zealand throughout the 1970s, both in Canada and in Australia it was largely the case that aboriginal writing was seen as some form of liberationist sociology, almost as ethnographic documentation. And here, the parallel with the outmoded perception that native visual art was no more than art and craft is an irresistible one.

The next stage occurred in the early 1980s, when the first serious attempts to publicize native literature occurred in Canada; here, the work of the non-native academic Penny Petrone was obviously significant. Petrone's anthology *First People, First Voices* (1983) was not the inaugural anthology of indigenous Canadian writing, but it was certainly one of the most influential.

The case of anthologies is in fact crucial to the whole phenomenon of indigenous writing in English. In Canada, no collections of native writing appeared between 1983 and 1987; between 1988 and 1995 there have been ten. In Australia, no collections of Aboriginal literature were

---

[23] Witi Ihimaera *et al.* (eds.), *Te Ao Marama: Contemporary Maori Writing*, vol. i (Auckland: Reed Books, 1992), 17.

released until 1988; by 1995 there were four. In New Zealand, two anthologies had been printed by 1980; by 1995 there were seven. I believe that a new phase began in the mid-1980s: one which I term the anthologizing of aboriginal people.

By this I do not just mean the aggregation of allegedly representative samples of native writing. By anthologizing I mean the process of decision-making which led, at a given point, to the conclusion by publishers: 'there is something here which is of major importance and cries out for public exposure.' Anthologies are pointless unless there is a substantial body of work to draw upon; an anthologist cannot create a tradition *ex nihilo*. What was important was the determination at a given historical moment that aboriginal literatures needed and deserved such treatment.

This can be argued in two ways. In one sense, this conforms to an organicist, humanist model of development in which the appearance of such books is seen as an inevitable and positive stage in a linear path. On the other hand, it can be maintained that the project of anthologizing is an attempt to *contain* a phenomenon which is growing so fast it has become threatening. If such books were able to make Aboriginality, Indianness, or Maoridom accessible commercially and fully known both in absolute and public terms this would be a real danger. Fortunately, the incredible heterogeneity of these works and of the ideology which underlies them makes this impossible.

If one adopts a purely descriptive perspective, one can line all of these books up side by side only to discover that they are all vastly different. Some are explicitly regional: Colleen Glass and Archie Weller's *Us Fellas* (1987) presents work only by West Australian Aborigines; Jeanne Perreault and Sylvia Vance's *Writing the Circle* (1990) is a collection of work solely by native women from western Canada. On the other hand, some editors have intentionally constructed a comprehensive, chronological survey of Aboriginal writing such as Agnes Grant's *Our Bit Of Truth* (1990), and Jack Davis and others' *Paperbark* (1990) the first national collection in Australia. Others like Moses and Goldie's *An Anthology of Canadian Native Literature in English* (1992) as well as *Paperbark* are the product of collaborative teams of native and non-native editors, while a few collections (like Thomas King's *All my Relations* (1990) and Kevin Gilbert's *Inside Black Australia* (1988) ) are compiled and edited by a single indigenous author. The case of New Zealand is a unique one because every collection of Maori literature to be published until 1995 with the exception of Margaret Orbell's *Contemporary Maori Writing* (1970) has been edited by one man: Witi Ihimaera. Ihimaera's contribution to the collection, production, and dissemination of Maori writing is, therefore, remarkable; in a real sense, he can be considered the doyen of indigenous authors in New Zealand.

So, there is no structural pattern which unites all of these works or even any two of them. However, there is a force which underpins the virtual explosion of such collections at a particular point in the history of all three nations. It is that the organizing principle of an anthology makes it especially attractive for native people because it combines, in a unique way, individual creativity with community support and involvement. Anthologies are politically useful, culturally representative, and symbolic of communal, co-operative work. As Thomas King puts it:

This idea of community and family is not an idea that is often pursued by non-Native writers who prefer to imagine their Indians as solitary figures poised on the brink of extinction. For Native writers, community—a continuous community—is one of the primary ideas from which our literature proceeds.

And this can have unexpected benefits:

For Native audiences, the twentieth-century phenomenon of Native storytellers from different tribes sharing their stories in a common language through the contemporary and non-traditional forms of written poetry, prose and drama has helped to reinforce many of the beliefs that tribes have held individually, beliefs that tribes are now discovering they share mutually.[24]

In this light, it is understandable why anthologies have recently become so popular; rather, it is surprising that it has taken so long for this stage to be reached. My conviction is that the ability and desire of indigenous writers for publication has always been there but the opportunities have not. One of the clearest conclusions that can be drawn is that Indian, Inuit, and Aboriginal and Maori writers are incredibly talented and that it is not a matter of any of them being discovered, in the Western sense, but simply of giving that talent an outlet. It is ironic that, in all three countries, this has been the biggest challenge of all.

Nevertheless, new cultural formations and new opportunities have emerged for native authors. The incredible impact of Maori writer Alan Duff's début novel *Once Were Warriors* (1990) both in its published form and as translated onto the screen as a feature film demonstrates the capacity for indigenous works to cross all boundaries, be they those of genre, political engagement, or national borders. While such narratives are rooted in the soil of their peoples' countries, the paper tracks they have gifted to the reader are now migrating as never before.

---

[24] Thomas King (ed.), *All my Relations: An Anthology of Contemporary Canadian Native Fiction* (Toronto: McClelland & Stewart, 1990), pp. xiv–xv, ix–x.

# Selected Bibliography

The bibliography is based mostly on the essays. Further bibliographical information can be found in the national literary histories, in such reference works as *Contemporary Novelists* and *Contemporary Poets*, and in the annual bibliographies in *PMLA*, *YES*, and the *Journal of Commonwealth Literature*.

### PRIMARY

ACHEBE, CHINUA. *Things Fall Apart*. London: Heinemann, 1958.
—— *No Longer at Ease*. London: Heinemann, 1963.
—— *Arrow of God*. London: Heinemann, 1964 (rev. edn. 1974).
—— *A Man of the People*. London: Heinemann Educational Books, 1966.
—— *Beware Soul Brother and Other Poems*. London: Heinemann Educational Books, 1971.
—— *Anthills of the Savannah*. New York: Anchor Books, 1988.
—— and INNES, C. L. (eds.). *African Short Stories*. Oxford: Heinemann, 1987.
ADCOCK, FLEUR (ed.). *The Oxford Book of Contemporary New Zealand Poetry*. Auckland: Oxford University Press, 1982.
AGARD, JOHN. *Limbo Dancer in Dark*. Lewes: Greenheart, 1983.
—— *Mangoes and Bullets*. 1985; London: Serpent's Tail, 1990.
AIDOO, AMA ATA. *The Dilemma of a Ghost*. London: Longman, 1965.
—— *Anowa*. London: Longman, 1970.
—— *No Sweetness Here*. London: Longman, 1970.
—— *Changes: A Love Story*. London: The Women's Press, 1991; New York: The Feminist Press, 1993.
ALLFREY, PHYLLIS SHAND. *The Orchid House*. 1953; London: Virago, 1982.
ANAND, MULK RAJ. *Untouchable*. 1935; London: Penguin, 1986.
ANDERSON, HUGH (ed.). *Colonial Ballads*. 2nd edn. Melbourne: Cheshire, 1962.
—— *The Story of Australian Folksong*. Melbourne: Hill of Content, 1970.
ANGAS, GEORGE FRENCH. *Savage Life and Scenes*, 1847.
ARASANAYAGAM, JEAN. *Reddened Water Flows Clear*. London: Forrest Books, 1991.
ARMAH, AYI KWEI. *Two Thousand Seasons*. London: Heinemann Educational Books, 1979.
ARMSTRONG, JEANNETTE. *Slash*. Penticton: Theytus Books, 1985.
ATKINSON, JAMES. *An Account of the State of Agriculture and Grazing in New South Wales*, 1826.
ATWOOD, MARGARET. *Surfacing*. 1972; Don Mills: Paperjacks, 1973.
—— *Survival*. Toronto: Anansi, 1972.

ATWOOD, MARGARET (comp.). *The New Oxford Book of Canadian Verse in English* [Robert Hayman, Charles Sangster, and other writers]. Toronto: Oxford University Press, 1982.

—— *Cat's Eye.* Toronto: McClelland & Stewart, 1988.

—— and WEAVER, ROBERT (eds.). *The Oxford Book of Canadian Short Stories in English.* Toronto: Oxford University Press, 1988.

AUCKLAND, MICHAEL (ed.). *The Penguin Book of 19th Century Australian Literature.* Ringwood: Penguin, 1993.

AWOONOR, KOFI. *This Earth, my Brother . . .* London: Heinemann Educational Books, 1971.

AYLMER, ISABELLA. *Distant Homes; or The Graham Family in New Zealand*, 1862.

B., W. M. *The Narrative of Edward Crewe; or Life in New Zealand.* London, 1874.

BAIL, MURRAY (ed.). *The Faber Book of Contemporary Australian Short Stories.* London: Faber & Faber, 1988.

BARKER, LADY MARY ANNE BROOME. *Station Life in New Zealand.* 1870; Auckland: Golden, 1973.

—— *Station Amusements in New Zealand*, 1873.

BARNES, JOHN (ed.). *The Writer in Australia: A Collection of Literary Documents 1856 to 1964.* Melbourne: Oxford University Press, 1969.

BATHGATE, ALEXANDER. *Waitaruna: A Story of New Zealand Life.* London: Sampson Low, Marston, Searle & Rivington, 1881.

BAYNTON, BARBARA. *Barbara Baynton* [*Bush Studies* and other writings], ed. Sally Krimmer and Alan Lawson. St Lucia: University of Queensland Press, 1980.

—— *Bush Studies.* Sydney: Angus & Robertson, 1983.

BISSOONDATH, NEIL. *Digging up the Mountains.* Toronto: Macmillan, 1986.

—— *A Casual Brutality.* Toronto: Macmillan, 1988.

—— *On the Eve of Uncertain Tomorrows.* Toronto: Macmillan, 1990.

—— *Selling Illusions: The Cult of Multiculturalism in Canada.* Toronto: Penguin, 1994.

BOLDREWOOD, ROLF. *Rolf Boldrewood*, ed. Alan Brissenden [*Robbery under Arms* and other writings]. St Lucia: University of Queensland Press, 1979.

BOWEN, C. C. *Poems*, 1861.

BOWN, LALAGE (ed.). *Two Centuries of African English.* London: Heinemann Educational, 1973.

BRACKEN, THOMAS. *Musings in Maoriland*, 1890.

BRANT, BETH (ed.). *A Gathering of Spirit: A Collection by North American Indian Women.* Toronto: The Women's Press, 1988.

BRATHWAITE, EDWARD KAMAU. *The Arrivants: A New World Trilogy.* London: Oxford University Press, 1973.

—— *Mother Poem.* London: Oxford University Press, 1977.

—— *X/Self.* Oxford: Oxford University Press, 1987.

BRODBER, ERNA. *Jane and Louisa Will Soon Come Home.* London: New Beacon Books, 1980.

—— *Myal: A Novel.* London: New Beacon, 1988.

BROOKE, FRANCES. *The History of Emily Montague*, 1769; ed. Mary Jane Edwards. Ottawa: Carleton University Press, 1985.

BROOME, FREDERICK NAPIER. *Poems from New Zealand*, 1868.

BROWN, STEWART, MORRIS, MERVYN, and ROHLEHR, GORDON (eds.). *Voiceprint: An Anthology of Oral and Related Poetry from the Caribbean.* Jamaica: Longman, 1989.

BRUNER, CHARLOTTE (ed.). *Unwinding Threads: Writing by Women in Africa.* London: Heinemann, 1983.

BRUTUS, DENNIS. *A Simple Lust*. 1963; London: Heinemann, 1973.

BURNETT, PAULA (ed.). *The Penguin Book of Caribbean Verse in English* [Francis Williams, M. J. Chapman, and other writers and examples of oral traditions]. Harmondsworth: Penguin, 1986.

BUSIA, ABENA P. A. *Testimonies of Exile*. Trenton, NJ: Africa World Press, 1990.

BUTLER, SAMUEL. *A First Year in Canterbury Settlement*. London, 1863.

CAMBRIDGE, ADA. *A Marked Man*. 1891; London: Pandora, 1987.

CAMPBELL, JOHN LOGAN. *Poenamo*, 1881.

CAMPBELL, MARIA. *Halfbreed*. Toronto: McClelland & Stewart, 1973.

CAMPBELL, WILFRED. *The Poetical Works of Wilfred Campbell*, ed. W. J. Sykes. London: Hodder & Stoughton, 1922.

CANTRELL, LEON (ed.). *Writing of the 1890s*. St Lucia: University of Queensland Press, 1977.

CHAMIER, GEORGE. *Philosopher Dick*, 1891.

—— *A South Sea Siren*, 1895; ed. Joan Stevens. Auckland: Auckland University Press/Oxford University Press, 1970.

CHAPMAN, ROBERT, and BENNETT, JONATHAN (eds.). *An Anthology of New Zealand Verse* [John Barr, William Pember Reeves, and other writers]. Wellington: Oxford University Press, 1956.

CHARLWOOD, DON. *The Long Farewell: Settlers under Sail*. Victoria: Allen Lane, 1981.

CHINODYA, SHIMMER. *Harvest of Thorns*. Oxford: Heinemann, 1989.

CHIPASULA, FRANK MKALAWILE (ed.). *When my Brothers Come Home: Poems from Central and Southern Africa*. Middletown, Conn.: Wesleyan University Press, 1985.

CLACY, ELLEN. *A Lady's Visit to the Gold Diggings of Australia*, 1853.

—— *Lights and Shadows of Australian Life*, 1854.

CLARKE, AUSTIN. *The Meeting Point*. Toronto: Macmillan, 1972.

—— *Nine Men Who Laughed*. Markham: Penguin, 1986.

CLARKE, MARCUS. *A Colonial City* [selected journalism], ed. L. T. Hergenhan. St Lucia: University of Queensland Press, 1972.

—— *His Natural Life*, 1870–2; ed. and introd. Stephen Murray-Smith. Harmondsworth: Penguin, 1970.

—— *Marcus Clarke* [*For the Term of his Natural Life* and other writings], ed. Michael Wilding. St Lucia: University of Queensland Press, 1976.

CLIFF, MICHELLE. *Abeng*. Trumansburg, NY: Crossing Press, 1984.

—— *The Land of Look Behind*. Ithaca, NY: Firebrand, 1985.

—— *No Telephone to Heaven*. New York: Dutton, 1987.

CLOUGH, ARTHUR HUGH. *Poems of Arthur Hugh Clough.* 2nd edn. Oxford: Clarendon, 1974.

COETZEE, J. M. *In the Heart of the Country.* Harmondsworth: Penguin, 1976.

COLLINS, DAVID. *An Account of the English Colony in New South Wales.* London, 1798.

CONNOR, RALPH. *The Man from Glengarry: A Tale of the Ottawa.* 1901; Toronto: McClelland & Stewart, 1993.

COUVREUR, J. C. ['Tasma']. *Uncle Piper of Piper's Hill*, 1889; ed. Cecil Hadgraft and Ray Bielby. Melbourne: Nelson, 1969.

COZENS, CHARLES. *Adventures of a Guardsman*, 1848.

DABYDEEN, CYRIL. *Coastland.* Oakville: Mosaic, 1989.

—— *Still Close to the Island.* Ottawa: Commoner's Publishing, 1980.

DABYDEEN, DAVID. *Slave Song.* Aarhus: Dangaroo, 1984.

—— *Coolie Odyssey.* London: Hansib, 1988.

—— *The Intended.* London: Secker & Warburg, 1991.

D'AGUIAR, FRED. *Mama Dot.* London: Chatto, 1985.

—— *Airy Hall.* London: Chatto, 1989.

—— 'Home', in Victor J. Ramraj, *Concert of Voices.* Peterborough: Broadview Press, 1995: 104–5.

—— 'Notting Hill', in *British Subjects.* Newcastle: Bloodaxe, 1993.

DANGAREMBGA, TSITSI. *Nervous Conditions.* Harare: Zimbabwe Publishing House, 1988.

DANSEY, HARRY. *Te Raukura: The Feathers of the Albatross.* Auckland: Longman Paul, 1974.

DAS, KAMALA. *The Old Playhouse and Other Poems.* Delhi: Orient Longman, 1973.

DAVEY, FRANK (ed.). *Tish No. 1–19.* Vancouver: Talonbooks, 1975.

DAVIS, JACK. *Kullark/The Dreamers.* Sydney: Currency Press, 1982.

—— *No Sugar.* Sydney: Currency Press, 1986.

—— *Barungin (Smell the Wind).* Sydney: Currency Press, 1989.

—— *et al.* (eds.). *Paperbark: A Collection of Black Australian Writings.* St Lucia: University of Queensland Press, 1990.

D'COSTA, JEAN, and LALLA, BARBARA (eds.). *Voices in Exile: Jamaican Texts of the 18th and 19th Centuries* [Francis Williams, Michael Scott, and other writers]. Tuscaloosa: University of Alabama Press, 1989.

DE LISSER, HERBERT G. *The White Witch of Rosehall.* 1929; Kingston: Macmillan Caribbean, 1982.

DE MILLE, JAMES. *A Strange Manuscript Found in a Copper Cylinder*, 1888; ed. Malcolm Parks. Ottawa: Carleton University Press, 1986.

DESAI, ANITA. *Cry, the Peacock.* 1963; New Delhi: Orient Paperbacks, 1983.

—— *Voices in the City.* 1965; New Delhi: Orient Paperbacks, 1982.

—— *Fire on the Mountain.* London: Penguin, 1977.

—— *Games at Twilight.* London: Penguin, 1978.

—— *Clear Light of Day.* London: Penguin, 1980.

—— *In Custody.* London: Heinemann; New York: Harper & Row, 1984.

—— *Baumgartner's Bombay.* London: Heinemann, 1988; New York: Knopf, 1989.

DESHPANDE, SHASHI. *That Long Silence*. London: Virago, 1988.

DE SOUZA, EUNICE. *Fix*. Bombay: Newground, 1979.

—— *Women in Dutch Painting*. Bombay: Praxis, 1988.

—— *Ways of Belonging: Selected Poems*. Edinburgh: Polygon, 1990.

DEWART, EDWARD HARTLEY (ed.). *Selections from Canadian Poets*. 1864; Toronto: University of Toronto Press, 1973.

DIEFFENBACK, ERNEST. *Travels in New Zealand*. London, 1843.

DOMETT, ALFRED. *Ranolf and Amohia*, 1872.

DRUMMOND, ALISON (ed.). *Married & Gone to New Zealand: Being Extracts from the Writings of Women Pioneers*. Auckland: Paul's Book Arcade; London: Oxford University Press, 1960.

DUFF, ALAN. *Once Were Warriors*. Auckland: Tandem Press, 1990.

DUNCAN, SARA JEANNETTE. *Selected Journalism*, ed. Thomas E. Tausky. Ottawa: Tecumseh, 1978.

—— *The Simple Adventures of a Memsahib*, 1893; ed. Thomas E. Tausky. Ottawa: Tecumseh, 1986.

EDWARDS, PAUL, and DABYDEEN, DAVID (eds.). *Black Writers in Britain 1760–1890* [Olaudah Equiano, Ignatius Sancho, Mary Prince, Mary Seacole, Edward Wilmot Blyden, and other writers]. Edinburgh: Edinburgh University Press, 1991.

ELLIOTT, BRIAN (ed.). *The Jindyworabaks*. Brisbane: University of Queensland Press, 1979.

—— and MITCHELL, ADRIAN (eds.). *Bards in the Wilderness: Australian Colonial Poetry to 1920*. Melbourne: Nelson, 1970.

EMECHETA, BUCHI. *Second-Class Citizen*. London: Fontana/Collins, 1977.

—— *The Slave Girl*. London: Allison & Busby, 1977.

—— *The Bride-Price*. London: Fontana/Collins, 1978.

—— *The Joys of Motherhood*. New York: Braziller, 1979.

EQUIANO, OLAUDAH. *Equiano's Travels*, ed. and abridged Paul Edwards. London: Heinemann Educational, 1966.

EZEKIEL, NISSIM. *Collected Poems 1952–1988*. Bombay: Oxford University Press, 1989.

FERGUSON, DUGALD. *Bush Life in Australia and New Zealand*, 1893.

—— *Mates*, 1911.

FIELD, BARRON. *First Fruits of Australian Poetry*, 1819.

FIFE, CONNIE (ed.). *The Colour of Resistance: A Contemporary Collection of Writing by Aboriginal Women*. Toronto: Sister Vision Press, 1993.

FISHER, PETER. *The Lay of the Wilderness*, 1833.

FOGARTY, LIONEL GEORGE. *Yoogum Yoogum*. Ringwood: Penguin, 1982.

FOOTT, MARY HANNAY. *Sketches of Life in the Bush; or Ten Years in the Interior*, 1872.

FORSTER, GEORGE. *Voyage round the World*. London, 1777.

FROST, LUCY (ed.). *No Place for a Nervous Lady: Voices from the Australian Bush*. Melbourne: McPhee Gribble/Penguin, 1984.

FURPHY, JOSEPH. *Such is Life*, in *Portable Australian Authors: Joseph Furphy*, ed. John Barnes. Brisbane: University of Queensland Press, 1981.

GALEANO, EDUARDO. *Memory of Fire: Genesis*, trans. Cedric Belfrage. New York: Pantheon, 1985.

GALLANT, MAVIS. 'The Ice Wagon Going down the Street', in Margaret Atwood and Robert Weaver (eds.), *The Oxford Book of Canadian Short Stories in English*. Toronto: Oxford University Press, 1988: 115–34.

GARRETT, SIMON (gen. ed.). *He Reo Hou: 5 Plays by Maori Playwrights*. Wellington: Playmarket, 1991.

GEDALOF, ROBIN (ed.). *Paper Stays Put: A Collection of Inuit Writing*. Edmonton: Hurtig, 1980.

GEOGHEGAN, EDWARD (ed.). *The Currency Lass*. Sydney: Currency Press, 1976.

GERSON, CAROLE, and MEZEI, KATHY (eds.). *The Prose of Life: Sketches from Victorian Canada*. Downsview: ECW, 1981.

GHOSE, ZULFIKAR. *Confessions of a Native-Alien*. London: Routledge & Kegan Paul, 1965.

—— *The Murder of Aziz Khan*. London: Macmillan, 1967.

—— *The Triple Mirror of the Self*. London: Bloomsbury, 1992.

—— 'Arrival in India', *Toronto Review of Contemporary Writing Abroad*, 12/1 (1993): 1–11.

GHOSH, AMITAV. *In an Antique Land*. London: Granta, 1992.

GILBERT, KEVIN (ed.). *Inside Black Australia: An Anthology of Aboriginal Poetry*. Ringwood: Penguin, 1988.

GILES, FIONA (ed.). *From the Veranda: Stories of Love and Landscape by Nineteenth Century Australian Women*. Victoria: McPhee Gribble Publishers, 1987.

GLASS, COLLEEN, and WELLER, ARCHIE (eds.). *Us Fellas: An Anthology of Aboriginal Writing*. Perth: Artlook Books, 1987.

GOLDSMITH, OLIVER. *The Rising Village of Oliver Goldsmith*, 1825, 1834; ed. Michael Gnarowski. Montreal: Delta Canada, 1968.

GOODISON, LORNA. *I Am Becoming my Mother*. London: New Beacon, 1986.

—— *Heartease*. London: New Beacon, 1988.

—— *Selected Poems*. Ann Arbor: University of Michigan Press, 1992.

GOODWIN, KEN, and LAWSON, ALAN (eds.). *The Macmillan Anthology of Australian Literature*. Melbourne: Macmillan, 1990.

GOONERATNE, YASMIN. 'How Barry Changed his Image', *Meanjin*, 48/1 (1989): 109–15.

GORDON, ADAM LINDSAY. *Adam Lindsay Gordon*, comp. Brian Elliott. Melbourne: Sun Books, 1973.

GORST, J. E. *The Maori King*, 1864.

GRACE, PATRICIA. *Waiariki*. Auckland: Longman Paul, 1975.

—— *Mutuwhenua: The Moon Sleeps*. Auckland: Longman Paul, 1978.

—— *Potiki*. Auckland: Penguin Books, 1986.

—— *Electric City*. Auckland: Penguin Books, 1987.

GRANT, AGNES (ed.). *Our Bit of Truth: An Anthology of Canadian Native Literature*. Winnipeg: Pemmican Publications, 1990.

GREGORY, LADY ISABELLA AUGUSTA. *Our Irish Theatre.* New York: Capricorn Books, 1965.

—— *Selected Plays.* Gerrards Cross: Colin Smythe, 1983.

GREY, GEORGE. *Mythology and Traditions of the New Zealanders,* 1854.

GUDGEON, T. W. *Reminiscences of the War in New Zealand,* 1879.

GUNNARS, KRISTJANA (ed.). *Unexpected Fictions: New Icelandic Canadian Writing.* Saskatoon: Turnstone, 1989.

GWARAM, HAUWA, and 'YARSHEHU, HAJIYA. *Alkalani A Hannun Matu,* ed. Beverly B. Mack. Zaria: Northern Nigerian Publishing Company, 1983.

HALIBURTON, THOMAS CHANDLER. *The Clockmaker: The Sayings and Doings of Samuel Slick of Slickville.* 1836; Toronto: McClelland & Stewart, 1993.

HAQ, KAISER (ed.). *Contemporary Indian Poetry.* Columbus: Ohio State University Press, 1990.

HARPUR, CHARLES. *Thoughts: A Series of Sonnets,* 1845.

—— *The Bushrangers, a Play in Five Acts, and Other Poems,* 1853.

—— *Selected Prose and Poetry,* ed. Michael Auckland. Ringwood: Penguin, 1986.

HARRIS, ALEXANDER. *Settlers and Convicts; or Recollections of Sixteen Years Labour in the Australian Backwoods,* 1847.

—— *The Emigrant Family; or The Story of an Australian Settler,* ed. W. S. Ramson. 1849; Canberra: Australian National University Press, 1967.

HARRIS, CLAIRE. *Travelling to Find a Remedy.* Fredericton: Goose Lane, 1986.

HARRIS, WILSON. *The Palace of the Peacock.* London: Faber, 1960.

—— *The Four Banks of the River of Space.* London: Faber & Faber, 1990.

HART, JULIA CATHERINE. *St. Ursula's Convent; or The Nun of Canada,* 1824.

HASLAM, ANTHONY (comp.). *Anthology of Empire.* London: Grayson & Grayson, 1932.

HAY, WILLIAM GOSSE. *The Escape of the Notorious Sir William Heans (and the Mystery of Mr. Daunt): A Romance of Tasmania.* 1919; Carlton: Melbourne University Press, 1955.

HEAD, BESSIE. *When Rain Clouds Gather.* London: Heinemann, 1968.

—— *Maru.* London: Heinemann, 1972.

—— *A Question of Power.* London: Heinemann, 1974.

—— *The Collector of Treasures.* London: Heinemann, 1977.

—— *Tales of Tenderness and Power.* London: Heinemann, 1989.

—— *A Woman Alone: Autobiographical Writings.* London: Heinemann, 1990.

HEATH, ROY. *Kwaku.* London: Allison & Busby, 1982.

—— *Shadows round the Moon.* London: Collins, 1990.

HEAVYSEGE, CHARLES. *Sonnets,* 1856.

HENNING, RACHEL. *The Letters of Rachel Henning,* ed. David Adams. Harmondsworth: Penguin, 1969.

HENRY, ALEXANDER. *Travels and Adventures in Canada and the Indian Territories between the Years 1760 and 1776.* London, 1809.

HIGHWAY, TOMSON. *The Rez Sisters.* Saskatoon: Fifth House, 1988.

—— *Dry Lips Oughta Move to Kapuskasing.* Saskatoon: Fifth House, 1989.

HODGE, MERLE. *Crick Crack Monkey.* 1970; London: Heinemann, 1981.

HODGSON, HEATHER (ed.). *Seventh Generation: Contemporary Native Writing.* Penticton: Theytus Books, 1989.

HOWITT, WILLIAM. *Land, Labour and Gold; or Two Years in Victoria,* 1855.

HULME, KERI. *The Silences Between: Moeraki Conversations.* Auckland: Auckland University Press, 1982.

—— *the bone people.* Wellington: Spiral, 1983; Suffolk: Picador, 1985.

—— *Lost Possessions.* Wellington: Victoria University Press, 1985.

—— *Te Kaihau/The Windeater.* Wellington: Victoria University Press, 1986.

HUNTER, JOHN. *An Historical Journal of the Transactions at Port Jackson and Norfolk Island,* 1793.

IHIMAERA, WITI. *Pounamu, Pounamu.* Auckland: Heinemann, 1972.

—— *The New Net Goes Fishing.* Auckland: Heinemann, 1977.

—— *The Matriarch.* Auckland: Heinemann, 1986.

—— *The Whale Rider.* Auckland: Heinemann, 1987.

—— *Bulibasha: King of the Gypsies.* Auckland: Penguin Books, 1994.

—— *et al.* (eds.). *Te Ao Marama: Contemporary Maori Writing,* vol. i. Auckland: Reed Books, 1992.

—— *et al.* (eds.). *Te Ao Marama: Contemporary Maori Writing,* vol. ii. Auckland: Reed Books, 1993.

—— *et al.* (eds.). *Te Ao Marama: Contemporary Maori Writing,* vol. iii. Auckland: Reed Books, 1993.

—— *et al.* (eds.). *Te Ao Marama: Contemporary Maori Writing for Children,* vol. iv. Auckland: Reed Books, 1994.

—— and LONG, D. S. *Into the World of Light: An Anthology of Maori Writing.* Auckland: Heinemann, 1982.

ITWARU, ARNOLD. *Entombed Survivals.* Toronto: Williams-Wallace, 1987.

—— *Shanti.* 1988; Toronto: Coach House, 1990.

JAMES, C. L. R. *Beyond a Boundary.* London: Stanley Paul, 1963.

—— *The Black Jacobins.* New York: Random House, 1963.

—— *Mariners, Renegades and Castaways.* London: Allison & Busby, 1985.

JAMESON, ANNA BRONWELL. *Winter Studies and Summer Rambles in Canada,* 1838.

JEWITT, JOHN R. *A Narrative of the Adventures and Sufferings of John R. Jewitt,* 1815.

JOHNSON, RICHARD. *An Address to the Inhabitants of the Colonies, Established in New South Wales and Norfolk Island,* 1794.

KANE, PAUL. *Wanderings of an Artist among the Indians of North America,* 1859.

KATIYO, WILSON. *A Son of the Soil.* 1976; Harlow: Longman, 1988.

KENDALL, HENRY. *Henry Kendall,* ed. Michael Ackland. St Lucia: University of Queensland Press, 1993.

KIDD, ADAM. *The Huron Chief,* 1830.

KINCAID, JAMAICA. *Annie John.* New York: American Library, 1983.

—— *A Small Place.* London: Virago, 1988.

KING, THOMAS. *Medicine River.* Markham: Viking, 1990.

—— (ed.). *All my Relations: An Anthology of Contemporary Canadian Native Fiction.* Toronto: McClelland & Stewart, 1990.

—— *One Good Story, That One.* Toronto: HarperPerennial, 1993.

—— *Green Grass, Running Water.* Toronto: HarperPerennial, 1994.

KINGSLEY, HENRY. *Henry Kingsley [Geoffry Hamlyn and other writings],* ed. J. S. D. Mellick. St Lucia: University of Queensland Press, 1982.

KIPLING, RUDYARD. *The Definitive Edition of Rudyard Kipling's Verse* [1885–1935]. 1940; repr. London: Hodder & Stoughton, 1969.

KIRBY, WILLIAM. *The Golden Dog (Le Chien d'or): A Romance of Old Quebec.* 1877; rev. edn. Toronto: Musson, 1925.

KRAMER, LEONIE, and MITCHELL, ADRIAN (eds.). *The Oxford Anthology of Australian Literature.* Melbourne: Oxford University Press, 1985.

KROETSCH, ROBERT. *Seed Catalogue.* Winnipeg: Manitoba, 1986.

KUREISHI, HANIF. 'Interview' with Marcia Pally, *Film Comment,* 22 (Sept.–Oct. 1986): 50–5.

—— *My Beautiful Laundrette,* dir. Stephen Frears. Orion Classics, 1986.

—— *Sammy and Rosie Get Laid,* dir. Stephen Frears. Cinecon Entertainment, 1987.

—— *The Buddha of Suburbia.* New York: Viking Penguin, 1990.

LAMMING, GEORGE. *The Emigrants.* 1954; London: Allison & Busby, 1980.

—— *The Pleasures of Exile.* London: Michael Joseph, 1960.

—— *In the Castle of my Skin.* London: Longmans, 1970.

—— 'Introduction' (1983) to *In the Castle of my Skin* (1970). Ann Arbor: University of Michigan Press, 1991: pp. xxxv–xlvi.

LAWSON, HENRY. *Collected Prose,* ed. Colin Roderick. 2 vols. Sydney: Angus & Robertson, 1972.

—— *Collected Verse,* ed. Colin Roderick. 3 vols. Sydney: Angus & Robertson, 1967–9.

—— *Portable Australian Authors: Henry Lawson,* ed. Brian Kiernan. St Lucia: University of Queensland Press, 1976.

LAWSON, LOUISA. *The First Voice of Australian Feminism: Excerpts from Louisa Lawson's 'The Dawn' 1888–1895,* ed. Olive Lawson. Brookvale: Simon & Schuster/New Endeavour, 1990.

LEE, DENNIS (ed.). *The New Canadian Poets 1970–1985.* Toronto: McClelland & Stewart, 1985.

LEPROHON, ROSANNA. *Antoinette de Mirecourt; or Secret Marrying and Secret Sorrowing,* ed. John C. Stockdale. 1864; Ottawa: Carleton University Press, 1989.

LIM, CATHERINE. *Little Ironies: Stories of Singapore.* Singapore: Heinemann, 1978.

LOVELACE, EARL. *The Dragon Can't Dance.* London: Longman, 1979.

LYCETT, JOSEPH. *Views in Australia; or New South Wales, and Van Dieman's Land Delineated,* 1824.

McCULLOCH, THOMAS. *The Mephibosheth Stepsure Letters,* 1821; ed. Gwendolyn Davies. Ottawa: Carleton University Press, 1990.

McGEE, THOMAS D'ARCY. *Canadian Ballads and Occasional Verses,* 1858.

MCKAY, CLAUDE. *Banana Bottom.* 1928; New York: Harcourt Brace Jovanovich, 1961.
—— *Home to Harlem.* 1928; Chatham, NJ: Chatham Book Seller, 1973.
—— *Gingertown.* New York, 1932.
MACKAY, J. *Quebec Hill; or Canadian Scenery: A Poem: In Two Parts,* 1797; ed. D. M. R. Bentley. London, Ont.: Canadian Poetry Press, 1988.
MACKENZIE, ALEXANDER. *Voyages.* London, 1801.
MCLAUGHLIN, ALEXANDER. *The Emigrant,* 1861.
MCMULLEN, LORRAINE (ed.). *Re(dis)covering our Foremothers: Nineteenth Century Canadian Women Writers.* Ottawa: University of Ottawa Press, 1990.
—— and Campbell, Sandra (eds.). *Pioneering Women: Short Stories by Canadian Women.* Ottawa: University of Ottawa Press, 1993.
MACPHERSON, EMMA. *My Experiences in Australia, by a Lady,* 1860.
MCQUEEN, HARVEY (ed.). *The New Place: The Poetry of Settlement in New Zealand, 1852–1914.* Wellington: Victoria University Press, 1993.
MAFI-WILLIAMS, LORRAINE (ed.). *Spirit Song: A Collection of Aboriginal Poetry.* Sydney: Omnibus Books, 1993.
MAHAPATRA, JAYANTA. *Temple.* Sydney: Dangaroo Press, 1989.
MALOUF, DAVID. *The Great World.* London: Chatto & Windus, 1990.
MANING, F. E. *History of the War in the North,* 1863.
—— *Old New Zealand,* 1863.
MARACLE, LEE. *Sojourner's Truth, & Other Stories.* Vancouver: Press Gang Publishers, 1990.
—— *Sundogs.* Penticton: Theytus Books, 1992.
MARECHERA, DAMBUDZO. *The House of Hunger.* London: Heinemann, 1984.
MARKANDAYA, KAMALA. *Nectar in a Sieve.* New York: Signet, 1954.
—— *A Handful of Rice.* 1966; Delhi: Orient Paperbacks, 1985.
—— *The Nowhere Man.* New Delhi: Orient Longman, 1972.
MARLEY, BOB. 'Bad Card', on *Uprising.* Kingston: Tugg Gong Records, 1980.
MARSDEN, SAMUEL. *Letters and Journals,* 1932.
MAZA, BOB. *The Keepers,* in *Plays from Black Australia.* Sydney: Currency Press, 1989: 167–229.
MEHROTRA, ARVIND KRISHNA. *The Oxford Indian Anthology of Twelve Modern Indian Poets.* Delhi: Oxford University Press, 1992.
MELVILLE, PAULINE. *Shape-Shifter.* London: The Women's Press, 1991.
MEREDITH, LOUISA ANNE. *Notes and Sketches of New South Wales,* 1844.
—— *My Home in Tasmania,* 1853.
—— *Tasmanian Friends and Foes: Feathered, Furred and Finned: A Family Chronicle of Country Life,* 1880.
MERRITT, ROBERT. *The Cake Man.* Sydney: Currency Press, 1978.
MIDGLEY, SARAH, and SKILBECK, RICHARD. *The Diaries of Sarah Midgley and Richard Skilbeck 1851–1864,* ed. H. A. McCorkell. Melbourne: Cassell Australia, 1967.
MISHRA, SUDESH. *Memoirs of a Reluctant Traveller.* Adelaide: CRNLE, 1995.
MISTRY, ROHINTON. *Tales of Ferozsha Baag.* Toronto: Penguin, 1987.

—— *Such a Long Journey*. Toronto: McClelland & Stewart, 1991.

MITCHELL, THOMAS. *Three Expeditions into the Interior of Eastern Australia.* London, 1838.

MO, TIMOTHY. *Sour Sweet*. London: Abacus, 1982.

MODARRESSI, TAGHI. *The Pilgrim's Rules of Etiquette*. New York: Doubleday, 1989.

MOODIE, SUSANNA. *Roughing it in the Bush; or Life in Canada*, 1852; ed. Carl Ballstadt. Ottawa: Carleton University Press, 1988.

—— *Life in the Clearings versus the Bush*, 1853.

MOOTOO, SHANI. *Out on Main Street and Other Stories*. Vancouver: Press Gang, 1993.

MORDECAI, PAMELA, and WILSON, BETTY (eds.). *Her True-True Name: An Anthology of Women's Writing from the Caribbean*. London: Heinemann, 1989.

MORGAN, SALLY. *My Place*. London: Virago, 1988.

MORRIS, MERVYN (ed.). *The Faber Book of Contemporary Caribbean Short Stories*. London: Faber & Faber, 1990.

MOSES, DANIEL DAVID. *Coyote City*. Stratford: Williams-Wallace, 1990.

—— and GOLDIE, TERRY (eds.). *An Anthology of Canadian Native Literature in English*. Toronto: Oxford University Press, 1992.

MUKHERJEE, BHARATI. 'Invisible Woman', *Saturday Night*, 96 (Mar. 1981): 36–40.

—— *Darkness*. New York: Penguin, 1985.

—— *The Middleman and Other Stories*. New York: Grove Press, 1988.

—— Plenary Lecture, Canadian Association of American Studies Conference. Ottawa, 4 Nov. 1994.

MULLOO, ANAND. *Watch Them Go Down*. Port Louis: Mauritius Writers' Association, 1967.

MURRAY, ANNA MARIA. *The Guardian: A Tale, by an Australian*, 1838.

MURRAY, LES (comp.). *The New Oxford Book of Australian Verse*. Melbourne: Oxford University Press, 1986.

NAIPAUL, V. S. *Miguel Street*. London: André Deutsch, 1959.

—— *A House for Mr Biswas*. London: André Deutsch, 1961.

—— *An Area of Darkness*. London: André Deutsch, 1964.

—— *The Mimic Men*. London: André Deutsch, 1967.

—— *The Overcrowded Barracoon*. London: André Deutsch, 1972.

—— *Finding the Centre: Two Narratives*. London: André Deutsch, 1984.

—— *The Enigma of Arrival*. Harmondsworth: Penguin, 1987.

—— *India: A Million Mutinies Now*. New York: Viking, 1991.

NAMJOSHI, SUNITI. *The Conversations of Cow*. London: The Women's Press, 1985.

—— *Because of India*. London: Onlywomen Press, 1989.

NANDAN, SATENDRA. *Voices in the River: Poems 1974–1984*. Suva: Vision International Publishers, 1985.

—— *The Wounded Sea*. Roseville: Simon & Schuster, 1991.

—— 'Return to a Certain Darkness', in Victor J. Ramraj (ed.), *Concert of Voices*. Peterborough: Broadview Press, 1995: 312–22.

274 *Selected Bibliography*

NARAYAN, R. K. *Mr Sampath: The Printer of Malgudi.* 1949; Chicago: University of Chicago Press, 1981.
—— *The Financial Expert.* 1952; Chicago: University of Chicago Press, 1981.
—— *Waiting for the Mahatma.* 1955; Chicago: University of Chicago Press, 1981.
—— *The Man-Eater of Malgudi.* Harmondsworth: Penguin, 1962.
—— *The Vendor of Sweets.* Harmondsworth: Penguin, 1967.
NAROGIN, MUDROOROO [Colin Johnson]. *Doctor Wooreddy's Prescription for Enduring the End of the World.* South Yarra: Hyland House, 1983.
—— *Long Live Sandawara.* Melbourne: Hyland House, 1979.
—— *Writing from the Fringe.* Melbourne: Hyland House, 1990.
—— *Master of the Ghost Dreaming.* Sydney: Angus & Robertson, 1991.
NGUGI WA THIONG'O. *A Grain of Wheat.* London: Heinemann, 1967.
—— 'Minutes of Glory', in Chinua Achebe and C. L. Innes (eds.), *African Short Stories.* Oxford: Heinemann, 1987: 71–84.
NICHOLS, GRACE. *Whole of a Morning Sky.* London: Virago, 1986.
NWAPA, FLORA. *Efuru.* London: Heinemann, 1966; repr. 1979.
NYAMFUKUDZA, S. *The Non-believer's Journey.* London: Heinemann, 1980.
OKARA, GABRIEL. *The Voice.* London: Heinemann, 1964.
OKRI, BEN. *The Famished Road.* London: Jonathan Cape, 1991; New York: Anchor Books, 1993.
—— *Songs of Enchantment.* London: Jonathan Cape, 1993.
ONDAATJE, MICHAEL. *The Collected Works of Billy the Kid.* Toronto: Anansi, 1970.
—— *Coming through Slaughter.* Toronto: Anansi, 1976.
—— *Running in the Family.* Toronto: McClelland & Stewart, 1982.
—— *Secular Love.* Toronto: Coach House, 1984.
—— *In the Skin of a Lion.* Toronto: McClelland & Stewart, 1987.
—— *The English Patient.* Toronto: McClelland & Stewart, 1992.
ORBELL, MARGARET (ed.). *Contemporary Maori Writing.* Wellington: A. H. & A. W. Reed, 1970.
OXLEY, JOHN. *Journals of Two Expeditions into the Interior of New South Wales.* London, 1820.
PARKER, SIR GILBERT. *The Seats of the Mighty.* New York: Appleton; London: Methuen; Toronto: Copp Clark, 1896; repr. of the 1926 edn. Ottawa: Tecumseh, 1981.
PARTHASARATHY, R. *Ten Twentieth-Century Indian Poets.* Delhi: Oxford University Press, 1976.
PATERSON, A. B. *The Old Bush Songs Composed and Sung in the Bushranging, Digging and Overlanding Days,* 1905.
PATERSON, ALISTAIR (ed.). *15 Contemporary New Zealand Poets.* New York: Grove Press, 1980.
PERKINS, CHARLES. *A Bastard Like Me.* Sydney: Ure Smith, 1975.
PERREAULT, JEANNE, and VANCE, SYLVIA (eds.). *Writing the Circle: Native Women of Western Canada.* Edmonton: NeWest, 1990.

PETRONE, PENNY (ed.). *First People, First Voices*. Toronto: University of Toronto Press, 1983.

PHILIP, M. NOURBESE. *She Tries her Tongue: Her Silence Softly Breaks*. Charlottetown: Ragweed, 1989.

—— *Looking for Livingstone: An Odyssey of Silence*. Stratford: Mercury, 1991.

PHILLIP, ARTHUR. *The Voyage of Governor Phillip to Botany Bay*. London, 1789.

PHILLIPS, CARYL. *The Final Passage*. London: Faber, 1985.

—— *A State of Independence*. London: Faber, 1986.

—— *Cambridge*. London: Bloomsbury, 1991.

—— *Crossing the River*. London: Bloomsbury, 1993.

—— 'Interview' with Carol Margaret Davison, *Ariel*, 25/4 (Oct. 1994): 91–9.

PILLAI, RAYMOND C. 'The Celebration', in Subramani (ed.), *The Indo-Fijian Experience*. St Lucia: University of Queensland Press, 1980: 91–6.

PRAED, ROSA. *An Australian Heroine*, 1880.

—— *Ariane; or The Bonds of Wedlock: A Tale of London Life*. 1887; London: Pandora, 1987.

—— *The Romance of a Station*, 1889.

PRICHARD, KATHARINE SUSANNAH. *Coonardoo*. 1929; Sydney: Angus & Robertson, 1975.

PRINGLE, THOMAS. *African Poems of Thomas Pringle*, ed. Ernest Pereira and Michael Chapman. Pietermaritzburg: University of Natal Press, 1989.

PURI, SHAMLAL. *The Dame of the Twilight*. Nairobi: Foundation Books, 1978.

RAMA RAU, SANTHA. *Remember the House*. London: Victor Gollancz, 1956.

RAMRAJ, VICTOR J. (ed.). *Concert of Voices: An Anthology of World Writing in English*. Peterborough: Broadview Press, 1995.

RAO, RAJA. *Kanthapura*. Bombay, 1937; New York: New Directions, 1984.

—— *The Serpent and the Rope*. Harmondsworth: Penguin, 1960.

REID, V. S. *New Day*. London: Heinemann, 1949.

RESISTANCE, BROTHER. *Rapso Explosion*. Karia Press, 1986.

RHYS, JEAN. *Wide Sargasso Sea*. London: André Deutsch, 1966.

—— *Tales of the Wide Caribbean*, ed. Kenneth Ramchand. London: Heinemann, 1986.

RICHARDSON, JOHN. *The Canadian Brothers; or The Prophecy Fulfilled: A Tale of the Late American War*, 1840; ed. Donald Stephens. repr. Ottawa: Carleton University Press, 1992.

—— *Wacousta*, 1832; ed. Douglas Cronk. Ottawa: Carleton University Press, 1987.

ROWCROFT, CHARLES. *Tales of the Colonies*, 1843.

RUSHDIE, SALMAN. *Midnight's Children*. London: Jonathan Cape, 1981.

—— *Shame*. London: Jonathan Cape, 1983.

—— *The Satanic Verses*. New York: Viking, 1989.

—— *East, West*. New York: Pantheon, 1994.

SAHGAL, NAYANTARA. *A Situation in New Delhi*. London: London Magazine Editions, 1977; repr. Penguin India, 1988.

276  *Selected Bibliography*

SALKEY, ANDREW. *Escape to an Autumn Pavement*. London: Hutchinson, 1970.
—— *Come Home, Malcolm Heartland*. London: Hutchinson, 1976.
SAMKANGE, STANLEY. *On Trial for my Country*. London: Heinemann, 1966.
SANGSTER, CHARLES. *The St. Lawrence and the Saguenay, and Other Poems*, 1861.
SARO-WIWA, KEN. *Sozaboy: A Novel in Rotten English*. Port Harcourt: Saros International, 1985.
SATCHELL, WILLIAM. *The Toll of the Bush*, 1905; ed. Kendrick Smithyman. Auckland: Auckland University Press; Oxford: Oxford University Press, 1985.
SAVERY, HENRY. *Quintus Servinton: A Tale Founded upon Incidents of Real Occurrences*, 1830–1; ed. Cecil Hadgraft. Brisbane: Jacaranda, 1962.
SAWAI, GLORIA. 'The Day I Sat with Jesus on the Sundeck and a Wind Came Up and Blew My Kimono Open and He Saw My Breasts', in Margaret Atwood and Robert Weaver (eds.), *The Oxford Book of Canadian Short Stories in English*. Toronto: Oxford University Press, 1988: 243–54.
SCHREINER, OLIVE. *An Olive Schreiner Reader: Writings on Women and South Africa*, ed. Carol Barash. London: Pandora, 1987.
—— *The Story of an African Farm*, introd. Doris Lessing. New York: Schocken, 1976.
—— *Trooper Peter Halket of Mashonaland*. 1897; London: Ernest Benn, 1959.
SCOTT, DUNCAN CAMPBELL. *In the Village of Viger and Other Stories*. 1896; Toronto: McClelland & Stewart, 1973.
SCOTT, LAWRENCE. *Witchbroom*. London: Allison & Busby, 1992.
SEALY, I. ALLAN. *The Trotter-Nama: A Chronicle 1977–1984*. New York: Knopf, 1988.
SELVON, SAM. *The Lonely Londoners*. 1956; London: Longman, 1972.
—— *Moses Migrating*. London: Longman, 1983.
—— *Moses Ascending*. London: Davis-Poynter, 1975; Oxford: Heinemann, 1984.
—— 'Turning Christian', in Victor J. Ramraj (ed.), *Concert of Voices*. Peterborough: Broadview Press, 1995: 378–84.
SENIOR, OLIVE. *Talking of Trees*. Kingston: Calabash Press, 1985.
—— *Summer Lightning and Other Stories*. London: Longman Caribbean Writers, 1986.
—— *Arrival of the Snake Woman and Other Stories*. London: Longman Caribbean, 1989.
—— *Gardening in the Tropics*. Toronto: McClelland Stewart, 1994.
SETH, VIKRAM. *A Suitable Boy*. London: Phoenix House, 1993.
SHORTLAND, EDWARD. *Traditions and Superstitions of the New Zealanders*, 1854.
SIDHWA, BAPSI. *The Crow Eaters*. Lahore: Ilmi Print Press, 1978; Minneapolis: Milkweed, 1992.
SIMCOE, ELIZABETH POSTHUMA. *Mrs. Simcoe's Diary*, ed. Mary Quayle Innis. Toronto: Macmillan, 1965.
SINGH, KHUSHWANT. *Train to Pakistan*. 1956; New York: Grove Press, 1981.

SISTREN with SMITH, HONOR FORD (eds.). *Lionheart Gal: Life Stories of Jamaican Women*. London: The Women's Press, 1986.

SLIPPERJACK, RUBY. *Honour the Sun*. Winnipeg: Pemmican Publications, 1987.

SOYINKA, WOLE. *The Forest of a Thousand Daemons*. 1968; Edinburgh: Nelson, 1982.

—— *Collected Plays*. 2 vols. Oxford: Oxford University Press, 1974.

SPARROW, The Mighty [Francisco Slinger]. 'Dan is the Man', in Stewart Brown, Mervyn Morris, and Gordon Rohlehr (eds.), *Voiceprint: An Anthology of Oral and Related Poetry from the Caribbean*. Kingston: Longman, 1989: 129–30.

SPENCE, CATHERINE HELEN. *Handfasted*, ed. Helen Thomson. Ringwood: Penguin, 1984.

—— *Catherine Helen Spence* [*Clara Morison* and other writings], ed. Helen Thomson. St Lucia: University of Queensland Press, 1987.

STONEY, HENRY BUTLER. *Taranaki: A Tale of the War. With a Description of the Province Previous to and during the War; also an Account (Chiefly Taken from the Despatches) of the Principal Contests with the Natives during that Eventful Period*. Auckland: W. C. Wilson, 1861.

STOREY, MARK (ed.). *Poetry and Ireland since 1800: A Source Book*. London: Routledge, 1988.

SUBRAMANI (ed.). *The Indo-Fijian Experience*. St Lucia: University of Queensland Press, 1980.

—— *The Fantasy-Eaters: Stories from Fiji*. Suva: University of South Pacific, 1990.

SYNGE, JAMES MILLINGTON. *Collected Works*, iv: *Plays*, Book II, ed. Ann Saddlemyer. London: Oxford University Press, 1968.

TAYLOR, DREW HAYDEN. *The Bootlegger Blues*. Saskatoon: Fifth House, 1991.

—— *Someday*. Saskatoon: Fifth House, 1993.

TAYLOR, RICHARD. *Te Ika a Maui*, 1855.

TENCH, WATKIN. *A Narrative of the Expedition to Botony Bay*. London, 1789.

THOMPSON, ARTHUR S. *The Story of New Zealand: Past and Present— Savage and Civilized*, 1859.

THOMPSON, DAVID. *David Thompson's Narrative of his Explorations in Western America, 1784–1812*, ed. J. B. Tyrrell. Toronto: The Champlain Society, 1916.

TLALI, MIRIAM. *Soweto Stories*. London: Pandora Press, 1989.

TRAILL, CATHARINE PARR. *The Backwoods of Canada: Being Letters from the Wife of an Immigrant Officer; Illustrative of the Domestic Economy of North America*, 1836.

—— *The Canadian Crusoes: A Tale of the Rice Lake Plains*, 1852; ed. Rupert Schieder. Ottawa: Carleton University Press, 1986.

—— *The Female Emigrant's Guide*, 1854.

—— *Canadian Wild Flowers*, 1868.

TUCKER, JAMES ROSENBERG. *The Adventures of Ralph Rashleigh, a Penal Exile in Australia, 1825–1844.* 1844–5; London: Jonathan Cape, 1929; rev. version, ed. Colin Roderick, Sydney: Angus & Robertson, 1952.

VASSANJI, M. G. *The Gunny Sack.* London: Heinemann, 1989.

—— *No New Land.* Toronto: McClelland & Stewart, 1991.

VOGEL, JULIUS. *Anno Domini 2000; or Woman's Destiny.* London: Hutchinson, 1889.

WAGNER, ANTON, and PLANT, RICHARD (eds.). *Canada's Lost Plays: The Nineteenth Century.* Toronto: CTR, 1978.

WAKEFIELD, EDWARD JERNINGHAM. *Adventure in New Zealand.* London, 1845. Abridgement by Joan Stevens. Auckland: Golden Press, 1975.

WALCOTT, DEREK. 'A Far Cry from Africa', in *In a Green Night.* London: Jonathan Cape, 1962: 19–20.

—— *The Gulf and Other Poems.* London: Cape, 1969.

—— *Dream on Monkey Mountain and Other Plays.* New York: Farrar Straus, 1970.

—— *Another Life.* London: Jonathan Cape, 1973.

—— *The Star-Apple Kingdom.* New York: Farrar, Straus & Giroux, 1979.

—— *The Fortunate Traveller.* London: Faber, 1982.

—— *Collected Poems: 1948–1984.* New York: Farrar, Straus, & Giroux, 1986.

—— *Omeros.* New York: Farrar, 1992.

—— *The Antilles: Fragments of Epic Memory.* New York: Farrar, Straus, & Giroux, 1993. ['The Nobel Lecture'.]

WALKER, KATH. [Oodgeroo Noonuccal]. *We Are Going.* Brisbane: The Jacaranda Press, 1964.

WALLEY, RICHARD. *Coordah,* in *Plays from Black Australia.* Sydney: Currency Press, 1989: 109–66.

WALROND, ERIC. *Tropic Death.* 1926; New York: Macmillan-Collier, 1972.

WARD, RUSSEL. *The Penguin History of Australian Ballads,* 1964.

WATLING, THOMAS. *Letters from an Exile at Botany-Bay, to his Aunt in Dumfries,* 1794. Australian Historical Monographs. Sydney: Review Publications, 1945.

WATSON, SAM. *The Kadaitcha Sung.* Ringwood: Penguin, 1990.

WEAVER, ROBERT, and TOYE, WILLIAM (eds.). *The Oxford Anthology of Canadian Literature.* 2nd edn. Toronto: Oxford University Press, 1981.

WEBBY, ELIZABETH (ed.). *Colonial Voices: Letters, Diaries, Journalism and Other Accounts of Nineteenth-Century Australia* [Henry Savery, Watkin Tench, Louisa Anne Meredith, Rosa Praed, and other writers]. Brisbane: University of Queensland Press, 1989.

—— and WEVERS, LYDIA (eds.). *Happy Endings: Stories by Australian and New Zealand Women, 1850s–1930s.* Port Nicholson: Allen & Unwin, 1987.

WELLER, ARCHIE. *The Day of the Dog.* Sydney: Allen & Unwin, 1981.

—— *Going Home.* 1986; Sydney: Allen & Unwin, 1990.

WELLS, THOMAS. *Michael Howe: The Last and Worst of the Bushrangers of Van Dieman's Land,* 1818.

WENTWORTH, WILLIAM CHARLES. *A Statistical, Historical, and Political Description of the Colony of New South Wales*, 1819.

WHEELER, JORDAN. *Brothers in Arms*. Winnipeg: Pemmican Publications, 1989.

WHITE, PATRICK. 'A Woman's Hand', in *The Cockatoos*. Harmondsworth: Penguin, 1974: 1–80.

—— *Patrick White Speaks*. London: Jonathan Cape, 1990.

WILKES, G. A. (ed.). *The Colonial Poets*. Sydney: Angus & Robertson, 1974.

WILLIAMS, DENIS. *Other Leopards*. 1963; London: Heinemann, 1983.

YEATS, WILLIAM BUTLER. *Yeats's Poems*, ed. A. N. Jeffares. London: Macmillan, 1989.

—— *Collected Plays*. London: Macmillan, 1965.

—— *Essays and Introductions*. London: Macmillan, 1970.

YUNUPINGU, MANDAWUY. 'My Kind of Life', on Yothu Yindi, *Tribal Voice*. Sydney: Mushroom Records, 1991.


SECONDARY


ACHEBE, CHINUA. 'The Role of the Writer in the New Nation', *Nigeria Magazine*, 81 (1964).

—— *Morning Yet on Creation Day*. London: Heinemann Educational Books, 1975.

—— *Hopes and Impediments: Selected Essays 1965–87*. London: Heinemann Educational, 1988.

—— 'African Literature as Restoration of Celebration', in *Chinua Achebe: A Celebration*, ed. Kirsten Holst Petersen and Anna Rutherford, *Kunapipi*, 12/2 (1990): 1–10.

ACHESON, JAMES (ed.). *The British and Irish Novel since 1960*. New York: St Martin's Press, 1991.

ADAM, IAN, and TIFFIN, HELEN (eds.). *Past the Last Post: Theorizing Post-colonialism and Post-modernism*. New York: Harvester Wheatsheaf, 1991.

ADELAIDE, DEBRA (ed.). *A Bright and Fiery Troop: Australian Women Writers of the Nineteenth Century*. Ringwood: Penguin, 1988.

AFZAL-KHAN, FAWZIA. *Cultural Imperialism and the Indo-English Novel: Genre and Ideology in R. K. Narayan, Anita Desai, Kamala Markandaya, and Salman Rushdie*. University Park: Pennsylvania State University Press, 1993.

AHMAD, AIJAZ. *In Theory: Classes, Nations, Literatures*. London: Verso, 1992.

ALDRIDGE, A. OWEN. *The Reemergence of World Literature: A Study of Asia and the West*. Newark: University of Delaware Press, 1986.

ALI, AHMED. 'Indians in Fiji: An Interpretation', in Subramani, *The Indo-Fijian Experience*. St Lucia: University of Queensland Press, 1980: 3–25.

ALLEN, H. C. *Bush and Backwoods: A Comparison of the Frontier in Australia and the United States*. Sydney: Angus & Robertson, 1959.

ALTBACH, PHILIP G. 'Education and Neocolonialism', *Teachers College Record*, 72/1 (May 1971): 543–58.

ALTBACH, PHILIP G. 'Literary Colonialism: Books in the Third World', *Harvard Educational Review*, 15/2 (May 1975): 226–36.
—— 'Publishing and the Intellectual System', in *Annals of the American Academy of Political and Social Science* (1975).
ALVAREZ-PÉREYRE, JACQUES. *Poetry of Commitment in South Africa*. London: Heinemann, 1984.
AMADIUME, IFI. *Male Daughters and Female Husbands: Gender and Sex in an African Society*. London: Zed Press, 1987.
AMOS, VALERIE, and PARMAR, PRATIBHA. 'Challenging Imperial Feminism', *Feminist Review*, 17 (Autumn 1984): 3–20.
AMRITHANAYAGAM, GUY, and HARREX, S. C. (eds.). *Only Connect: Literary Perspectives East and West*. Adelaide: Center for Research in the New Literatures in English and East–West Center, 1981.
AMUR, G. S., and DESAI, S. K. (eds.). *Colonial Consciousness in Commonwealth Literature*. Bombay: Somaiya, 1984.
ANDERSON, BENEDICT. *Imagined Communities: Reflections on the Origins and Spread of Nationalism*. London: Verso, 1983.
APPIAH, KWAME ANTHONY. 'Is the Post- in Postmodernism the Post- in Postcolonial?', *Critical Inquiry*, 17/2 (Winter 1991): 336–57.
—— *In my Father's House: Africa in the Philosophy of Culture*. London: Methuen, 1992.
ARGYLE, BARRY. *An Introduction to the Australian Novel, 1830–1930*. Oxford: Clarendon Press, 1972.
ARVIDSON, KEN O. 'Cultural Interaction in the Literature of New Zealand', in Guy Amrithanayagam and S. C. Harrex (eds.), *Only Connect: Literary Perspectives East and West*. Adelaide: CRNLE/East–West Center, 1981.
—— 'Aspects of Contemporary Maori Writing in English', in Graham McGregor and Mark Williams (eds.), *Dirty Silence: Aspects of Language and Literature in New Zealand*. Auckland: Oxford University Press, 1991: 116–28.
ASHCROFT, BILL. 'Constitutive Graphonomy: Post-colonial Theory of Literary Writing', in Stephen Slemon and Helen Tiffin (eds.), *After Europe: Critical Theory and Post-colonial Writing*. Sydney: Dangaroo, 1989: 58–73.
—— GRIFFITHS, GARETH, and TIFFIN, HELEN. *The Empire Writes Back: Theory and Practice in Post-colonial Literatures*. London: Routledge, 1989.
—— GRIFFITHS, GARETH, and TIFFIN, HELEN. (eds.). *The Post-colonial Studies Reader*. London: Routledge, 1995.
*Atlantic Provinces Literature Colloquium Papers* [essays by Cyril Byrne *et al.*, on early Newfoundland and Maritime poetry and journalism]. Saint John: Atlantic Canada Institute, 1977.
AVIS, WALTER S. 'A Note on the Speech of Sam Slick', in *The Sam Slick Anthology*, ed. R. E. Watters. Toronto: Clarke Irwin, 1969: pp. xix–xxix.
—— *et al.* (eds.). *A Concise Dictionary of Canadianisms*. Toronto: Gage, 1973.
BAKER, RAY PALMER. *A History of English-Canadian Literature to the Confederation: Its Relation to the Literature of Great Britain and the United States*. Cambridge, Mass.: Harvard University Press, 1920.
BAKER, SIDNEY J. *The Australian Language*. Sydney: Currawong, 1966.

BALLSTADT, CARL (ed.). *The Search for English-Canadian Literature*. Toronto: University of Toronto Press, 1975.

BARKER, FRANCIS (ed.). *The Politics of Theory*. Colchester: University of Essex, 1983.

—— et al. (eds.). *Europe and its Others*. 2 vols. Colchester: University of Essex, 1985.

——HULME, PETER, and IVERSEN, MARGARET (eds.). *Colonial Discourse/Postcolonial Theory*. Manchester: Manchester University Press, 1994.

BARNES, JOHN (ed.). *The Writer in Australia: A Collection of Literary Documents 1856 to 1964*. Melbourne: Oxford University Press, 1969.

—— *Henry Kingsley and Colonial Fiction*. Melbourne: Oxford University Press, 1971.

BARRETT, MICHELLE. *Women's Oppression Today: Problems in Marxist Feminist Analysis*. London: Verso, 1980.

BAUDET, HENRI. *Paradise on Earth: Some Thoughts on European Images of Non-European Man*, trans. Elizabeth Wentholt. New Haven: Yale University Press, 1965.

BAYARD, CAROLINE. *The New Poetics in Canada and Quebec: From Concretism to Post-modernism*. Toronto: University of Toronto Press, 1989.

BÉJI, HÉLÉ. *Désenchantement national: Essai sur la décolonisation*. Paris: François Maspéro, 1982.

BELICH, JAMES. *The New Zealand Wars and the Victorian Interpretation of Racial Conflict*. Auckland: Penguin, 1986.

BELL, LEONARD. *Colonial Constructs: European Images of Maori 1840–1914*. Auckland: Auckland University Press, 1992.

BENITEZ-ROJO, ANTONIO. *The Repeating Island: The Caribbean and the Postmodern Perspective*, trans. James Maraniss. Durham, NC: Duke University Press, 1992.

BERNABÉ, JEAN, CHAMOISEAU, PATRICK, and CONFIANT, RAPHAËL. *Éloge de la créolité/In Praise of Creoleness*. Bilingual edition, trans. M. B. Taleb-Khyar. Paris: Editions Gallimard, 1993.

BHABHA, HOMI K. 'Of Mimicry and Man: The Ambivalence of Colonial Discourse', *October*, 28 (Spring 1984): 125–33.

—— 'Signs Taken for Wonders: Questions of Ambivalence and Authority under a Tree outside Delhi', *Critical Inquiry*, 12/1 (Autumn 1985): 144–65.

—— 'The Other Question: Difference, Discrimination and the Discourse of Colonialism', in Francis Barker et al. (eds.), *Literature, Politics and Theory*. London: Methuen, 1986: 148–72.

—— 'The Commitment to Theory', *New Formations*, 5 (1988): 5–23.

—— 'Dissemination: Time Narrative, and the Margins of the Modern Nation', in Homi K. Bhabha (ed.), *Nation and Narration*. London: Routledge, 1990: 291–322.

—— 'Postcolonial Criticism', in Stephen Grenblatt and Giles Gunn (eds.), *Redrawing the Boundaries: The Transformation of English and American Literary Studies*. New York: MLA, 1992: 437–65.

—— *The Location of Culture*. London: Routledge, 1994.

BHABHA, HOMI K. 'In a Spirit of Calm Violence', in Gyan Prakash (ed.), *After Colonialism: Imperial and Postcolonial Displacements*. Princeton: Princeton University Press, 1995: 326–43.

BICKERTON, DEREK. 'On the Nature of a Creole Continuum', *Language*, 49/3 (1973): 640–9.

BIRD, DELYS. 'Women in the Wilderness: Gender, Landscape and Eliza Brown's Letters and Journal', *Westerly*, 36/4 (Dec. 1991).

BISHOP, ALAN J. 'Western Mathematics: The Secret Weapon of Cultural Imperialism', *Race and Class*, 32/2 (1990): 51–65.

BOEHMER, ELLEKE. *Colonial and Postcolonial Literature*. Oxford: Oxford University Press, 1995.

BOLAND, EAVAN. *A Kind of Scar: The Woman Poet in a National Tradition*. Dublin: Attic Press LIP Pamphlet, 1989.

BOLLAND, NIGEL. 'Creolisation and Creole Societies', in A. Hennessey, *Intellectuals in the Twentieth-Century Caribbean*. Basingstoke: Macmillan, 1992: 50–79.

BOOTH, JAMES. *Writers and Politics in Nigeria*. New York: Africana Publishing Co., 1981.

BOURDIEU, PIERRE. *Language and Symbolic Power*, ed. and introd. John B. Thompson, trans. Gino Raymond and Matthew Adamson. Cambridge: Polity Press and Basil Blackwell, 1991.

BOYCE DAVIES, CAROL, and GRAVES, ANNE ADAMS (eds.). *Ngambika: Studies of Women in African Literature*. Trenton, NJ: Africa World Press, 1986.

BRATHWAITE, EDWARD KAMAU. *The Development of Creole Society in Jamaica*. London: Oxford University Press, 1971.

—— 'Caribbean Man in Time and Space', *Savacou*, 11–12 (1975): 1–11. Republished in *Carifesta Forum*. Kingston: Institute of Jamaica, 1976: 199–208.

—— *History of the Voice: The Development of Nation Language in Anglophone Caribbean Poetry*. London: New Beacon Books, 1984.

—— 'English in the Caribbean: Notes on Nation Language and Poetry: An Electronic Lecture', in Leslie A. Fiedler and Houston A. Baker, Jr. (eds.), *English Literature: Opening up the Canon*. Selected Papers from the English Institute, 1979, NS 4. Baltimore: Johns Hopkins University Press, 1981: 15–53.

BREITINGER, ECKHARD (ed.). *Theatre and Performance in Africa*. Bayreuth: Bayreuth African Studies 31, 1994.

BREWER, ANTHONY. *Marxist Theories of Imperialism: A Critical Survey*. 2nd edn. New York: Routledge, 1987.

BRODBER, ERNA. 'Sleeping's Beauty and the Prince Charming', *Kunapipi*, 11/3 (1989): 1–4.

BRODSKY, JOSEPH. 'On Derek Walcott', *New York Review of Books*, 30/17 (10 Nov. 1983): 39–41.

—— 'The Sound of the Tide', in *Less Than One: Selected Essays*. New York: Farrar, Straus, 1986: 164–75.

BROWN, LLOYD W. *Women Writers in Black Africa*. Westport, Conn.: Greenwood Press, 1981.

BRUTUS, DENNIS. 'English and the Dynamics of South African Creative Writing', in Leslie A. Fiedler and Houston A. Baker, Jr. (eds.), *English Literature: Opening up the Canon*. Selected Papers from the English Institute, 1979, NS 4. Baltimore: Johns Hopkins University Press, 1981: 1–14.

BRYDON, DIANA. 'Landscape and Authenticity', *Dalhousie Review*, 61/2 (Summer 1981): 278–90.

—— ' "The Thematic Ancestor": Joseph Conrad, Patrick White, Margaret Atwood', *World Literature Written in English*, 24/2 (Autumn 1984): 386–97.

—— 'The Myths that Write Us: Decolonising the Mind', *Commonwealth*, 10/1 (1987): 1–14.

CAIRNS, DAVID, and RICHARDS, SHAUN. *Writing Ireland: Colonialism, Nationalism and Culture*. Manchester: Manchester University Press, 1988.

*Canadian Literature*, 131 [Discourse in Early Canada, introd. Germaine Warkentin and Heather Murray] (Winter 1991): 7–167.

Canadian Multiculturalism Act, in *Statutes of Canada*, vol. i. Ottawa: Queen's Printers, 1989: 835–41.

CANTRELL, LEON (ed.). *Bards, Bohemians, and Bookmen*. St Lucia: University of Queensland Press, 1976.

CARBY, HAZEL. 'White Woman Listen! Black Feminism and the Boundaries of Sisterhood', in *The Empire Strikes Back: Race and Racism in 70s Britain*. London: Hutchinson, 1982: 212–35.

CARRINGTON, C. E. *The British Overseas: Exploits of a Nation of Shopkeepers*. Cambridge: Cambridge University Press, 2nd edn. 1968.

CARTER, PAUL. *The Road to Botany Bay: An Essay in Spatial History*. Chicago: University of Chicago Press. 1987.

CASSIDY, F. G. and LE PAGE, ROBERT B. (eds.). *Dictionary of Jamaican English*. Cambridge: Cambridge University Press, 1967; 2nd edn. 1980.

CHAMBERLAIN, J. EDWARD. *Come Back to Me my Language: Poetry and the West Indies*. Urbana: University of Illinois Press, 1993.

CHAND, MEIRA. 'The Experience of Writing in an Expatriate Situation', in Mimi Chan and Roy Harris (eds.), *Asian Voices in English*. Hong Kong: Hong Kong University Press, 1991: 51–4.

CHATTERJEE, PARTHA. *The Nation and its Fragments: Colonial and Postcolonial Histories*. Princeton: Princeton University Press, 1993.

CHINWEIZU, JEMIE ONWUCHEKWA, and MADUBIKE, IHECHUKWU. *Toward the Decolonization of African Literature: African Fiction and Poetry and their Critics*. London: Kegan Paul International, 1985.

CHOMSKY, NOAM. *Aspects of the Theory of Syntax*. Cambridge, Mass.: MIT Press, 1965.

CHRISTIAN, BARBARA. 'The Race for Theory', *Cultural Critique*, 6 (1987): 51–63.

CLAYTON, CHERRY (ed.). *Olive Schreiner*. Johannesburg: McGraw-Hill, 1983.

CLIFFORD, JAMES. *The Predicament of Culture: Twentieth-Century Ethnography, Literature, and Art*. Cambridge, Mass.: Harvard University Press, 1988.

—— 'Diasporas', *Cultural Anthropology*, 9/2 (1994): 302–38.

COBHAM, RHONDA. 'Revisioning our Kumblas: Transforming Feminist and Nationalist Agendas in Caribbean Women's Texts', *Callaloo*, 16/1 (Spring 1993): 44–64.

CONOLLY, L. W. (ed.). *Theatrical Touring and Founding in North America.* Westport Conn.: Greenwood, 1982.

COOMBS, ORDE (ed.). *Is Massa Day Dead? Black Moods in the Caribbean.* Garden City, NY: Anchor Books, 1974.

COOPER, CAROLYN. 'Writing Oral History: SISTREN Theatre Collective's *Lionheart Gal*', *Kunapipi*, 11/1 (1989): 49–58.

—— *Noises in the Blood: Orality, Gender and the 'Vulgar' Body of Jamaican Popular Culture.* Warwick University Caribbean Studies. Warwick: Macmillan Caribbean, 1993.

CRAWFORD, ROBERT. *Devolving English Literature.* Oxford: Clarendon Press, 1992.

CRONIN, RICHARD. *Imagining India.* New York: St Martin's, 1989.

CROSBY, ALFRED W. *Ecological Imperialism: The Biological Expansion of Europe, 900–1900.* Cambridge: Cambridge University Press, 1986.

CROWLEY, TONY. *Standard English and the Politics of Language.* Urbana: University of Illinois Press, 1989.

CUDJOE, SELWYN R. *Resistance and Caribbean Literature.* Athens, Oh.: Ohio University Press, 1980.

—— (ed.). *Caribbean Women Writers.* Wellesley: Callaloux Publications, 1990.

CURTIS, L. P. *Anglo-Saxons and Celts.* Bridgeport, Conn.: Conference on British Studies, 1968.

CUTTERIDGE, CAPT. O. *Royal Readers*, First Series. London: Nelson, 1952.

—— *Nelson's West Indian Readers*, Book I. London: Nelson, 1971.

DALE, LEIGH. 'Courting Captivity: The Teaching of English Literature and the Inculcation of Englishness in Australian Universities', University of Queensland, 1993.

DALGLISH, GERARD M. *A Dictionary of Africanisms.* Westport, Conn.: Greenwood, 1982.

DANCE, DARYL (ed.). *Fifty Caribbean Writers: A Bio-bibliographical Critical Sourcebook.* New York: Greenwood Press, 1986.

DAS, VEENA. 'Subaltern as Perspective', in Ranajit Guha (ed.), *Subaltern Studies VI: Writings in South Asian History and Society.* New Delhi: Oxford University Press, 1989: 310–28.

DATHORNE, O. R. *Dark Ancestor: The Literature of the Black Man in the Caribbean.* Baton Rouge: Louisiana State University Press, 1981.

DAVEY, FRANK. *Post-national Arguments: The Politics of the Anglophone Canadian Novel since 1967.* Toronto: University of Toronto Press, 1993.

DAVIES, R. A. (ed.). *On Thomas Chandler Haliburton.* Ottawa: Tecumseh, 1979.

DAVIS, DAVID BRION. *The Problem of Slavery in Western Culture.* Ithaca, NY: Cornell University Press, 1966.

DAVIS, GEOFFREY, and MAES-JELINEK, HENA (eds.). *Crisis and Creativity in the New Literatures in English.* Amsterdam: Rodopi, 1990.

DAVIS, JACK, and HODGE, BOB (eds.). *Aboriginal Writing Today*. Canberra: Australian Institute of Aboriginal Studies, 1985.

DAYMOND, DOUGLAS M., and MONKMAN, LESLIE G. (eds.). *Towards a Canadian Literature: Essays, Editorials & Manifestos*, vol. i. 1752–1940. Ottawa: Tecumseh, 1984.

DEANE, SEAMUS. *Celtic Revivals*. London: Faber, 1985.

DELBAERE, JEANNE (ed.). *The Ring of Fire: Essays on Janet Frame*. Sydney: Dangaroo Press, 1992.

DELEUZE, GILLES, and GUATTARI, FÉLIX. *Kafka: Toward a Minor Literature*, trans. Dana Polan. Minneapolis: University of Minnesota Press, 1988.

DENNEY, REUEL. 'Breathing the Sublime: Respiration and Inspiration in the Poetics of Allen Ginsberg', in Guy Amrithanayagam and S. C. Harrex (eds.), *Only Connect: Literary Perspectives East and West*. Adelaide: Center for Research in the New Literatures in English and East–West Center, 1981: 64–74.

DERRIDA, JACQUES. *Of Grammatology*, trans. Gayatri Spivak. Baltimore: Johns Hopkins University Press, 1974.

—— *Writing and Difference*, trans. Alan Bass. London: Routledge, 1978.

DEVONISH, HUBERT. *Language and Liberation: Creole Language Politics in the Caribbean*. London: Karia, 1986.

DHARWADKER, APARNA, and DHARWADKER, VINAY. 'Language, Identity, and Nation in Postcolonial Indian-English Literature', in Gita Rajan and Radhika Mohan Ram (eds.), *English Postcoloniality: Literatures from around the World*. Westport, Conn.: Greenwood Press, 1996.

DHARWADKER, VINAY (trans.). 'Twenty-Nine Modern Indian Poems', *TriQuarterly*, 77 (1990): 119–228.

—— 'The Poems of Sujata Bhatt Are Such', *Arc*, 26 (1990): 78–82.

—— 'Some Contexts of Modern Indian Poetry', *Chicago Review*, 38/1–2 (1992): 218–31.

—— 'The Contemporary Urdu Short Story: A Review Article', *Annual of Urdu Studies*, 8 (1993): 169–79.

—— 'Orientalism and the Study of Indian Literatures', in Carol A. Breckenridge and Peter van der Veer (eds.), *Orientalism and the Postcolonial Predicament: Perspectives on South Asia*. Philadelphia: University of Pennsylvania Press, 1993: 158–85.

—— 'Trials of a Nation', *The World and I* (Nov. 1993): 283–97.

—— and RAMANUJAN, A. K. (eds.). *The Oxford Anthology of Modern Indian Poetry*. Delhi: Oxford University Press, 1994.

DICKASON, OLIVE PATRICIA. *The Myth of the Savage*. Edmonton: University of Alberta Press, 1984.

DICKSON, ROBERT. *The Course of Empire: Neo-Classical Culture in New South Wales 1788–1860*. Melbourne: Oxford University Press, 1986.

DIXON, ROBERT. 'Public and Private Voices', in *The Penguin New Literary History of Australia*. Ringwood: Penguin Books, 1988.

DOCKER, JOHN. 'The Neocolonial Assumption in University Teaching of English', in Chris Tiffin (ed.), *South Pacific Images*. St Lucia: SPACLALS, 1978.

—— *The Nervous Nineties*. Melbourne: Oxford University Press, 1991.

DRAYTON, ARTHUR. 'Francis Williams (1700–1770)', in Daryl Cumber Dance (ed.), *Fifty Caribbean Writers*. Westport, Conn.: Greenwood, 1986: 493–7.

DURING, SIMON. 'Postmodernism or Postcolonialism?', *Landfall*, 39/3 (1985): 366–80.

—— 'Postmodernism or Post-colonialism Today', *Textual Practice*, 1/1 (1987): 32–47.

DURIX, JEAN-PIERRE. *The Writer Written: The Artist and Creation in the New Literatures in English*. Contributions to the Study of World Literature 21. New York: Greenwood Press, 1987.

DUTTON, GEOFFREY (ed.). *The Literature of Australia*. Harmondsworth: Penguin, 1964; 2nd edn. 1976.

EADEN, P. R. and MARES, F. H. (eds.). *Mapped but not Known: The Australian Landscape of the Imagination*. Netley: Wakefield, 1986.

EAGLETON, TERRY. *Literary Theory: An Introduction*. Oxford: Blackwell, 1983.

—— JAMESON, FREDRIC, and SAID, EDWARD W. *Nationalism, Colonialism, and Literature*. Minneapolis: University of Minnesota Press, 1990.

EDWARDS, MURRAY D. *A Stage in our Past*. Toronto: University of Toronto Press, 1968.

EGEJURU, P. A. *Black Writers, White Audience: A Critical Approach to African Literature*. New York: Exposition, 1978.

ELLIOTT, BRIAN. *Marcus Clarke*. Oxford: Clarendon Press, 1958.

ELLMAN, RICHARD, and O'CLAIR, ROBERT. 'Introduction', *The Norton Anthology of Modern Poetry*. 2nd edn. New York: W. W. Norton, 1988.

EVANS, CHAD. *Frontier Theatre*. Victoria: Sono Nis, 1983.

FANON, FRANTZ. *The Wretched of the Earth*, trans. Constance Farrington. New York: Grove Press, 1961; repr. 1977.

FARAH, NURUDDIN. 'Homing in on the Pigeon', *Brick*, 48 (Spring 1994): 4–9.

FERRIER, CAROLE (ed.). *Gender, Politics and Fiction: Twentieth-Century Women's Novels*. St Lucia: Queensland University Press, 1991.

FIEDLER, LESLIE A., and BAKER, HOUSTON A., Jr. (eds.). *English Literature: Opening up the Canon*. Selected Papers from the English Institute, 1979, NS 4. Baltimore: Johns Hopkins University Press, 1981.

FINNEGAN, RUTH. *Oral Literature in Africa*. Oxford: Clarendon Press, 1970.

—— *Oral Poetry*. Cambridge: Cambridge University Press, 1977.

—— *Literacy and Orality*. Oxford: Basil Blackwell, 1988.

FIRST, RUTH, and SCOTT, ANN. *Olive Schreiner*. London: André Deutsch, 1980.

FOLEY, JOHN MILES (ed.). *Oral Traditional Literature: A Festschrift for Albert Bates Lord*. Columbus, Oh.: Slavica Publishers, 1989: 347–74.

FOUCAULT, MICHEL. *The Archaeology of Knowledge*, trans. A. M. Sheridan. London: Tavistock, 1972.

FRASER, ROBERT. *West African Poetry: A Critical History*. Cambridge: Cambridge University Press, 1986.

GEE, JAMES. *Social Linguistics and Literacies: Ideology in Discourses: Critical Perspectives on Literacy and Education*. London: Falmer, 1990.

GÉRARD, ALBERT. *African Language Literatures: An Introduction to the Literary History of Sub-Saharan Africa*. Harlow: Longman, 1981.

—— (ed.). *European-Language Writing in Sub-Saharan Africa*. Budapest: Akademiai Kiadó, 1986.

GHOSE, ZULFIKAR. 'Going Home', *The Toronto South Asian Review*, 9/2 (1991): 15–22.

—— *The Art of Creating Fiction*. London: Macmillan, 1991.

GIKANDI, SIMON. *Reading the African Novel*. London: James Currey, 1987.

—— *Reading Chinua Achebe: Language and Ideology in Fiction*. Portsmouth, NH: Heinemann, 1991.

—— *Writing in Limbo: Modernism and Caribbean Literature*. Ithaca, NY: Cornell University Press, 1992.

GILDERDALE, BETTY. *A Sea Change: 145 Years of New Zealand Junior Fiction*. Auckland: Longman Paul, 1982.

GILROY, PAUL. *The Black Atlantic: Modernity and Double Consciousness*. London: Verso, 1993.

GLASER, MARLIES, and PAUSCH, MARION (eds.). *Caribbean Writers. Between Orality and Writing. Les Auteurs caribéens entre l'oralité et l'écriture*. Amsterdam: Rodopi, 1994.

GLISSANT, ÉDOUARD. *Caribbean Discourse*, trans. J. Michael Dash. Charlottesville: University of Virginia Press, 1989.

GOLDIE, TERRY. *Fear and Temptation: The Image of the Indigene in Canadian, Australian and New Zealand Literatures*. Montreal: McGill-Queen's University Press, 1989.

GOODWIN, KEN. *Understanding African Poetry: A Study of Ten Poets*. London: Heinemann, 1982.

—— *A History of Australian Literature*. New York: St Martin's Press, 1986.

GOODY, JACK, and WATT, IAN. 'The Consequences of Literacy', in Jack Goody and Ian Watt (eds.), *Literacy in Traditional Societies*. Cambridge: Cambridge University Press, 1968.

GOONERATNE, M. Y. *English Literature in Ceylon 1815–1878*. Dehiwala: Tisara Prakasakayo, 1968.

GOONETILLEKE, D. C. R. A. *Developing Countries in British Fiction*. London: Macmillan, 1977.

GORDON, SHIRLEY. *A Century of West Indian Education*. London: Longman, 1963.

GRAMSCI, ANTONIO. *Selections from the Prison Notebooks of Antonio Gramsci*, ed. Quintin Hoare and Geoffrey Nowell Smith. London: Lawrence & Wishart, 1971.

GREEN, H. M. *A History of Australian Literature*. 2 vols. Sydney: Angus & Robertson, 1961; rev. 1984.

GREENBERGER, ALLEN J. *The British Image of India: A Study in the Literature of Imperialism*. London: Oxford University Press, 1969.

GREET, ANNIE, et al. (eds.). *Raj Nostalgia: Some Literary and Critical Implications*. Adelaide: CRNLE, 1992.

GRIFFITHS, GARETH. 'The Myth of Authenticity', in Chris Tiffin and Alan Lawson (eds.), *De-scribing Empire: Post-colonialism and Textuality*. London: Routledge, 1994.

GUMPERZ, JOHN J., and COOK-GUMPERZ, J. 'Introduction', in *Language and Social Identity*. Cambridge: Cambridge University Press, 1982: 1–21.

GUNEW, SNEJA. *Displacements: Migrant Story-Tellers*. Geelong: Deakin University, 1982.

GURNAH, ABDULRAZAK (ed.). 'Transformative Strategies in the Fiction of Ngugi wa Thiong'o', in Abdulrazak Gurnah, *Essays on African Writing: A Re-evaluation*. Oxford: Heinemann, 1993: 142–58.

GURR, ANDREW. *Writers in Exile: The Identity of Home in Modern Literature*. Brighton: Harvester Press, 1981.

HABEKOST, CHRISTIAN. *Verbal Riddim: The Politics and Aesthetics of African-Caribbean Dub Poetry*. Amsterdam: Rodopi, 1993.

HADJOR, KOFI BUENOR. *The Penguin Dictionary of Third World Terms*. London: Penguin, 1992.

HAFKIN, NANCY, and BAY, EDNA (eds.). *Women in Africa: Studies in Social and Economic Change*. Stanford, Calif.: Stanford University Press, 1976.

HALL, STUART. 'Cultural Identity and Diaspora', in Patrick Williams and Laura Chrisman (eds.), *Colonial Discourse and Post-colonial Theory: A Reader*. New York: Columbia University Press, 1994: 392–403.

HALLIDAY, M. A. K. *Language as a Social Semiotic: The Social Interpretation of Language and Meaning*. London: Edward Arnold, 1978.

HALPENNY, FRANCESS (ed.). *Dictionary of Canadian Biography*. 12 vols. + Index. Toronto: University of Toronto Press, 1966–91.

HAMNER, ROBERT D. (ed.). *Critical Perspectives on Derek Walcott*. Washington: Three Continents Press, 1993.

HANNA, CLIFF. 'The Ballads', in *The Penguin New Literary History of Australia*. Ringwood: Penguin Books, 1988.

HARLOW, BARBARA. *Resistance Literature*. New York: Methuen, 1987.

HARRIS, WILSON. *Tradition, the Writer and Society*. London: New Beacon, 1967.

—— *History, Fable and Myth in the Caribbean and Guianas*. Georgetown: Ministry of Information and Culture, 1970. Reprinted in *Explorations*. Mundelstrup: Dangaroo Press, 1981: 20–42.

—— 'A Talk on the Subjective Imagination', in Hena Maes-Jelinek (ed.), *Explorations: A Selection of Talks and Articles 1966–1981*. Mundelstrup: Dangaroo, 1981: 57–67.

—— *The Womb of Space: The Cross-cultural Imagination*. Westport, Conn.: Greenwood, 1983.

—— 'Adversarial Contexts and Creativity', *New Left Review*, 154 (Nov.–Dec. 1985): 124–8.

—— 'A Note on Zulfikar Ghose's "Nature Strategies" ', *Review of Contemporary Fiction*, 9/2 (Summer 1989): 172–8.

HARTZ, LOUIS. *The Founding of New Societies*. New York: Harcourt, Brace & World, 1964.

HASSAM, ANDREW. ' "As I Write": Narrative Occasions and the Quest for Self-Presence in the Travel Diary', *Ariel: A Review of International English Literature*, 21/4 (Oct. 1990).

—— 'Writing the Coastline of Australia: Emigrants' Diaries and "The Long Looked for Shores" ', *University of Toronto Quarterly*, 61/2 (Winter 1991/2).

HAVELOCK, ERIC A. *The Muse Learns to Write: Reflections on Orality and Literacy from Antiquity to the Present*. New Haven: Yale University Press, 1986.

HAVEMANN, PAUL. 'What's in the Treaty? Constitutionalizing Maori Rights in Aotearoa/New Zealand, 1975–1993', in Kayleen Hazlehurst (ed.), *Legal Pluralism and the Colonial Legacy*. Aldershot: Avebury, 1995: 73–101.

HAYNES, JOHN. *African Poetry and the English Language*. Basingstoke: Macmillan, 1987.

HEALY, J. J., *Literature and the Aborigine in Australia*. St Lucia: University of Queensland Press, 1989.

HEATH, ROY. 'Night Rain on the Parapet', *Guardian*, 17 May 1990, p. 21.

HENNESSEY, ALISTAIR. *Intellectuals in the Twentieth Century Caribbean I*. Basingstoke: Macmillan, 1992.

HERGENHAN, LAURIE. *Unnatural Lives: Studies in Australian Fiction about the Convicts, from James Tucker to Patrick White*. St Lucia: University of Queensland Press, 1983.

—— (ed.). *The Penguin New Literary History of Australia*. Ringwood: Penguin, 1988.

HODGE, BOB, and MISHRA, VIJAY. 'Multiculturalism and the Fragment Society', in *Dark Side of the Dream: Australian Literature and the Postcolonial Mind*. Sydney: Allen & Unwin, 1990: 178–203.

HOLT, PATRICIA. 'Mukherjee's Vision of America', *San Francisco Sunday Examiner and Chronicle*, 17 Feb. 1991, pp. 1–2.

HUGGAN, GRAHAM. 'Creolisation and the Post-colonial Text', in Stephen Slemon and Helen Tiffin (eds.), *After Europe*. Sydney: Dangaroo Press, 1989: 27–40.

HULME, KERI A. L. 'Mauri: An Introduction to Bicultural Poetry in New Zealand', in Guy Amrithanayagam and S. C. Harrex (eds.), *Only Connect: Literary Perspectives East and West*. Adelaide: Centre for Research in the New Literatures in English, 1981: 290–310.

HULME, PETER. *Colonial Encounters: Europe and the Native Caribbean, 1492–1797*. London: Methuen, 1986.

—— 'Subversive Archipelagoes: Colonial Discourse and the Break-Up of Continental Theory', *Disposite*, 14 (Autumn 1989).

HURLEY, MICHAEL. *The Borders of Nightmare: The Fiction of John Richardson*. Toronto: University of Toronto Press, 1992.

HUSSEIN, AAMER. 'The Echoing of Quiet Voices', in Mimi Chan and Roy Harris (eds.), *Asian Voices in English*. Hong Kong: Hong Kong University Press, 1991: 101–8.

HUTCHEON, LINDA. *A Poetics of Postmodernism: History, Theory, Fiction*. New York: Routledge, 1988.

HUTCHEON, LINDA. 'Introduction: Complexities Abounding', *PMLA*, 110/1 (Jan. 1995): 1–16. ['Special Topic: Colonialism and the Postcolonial Condition'.]

—— and RICHMOND, MARION (eds.), *Other Solitudes: Canadian Multicultural Fictions*. London: Oxford University Press, 1990.

INNES, C. L. *The Devil's Own Mirror: The Irishman and the African in Modern Literature*. Washington: Three Continents Press, 1990.

IRVIN, ERIC. *Australian Melodrama: 80 Years of Popular Theatre*. Sydney: Hale & Iremonger, 1981.

—— *A Dictionary of Australian Theatre 1788–1914*. Sydney: Hale & Iremonger, 1985.

—— *Theatre Comes to Australia*. St Lucia: University of Queensland Press, 1971.

ITWARU, ARNOLD. 'Exile and Commemoration', in Frank Birbalsingh (ed.), *Indenture and Exile: The Indo-Caribbean Experience*. Toronto: *Toronto South Asia Review*, 1989: 202–6.

IYENGAR, K. R. SRINIVASA. *Indian Writing in English*. New Delhi: Sterling Press, 1961; 4th edn. 1984.

JACOBY, RUSSELL. 'Marginal Returns: The Trouble with Post-colonial Theory', *Lingua Franca* (Sept.–Oct. 1995): 30–7.

JAHN, JANHEINZ. *Muntu: An Outline of the New African Cultures*. New York: Grove Press, 1961.

—— *A History of Neo-African Literatures: Writing in Two Continents*. London: Faber, 1968.

JAMES, ADEOLA (ed.). *In their Own Voices: African Women Writers Talk*. London: Heinemann, 1990.

JAMES, C. L. R. *Spheres of Influence*. London: Alison & Busby, 1980.

JAMESON, FREDRIC. *The Political Unconscious*. Ithaca, NY: Cornell University Press, 1981.

—— 'Third-World Literature in the Era of Multinational Capitalism', *Social Text*, 15 (Fall 1986): 65–88.

JANMOHAMED, ABDUL R. *Manichean Aesthetics: The Politics of Literature in Colonial Africa*. Amherst: University of Massachusetts Press, 1983.

—— 'The Economy of Manichean Allegory: The Function of Racial Difference in Colonialist Literature', *Critical Inquiry*, 12/1 (1985): 59–87.

—— and LLOYD, DAVID (eds.). *The Nature and Context of Minority Discourse*. New York: Oxford University Press, 1990.

JAYAWARDENA, KUMARI. *Feminism and Nationalism in the Third World*. London: Zed Press, 1986.

JONES, JOSEPH. *Terranglia: The Case for English as World Literature*. New York: Twayne, 1965.

—— and JONES, JOHANNA. *New Zealand Fiction*. Boston: Twayne, 1983.

JORDENS, ANN-MARI. *The Stenhouse Circle: Literary Life in Mid-Nineteenth Century Sydney*. Carlton: Melbourne University Press, 1979.

JULIEN, EILEEN. *African Novels and the Question of Orality*. Bloomington: Indiana University Press, 1992.

JUSSAWALLA, FEROZA, and DASENBROCK, REED WAY (eds.). *Interviews with Writers of the Post-colonial World*. Jackson: University Press of Mississippi, 1992.

KACHRU, BRAJ (ed.). *The Other Tongue: English across Cultures*. Urbana: University of Illinois Press, 1982.

—— *The Indianization of English: The English Language in India*. Oxford: Oxford University Press, 1983.

KEDGLEY, SUE (ed.). *Our Own Country: Leading New Zealand Women Writers Talk about their Writing and their Lives*. Auckland: Penguin Books, 1989.

KENT, GEORGE E. 'A Conversation with George Lamming', *Black World*, 22/5 (1973): 88–9.

KIERNAN, BRIAN. 'Realism and Romance', in Ken Goodwin and Alan Lawson (eds.), *The Macmillan Anthology of Australian Literature*. Melbourne: Macmillan, 1990: 409–14.

KING, ANTHONY (ed.). *Culture, Globalization and the World System*. Binghampton: State University of New York, 1991.

KING, BRUCE (ed.). *Introduction to Nigerian Literature*. Lagos: University of Lagos Press, 1971.

—— (ed.). *Literatures of the World in English*. London: Routledge & Kegan Paul, 1974.

—— 'Varieties of African Literature', in H. H. Anniah Gowda (ed.), *Powre above Powres 3: Essays in African Literature*. Mysore: The Centre for Commonwealth Literature and Research, 1978: 1–17.

—— (ed.). *West Indian Literature*. Basingstoke: Macmillan, 1979; 2nd edn. 1995.

—— *New English Literatures: Cultural Nationalism in a Changing World*. London: Macmillan, 1980.

—— 'Nationalism, Internationalism, Periodisation and Commonwealth Literature', in Dieter Riemenschneider (ed.), *The History and Historiography of Commonwealth Literature*. Tübingen: Gunter Narr Verlag, 1983: 10–18.

—— *Modern Indian Poetry in English*. New Delhi: Oxford University Press, 1987, 1994.

—— *Three Indian Poets: Nissim Ezekiel, A. K. Ramanujan and Dom Moraes*. New Delhi: Oxford University Press, 1991.

—— (ed.). *The Commonwealth Novel since 1960*. London: Macmillan, 1991.

—— 'The New Internationalism', in J. Acheson (ed.), *The British and Irish Novel since 1960*. London: Macmillan, 1991: 193–210.

—— (ed.). *Post-colonial English Drama*. London: Macmillan, 1992.

—— *V. S. Naipaul*. London: Macmillan, 1993.

—— 'Introduction: A Changing Face', in Bruce King (ed.), *The Later Fiction of Nadine Gordimer*. London: Macmillan, 1993: 1–17.

—— *Derek Walcott and West Indian Drama/'Not Only a Playwright But a Company'/The Trinidad Theatre Workshop 1959–1993*. Oxford: Clarendon, 1995.

KING, RUBY, and MORRISSEY, MIKE. *Images in Print: Bias and Prejudice in Caribbean Textbooks*. Kingston: Institute of Social and Economic Research, 1988.

KIRKBY, JOAN (ed.). *The American Model: Influence & Independence in Australian Poetry*. Sydney: Hale & Iremonger, 1982.

KLINCK, CARL F. (gen. ed.). *Literary History of Canada: Canadian Literature in English*. 2nd edn. 3 vols. Toronto: University of Toronto Press, 1976.

KOCH, C. J. 'Literature and Cultural Identity', *Tasmanian Review*, 4 (1980).

KOLODNY, ANNETTE. *The Lay of the Land*. Chapel Hill: University of North Carolina Press, 1975.

KOTEI, S. I. A. *The Book Today in Africa*. Paris: Unesco, 1981.

KRAMER, LEONIE (ed.). *The Oxford History of Australian Literature*. Melbourne: Oxford University Press, 1981.

KRÖLLER, EVA-MARIE. 'The Politics of Influence: Canadian Post-modernism in an American Context', in M. J. Valdes (ed.), *InterAmerican Literary Relations*, vol. iii. New York: Garland, 1985.

—— 'First Impressions: Rhetorical Strategies in Travel Writing by Victorian Women', *Ariel: A Review of International English Literature*, 21/4 (Oct. 1990).

LAMMING, GEORGE. *The Pleasures of Exile*. London: Michael Joseph, 1960; Allison & Busby, 1984.

LANSBURY, CORAL. *Arcady in Australia: The Evocation of Australia in Nineteenth-Century English Literature*. Carlton: Melbourne University Press, 1970.

LARSON, CHARLES. 'Heroic Ethnocentrism: The Idea of Universality in Literature', *American Scholar*, 43/3 (1973): 463–75.

LAWRENCE, KAREN R. (ed.). *Decolonizing Tradition: New Views of Twentieth-Century 'British' Literary Canons*. Urbana: University of Illinois Press, 1992.

LAWSON, ALAN. 'A Cultural Paradigm for the Second World', *Australian-Canadian Studies*, 9/1–2 (1991): 67–78.

LAZARUS, NEIL. *Resistance in Postcolonial African Fiction*. New Haven: Yale University Press, 1990.

LEFEVERE, A. 'Interface: Some Thoughts on the Historiography of African Literature Written in English', in D. Riemenschneider (ed.), *The History and Historiography of Commonwealth Literature*. Tübingen: Gunter Narr Verlag, 1983: 99–107.

LÉVI-STRAUSS, CLAUDE. *The Savage Mind*, trans. Weidenfeld & Nicolson. Welwyn Garden City: Garden City Press, 1966.

LEWIS, IVOR. *Sahibs, Nabobs and Boxwallahs: A Dictionary of the Words of Anglo-India*. Oxford: Oxford University Press, 1991.

LEWIS, JEFF. 'Putu Goes to Paris: Global Communication and Australian Imaginings of the East', *Kunapipi*, 14/3 (1994): 54–75.

LIM, SHIRLEY GOEK-LIN. *Nationalism and Literature: English-Language Writing from the Philippines and Singapore*. Quezon City: New Day Publishers, 1993.

LINDFORS, BERNTH. *Black African Literature in English, 1977–81.* New York: Africana Publishing, 1986.

—— *Black African Literature in English, 1981–1986.* New York: Hans Zell, 1989.

—— and SANDER, REINHARD (eds.). *Twentieth-Century Caribbean and Black African Writers.* 2nd Series. Detroit: Gale Research, 1993. [*Dictionary of Literary Biography,* vol. cxxv.]

LLOYD, DAVID. *Anomalous States: Irish Writing and the Post-colonial Moment.* Durham, NC: Duke University Press, 1993.

LOCKSLEY, LINDO. 'Francis Williams: A "Free" Negro in a Slave World', *Savacou,* 1 (June 1970): 75–80.

LONG, EDWARD. *A History of Jamaica.* London: T. Lowndes, 1774.

LOVE, HAROLD (ed.). *The Australian Stage: A Documentary History.* Kensington: University of New South Wales Press, 1984.

LOWE, LISA. *Critical Terrains: French and British Orientalisms.* Ithaca, NY: Cornell University Press, 1991.

LUTZ, HARTMUT. *Contemporary Challenges: Conversations with Canadian Native Authors.* Saskatoon: Fifth House, 1991.

LYONGA, NALOVA, BREITINGER, ECKHARD, and BUTAKE, BOLE (eds.). *Anglophone Cameroon Writing.* Bayreuth: Bayreuth African Studies 30, 1993.

MACAULAY, THOMAS R. 'Indian Education: Minute of the 2nd February, 1835', in *Macaulay: Prose and Poetry,* ed. G. M. Young. London: Rupert Hart-Davis, 1952.

McCLINTOOK, ANNE. *Imperial Leather: Race, Gender and Sexuality in the Colonial Contest.* New York: Routledge, 1995.

McCORMICK, E. H. *New Zealand Literature: A Survey.* London: Oxford University Press, 1959.

MACHEREY, PIERRE. *A Theory of Literary Production,* trans. Geoffrey Wall. London: Routledge & Kegan Paul, 1978.

MacDONALD, ROBERT H. *Sons of the Empire: The Frontier and the Boy Scout Movement, 1890–1918.* Toronto: University of Toronto Press, 1993.

McGIFFORD, DIANE. 'Suniti Namjoshi', in Emmanuel S. Nelson (ed.), *Writers of the Indian Diaspora: A Bio-bibliographical Critical Sourcebook.* Westport, Conn.: Greenwood Press, 1993: 291–8.

McGREGOR, GAILE. *The Wacousta Syndrome.* Toronto: University of Toronto Press, 1985.

McGREGOR, GRAHAM, and WILLIAMS, MARK (eds.). *Dirty Silence: Aspects of Language and Literature in New Zealand.* Auckland: Oxford University Press, 1991.

McKENZIE, D. F. *Oral Culture, Literacy & Print in Early New Zealand: The Treaty of Waitangi.* Wellington: Victoria University Press/Alexander Turnbull Library, 1985.

McLAREN, JOHN. *Australian Literature: An Historical Introduction.* Melbourne: Longman, 1989.

McLUHAN, MARSHALL. *The Gutenberg Galaxy.* Toronto: Toronto University Press; London: Routledge & Kegan Paul, 1962.

294  *Selected Bibliography*

MACMECHAN, ARCHIBALD. *Headwaters of Canadian Literature.* 1924; repr. Toronto: McClelland & Stewart, 1974.

MCMULLEN, LORRAINE. *An Odd Attempt in a Woman: The Literary Life of Frances Brooke.* Vancouver: University of British Columbia Press, 1983.

—— (ed.). *Re(dis)covering our Foremothers: Nineteenth-Century Canadian Women Writers.* Ottawa: University of Ottawa Press, 1990.

MCNAUGHTON, HOWARD. *New Zealand Drama.* Boston: Twayne, 1981.

MAES-JELINEK, HENA (ed.). *Wilson Harris: The Uncompromising Imagination.* Sydney: Dangaroo Press, 1991.

—— PETERSEN, KIRSTEN HOLST, and RUTHERFORD, ANNA. *A Shaping of Connections: Commonwealth Literature Studies—Then and Now.* Sydney: Dangaroo Press, 1989.

MAGAREY, SUSAN, ROWLEY, SUE, and SHERIDAN, SUSAN (eds.). *Debutante Nation: Feminism Contests the 1890s.* Sydney: Allen & Unwin, 1993.

MAHOOD, M. M. *The Colonial Encounter: A Reading of Six Novels.* London: Rex Collings, 1977.

MAJA-PEARCE, ADEWALE. *Who's Afraid of Wole Soyinka?* London: Heinemann, 1991.

—— *A Mask Dancing: Nigerian Novelists of the Eighties.* London: Hans Zell, 1992.

MARCUS, PHILIP. *Yeats and the Irish Renaissance.* Ithaca, NY: Cornell University Press, 1970.

—— *Marx/Engels: The First Indian War of Independence 1857–1859.* Moscow: Progress Publishers, 1959.

MATTHEWS, BRIAN. *The Receding Wave: Henry Lawson's Prose.* Melbourne: Melbourne University Press, 1972.

MATTHEWS, JOHN PENGWERNE. *Tradition in Exile.* Toronto: University of Toronto Press; Melbourne: Cheshire, 1962.

MAUGHAN-BROWN, DAVID. *Land, Freedom and Fiction: History and Ideology in Kenya.* London: Zed, 1985.

MAXWELL, D. E. S. 'Landscape and Theme', in John Press (ed.), *The Commonwealth Pen: Unity and Diversity in a Common Culture.* London: Heinemann, 1965: 82–9.

MAZRUI, ALI. *The Political Sociology of the English Language: An African Perspective.* The Hague: Mouton, 1975.

MEIRING, JANE. *Thomas Pringle: His Life & Times.* Cape Town: A. A. Balkema, 1968.

MISHRA, VIJAY. 'Indo-Fijian Fiction and the *Girmit* Ideology', in Subramani (ed.), *The Indo-Fijian Experience.* St Lucia: University of Queensland Press, 1980: 171–83.

—— 'The Girmit Ideology Revisited: Fiji Indian Literature', in Emmanuel S. Nelson (ed.), *Reworlding.* New York: Greenwood Press, 1992: 1–12.

—— and HODGE, BOB. 'What Is Post(-)colonialism?', *Textual Practice,* 5/3 (Dec. 1991): 399–414.

MITCHELL, W. J. T. 'Postcolonial Culture, Postimperial Criticism', *Transition,* 56 (1992): 11.

MODARRESSI, TAGHI. 'Writing with an Accent', *Chanteh* (Fall 1992): 7–9.

MOHANTY, CHANDRA, *et al*. (eds.). *Third World Women and the Politics of Feminism*. Bloomington: Indiana University Press, 1990.

MOHANTY, S. P. 'Us and Them: On the Philosophical Bases of Political Criticism', *New Formations*, 8 (Summer 1989): 55–80.

MOMMSEN, WOLFGANG J. 'Theories of Imperialism', trans. P. S. Falla. Chicago: University of Chicago Press, 1977.

MOORE, T. INGLIS. *Social Patterns in Australian Literature*. Sydney: Angus & Robertson, 1971.

MOSS, JOHN (ed.). *The Canadian Novel: Beginnings*. Toronto: NC Press, rev. edn. 1984.

—— *Future Indicative: Literary Theory and Canadian Literature*. Ottawa: University of Ottawa Press, 1987.

MUECKE, STEPHEN. 'Aboriginal Literature: Oral', in *The Penguin New Literary History of Australia*. Ringwood: Penguin Books, 1988.

—— *Textual Spaces: Aboriginality and Cultural Studies*. Kensington: New South Wales University Press, 1992.

MUKHERJEE, ARUN P. 'Ideology in the Classroom: A Case Study in the Teaching of English Literature in Canadian Universities', *Dalhousie Review*, 66/1–2 (1986): 22–30.

MUKHERJEE, MEENAKSHI. *The Twice-Born Fiction: Themes and Techniques of the Indian Novel in English*. Delhi: Heinemann, 1971.

—— *Realism and Reality*. Delhi: Oxford University Press, 1986.

NAIK, M. K. *A History of Indian English Literature*. New Delhi: Sahitya Akademi, 1982.

NAIRN, BEDE, *et al*. (eds.). *Australian Dictionary of Biography*. 12 vols. Carlton: Melbourne University Press, 1966–.

NAROGIN, MUDROOROO [Colin Johnson]. 'Guerilla Poetry: Lionel Fogarty's Response to Language Genocide', *Westerly*, 31/3 (1986): n.p.

—— 'White Forms, Aboriginal Content', in Jack Davis and Bob Hodge (eds.), *Aboriginal Writing Today*. Canberra: Australian Institute of Aboriginal Studies, 1985.

NASTA, SUSHEILA (ed.). *Motherlands: Black Women's Writing from Africa, the Caribbean and South Asia*. London: The Women's Press, 1991.

NATH, DWARKA. *A History of the Indians in Guyana*. 1950; London: Author, 1970.

NDEBELE, NJABULO S. *South African Literature and Culture: Rediscovery of the Ordinary*, introd. by Graham Pechey. Manchester: Manchester University Press, 1994.

NELSON, EMMANUEL S. (ed.). *Reworlding: The Literature of the Indian Diaspora*. New York: Greenwood Press, 1992.

—— (ed.). *Writers of the Indian Diaspora: A Bio-bibliographical Critical Sourcebook*. New York: Greenwood, 1993.

NEW, WILLIAM H. *Among Worlds: An Introduction to Modern Commonwealth and South African Fiction*. Erin: Press Procepic, 1975.

—— *A History of Canadian Literature*. London: Macmillan Education, 1989.

NEW, WILLIAM H. (ed.). *Canadian Writers before 1890*: Dictionary of Literary Biography, vol. xcix. Detroit: Bruccoli-Clark-Layman/Gale, 1990.

NGUGI WA THIONG'O. *Homecoming: Essays on African and Caribbean Literature, Culture and Politics*. London: Heinemann, 1972.

—— *Decolonizing the Mind: The Politics of Language in African Literature*. London: James Currey, 1986.

OBBO, CHRISTINE. *African Women: Their Struggle for Economic Independence*. London: Zed Press, 1980.

OBIECHINA, EMMANUEL. *An African Popular Literature: A Study of Onitsha Market Pamphlets*. Cambridge: Cambridge University Press, 1973.

OGUNDIPE-LESLIE, MOLARA, and BOYCE DAVIES, CAROL (eds.). *Women as Oral Artists*. Special Issue of *Research in African Literatures*, 25/3 (1994).

OKPEWHO, ISIDORE. *The Epic in Africa: Towards a Poetics of Oral Performance*. New York: Columbia University Press, 1979.

ONG, WALTER J. *Interfaces of the Word: Studies in the Evolution of Consciousness and Culture*. Ithaca, NY: Cornell University Press, 1977.

—— *Orality and Literacy: The Technologizing of the Word*. London: Methuen, 1982.

*Oxford Literary Review*, 9/1–2 [*Colonialism & Other Essays* by Benita Parry *et al.*] (1987).

PALA, ACHOLA. 'Definitions of Women and Development: An African Perspective', in Filomena Steady (ed.), *The Black Woman Cross-Culturally*. Cambridge, Mass.: Schenkman Publishing, 1981: 185–208.

PARRY, BENITA. 'Problems in Current Theories of Colonial Discourse', *Oxford Literary Review*, 9/1–2 (1987): 27–58.

PASCOE, ROB. *The Manufacture of Australian History*. Melbourne: Oxford University Press, 1979.

PATHAK, ZAKIA, SENGUPTA, SASWSATI, and PURKAYASTHA, SHARMILA. 'The Prisonhouse of Orientalism', *Textual Practice*, 5/2 (June 1991): 195–218.

PEARLMAN, MICKEY (ed.). *Canadian Women Writing Fiction*. Jackson: University Press of Mississippi, 1993.

PEARSON, BILL. *Rifled Sanctuaries: Some Views of the Pacific Islands in Western Literature*. Auckland: Auckland University Press/Oxford University Press, 1984.

PÊCHEUX, MICHEL. *Language, Semantics and Ideology: Stating the Obvious*, trans. Harbans Nagpal. 1975; London: Macmillan, 1982.

PETERMAN, MICHAEL. 'Susanna Moodie (1803–1885)', in Robert Lecker, Jack David, and Ellen Quigley (eds.), *Canadian Writers and their Works*, vol. i. Toronto: ECW, 1983.

PETERSEN, KIRSTEN HOLST (ed.). *Criticism and Ideology: Second African Writers' Conference* [Stockholm, 1986]. Uppsala: Scandinavian Institute of African Studies, 1988.

—— and RUTHERFORD, ANNA (eds.). *In Celebration of Chinua Achebe*, *Kunapipi*, 12/2 (1990).

—— *New Art and Literature from South Africa*, *Kunapipi*, 13/1–2 (1991).

PETRONE, PENNY. *Native Literature in Canada: From the Oral Tradition to the Present.* Toronto: Oxford University Press, 1987.

PHILLIPS, A. A. *The Australian Tradition: Studies in a Colonial Culture.* Melbourne: Cheshire/Lansdowne, 1958; 2nd edn. 1966.

PHILLIPS, CARYL. *The European Tribe.* New York: Farrar, Straus & Giroux, 1987.

PIERCE, LORNE. *William Kirby: The Portrait of a Tory Loyalist.* Toronto: Macmillan, 1929.

PIETERSE, COSMO, and DUERDIN, DENNIS (eds.), *African Writers Talking: A Collection of Radio Interviews.* London: Heinemann, 1972.

POLLARD, VELMA. 'The Social History of Dread Talk', in Laurence D. Carrington (ed.), *Studies in Caribbean Language.* St Augustine: School of Education, UWI, 1983: 46–62.

PRATT, MARY LOUISE. *Imperial Eyes: Travel Writing and Transculturation.* London: Routledge, 1992.

PRESS, JOHN (ed.). *The Commonwealth Pen: Unity and Diversity in a Common Culture.* London: Heinemann, 1965.

PRIEBE, RICHARD K. (ed.). *Ghanaian Literatures.* New York: Greenwood Press, 1988.

RAHIMIEH, NASRIN. *Oriental Responses to the West: Comparative Essays in Select Writers from the Muslim World.* Leiden: E. J. Brill, 1990.

RAMCHAND, KENNETH. *The West Indian Novel and its Background.* London: Faber & Faber, 1970; Heinemann, 1983.

RAMRAJ, VICTOR. 'Denis Williams', in Daryl Cumber Dance (ed.), *Fifty Caribbean Writers: A Bio-bibliographical Critical Sourcebook.* New York: Greenwood Press, 1986: 481–92.

RASHLEY, R. E. *Poetry in Canada: The First Three Steps.* Toronto: Ryerson, 1958.

RASKIN, JONAH. *The Mythology of Imperialism.* New York: Random House, 1971.

REID, J. C., and WILKES, G. A. *Australia and New Zealand.* University Park, Pennsylvania: Pennsylvania State University Press, 1970.

RICHARDS, THOMAS. *The Imperial Archive: Knowledge and the Fantasy of Empire.* London: Verso, 1993.

RIEMENSCHNEIDER, DIETER (ed.). *The History and Historiography of Commonwealth Literature.* Tübingen: Gunter Narr Verlag, 1983.

—— (ed.). *Critical Approaches to the New Literatures in English: A Selection of Papers of the 10th Annual Conference on 'Commonwealth' Literature and Language Studies, Koenigstein, 11–14 June 1987.* Essen: Verlag Die Blaue Eule, 1989.

ROBERTSON, ROBERT T. 'Harvesters in May: Commonwealth Literary Studies 1970–1980', *Commonwealth*, 2 (1976).

ROMAINE, SUZANNE (ed.). *Language in Australia.* Cambridge: Cambridge University Press, 1991.

ROSS, ANDREW. *No Respect: Intellectuals and Popular Culture.* New York: Routledge, 1989.

ROSS, ROBERT (ed.). *International Literature in English: Essays on the Major Writers.* New York: Garland Publishing, 1991.

RUSHDIE, SALMAN. *Imaginary Homelands.* Harmondsworth: Penguin, 1992.

RUTHERFORD, ANNA (ed.). *Colonial and Post-colonial Women's Writing, Kunapipi,* 7/2–3 (1985).

—— (ed.). *Aboriginal Culture Today.* Sydney: Dangaroo Press, 1988 [Special issue of *Kunapipi,* 10/1–2.]

—— (ed.). *From Commonwealth to Post-colonial.* Sydney: Dangaroo, 1992.

—— (ed.). *Post-colonial Women's Writing, Kunapipi,* 14/1 (1994).

SAAKANA, AMON SABA. *The Colonial Legacy in Caribbean Literature.* Trenton, NJ: Africa World Press, 1987.

SAFRAN, WILLIAM. 'Diasporas in Modern Societies: Myth of Homeland and Return', *Diaspora: A Journal of Transnational Studies,* 1 (1991): 83–99.

SAID, EDWARD. *Orientalism.* London: Routledge; New York: Pantheon, 1978.

—— *The World, the Text, and the Critic.* Cambridge, Mass.: Harvard University Press, 1983.

—— 'Figures, Configurations, Transfigurations', in Anna Rutherford (ed.), *From Commonwealth to Post-colonial.* Aarhus: Dangaroo, 1992: 1–16.

—— *Culture and Imperialism.* London: Chatto & Windus; New York: Knopf, 1993.

SANDIFORD, KEITH A. *Measuring the Moment: Strategies of Protest in Eighteenth-Century Afro-English Writing.* Selinsgrove: Susquehanna University Press; London and Toronto: Associated University Presses, 1988.

SANGARI, KUMKUM. 'The Politics of the Possible', in Abdul R. JanMohamed and David Lloyd (eds.), *The Nature and Context of Minority Discourse.* New York: Oxford University Press, 1990: 216–45.

—— and VAID, SUDESH. *Recasting Women: Essays in Colonial History.* New Delhi: Kali for Women Press, 1989.

SATTAR, ARSHIA. 'Does Television Exist If You Don't Watch It?', *Literary Criterion* [Bangalore], 28/4 (1993): 62–71.

SCHAFFER, KAY. *Women and the Bush: Forces of Desire in the Australian Cultural Tradition.* Cambridge: Cambridge University Press, 1988.

SCHERZER, JOEL, and WOODBURY, ANTHONY C. (eds.). *Native American Discourse: Poetics, Rhetoric and Literate Culture.* Cambridge: Cambridge University Press, 1987.

SEKORA, JOHN, and TURNER, DARWIN T. (eds.). *The Art of Slave Narrative.* Macomb: University of Western Illinois Press, 1982.

SENIOR, OLIVE. *Working Miracles: Women's Lives in the English-Speaking Caribbean.* Bloomington: Indiana University Press, 1991.

SHARPE, JENNY. 'Figures of Colonial Resistance', *Modern Fiction Studies,* 35/1 (Spring 1989): 137–55.

SHERIDAN, SUSAN. 'Women Writers', in *The Penguin New Literary History of Australia.* Ringwood: Penguin Books, 1988.

SHOEMAKER, ADAM. *Black Words, White Page: Aboriginal Literature, 1929–1988.* St Lucia: University of Queensland Press, 1989.

—— *Mudrooroo: A Critical Study.* Sydney: Collins/Angus & Robertson, 1993.

SHUSTERMAN, RICHARD. 'Aesthetics between Nationalism and Internationalism', *The Journal of Aesthetics and Art Criticism*, 51/2 (1993): 157–67.

SICHERMAN, CAROL. *Ngugi wa Thiong'o: The Making of a Rebel: A Sourcebook in Kenyan Literature and Resistance*. New York: Hans Zell, 1990.

SIMMS, NORMAN. *Points of Contact: A Study of the Interplay and Intersection of Traditional and Non-traditional Literatures, Cultures and Mentalities*. New York: Pace University Press, 1991.

SINCLAIR, KEITH (ed.). *Distance Looks our Way: The Effects of Remoteness on New Zealand*. Auckland: Paul's Book Arcade/University of Auckland, 1961.

SINNETT, FREDERICK. *The Fiction Fields of Australia*. 1856; repr. Brisbane: University of Queensland Press, 1966.

SINNETT, JAMES. 'The Fiction Fields of Australia', in John Barnes (ed.), *The Writer in Australia*. Melbourne: Oxford University Press, 1969.

SLEMON, STEPHEN. 'Cultural Alterity and Colonial Discourse', *Southern Review*, 20 (Mar. 1987): 102–7.

—— 'Monuments of Empire: Allegory/Counter-discourse/Post-colonial Writing', *Kunapipi*, 9/3 (1987): 1–16.

—— 'The Scramble for Post-colonialism', in Chris Tiffin and Alan Lawson (eds.), *De-scribing Empire: Post-colonialism and Textuality*. London: Routledge, 1994: 15–32.

—— and TIFFIN, HELEN (eds.). *After Europe*. Kunapipi, 11/1 (1989). [Special issue on post-colonial criticism.]

SMITH, BERNARD. *European Vision and the South Pacific: 1768–1850: A Study in the History of Art and Ideas*. Oxford: Clarendon, 1969.

—— *Imagining the Pacific in the Wake of the Cook Voyages*. Melbourne: Melbourne University Press, 1992.

SODERLIND, SYLVIA. *Margin/Alias: Language and Colonization in Canadian and Québécois Fiction*. Toronto: University of Toronto Press, 1991.

SOYINKA, WOLE. *Myth, Literature and the African World*. Cambridge: Cambridge University Press, 1976.

—— *Art, Dialogue and Outrage: Essays on Literature and Culture*, ed. Biodun Jeyifo. Ibadan: New Horn Press, 1988.

SPIVAK, GAYATRI CHAKRAVORTY. 'Three Women's Texts and a Critique of Imperialism', *Critical Inquiry*, 12/1 (1985): 43–61.

—— *In Other Worlds: Essays in Cultural Politics*. New York: Methuen, 1987.

—— 'Can the Subaltern Speak?', in Cary Nelson and Lawrence Grossberg (eds.), *Marxism and the Interpretation of Culture*. Urbana: University of Illinois Press, 1988: 271–313.

—— *The Post-colonial Critic: Interviews, Strategies, Dialogues*, ed. Sarah Harasym. New York: Routledge, 1990.

STEAD, C. K. *In the Glass Case: Essays on New Zealand Literature*. Auckland: Auckland University Press, 1981.

STEADY, FILOMENA. *The Black Woman Cross-culturally*. Cambridge, Mass.: Schenkman Publishing, 1981.

STEADY, FILOMENA. 'African Feminism: A Worldwide Perspective', in Rosalyn Terborg-Penn *et al.* (eds.), *Women in Africa and the African Diaspora.* Washington: Howard University Press, 1989: 3–24.

STEVENS, JOAN. *The New Zealand Novel 1860–1965.* 2nd rev. edn. Wellington: Reed, 1966.

STEVENSON, LIONEL. *Appraisals of Canadian Literature.* Toronto: Macmillan, 1926.

STEWART, DOUGLAS. *The Broad Stream: Aspects of Australian Literature.* Sydney: Angus & Robertson, 1975.

STOUCK, DAVID. *Major Canadian Authors: A Critical Introduction to Canadian Literature in English.* 2nd edn. rev. and exp. Lincoln: University of Nebraska Press, 1988.

STREET, BRIAN. *The Savage in Literature.* London: Routledge & Kegan Paul, 1975.

STURM, TERRY (ed.). *The Oxford History of New Zealand Literature.* Auckland: Oxford University Press, 1991.

SULERI, SARA. *The Rhetoric of English India.* Chicago: University of Chicago Press, 1992.

SUMMERS, ANNE. *Damned Whores and God's Police.* Ringwood: Penguin, 1975.

SUTCLIFFE, DAVID. *British Black English.* Oxford: Blackwell, 1982.

TAM, SEE KAM, *Span* 33 (May 1992): 152–4. [Review of Ian Adam and Helen Tiffin (eds.), *Past the Last Post: Theorizing Post-colonialism and Post-modernism.* New York: Harvester Wheatsheaf, 1991.]

TERADA, REI. *Derek Walcott's Poetry: American Mimicry.* Boston: Northeastern University Press, 1992.

TERBORG-PENN, ROSALYN, *et al.* (eds.). *Women in Africa and the African Diaspora.* Washington: Howard University Press, 1989.

TERDIMAN, RICHARD. *Discourse/Counter Discourse: The Theory and Practice of Symbolic Resistance in Nineteenth-Century France.* Ithaca, NY: Cornell University Press, 1985.

THOMAS, NED. *Derek Walcott: Poet of the Islands.* Cardiff: Welsh Arts Council, 1980.

TIERNEY, FRANK (ed.). *The Thomas Chandler Haliburton Symposium: Reappraisals.* Ottawa: University of Ottawa Press, 1985.

TIFFIN, CHRIS. 'Progress and Ambivalence in the Colonial Novel', in Gillian Whitlock and Helen Tiffin (eds.), *Re-siting Queen's English: Text and Tradition in Post-colonial Literatures.* Amsterdam: Rodopi, 1992: 1–9.

—— and LAWSON, ALAN (eds.). *De-scribing Empire: Post-colonialism and Textuality.* London: Routledge, 1994.

TIFFIN, HELEN. 'Commonwealth Literature and Comparative Methodology', *World Literature Written in English*, 23/1 (Winter 1984): 26–30.

—— 'Post-colonial Literatures and Counter-discourse', *Kunapipi*, 9/3 (1987): 17–34.

TODOROV, TZVETAN. *The Conquest of America: The Question of the Other*, trans. Richard Howard. New York: Harper & Row, 1987.

TRAUGOTT, ELIZABETH C., and PRATT, MARY-LOUISE. *Linguistics for Students of Literature.* New York: Harcourt, Brace, Jovanovich, 1980.

TURNER, VICTOR. 'Betwixt and Between: The Liminal Period in *Rites de Passage*', in Victor Turner, *The Forest of Symbols: Aspects of Ndembu Ritual.* Ithaca, NY: Cornell University Press, 1967.

VANSINA, IAN. *Oral Tradition: A Study in Historical Methodology.* Chicago: Aldine, 1965.

VAUGHAN, ALDEN T., and VAUGHAN, VIRGINIA MASON. *Shakespeare's Caliban: A Cultural History.* Cambridge: Cambridge University Press, 1991.

VIET-WILD, FLORA. *Teachers, Preachers, Non-believers: A Social History of Zimbabwean Literature.* Harare: Baobab Books, 1993.

VISWANATHAN, GAURI. *Masks of Conquest: Literary Study and British Rule in India.* New York: Columbia University Press, 1989.

WALCOTT, DEREK. 'The Caribbean: Culture or Mimicry?', *Journal of Interamerican Studies and World Affairs*, 16/1 (Feb. 1974): 3–13. Republished in Robert D. Hamner (ed.), *Critical Perspectives on Derek Walcott.* Washington: Three Continents Press, 1993: 51–7.

—— 'The Muse of History', in *Is Massa Day Dead?* ed. Orde Coombs. New York: Doubleday, 1974: 1–28. Republished in *Carifesta Forum.* Kingston: Institute of Jamaica, 1976: 111–28.

—— 'Caligula's Horse', in Stephen Slemon and Helen Tiffin (eds.), *After Europe: Critical Theory and Post-colonial Writing.* Aarhus: Dangaroo, 1989: 138–42.

WALLACE-CRABBE, CHRIS (ed.). *The Australian Nationalists: Modern Critical Essays.* Melbourne: Oxford University Press, 1971.

WALMSLEY, ANNE. *The Caribbean Artists Movement 1966–72.* London: New Beacon Books, 1992.

WALSH, WILLIAM. *A Manifold Voice: Studies in Commonwealth Literature.* London: Chatto and Windus, 1970.

—— *Commonwealth Literature.* London: Oxford University Press, 1973.

WARD, RUSSEL. *The Australian Legend.* Melbourne: Oxford University Press, 1958; 2nd edn. 1965.

WARE, VRON. *Beyond the Pale: White Women, Racism and History.* London: Verso, 1992.

WEBB, BARBARA J. *Myth and History in Caribbean Fiction: Alejo Carpentier, Wilson Harris, and Edouard Glissant.* Amherst: University of Massachusetts Press, 1992.

WEBBY, ELIZABETH. 'Writers, Printers, Readers', in *The Penguin New Literary History of Australia.* Ringwood: Penguin Books, 1988.

WEISS, THEODORE. 'Ezra Pound and the Cross-Cultural Sources of Modern Poetry', in Guy Amrithanayagam and S. C. Harrex (eds.), *Only Connect: Literary Perspectives East and West.* Adelaide: Center for Research in the New Literatures in English and East–West Center, 1981: 45–57.

WEST, CORNELL. *Keeping Faith: Philosophy and Race in America.* New York: Routledge, 1993.

WHITE, RICHARD. *Inventing Australia: Images and Identity 1688–1980.* Sydney: George Allen & Unwin, 1981.

WHITEMAN, MARCIA FARR (ed.). *Variation in Writing: Functional and Linguistic-Cultural Differences*, vol. i of *Writing: The Nature, Development, and Teaching of Written Communication*. 2 vols. Hillsdale, NJ: Laurence Erlbaum, 1981.

WIELAND, JAMES. *The Ensphering Mind: History, Myth, and Fictions in the Poetry of Allen Curnow, Nissim Ezekiel, A. D. Hope, A. M. Klein, Christopher Okigbo, and Derek Walcott*. Washington: Three Continents Press, 1988.

WILENTZ, GAY. 'English Is a Foreign Anguish', in Karen R. Lawrence (ed.), *Decolonizing Tradition: New Views of Twentieth-Century 'British' Literary Canons*. Urbana: University of Illinois Press, 1992: 261–78.

WILKES, G. A. *A Dictionary of Australian Colloquialisms*. London: Routledge & Kegan Paul, 1978.

—— *The Stockyard and the Croquet Lawn: Literary Evidence for Australia's Cultural Development*. London: Edward Arnold, 1981.

WILKINSON, JANE. 'Between Orality and Writing: *The Forest of a Thousand Daemons* as a Self-Reflexive Text', *Commonwealth*, 9/2 (1987): 41–51.

—— *Talking with African Writers: Interviews by Jane Wilkinson*. London: James Currey and Heinemann Educational Books, 1992.

WILLIAMS, MARK. *Leaving the Highway: Six Contemporary New Zealand Novelists*. Auckland: Auckland University Press, 1990.

WILLIAMS, PATRICK, and CHRISMAN, LAURA (eds.). *Colonial Discourse and Post-colonial Theory: A Reader*. Brighton: Harvester Wheatsheaf, 1993.

WOODS, GREGORY. 'Aimless Snippets', *Times Literary Supplement*, 5 Feb. 1994, p. 10.

WOOLCOCK, HELEN R. *Rights of Passage: Emigration to Australia in the Nineteenth Century*. London: Tavistock, 1986.

WREN, ROBERT M. *Those Magical Years: The Making of Nigerian Literature at Ibadan: 1948–1966*. Washington: Three Continents Press, 1991.

WRIGHT, DEREK. 'Unwritable Realities: The Orality of Power in Nuruddin Farah's *Sweet and Sour Milk*', *Journal of Commonwealth Literature*, 24 (1989): 185–92.

—— *The Novels of Nuruddin Farah*. Bayreuth: Bayreuth African Studies 32, 1994.

YOUNG, ROBERT. *White Mythologies: Writing History and the West*. New York: Routledge, 1990.

ZABUS, CHANTAL. *The African Palimpsest. Indigenization of Language in the West African Europhone Novel*. Amsterdam: Rodopi, 1990.

ZELL, HANS M., BUNDY, CAROL, and COULON, VIRGINIA (eds.). *A New Reader's Guide to African Literature*. 2nd edn. New York: Africana Publishing Co., 1983.

ZUMTHOR, PAUL. *Introduction à la poésie orale*. Paris: Seuil, 1983.

# Index

Achebe, Chinua 6, 14, 25, 37, 70, 124–5,
    133–6, 147, 236
  and language 134–6
  use of proverbs 32–3, 133
  *Anthills of the Savannah* 71
  *Arrow of God* 32, 35
  *A Man of the People* 125
  *No Longer at Ease* 68
  *Things Fall Apart* 22–3, 32–5, 67, 71, 124
Adam, Ian 21
Adcock, Fleur 72
Africa 144
  African literature 14, 30, 31, 69, 231
  anthologies of literature 74
  as desire 215–16
  influences others 12–13, 74–5
  literary criticism 32, 68, 176, 241, 321
  poetry 31–2
  views of writers 15
  *see also*: Ghana; Kenya; Malawi; Nigeria;
    Somalia; South Africa; Zimbabwe
African-American influence 74
Afzal-Khan, Fawzia 66, 67, 70
Agard, John 19
Ahmad, Aijaz 19, 137, 169–72
  criticism of Jameson 137–8
  criticism of Said 169–70
  on Marx 190–1
Aidoo, Ama Ata 230, 234, 239, 240, 242,
    243
  oral stories 232
Akan 39
Alexis, Jacques Stephen 73
Ali, Ahmed 218, 220
Alkali, Zaynab 44
Allen, Lillian 40
Allfrey, Phyllis Shand 215
Altbach, Philip 143, 176
American influence 11–14, 23, 72–3, 160
  confessional poetry 73, 76
  open form poetry 12, 73
Amos, Valerie 237, 238
Anand, Mulk Raj 34, 67
Anderson, Benedict 138, 215
Angas, George French 98
Anglo-Irish 120, 126–7
anthologies of literature 8, 260–1
Anyidoho, Kofi 14
Appiah, Kwame Anthony 23

Arabic 37, 60
Arasanayagam, Jean 206
*ARIEL* 15
Armah, Ayi Kwei 125
Armstrong, Jeannette 247, 256
Arnold, Matthew 123
Arvidson, Ken 254
Ashcroft, Bill 32
  *see also The Empire Writes Back*
Association of Commonwealth Literature
    and Language Studies 15, 159, 172
  founding 157–61, 185
Atkinson, James 97
*Atlantic Provinces Literature Colloquium*
    119
Atwood, Margaret 13, 72, 77, 110, 150
Australia 18, 81, 121, 128–33
  anthologies of literature 68, 85, 89, 91,
    93, 259, 261
  and Ireland 128
  literary histories and criticism 8, 72, 86,
    90, 93, 131
  literary realism in 66
  and race 130–2
  writers 6, 247
  *see also* Baynton; Boldrewood; Boyd;
    Field; Furphy; Harpur; Hope;
    Ingamells; Koch; Henry Lawson;
    Merritt; Morgan; Les Murray;
    Mudrooroo Narogin; Banjo Paterson;
    Praed; Prichard; Henry Handel
    Richardson; Christina Stead; Walker;
    Ward; Sam Watson; Weller; White;
    Wright; *The Bulletin*; Jindyworabak
Awoonor, Kofi 14, 31–2, 125
Aylmer, Isabella 90

Ballantyne, R. M. 111
Barbados 48, 111, 149
  *see also* Brathwaite; Austin Clarke;
    Lamming
Barker, Francis 25
Barker, Mary Anne Broome, Lady 111
Barnes, John 129
Barr, John 110
Barthes, Roland 18
Bathgate, Alexander 94, 115
Bayard, Caroline 74
Baynton, Barbara 91, 117, 118, 131

Bayreuth African Studies 15
Bean, C. E. W. 130
Béji, Hélé 9
Benitez-Rojo, Antonio 51
Bennett, Jonathan 110, 117
Bennett, Louise 40
Bernabé, Jean 22
Berry, James 75
Bhabha, Homi 175, 179, 189, 195, 217
    *The Location of Culture* 153, 165–6,
    196
Bhatt, Sujata 16, 76, 77
biculturalism 6
bilingualism 76
    contrasted to creolization 75–6
Bird, Delys 89
Birney, Earle 77
Bissoondath, Neil 24, 225–7
'Black British' 37
    see also Agard; Berry; David Dabydeen;
    D'Aguiar; Linton Kwesi Johnson; Caryl
    Phillips; Zephaniah
Bloom, Harold 125
Boldrewood, Rolf 113–14, 129
Bolland, Nigel 47
Bowen, C. C. 96
Bowering, George 12, 41
Boyd, Martin 6
Bracken, Thomas 91
Brand, Dionne 226–7
Brathwaite, Edward Kamau 13, 75, 220
    'Creole Man in Time and Space' 48
    *History of the Voice* 38, 39
Breeze, Jean 'Binta' 40
Brewer, Anthony 180
Brodber, Erna 42
    *Myal* 39, 151–3, 162
Brodsky, Joseph 10
Brontë, Charlotte 109
Brooke, Frances 92, 115
Broome, Frederick Napier 96
Brown, Eliza 88
Brown, Lloyd W. 231
Brutus, Dennis 74, 202, 207
Brydon, Diana 174
    *The Bulletin* 128–9, 131
Burke, Johnny 118
Burnett, Paula 107–8
Busia, Abena P. A. 201, 203
Byrne, Cyril 119

Cambridge, Ada 116
Campbell, John Logan 98
Campbell, Maria 260
Campbell, Sandra 91
Campbell, Wilfred 102
Canada 62, 68, 83, 181

anthologies of literature 62, 82, 91, 259,
    260, 261
literary histories and criticism 8, 72, 74,
    90, 261
Multiculturalism Act 225
politics and literature 96
writers 6, 12, 62, 72, 225–8, 247, 250,
    256–7
see also Armstrong; Atwood; Birney;
    Bissoondath; Bowering; Brand; Brooke;
    Austin Clarke; Cyril Dabydeen; Davey;
    Duncan; Findley; Gallant; Goldsmith;
    Haliburton; Highway; Claire Harris;
    Highway; Thomas King; Kroetsch; Lee;
    McClung; Mistry; Moodie; Bharati
    Mukherjee; Ondaatje; Parr; N. M.
    Philip.; Richler; Sawai; Slipperjack;
    Traill; Vassanji; Wah; Wayman; and
    *Open Letters*; *Tish*; *and* Cree
Carby, Hazel 232, 238
Caribbean 4, 5, 46
anthologies of literature 107, 108, 119,
    153
contrasted to India 75–6
as Creole paradigm 42
education in 143–9, 151–2
and English language 38–40
Francophone, *see* Haiti; Martinique; *and*
    Alexis; Chamoiseau; Césaire; Confiant;
    Fanon; Glissant; Perse
literary criticism and histories 8, 18, 22,
    51, 52, 74, 75
plantation as capitalist industry 46
writers 6, 9, 39, 53
see also Barbados; Dominica; Guyana;
    Jamaica; St Lucia; Trinidad; *and*
    Michelle Cliff; Kincaid; Pauline
    Melville; Caryl Phillips; Sparrow
Carter, Angela 58
Carter, Paul 84
Cary, Joyce 125
Cassidy, F. G. 39
Césaire, Aimé 8, 13, 49, 52
Chamier, George 94
Chamoiseau, Patrick 22
Chand, Meira 204
Chapman, M. J. 110
Chapman, Robert 110, 117
Charlwood, Don 85
Chatterjee, Partha 192
Cheney-Coker, Syl 13
Chi, Jimmie 251
Chinweizu, Jemie Onwuchekwa 32, 68
Chipasula, Frank Mkalawile 74
Chitre, Dilip 14, 76
Chomsky, Noam 31
Christian, Barbara 173

Clacy, Ellen 92
Clark, J. P. 37
Clarke, Austin 11, 225
Clarke, Marcus 97, 113, 116
Cliff, Michelle 209–10
Clifford, James 46, 75
Clough, Arthur Hugh 109
Coetzee, J. M. 109, 150, 188
colonial literature 15, 21
  adventure and travel writing 5, 82, 84,
    87–8, 93, 111–14
  children's literature 111
  diaries and letters 84, 88–9
  and economics 106–7, 109, 115
  folksong 118
  and gender 111–17
  and independence 103–4
  irony and satire 108, 116
  and metropolis 83
  and paintings 107
  readers and market 100
  and religion 112, 119
  romance and gothic 93
  and slavery 106–7, 119
  and sublime 85, 92
  and utopia 116, 118
  and vernacular 110, 119
  women writers 81–2, 89–92, 93, 115–17,
    118, 131–2
Commonwealth literature 4, 13, 15, 62–3,
  65–6, 71, 72, 74, 157–9, 169, 174,
  185–6, 214
  *see also* Association of Commonwealth
    Literature and Language Studies
Connor, Ralph, *see* Gordon, Charles William
Conrad, Joseph 70, 109, 125, 143, 144
Cooper, Carolyn 40, 43
Cooper, James Fenimore 112
Corkery Daniel 137
Cozens, Charles 94
Crawford, Robert 10
Cree 42
Creeley, Robert 10, 73
Cuba 51
Cudjoe, Selwyn 69, 189
Curnow, Allen 72
Curtis, L. P. 122
Cutteridge, Capt. O. 147–9

Dabydeen, Cyril 227
Dabydeen, David 11, 24, 37, 223
  *Slave Song* 39, 223
D'Aguiar, Fred 24, 223
Dale, Leigh 148
Dangarembga, Tsitsi 231–3, 238–9
Dangaroo Press 15
Dansey, Harry 249, 252

Dante Alighieri 38
Das, Kamala 14, 76
Das, Veena 191
Dasenbrock, Reed Way 63
Davey, Frank 12
Davies, Boyce 231–2, 241
Davis, Jack 250, 261
D'Costa, Jean 108, 119
Defoe, Daniel (*Robinson Crusoe*) 108, 109,
  143, 144, 155
de Lisser, Herbert G. 105
De Mille, James 118
Denney, Reuel 73
Derrida, Jacques 31, 53
Desai, Anita 67, 230, 231, 234
De Souza, Eunice 76, 233–4, 239
Devonish, Hubert 144, 145
Dewes, Henare 43
Dharker, Imtiaz 76
Dharwadker, Vinay 69, 71, 74, 77
Dickens, Charles 109
Dieffenback, Ernest 87
Disraeli, Benjamin 134
Dixon, Robert 86, 87, 90, 97
Domett, Alfred 96
Dominica, *see* Allfrey, Rhys
Dub poets 40
DuBois, W. E. B. 55
Duerden, Dennis 14, 15, 232
Duff, Alan 247, 262
Duffy, Charles Gavin 128
Duncan, Sara Jeannette 116, 117
Durach, Dame Mary 260
During, Simon 156

Eagleton, Terry 158
Ellman, Richard 73
*Éloge de la créolité* 22
Emecheta, Buchi 36, 230, 234, 239, 242
*The Empire Writes Back* 20, 34, 46, 68, 69,
  74, 75, 83, 162, 176, 188
Ewe 32
Ezekiel, Nissim 4, 6, 11, 72

Fagunwa, D. O. 32
Fanon, Frantz 13, 122
Farah, Nuruddin 10, 33, 203, 213
feminisms:
  African 240–1
  Third World 230, 234, 236, 237, 239
Ferguson, Dugald 94
Ferrier, Carole 286
Field, Barron 92, 110, 116
Fiji 181–2, 202, 207, 214, 219
  Indo-Fijians 216, 218–20
  see also *girmit*
Findley, Timothy 188

Foott, Mary Hannay 90
Forster, George 87
Foucault, Michel 53, 166, 169, 193, 196
Frame, Janet 68
Furphy, Joseph 128–30

Gaelic League 137
Galeano, Eduardo 189, 197
Gallant, Mavis 68
Garcia Marquez, Gabriel 13
Gérard, Albert 176
Gerson, Carole 86
Ghana 121
  see also Aidoo; Anyidoho; Armah;
    Awoonor; Nkrumah; Akan; Ewe
Ghose, Zulfikar 187, 202, 203, 208–10, 221
Ghosh, Amitav 13, 16, 25
Gikandi, Simon 67, 74
Gikuyu 37, 38, 136
Gilbert, Kevin 259, 261
Giles, Fiona 91
Gilroy, Paul 23
Ginsberg, Allen 73
*girmit* 219
Glass, Colleen 261
Glissant, Édouard 51
globalization 7, 10, 15–16
  of creolization 46
  of English language 29, 61
  of marginality 58
  and nationalism 63–9
  in the past 25, 60
  reaction to 23
Goldie, Terry 261
Goldsmith, Oliver 110
Goodison, Lorna 72
Goody, Jack 30
Gordimer, Nadine 9
Gordon, Charles W. ('Ralph Connor') 112
Gordon, Shirley 145
Gorst, J. E. 98
Grace, Patricia 42, 252, 254
Grainger, James 110
Grant, Agnes 261
Grass, Günter 13
Green, H. M. 8
Gregory, Lady Isabella Augusta 120, 121,
  126, 128
Grey, George 98
Griffiths, Gareth, see *The Empire Writes
  Back*
Gudgeon, T. W. 98
Gurr, Andrew 201–2, 203, 205, 213
Guyana 48, 201, 204, 205, 215, 223, 227
  see also David Dabydeen; Wilson Harris;
    Heath; Waldron; Denis Williams
Gwaram, Hauwa 44

Haberkost, Christian 40
Hadjor, Kofu 180
Haiti 54, 73
Haldane, George 107
Haliburton, Thomas Chandler 119
Hall, Stuart 214–16
Hanna, Cliff 95
Haq, Kaiser 77
Harlow, Barbara 189
Harpur, Charles 95, 110, 116
Harris, Alexander 94, 114
Harris, Claire 24, 221
Harris, Wilson 54, 55, 172, 187
  C. L. R. James, about 54–5
  *The Four Banks of the River Space* 38
  'History, Fable and Myth' 48–9
  *The Palace of the Peacock* 205
Hart, Julia Catherine 92
Haslam, Anthony 110
Hassam, Andrew 84, 85, 86, 100, 101
Hausa 39, 44
Havelock, Eric 30–1
Havemann, Paul 251–2
Hayman, Robert 105
Haynes, John 32
Head, Bessie 230, 231, 232, 234, 242
Heaney, Seamus 11, 128
Hearne, John 38
Heath, Roy 201, 204–5
Heavysege, Charles 110
Hennessey, Alistair 47
Henning, Rachel 88
Henry, Alexander 87
Heriot, George 88
Highway, Tomson 250
Hillard, Noel 266
Hindi 220
Hodge, Bob 183
Holt, Patricia 228
'home' 209, 226, 228
  Africa as 215
  and diasporas 214–15, 228
  England as 6
  Harlem as 55
  visions of 205–6
Hope, A. D. 6, 71, 72
Hulme, Keri 42–3, 253–4, 256
  *the bone people* 43, 248, 253
Hulme, Peter 159, 193–4
Hussein, Aamer 202–3
Hutcheon, Linda 51, 71
Hyde, Douglas 136–7

Igbo 32, 34, 35, 133, 134, 135, 136
Ihimaera, Witi 252, 254–5, 260, 261
  *The Matriarch* 41, 254–5
Ijọ 36, 37, 67

imperialism 179–80
India 13–14, 66, 210, 216
  anthologies of literature 14, 16, 77
  biculturalism and translation 76
  literary histories and criticism 8, 66, 152
  Marx concerning 190
  *see also* Anand; Chitre; Kamala Das;
    Desai; de Souza; Ezekiel; Ghose;
    Ghosh; Kolatkar; Makandaya;
    Mahapatra; Moraes; Narayan;
    Ramanujan; Rao; Rushdie; Seth; *and*
    Kannada; Malayalam; Marathi;
    Sanskrit; Urdu; subaltern studies
Indo-Fiji, *see* Fiji; *and* Ali; Nandan; Sudesh
    Mishra; Pillai; Subramani
Ingamells, Rex 131–2
Ireland 29, 120–8, 138
  *see also* Gregory; Hyde; Mangan; Heaney;
    Joyce; Synge; Yeats *and* Anglo-Irish
Ishiguro, Kazuo 37
Itwaru, Arnold 203, 208, 227
Iyengar, K. R. Srinivasa 8

Jacoby, Russell 178
Jahn, Janheinz 176
Jamaica 39, 40, 42, 107, 151–2, 230
  anthologies of literature 108
  *see* Louise Bennett; Breeze; Brodber; de
    Lisser; Goodison; Hearne; Claude
    McKay; Marley; V. S. Reid; Senior;
    Sistren; Francis Williams
James, C. L. R. 6, 53–4
Jameson, Anna Bronwell 88
Jameson, Fredric 69, 170
  Ahmad's criticism of 137–8
  *The Political Unconscious* 18, 30
  'Third World Literature' 69, 137–8
JanMohamed, Abdul R. 70
Jindyworabak 131–2
Johnson, Colin, *see* Narogin, Mudrooroo
Johnson, Linton Kwesi 37, 40
Johnson, Richard 97
*Journal of Commonwealth Literature* 159
Joyce, James 29, 69, 124, 138
Jussawalla, Adil 16
Jussawalla, Feroza 63

Kana 41
Kane, Paul 88
Kannada 76
Keeshig-Tobias 258–9
Kelly, Ned 128
Kendall, Henry 110, 116
Keneally, Thomas 6
Kent, George 151
Kenya 18, 37, 69, 131
  literary history and criticism 18, 69

  *see also* Ngugi; Vassanji; *and* Gikuyu
Khan, Ismith 217–18, 220, 225
Kiernan, Brian 66
Kincaid, Jamaica 113
King, Bruce 7, 8, 16, 18, 69, 72, 81
King, Ruby 143
King, Thomas 257, 261, 262
Kingsley, Charles 122, 148
Kingsley, Henry 114–15, 129
Kipling, Rudyard 110, 111, 151, 184–5
Kirby, William 113
Kirkby, Joan 12
Klein, A. M. 72
Klinck, Carl F. 72
Koch, C. J. 149
Kolatkar, Arun 14, 76, 77
Kolodny, Annette 95
Kotei, S. I. A. 176
Kramer, Leonie 8, 72, 116
Kroetsch, Robert 12
Kröller, Eva-Marie 82
*Kunapipi* 15, 159
Kunene, Mazisi 14, 31
Kureishi, Hanif 203, 224

Ladoo, Sonny 216, 218–20
Lalla, Barbara 108, 119
Lamming, George 6, 8, 152, 221
  *In the Castle of My Skin* 68, 111, 150
  *The Pleasures of Exile* 38, 221
  *Water with Berries* 109
Lawson, Henry 95, 112, 118, 129–30, 133
Lawson, Louisa 116
Lazarus, Neil 69
Lee, Dennis 62, 77
Lefevere, A. 176
Lenin, Vladimir 179–80
Leprohon, Rosanna 93, 115
Leslie, Molara Ogundipe 241
Lesperance, John Talon 110
Levi-Strauss, Claude 30
Lewis, Jeff 18
Lim, Catherine 206
liminal 216–17, 229
literary genres:
  drama 16, 126, 128, 249–51
  novel 66–71, 92, 128–9
  mixed 9, 90, 94
  poetry 71–7, 92, 95–6
  *see also* Colonial literature
literary histories 7–8
literary markets 6, 14–16, 62–5, 88–9, 93,
    187, 232, 248, 261
  nationalist 120
Lloyd, David 70
Long, D. S. 260
Long, Edward 107

Lovelace, Earl  11, 57
Lowe, Lisa  18
Lowell, Robert  73
Lutz, Hartmut  258–9
Lycett, Joseph  97
Lyttelton, Edith (G. B. Lancaster)  93

McAuley, James  71
Macaulay, Thomas R.  144, 145, 154
McClintock, Anne  183
McClung, Nellie  91
MacConmara, Donncha Ruah  119
McCormick, E. H.  86
McGifford, Diane  210
McKay, Claude  6, 53–7, 227
  *Banana Bottom*  55–6
Mackay, J.  110
McLaren, John  131
McLuhan, Marshall  30
McMullen, Lorraine  91
Macpherson, Emma  90
Maes-Jelinek, Hena  185
magic realism  69–71, 73
Mahapatra, Jayanta  11, 14
Maja-Pearce, Adewale  25, 68, 70
Malawi, *see* Chipasula, Mapanje
Malayalam  14, 76
Malouf, David  202
Mangan, James Clarence  125
Mani, Lati  235
Maning, F. E.  98
Mansfield, Katherine  6, 118
Maori  41–3, 249, 251, 252, 254, 260–1
Mapanje, Jack  24
Marathi  14, 76
Marechera, Dambudzo  212
Markandaya, Kamala  221, 232, 234
Marley, Bob  39, 40
Martinique  51
Marxist  53, 136, 160, 169, 171, 173, 190
Maughan-Brown, David  18
Maxwell, D. E. S.  159
Maza, Bob  251
Mehrotra, Arvind Krishna  14
Melville, Herman  54
Melville, Pauline  223–34
Meredith, Louisa Anne  89, 90
Merritt, Robert  249, 250
Mezei, Kathy  89
Midgley, Sarah  85
Mishra, Sudesh  218
Mishra, Vijay  183, 219
Mistry, Rohinton  208, 227
Mitchell, Adrian  116
Mitchell, Thomas  87, 98
Mitchell, W. J. T.  162, 166
Mo, Timothy  37, 203, 224–5

Modarressi, Taghi  37
*The Modern Language Association*  158
Mohanty, Chandra  235, 238
Mommsen, Wolfgang  179
Moodie, Susanna  96
  *Life in the Clearing*  85, 90
  literary concerns  90
  *Roughing it in the Bush*  82–3, 85, 90, 97, 111
Moorhouse, Frank  6
Moraes, Dom  11, 71, 72
Morgan, Sally  132
Morrissey, Mike  143
Moses, Daniel David  259, 261
Mphahlele, Ezekiel  74
Mudrooroo, *see* Narogin
Muecke, Stephen  99, 256, 257
Mukherjee, Bharati  24, 217, 228
Mukherjee, Meenakshi  66
Murray, Anna Maria  92
Murray, Les  149
Mutabaruka  40

Naik, M. K.  8
Naipaul, V. S.  6, 19, 54, 70, 109, 215, 220
  *A Bend in the River*  56
  'A Christmas Story'  217, 218
  'Conrad's Darkness'  109
  *The Enigma of Arrival*  9, 56, 203–4
  *A House for Mr Biswas*  19, 67, 68, 217
  *In a Free State*  8
  *India: A Million Mutinies Now*  215, 216
  *Miguel Street*  147
  *The Mimic Men*  188, 221
  *A Way in the World*  9
Namjoshi, Suniti  210–12
Nandan, Satendra  202, 207, 219, 220
Narayan, R. K.  35, 67, 70, 206
Narogin, Mudrooroo (Colin Johnson)  248, 255
  *Doctor Wooreddy's Prescription*  41, 133
  *Master of the Ghost Dreaming*  42, 255
  *Wild Cat Falling*  256, 260
Nath, Dwarka  215
nationalism  7, 62, 160, 168
  as antithesis  123
  and generational conflict  124
  and land  124
  and middle class  127
  and the postcolonial  10
  and violence  126
Ndebele, Njabulo  14
neo-colonialism  17, 19, 168, 181
Neruda, Pablo  49, 74
New, William H.  68, 69, 90, 92, 96, 180

New Zealand 72, 96, 98, 247, 261
  anthologies of literature 65, 72, 249, 260
  literary histories and criticism 8, 59, 86,
    90, 253, 254
  early literature about Maori 98
  *see also* Adcock; Aylmer; Chamier;
    Curnow; Dansey; Alan Duff; Frame;
    Grace; Keri Hulme; Ihimaera; Owen;
    Alistair Paterson; Renée; Sargeson;
    H. B. Stoney; Wakefield; *and* Maori
Nigeria 7, 121, 136, 168
  literary criticism 15, 18, 32, 68
  writers 36, 44, 74, 125, 133–8, 168, 230
  *see also* Achebe; Alkali; Chinweizu; J. P.
    Clark; Emecheta; Fagunwa;
    Maja-Pearce; Nwapa; Ogunyemi;
    Okara; Okigbo; Okri; Saro-Wiwa;
    Soyinka; Tutuola; *and* Hausa; Igbo; Ijọ;
    Kana; Yoruba
Ngcobo, Lauretta 240–1
Ngugi wa Thiong'o 37, 38, 67–9, 136, 137,
  187
  *Decolonizing the Mind* 37, 136
Nkosi, Lewis 188
Nkrumah, Kwame 121, 181
Nwapa, Flora 231, 242

O'Clair, Robert 73
Ogunyemi, Wale 33
Okara, Gabriel 31, 36, 37, 124
Okigbo, Christopher 31, 72, 74, 125
Okri, Ben 9, 37, 69
Olson, Charles 73
Ondaatje, Michael 206–7, 227
Onuora, Oku 40
Oodgeroo, *see* Walker, Kath
*Open Letters* 12
Orbell, Margaret 261
Owen, Rena 251

Pakistan 208
Pala, Achola 236
Parker, Sir Gilbert 113
Parmar, Pratibha 237, 238
Parsi writers 208, 227
Parthasarathy, R. 16
Paterson, A. Banjo 95, 118
Paterson, Alistair 65, 71
Pathak, Zakia 194
p'Bitek, Okot 31
Pêcheux, Michel 154
Pere, Vernice Wineera 252
Perkins, Charles 260
Perreault, Jeanne 261
Persaud, Sasenarine 220
Perse, St John 49, 51, 52
Persian 37, 60

Pessoa, Fernando 76
Petersen, Kirsten Holst 185
Petrone, Penny 260
Philip, M. Nourbese 24, 225–7
Phillips, Caryl 24, 39, 57–8, 221–3
Pieterse, Cosmo 15, 16, 232
Pillai, Raymond 218–20
Plath, Sylvia 73
post-colonial:
  as Americanization 11
  and colonial 158
  as cultural imperialism 25
  cultural studies 20–1
  as post-national 4, 6, 12–13, 17, 24
post-modernism 8–9
  and creolization 51–3, 57, 58
  market for 187
  and postcolonialism 8–9, 20–1, 71, 156,
    248
  *see* Walcott
Potiki, Roma 249
Pound, Ezra 12, 73
Praed, Rosa 93
Pratt, Mary Louise 5
Press, John 159
Preston, Richard 143
Prichard, Katharine Susannah 91, 131–2
Pringle, Thomas 106
Punjabi 34
Purkeyastha, Shermila 194

Rahimieh, Nasrin 37
Ramanajun, A. K. 14, 72, 76
Ramsden, Irihapeti 260
Rao, Raja 34, 68, 160, 173
Rattray, R. S. 32
Rau, Santha Rama 68
realism, types of 66–8
Reeves, William Pember 110, 117
regionalism 17
Reid, J. C. 90
Reid, V. S. 40, 41, 55, 68
Renée 251
Resistance, Brother 40
Rhys, Jean 6, 109, 188, 214
Richards, Thomas 82
Richardson, Henry Handel 6, 131
Richardson, John 93, 113
Richler, Mordecai 217
Robertson, Robert 150
Roe, Paddy 259
Ross, Sinclair 68
Rushdie, Salman 24, 37, 58
  contrasted to Vikram Seth 207
  and hybridity 45
  *Imagined Homelands* 45
  *Midnight's Children* 8, 13, 69, 71, 207

Rushdie, Salman (*cont.*)
  *Satanic Verses* 45, 69, 71
  *Shame* 207–8
Rutherford, Anna 172, 185

Safran, William 214
Said, Edward 215
  Ahmad's criticism of 169–70
  *Culture and Imperialism* 64, 126, 162,
    180
  *Orientalism* 18, 159–60, 162, 165–6, 193
  *The Word, the Text, and the Critic* 115
St Lucia, *see* Walcott
Salih, Tayeb 37
Samkange, Stanley 212
Sangarai, Kumkum 70
Sanskrit 34, 60, 76
Sangster, Charles 110
Sargeson, Frank 13
Saro-Wiwa, Ken 24, 36, 41
Sartre, Jean-Paul 165
Sattar, Arisha 2
Saussure, Ferdinand 31
Sawai, Gloria 70
Schaffer, Kay 82, 91
Schreiner, Olive 117
Scott, D. C. 118
Scott, Lawrence 9, 57–8
Selvon, Sam 6, 41, 153–5, 203, 218, 220–1
Senghor, L. S. 8, 123–4, 125, 133
Sengupta, Saswsati 194
Senior, Olive 23, 58, 230, 233, 235–7, 239
Service, Robert 118
Seth, Vikram 9, 16, 202, 207
Shakespeare, William 155
  *The Tempest* 38, 56, 108, 109, 151
Sheridan, Susan 99
Shortland, Edward 98
Sicherman, Carol 69
Sidhwa, Bapsi 208
Simcoe, Elizabeth Posthuma 89
Singapore 206
Sinnett, Frederick 93, 95
Sistren Theatre Collective 43, 232, 235,
    243
Skilbeck, Richard 85
Slemon, Stephen 157, 166, 175
Slipperjack, Ruby 42
Smith, Honor Ford, *see* Sistren
Smith, Mikey 40
Somalia 33
South Africa 5, 74, 207, 230
  literary criticism of 15
  *see also* Brutus; Coetzee; Duerden;
    Gordimer; Head; Kunene; Mphahlele;
    Ndebele; Pieterse; Schreiner; Tlali; Zulu
*Southern African Review of Books* 19

Soyinka, Wole 6, 8, 14, 24–5, 31–2, 74, 124–5
Sparrow, The Mighty (Francisco Slinger)
    148, 153
Spence, Catherine Helen 91, 94, 116
Spivak, Gayatri Chakravorty 165, 192
Sri Lanka 206–7
  *See* Arasanayagam, Ondaatje
Stead, Christina 6, 131
Steady, Filomena 241
Stephens, A. G. 129
Stoney, Henry Butler 92, 98, 113
Stoney, Mark 137
Sturm, Terry 8
subaltern studies 191, 192
Subramani 218, 219
Suleri, Sara 152
Swift, Jonathan 108
symbolism of houses 68
symbolism of motherland 125–6, 138
Synge, James Millington 120, 124, 128,
    129, 133–5

Tam, See Kam 20, 21
Taylor, Drew Hayden 251
Taylor, Richard 98
*Tel quel* 18
Terada, Rei 51, 57
Terdiman, Richard 188–9
Thomas, Ned 26
Thompson, Arthur 98
Tiffin, Helen 21, 174, 189
  see also *The Empire Writes Back*
*Tish* 12
Tlali, Miriam 240
Traill, Catharine Parr 89, 90, 111
Trinidad 39, 50, 204, 215, 218
  writers 11, 153
  *see also* C. L. R. James; Khan; Laddo;
    Lovelace; Naipaul; Brother Resistance;
    Lawrence Scott; Selvon
Tucker, James Rosenberg 94, 114
Tunisia 9
Turner, Victor 216–17, 223, 229
Tutuola, Amos 37

Udu 34, 71, 170–1
'usable past' 7, 23, 25, 123

Vance, Sylvia 261
Vassanji, M. G. 203, 227–8
Viswanathan, Gauri 18, 144
Vogel, Julius 115
*Voiceprint* 153
Voltaire (François Marie Arouet) 108, 115

Wah, Fred 12
Wakefield, Edward Jerningham 87

Walcott, Derek 6, 8, 11, 20, 57, 71, 72, 150
    *Another Life* 51
    *The Antilles* 4
    'Blues' 39
    'Caligula's Horse' 52
    'The Caribbean: Culture or Mimicry?' 26
    critics on 26, 51
    'A Far Cry from Africa' 144, 216, 220
    'Midsummer' 186
    'The Muse of History' 49, 50, 52
    *Omeros* 9, 52, 220, 225
    and postmodernism 51–2
    'The Schooner Flight' 50–1
    'The Spoiler's Return' 50
Walker, Kath 252
Walley, Richard 251
Walmsley, Anne 18
Walrond, Eric 225
Walsh, William 164
Ward, Russel 130
*Wasafiri* 15
Watling, Thomas 88, 97
Watson, Sam 247, 253
Watt, Ian 30
Wayman, Tom 77
Webby, Elizabeth 86, 89, 93, 95, 99, 100
Weiss, Theodore 73
Weller, Archie 202, 261
Wells, Thomas 92
Wentworth, William 97
West, Cornell 197
West Indies, *see* Caribbean
Wevers, Lydia 93
White, Patrick 6, 8, 68, 109, 204

White, Richard 130, 131
Whitman, Walt 49
Wieland, James 72, 74
Wilentz, Gay 42
Wilkes, G. A. 90
Wilkinson, Jane 15, 32
Williams, Denis 220–1, 225
Williams, Francis 107–8
Williams, Haare 260
Williams, Mark 253
Williams, William Carlos 12, 73
women colonial writers 81–2, 89–92, 93,
    115–17, 118, 131–2
Woods, Gregory 21
Wordsworth, William 4
*World Literature Written in English* 158
Wren, Robert W. 18
Wright, Derek 23
Wright, Judith 71
Wyss, J. R. 111

Yarshehu, Hajiya 44
Yeats, William Butler 120, 123–8, 133,
    134, 138
    and language 137
Yoruba 33
Young, Robert 190, 191
Yunupingu, Mandawuy 120, 258

Zephaniah, Benjamin 40
Zimbabwe 212
    *see* Dangarembga, Marechera
Zulu 14, 168
Zumthor, Paul 31, 32